THE MANCHESTER CHRONICLES

THE MANCHESTER CHRONICLES

TRUE TALES OF MUSIC, MADNESS AND MAYHEM 1976–2006

CLINT BOON

With assistance from Luke Bainbridge

monoray

First published in Great Britain in 2026 by Monoray,
an imprint of Octopus Publishing Group Ltd
Carmelite House
50 Victoria Embankment
London EC4Y 0DZ
www.octopusbooks.co.uk

An Hachette UK Company
www.hachette.co.uk

The authorized representative in the EEA is Hachette Ireland,
8 Castlecourt Centre, Dublin 15, D15 XTP3, Ireland (email: info@hbgi.ie)

Distributed in the US by Hachette Book Group,
1290 Avenue of the Americas, 4th and 5th Floors,
New York, NY 10104

Distributed in Canada by Canadian Manda Group,
664 Annette St, Toronto, Ontario, Canada M6S 2C8

ISBN: 978-1-80096-282-8
eISBN: 978-1-80096-284-2

A CIP catalogue record for this book is available from the British Library.

Typeset in 11.25/16pt Heldane Text by Six Red Marbles UK, Thetford, Norfolk.

Printed and bound in Great Britain.

1 3 5 7 9 10 8 6 4 2

This FSC® label means that materials used for
the product have been responsibly sourced.

MIX
Paper | Supporting
responsible forestry
FSC® C104740

For Mani, Imelda, George and Gene.
And every kid who ever grew up dreaming about being a pop star.

Contents

DRAGGING ME DOWN

LIFE IN TRANSITION

LAST NIGHT, DJING SAVED MY LIFE

Foreword

by Shaun Ryder

Clint's a fuckin' dude, man. He's a geezer and he's a fuckin' artist.

Back in the day, we were just kids – we were just babies – havin' a fuckin' laugh. We've both had our ups and downs along the way, but we've survived, and it's all in this book.

There was 12 fuckin' mad years when I got all my dough took off me because of a 'receivership', or some bollocks. I was a bit raw then, but Clint really helped me out.

We used to talk about starting an Engie Benjy band. That still sounds like a good idea to this day! We're lucky to still be doing this at our age. Fuckin' absolutely. But you make your own luck. People like me and Clint are real. Kids these days can't even close the fuckin' cupboard doors in the kitchen.

Total respect to Clint and the Inspirals.

Shaun Ryder

Introduction

I was on tour with the Inspiral Carpets in November 2025 when I got a text from my son Oscar, who was on tour with Peter Hook. I was lying in my bunk on the tour bus, when I opened Oscar's text and read the news that Mani had died. I couldn't believe it. I was floored. Mani had suffered with his health for a while and was still mourning the death of his beautiful wife Imelda, who had died of cancer just two years earlier. We all knew he was still absolutely heartbroken, but nobody expected this. Mani had always been so full of life, ever since I'd first met him over 40 years earlier. He was always the biggest heart and soul in any room he happened to be in. He always brought the party. It didn't seem possible that a human being so full of love and life could be gone.

Fittingly, for one of Manchester's greatest sons, Mani's funeral service was at Manchester Cathedral, which was full to capacity, while the streets outside were packed with thousands of people standing shoulder to shoulder. The rest of The Stone Roses and Primal Scream were there, and it seemed like every Manchester band that ever mattered had members in the congregation. Liam Gallagher and Bonehead from Oasis, Mike Joyce from The Smiths, New Order and their former bass-man Peter Hook, Dermo and the lads from Northside, Steve Diggle from Buzzcocks, Bez, Rowetta and other artists that were always part of Manchester's extended music family, like Paul Weller and The Farm.

Sir David Beckham was in attendance, as was Gary Neville, who'd fought to get 'This is the One' installed as the walk-out music at Old Trafford when he was captain of Manchester United. As I walked into the cathedral, Ian Brown came straight up to me and said, 'I bet you need a big hug, don't you?' before wrapping his arms around me with a huge warm squeeze. I was overcome by a wave of emotions for one of my oldest friends, Gary 'Mani' Mounfield, one of the greatest humans you could ever wish to meet, and for his sons, Gene and

George, who had now lost their dad, only two years after losing their mum. In the cathedral service, Ian Brown and Bobby Gillespie both gave breathtakingly beautiful eulogies, not just about their love for Mani, but about how he'd elevated each of their bands to even greater heights. As I looked around the cathedral, at the great and good of Manchester music, I thought about the journey we'd all been on over the last half a century. How our lives, the music scene, and the city itself were unrecognisable from what we knew as youngsters. We'd come up through the ranks with our bands at the same time as the city was reinventing itself. Mani was such a big part of that, for so many of us.

Manchester is a wonderful place to write your own story. It's a relatively young city, so there's no old money, and it's more egalitarian than any other city I know. There's fewer barriers. It's easier to wipe the slate clean and start again in Manchester.

I've always loved a good story and I've always thought of myself as a storyteller. Maybe that's what drew me to pop music in the first place. Most of my favourite records are just great stories set to great music. Over time, as the Inspirals started our journey that took us off around the world, I knew instinctively that, one day, I'd need to write it all down.

So, I always knew there'd be a book. I just needed to work out what kind of book it would be and who'd want to read it. When the time came, I wanted to write something different to the standard rock 'n' roll memoir. I wanted to tell the story of Manchester and its music, alongside my story, as well as the tales of people I'd met along the way. I toyed around with this idea, and it seemed to work. I thought about calling it *The Boon Chronicles*, or *The Book of Boon*, but in the end *The Manchester Chronicles* seemed more fitting, because it's not just about me, it's about this special city, and the incredible halcyon days we lived through. I was remarkably lucky to be part of that scene. The Inspirals came up with a bunch of amazing groups, including The Stone Roses, Happy Mondays, James, 808 State, The Charlatans and others, in a huge creative moment just as the 1980s morphed into the 1990s. Some people thought this huge kaleidoscopic explosion came from nowhere. But the truth was, it was the glorious culmination of something that had been bubbling under since the mid-1970s. That's the story I wanted to tell. How me, my friends and other like-minded souls across Manchester started to experiment with music, form bands, swap personnel, make records, set up labels and promote gigs and raves. To me, it's the greatest musical story of the last half-century. But I would say that, wouldn't I?

That's not to say this is a history book. It's a fragmented history, a sort of modern folk history from the street. It's how I saw it – and, to understand it, I need to talk about my life. Which I will do as honestly as I can.

My life has been extraordinary. It's been a wild trip. I still can't quite believe everything that has happened to me. A kid from Oldham like me was never supposed to be on *Top of the Pops* and on the cover of magazines. If you'd have told any teacher at my school that Clinton Boon was going to be a pop star one day they would've laughed. I still laugh about it myself sometimes. But I did it. Why shouldn't a kid from Oldham become a pop star?

So, within this book you're holding, I've written about how I was affected by the punk movement, forming my first band, t'Mill, with Mani and Chris Goodwin, joining Inspiral Carpets and eventually finding mainstream success. I've also written about how that dream turned sour, my years in the wilderness, how I got back on track again as a solo artist, and how Inspiral Carpets came back together after years apart.

I was lucky enough to be part of not one, but two of the biggest musical revolutions in my lifetime. I've also seen Manchester itself undergo a revolution, from being the world's first industrial city to becoming the world's first post-industrial city. Manchester had suffered in the 1960s and 1970s, but by the late 1980s it had rediscovered its zeal. I've watched as the city has reinvented itself around me, drawing no little inspiration and confidence from a music scene that brought the eyes of the world back on our city. Music and culture replaced cotton as the city's greatest export and laid the foundations for its excess of civic pride and reinvigorated international reputation. The seeds of those sweeping changes, for me, date back to the birth of punk and the knock-on effect it had from 1976 onwards. When my generation suddenly realised that they could reimagine the city in their own vision of the future. It was the likes of Buzzcocks, Joy Division, New Order and Factory who first showed us what was possible to achieve in Manchester, and then a whole new generation took up the mantle. I was lucky enough to become friends with and hang out with all the main players, play in bands with some of them, and play my own part in helping reinvent the city.

I've got to admit: my recollections will be lucid in parts and vague in others! My chronology may be wobbly, as there's been lots of alcohol at various stages of the journey. I'll do my best to tell these stories honestly and from my point of view. This is what I saw and remember. Through the haze of sheer determination, through success and stardom, to the pain of being on my arse and being seen as yesterday's man. You'll see me slapping one of my heroes across the face backstage at *Top of the Pops*, and you'll see me knelt on a motorway covered in blood. A lot of these stories I've never told before, even to the people I've been in a band with for 40 years.

I've had some exhilarating highs and some crushing lows. But you need the dark to appreciate the light. I've loved my life. I still love life. Somehow, I'm still in the game, 50 years after I first started making music and playing records to people for money. This city has never let me down. So, strap in, let me tell you my Manchester chronicles. First, we have to go back to the 1970s . . . Let's do it!

GROUND ZERO

1/
I'm in the Room

I'm in the room. In the thick of it. Ten feet from the stage. The condensation is dense. The pushing intense. The place stinks of mould, sweat, cigarette smoke and Newcastle Brown Ale. The atmosphere is electric. I feel like I'm in the absolute centre of the world, time – life itself. It's one of those rare moments in life when you know with absolute certainty that there's nowhere on Earth that you'd rather be right now; squashed in with hippies, rockers, early punks and kids who've not decided on their subculture of choice yet.

The frontman, John, isn't happy. He's not enjoying the gig. He spends much of the set sat down, stage left, back against the wall, facing the band, head in his hands, sulking at those in the crowd who think it's still cool to spit at musicians on stage because they've read it in the *NME*. Fuckin' morons. I'd be pissed off too. He shouts into the mic, '*Stop spitting! Stop fuckin' spitting!*'

Glen, stage right, bass guitar, dark red Rickenbacker, holding things together, cool as fuck. He looks about 15. Paul at the back, knocking out the rhythms, keeping everyone in line. His hair, an unkempt and lively blond explosion. Steve, stage left, guitar. He's angry too: 'Stop fuckin' gobbin' or we're off!' Midway through the set, his black PVC trousers split under the crotch. He's obviously 'going commando' tonight because I can clearly see his cock slapping against the back of his Gibson Les Paul in time with the music.

I'm surprised at the covers in their set: 'Substitute' by The Who, and '(I'm Not Your) Steppin' Stone' by Paul Revere & the Raiders (via The Monkees). This does feel like the remnants of the 'pub rock' thing I've been reading about in the weekly music papers. But that doesn't matter, this is all new and exciting to me. I've never seen or felt anything like this before. This is punk. I'm 17 and smitten. It's Thursday 9 December, 1976. I'm in the room. With the Sex Pistols.

The Electric Circus was a crumbling old Victorian music hall in Collyhurst, just a few minutes' walk from Manchester's city centre. Until punk, it'd hosted mainly rock groups and rock discos. Those attending gigs at the Electric Circus were often brutalised by the local psychotic and devilish kids who would pelt us with bottles and bricks as we queued to get in. They were hungry for punk blood and had the advantage of elevation as they'd position themselves on the first- and second-floor walkways of the run-down flats directly opposite the venue. Even unsuspecting bands, arriving in the afternoon to soundcheck, would receive the same welcome. Collyhurst wasn't the friendliest part of Manchester back then.

That Thursday night in December was my first time at the venue. I'd come on the bus with a bunch of my art-college mates. We hadn't even bought tickets in advance – just paid £1.50 on the door. The best £1.50 I've ever spent in my life. On entering the venue, I got an overwhelming sense of lawlessness. I didn't feel scared or in danger – I never felt that at any of the punk gigs I would go to over subsequent years; there was always a calmness I felt in the moment – but at the same time, it felt like stepping into a *Lord of the Flies* kind of netherworld.

First on were Buzzcocks: Howard Devoto still fronting the band, Steve Diggle on bass, Pete Shelley on guitar, John Maher on drums. An absolute fucking revelation. Simple pop songs but played with an attitude I'd not seen before. I was transfixed by Pete's guitar. It looked like he'd sawn the body off, just above the strings, and stuck a piece of paper on which I assumed contained a setlist or backing vocal notes. I later found out he hadn't sawn it off, he'd just dropped it in rehearsals and, because it was such a cheap guitar, a 'Starway' from Woolworths, the timber just snapped off along the grain.

After the Buzzcocks' set, another band took to the stage: Johnny Thunders and the Heartbreakers. They looked ultra-cool. We knew their backstory from the music papers. They'd risen from the ashes of the New York Dolls but looked nothing like them. They had shorter hair and looked as if glam rock had never existed. My memories of the band on that night are of a more monochrome look – a suit jacket here, a biker jacket there, a couple of thin black ties, maybe a bootlace tie. Whatever the fashion detail, they had a real fifties vibe to their sound and style. They came from New York, which made the whole thing feel even more special.

After a quick changeover, another band stepped out onto the stage and took charge of the room in a split second. Straight into the first song: '*One, two, three, four . . .!*' They'd not made a record or been on the radio yet, so I didn't know their songs, but I'd seen them in the music press. They started with a song about rioting. I couldn't hear the lyrics in the verses as the singer's accent and anger prevented any such luxury. But the repetition in the chorus '*White riot, I wanna riot/White riot, a riot of my own!*' was all I needed to hear. Never being the kind of kid who'd be up for an actual riot, bouncing off other kids in that moment and having yet another life-affirming anthem to learn the words to was enough. The band had numbers and slogans pinned and painted onto their clothes, particularly the bass player (stage left). I'd never seen this before but decided it was the way forward. I made a mental note to update my wardrobe the next day. I'd need safety pins, some newspaper cuttings, a roll of Sellotape and some thin cardboard. A Corn Flakes box would be perfect. The band sung about London being on fire, America being boring, and how we'd never need the music of Elvis, the Beatles or the Stones ever again after this moment. They seemed way more politically aware than me or my mates, though were only a couple of years older. They were called The Clash.

Then the Sex Pistols. Sometimes you only realise years later how momentous one moment in your life can be. Not that night. I knew right away that it was an important moment. I could feel my life changing direction as I stood facing the stage, with every ear-splitting beat, every dirty bar chord, every angry, snarling, petulant lyric, every profanity. I soaked it up. I wanted it so bad. Apart from the spit! I wanted to be on that stage. Until then, I was always destined to just be a spectator in life, a kid in the crowd. In the mid-1970s, working-class boys like me from Oldham, with no musical ability whatsoever, weren't in bands. They didn't make records or get on the television. Until then, I was vaguely hoping for a career as an art teacher (at best), a struggling artist (at worst), or perhaps a photographer or someone in the world of film-making. Although, to be honest, I'd not really spent too much time thinking about my future at all until that moment.

But right there in front of me were kids singing out of tune, songs made up of just three or four chords, playing cheap guitars from Woolworths. The Buzzcocks' guitarist, Steve Diggle, was my art-college mate Phil's older brother. They were the sons of a truck driver who would soon enjoy the privilege of being jumped ahead of other trucks when doing his rounds, because the warehouse lads all knew he was the dad of a Buzzcock. The lads on stage at the Circus that night had never heard of singing lessons or guitar tuition. They weren't dressed in posh stage gear. There was a slight glam flavour to the whole thing, but these were no Rubettes or Showaddywaddys.

As the Pistols stepped on stage, there was a surge forward. They opened the set with 'Anarchy in the UK', which had been released only two weeks earlier and was beginning to worry the authorities, royalists and religious leaders up and down the UK. This was only eight nights after the Sex Pistols had appeared on the Bill Grundy TV show in London, which, for our generation, was one of *the* defining moments in British popular culture. The first day of December 1976. We missed that broadcast in the north, but we felt its beautiful repercussions for many years after the event.

The Sex Pistols ended their set and disappeared off stage, leaving me shellshocked, trying to grasp the enormity of what I'd just seen. I suddenly had an urge to get something to celebrate this occasion. Something tangible. I hadn't brought my camera with me. I found a small wooden stool at the side of the room. The top was upholstered in thick red vinyl. I tore a piece off and stuck it in my pocket, so I could prove to myself, when I woke up the next morning, that all of this had actually happened. Here's the evidence. I was there.

This was my ground-zero moment. My life had just changed for ever.

2/
M74, Northbound, Scotland
Wednesday 8 April, 1999

Twenty-nine miles south of Glasgow. Northbound carriageway. 4.35pm. I'm covering the laceration on Kathryn's head with my left hand, while using my right hand to try to prevent the clouds of thick dust getting into the gaping wound. I'm also doing my absolute best to avoid letting the others see how badly injured she is. I've just seen the white of her skull. The motorway has come to a standstill. Fifteen feet away lies Tony. I believe he'll lose his eye, it's so badly damaged.

Some of the others are trying to release Danny (he's just turned 21 years old on the day this is happening) from the wreckage of the Mercedes tour bus. The vehicle is a 'splitter' bus, meaning the rear compartment is divided into two sections, one for the passengers, the other (directly above the back axle) for all the band's equipment. Danny's pinned down by his arm, which went through the passenger window as we rolled over. His arm is stuck between the twisted metal and the ground. I'm going to have to leave him here in the wreckage, with the fuel fumes growing stronger, looking scared, straight into my eyes. Both of us shocked and frightened. I'm suspended above him, still gripping onto the steering wheel for dear life, held in the air by my seatbelt.

I know Kathryn has been thrown from the vehicle because I can hear her older brother Richard screaming her name from the back of the van. Tony's gone too. As I release the seatbelt, I land, feet either side of Danny's head. 'Close your eyes, Dan!' I kick the shattered, laminated windscreen out and step out of the wreckage looking for Kathryn and Tony. Tony is lying a few feet away, groaning and barely conscious. Kathryn is further down the hard shoulder, almost on the inside lane of the motorway. She's lying completely still with a severely damaged back and the worst head wound I'll probably ever witness in my life.

The paramedics eventually arrive. They gently move me from Kathryn's side and take over. I can hardly stand. I'm covered in blood. Mine and hers. The air ambulance arrives and lands on the motorway. Kathryn is stretchered into the helicopter while I'm breathalysed on the hard shoulder by a sympathetic-looking policeman who asks, 'What's your name, mate?'

'Clint Boon.'

3/
Mills and Boon

My whole life has revolved around mills. My mum and dad met in a mill; I was conceived round the back of a mill; my first job was in a mill; my first band practice was in a mill; my first recording studio was in a mill; and I still rehearse in a mill today. Mills have shaped my life, in so many ways.

Mum and Dad met at the Lilac cotton mill in Shaw, to the northeast of Oldham, back in the mid-1950s. I was conceived on a deckchair in a shed behind the mill in their lunch-hour, sometime in the autumn of 1958, and was born Clinton David Boon on 28 June 1959. Not many people know my full name is Clinton, and a lot of people assume Clint Boon is a made-up stage name. I was always destined to stand out with a name like Clinton, especially growing up in the industrial north of the 1960s.

My first home was at 61 Linney Lane in Shaw, a small mid-terraced house nestled deep in the shadow of the Rutland Mill. Cotton mills were still among the biggest employers in the region and, as such, sat right at the heart of Oldham's culture and communities. From minute one, mine was a real working-class upbringing. I was raised by, and surrounded by, real grafters – people who worked every hour to make for a better life.

When I was four, my mum and dad took over the corner shop at 287 Higginshaw Lane in Heyside, a village halfway between Oldham and Shaw, and we settled into a new life, living directly above the shop. That's where we lived throughout my formative years, with my little brother and sister, Craig and Lynda, until Mum and Dad later bought a newbuild house just down the road. Me, Craig and Lynda always called each other 'Booney' – we still do to this day, which amuses us, but can cause confusion if one of us starts talking about what 'Booney' has been up to when checking in with Mum. Craig (or Booney) and I shared bunk beds and a bedroom.

We had a length of hosepipe that we used to whisper to each other through, bunk to bunk, until one night when I was about nine and he was only about five, I decided to piss down the hosepipe onto poor little Booney when he was mid-chat. That didn't go down too well.

The kitchen was downstairs and there was no bathroom. This wasn't unusual in our part of the world in the late 1950s and early 1960s. Most people I knew had an outside toilet. Ours sat in a communal yard behind the shop, a ramshackle brick building with an asbestos roof. Those four toilets were shared between the families in our terrace, about 15 homes in all. Each family would have a key for their shared toilet. One of the people we shared with was an old lady called Nelly. On more than one occasion, I was sat doing my business when there was a knock on the door. 'Clinton, is that you? It's Nelly. Can you hurry up?'

Hardly anyone in our world used toilet paper, especially in outside toilets. Torn-up pieces of newspaper hung on a loop of string behind the door was the norm. There was no electricity in the toilets either, so you'd need to take a torch or a candle after dark. The toilets were long drop, meaning no sophisticated plumbing was involved. Everything dropped directly into the sewer. Them were t'days. I'd scrape my arse clean on the 'Births, Deaths and Marriages' column of a recent *Oldham Chronicle* and leave Nelly to evacuate her bowels in the dark.

We lived in the shadow of the moors, literally. Right across from our shop was Moss Lane, and the Pennines started at the end of Moss Lane. We also lived in the more sombre shadow of the Moors Murders, which happened when I was around the age of four or five. Ian Brady and Myra Hindley abducted five children from around Manchester, murdered them and buried their bodies on Saddleworth Moor. I was too young to realise what had really happened to the poor victims at the time it hit the news, but I do remember Mum driving us over the moors once, and hearing my dad say to her, 'This is where they buried the kids, round here.'

Despite the shadow of the Moors Murders, all the kids round our way still played out until late at night. We'd spend most of our days having adventures and getting up to no good around the neighbourhood. When the school summer holidays started, it felt like we went out on our bikes on the Friday and didn't come back in until September.

My dad was the local Dr Dolittle. He loved all animals, and our home above the shop was always full of various birds and beasts. Dad was always taking in injured animals and nursing them back to health. We even had a kestrel once. A full-size bloody kestrel living above a shop. Dad adored that kestrel; he was like an adult Billy Casper. We had to get rid of it in the end, though, as it kept shitting on the carpet. Dad rented a couple of pens* down the street where he kept his chickens and some geese. He once bought a Shetland pony off a traveller who'd come into the shop to buy a sandwich and said to my dad, 'D'you know anyone who wants to buy an 'orse? I need to get rid of it.' Dad said, 'What kind of horse is it?' 'It's a small 'orse. It's in me van outside.' He took my dad outside and showed him this dishevelled pony in the back of his knackered old van. It had loads of its coat missing and its hooves were curled up at the front. My dad felt that sorry for the poor creature and bought it off him for a tenner there and then. I came downstairs, and there was Dad stood in the shop with this scraggy pony on the end of a short rope. I held onto the rope and waited in the shop with the pony while Dad toddled off down the street to rent another pen.

We rarely went into Manchester. Shaw had everything you wanted: a Woolworths, a hardware shop, a couple of grocer shops and the gas shop where you went to pay your gas bill. If she needed to, Mum would sometimes pop into Oldham, but we rarely ventured as far as Manchester.

I didn't do too well at school. I started off OK, at St Joseph's Primary School near Shaw, with all my mates. Even at that tender age, I already loved music. I'd be listening to the girls in the playground chanting their quirky little skipping songs to the rhythm of the rope whipping the ground. Some of the songs felt like old folk songs that might have been around for generations, others seemed to have been made up on the day:

---

* Small fields or enclosures, used for keeping small farm animals like chickens, geese or ponies.

Mary had a daughter; its name was double-jointed. . .
Eeney Meeney Makkeracker. . .
Gilly Gally whiskers. . .
—Anonymous

I didn't know what was going on, but I liked it. I was also mesmerised at the sight and sound of someone sitting or standing in the same room as me, singing. At nine years old, I sat in the school hall one afternoon and watched one of my classmates, Joan Malone, and my older cousin Julie Scarsbrook perform 'Scarborough Fair' as part of a school show. Joan stood nervously swaying in time with the music as she sang, Julie sat to her side, gently strumming a huge acoustic guitar balanced on her lap. Their harmonies that afternoon were gorgeous and stayed in my head for weeks. I also loved writing poetry at primary school. Even then, the process of writing excited me. The challenge of trying to squeeze a story or an emotion into a finite number of words or verses. Whether or not to make the words rhyme. Counting the syllables – too many will sound clumsy, too few might not be enough.

I loved my time at primary school, until we had to sit something called the 11 Plus. Nobody told us how important it was. Somehow, I passed it, while the majority of my mates didn't, which meant I was separated from most of them and shipped off to the Cardinal Langley Grammar School for Boys, which was an eight-mile bus ride away, in Middleton. I was there from 1970 until 1975. That's when things went downhill for me, academically. It wasn't the happiest five years of my life.

Cardinal Langley had a strict uniform policy. The uniforms – including a black blazer with the school's crest on the breast pocket and red braid around the edges of the collar and pockets – could only be bought from a shop called Broadbents in Middleton and were expensive. To save a bit of money, Mum bought a plain black blazer from Oldham Market and stitched some red braid onto it. The braid she used was slightly wider and a much brighter red than the official garments, which meant my schoolmates and teachers took the piss for a few months until I outgrew it, and Mum could afford to get me the proper uniform from Broadbents.

I never felt I fitted in at Cardinal Langley. It didn't help that the school was a big rugby establishment, which meant skinny, pale little buggers like me, with not much muscle or stamina, were low on the lists of certain teachers' favourite pupils. It was also a time when teachers could freely abuse kids, mentally and physically, in the name of education and religion. Being something of a class clown, I often found myself on the wrong end of the cane, strap, plimsoll or blackboard duster wielded as a fierce form of correction. The bruising would fade with time but, as with a lot of young men of that generation, the mental scars would live in my head for the rest of my life. As it was a Roman Catholic school, we also had to go to regular 'confession' in the chapel, which was attached to the school, even if we hadn't done anything worth confessing. You had to go and sit in the confession box, and most weeks, I'd be thinking, 'I've not even done 'owt wrong this week!' So you'd have to make something up, then the priest would tell you to go and do three 'Our Father's and three 'Hail Mary's.

I tried to keep up with fashion, but we weren't a wealthy family, so I'd usually be a few months behind the latest trends, always the last to turn up in a pair of Oxford bags or penny round shirt, sometimes given to me by friends as they were superseded by the next 'must have' apparel. But music was always my thing. In my second year at Cardinal Langley, 1971, I befriended a lad in the first year who was an incredible pianist. His name was Stephen Buckley. He lived in Lees, just outside Oldham, so we'd share part of our daily bus journeys to and from school chatting enthusiastically about music. We'd discuss the hits of the day, his beloved T. Rex, my beloved Elvis, and, on Fridays, the previous night's *Top of the Pops*.

This being a grammar school, the obligatory grand piano sat in the corner of the school hall, just in front of the stage. It would spend most of its days beneath a heavy canvas protective cover in a grim shade of dark green, only to be revealed for the occasional theatrical performance or mayoral visit. The school's policy at break times was generally, 'Get outside, you lazy useless sods! We don't care if it's raining, it'll do you good! Might even give you a bit of character!' Me and Ste soon figured out that the staff seemed to turn a blind eye to us sitting, playing and singing at the piano for the entire length of the lunchbreak. Maybe they thought we were working on a forthcoming school play? Whatever their thinking, they did us a massive favour. Ste would play any song I suggested while I'd sing along at the top of my voice. Lots of Elvis, Little Richard and Jerry Lee Lewis. We took the lyrics from the Cliff Richard tune 'Travellin' Light' and put it to a more 'boogie-woogie' piano backing. We told all passers-by that it was 'one of ours!' and no one questioned it. Ste showed me how to play basic piano patterns. The old classic 'C', 'Am', 'F' and 'G' chord sequence used on so many of my favourite rock 'n' roll songs.

In some ways, you can blame Stephen Buckley for pretty much my entire output as a keyboard player from 1971 until the present day. Stephen went on to become Lisa Stansfield's sound engineer and producer at her home studio in Rochdale, which she named Gracielands, as a jokey reference to Elvis and the Dale's own superstar Gracie Fields. Stephen would also later become the in-house sound engineer at Square One Studios in nearby Bury, where the Inspirals would finish and mix our debut album *Life* in late 1989.

A bunch of older students, fifth years and sixth formers, would hold regular jam sessions in the physics classroom during break times. The room was tucked away in a part of the school that wasn't as visible to whichever teacher might be on 'Get outside, you useless lazy sods!' duty. There'd be half a dozen or so lads, three or four of them playing acoustic guitars, and all singing. The songs were usually a mix of contemporary radio songs and older classics by the Beatles, the Stones, and The Kinks. For me, though, the icing on the cake was the recent hit songs of Lindisfarne, which they'd play and sing with sheer passion. I'd heard vocal harmonies like these on record but had never stood next to people doing it in real time. It was like nothing I'd ever experienced. 'Meet Me on the Corner', 'Lady Eleanor', 'Fog on the Tyne' – the sound was heavenly and moved me to the core. I don't have many fond memories of my time at Cardinal Langley, but the lunchtime piano jams with Ste and the Lindisfarne physics-lab sessions were truly joyous moments, which most certainly helped steer me along my path through life.

We used to gamble a bit at school, mainly poker, and one Monday morning when I was 13, I put all my dinner money for that week on what I thought was a winning hand. I lost. Which meant I had no dinner money for the week and went without school dinners. On the Thursday, I fell ill on the bus home and started spewing up. I knew exactly why, but played it up a bit when I got home hoping I'd get the Friday off school. Mum took me to the doctor's the next day, he examined me, found a lump, and discovered I had a duplex, or 'horseshoe', kidney, which is when you have both kidneys stuck together, operating as one. He gave me a note for school to say I should be excused from rugby or any other heavy-contact sport. I was made up. When I gave the note to the PE teacher, I chanced my arm and said, 'The doctor said I shouldn't really do cross-country either' and he bought it, which was a right result, as I hated PE, rugby and cross-country and never had to do them again. I've never had any issues with my funky kidney – as I got older, I was never told I should go easy on the drink, or anything like that, and thankfully it's never been a problem.

There were a few teachers at the school who were good souls and they stuck out among the rest. Our English teacher was called Chris Giblin; thinking back, he was like a schoolteacher version of Gene Hunt, the edgy seventies cop from the TV series *Life on Mars*, but not as crude. He used to wear light-brown Chelsea boots, and on the first day he taught us he came into the classroom, sat on his desk, with his boots resting on the desk of the kid on the front row, and said, 'Right, gents, who's got any jokes?' There were two teachers called Mr Murphy that I got on with too. P K Murphy was my geography teacher, a bit of a hippy with a beard, who kept part of his personal record collection in school. He had a little storeroom to the side of the classroom that he'd turned into a record library. He set up a system where he'd lend us his records for a couple of pence, usually on Monday, to bring back the following Monday. He kept a hand-drawn diagram of each side of each vinyl record and marked any scratches on it, then, when you'd return it, he'd compare the record to the diagram to make sure there weren't any new scratches, a bit like when you hire a car now and they check if there's any fresh scratches when you bring it back. For each new scratch, you'd pay a halfpenny or something. P K was heavily into rock (makes sense being a geography teacher, I suppose), so a big part of his collection was made up of rock music. It was a genre I wasn't too familiar with, so a great opportunity for me to see what all the fuss was about. On my first visit to his library I borrowed King Crimson and Steppenwolf records, but they didn't do much for me. I wasn't ready for music like that yet – but fair play to him for lending his personal record collection out to pupils. I'm still not that keen on lending my records to anyone, even now. The other teacher I liked was Pete 'Art' Murphy, who was my art teacher. My memory of him is that he was a bit like the actor Bill Murray – dry humour and a very likeable character – and it was no surprise that art became my best subject.

I left school in the summer of 1975 with a grand total of three O-level exam passes – art (obviously), religion (randomly) and physics (bizarrely). Not a great result considering I took ten exams. I was never the most intellectual of pupils, my passions leaning mainly towards music, art and making my classmates laugh. Many of my schoolfriends came away with eight or nine O-level passes compared to my three. I wasn't arsed, though. Just happy to be out of the place.

I'd not given much thought to what I would do next. I'd not applied for any job interviews and hadn't considered further education. I simply jumped on the number 17 bus on Friday 20 June, 1975 after my final exams and got the fuck out, went home and played Scalextric.

A week later, on 28 June, my sixteenth birthday, Mum and Dad drove me over to Kingsway Autos in Rochdale and bought me a moped. Me and my best mate, Kenny Berry, shared the same birthday; we were born just a couple of hours apart and pretty much grew up together from around five years old. Growing up, we used to say we were 'twins but not brothers!', which at some point became 'twits but not buggers!' We'd spent our primary-school years together, until we were separated by the dreaded 11 Plus virus, but we were still best mates.

For some time, we'd planned on getting matching bikes as soon as we were old enough, and our parents seemed supportive of the idea. The bike-shop owner, also called Ken, delivered my moped to our house in Heyside in the back of his van. It was a gorgeous 50cc Italian machine called a Fantic Caballero (JBN 14N) in a cool shade of blue. Kenny came back from holiday a week or so later and his parents drove him over to Rochdale and bought him one exactly the same (JBN 15N).

We thought we were the dog's bollocks cruising around Royton, Oldham and Manchester, side by side, feeling like Peter Fonda and Dennis Hopper in *Easy Rider*, or Jon and Poncherello in the American cop show *CHiPs*. I hadn't particularly dreamt of being a biker as a kid, but the law allowed you to ride a 50cc moped from 16 years old, as long as you had 'L' plates, so it was a great option. As the Merton Parkas once sang, '*You need wheels!*' I didn't fancy waiting another year to be old enough to get a car. By 16 I wanted to be mobile and start exploring the wider world, or at least wider Manchester, even if it meant having to explain the Fantic's legally required 'pedals' to anyone who asked.

I got a bit obsessed with the whole American motorbike-cop thing. I even went to the extent of dressing a bit like an American bike cop. I got an open-face crash helmet, painted it black and white and bought some long leather gauntlets, again in black and white. I was living the dream, baby. So was Kenny. Although he was channelling the spirit of American superbike hero Kenny Roberts.

As we approached 17 we knew we needed to take a proper driving test to allow us to upgrade to a full motorbike licence and bigger bikes. The problem was, you couldn't take a motorbike test on a moped. You could only take it on a motorbike. So I took the left-hand-side pedal and arm completely off the shaft and removed the black rubber bit from the right-side pedal, leaving an 'L'-shaped metal arm that looked a bit like a kick-starter pedal. I then bought some regular motorbike footrests and screwed them to the frame just below the engine. My moped now looked like a real motorbike.

Nobody noticed. I took my test, passed first time and rode off into the sunset. The world was opening up to me, and I was on the hunt for my next chapter.

4/
Follow Your Art

By the time I left school, music was my obsession. I was constantly playing records, buying records, swapping records, or borrowing records from Oldham Record Library. I had *Disco 45* delivered every week, a great little magazine with printed lyrics to all the current pop hits for kids like me to obsess over and memorise. Like thousands of other boys growing up in the era of pop, glam and prog, I spent endless hours dreaming of being a pop star. One of the biggest dreams of every kid growing up in the sixties and seventies was to be rich and famous one day. We all imagined ourselves as a future George Best, David Bowie or Little Jimmy Osmond. I was no exception. Our worlds revolved around these people in a focused and positive-minded way that today's celebrity culture doesn't seem to enjoy, with all the distraction of social media and the noise and negativity that brings. But they were just pipe dreams. It wasn't a serious option I could discuss with my careers teacher Mr Bates (aka Bully Bates) at Cardinal Langley. He'd aquired the nickname 'Bully' partly due to his stern and condescending way of addressing the pupils, but also for the way he gleefully administered corporal punishment at every opportunity. Mr Bates was also the head of the engineering drawing class, so was quite encouraging when I mentioned maybe training as an architect or designer, but he'd openly laugh if me or any other kid ever dared suggesting getting into music, theatre or comedy. Ask the actor and comedian Steve Coogan. He and his brothers*

* Steve Coogan's older brother Martin Coogan later formed the band The Mock Turtles, who scored chart hits with 'Can You Dig It?' and 'Lay Me Down'. Some of Steve Coogan's earliest stand-up gigs were supporting The Mock Turtles at gigs around Manchester, including the Haçienda. Alongside writing this book, I've been working on a musical (film) with Mock Turtles drummer Steve Cowen . . . watch this space!

went to the same school as me, so they also had Bully Bates laughing at any dreams they had of doing anything creative.

The reality was working-class kids like me weren't allowed to be pop stars. On top of that, having a thick Oldham accent guaranteed I'd never be taken seriously if I ever found myself on the radio or television. Being totally consumed by and obsessed with music didn't mean I'd get a one-way ticket to *Top of the Pops*. Having every square inch of my bedroom walls covered with images of my music heroes (mainly Elvis) didn't ensure I'd win a major-label record deal somewhere down the road.

As my first summer as a free man started, I still didn't have a clue what I was going to do next. Kenny had signed up for an apprenticeship at Hawker Siddeley in Chadderton, the legendary aircraft manufacturers who had produced the Lancaster Bomber, Avro Vulcan and Harrier Jump Jet. He seemed to know what he wanted to do with his life. I was still floundering.

Then, halfway through the summer, I heard about a couple of the lads from my class going to art college. There were only two colleges nearby that offered basic and foundation courses for 16- and 17-year-olds who fancied going down the university route. One was based in Oldham, the other in Rochdale. The Rochdale College of Art was rated as one of the best of its kind in the country. I thought I'd give it a shot as a way of buying a bit of time until I decided what to do with my future.

I posted an eleventh-hour application to Rochdale College of Art and got a quick reply inviting me in for an interview. I turned up and had a chat with a couple of members of staff and the college principal, a kind and soft-natured chap called Leo Solomon, who was a very well-respected figure, not only in education, but in the art world in general. He was even a close friend of the legendary L S Lowry, who he'd recently persuaded to visit the college to meet and talk with students. A bronze bust of Lowry, sculpted by Mr Solomon, still sits on display in Rochdale Art Gallery. Mr Solomon was also an old acquaintance of Dylan Thomas. Quite the dude. The interview went well. My artwork and ideas seemed to persuade them I had some potential, and they told me on the spot that I could have a place on the basic course. I rode away on my moped, quite chuffed with myself. I didn't know it yet, but

Mr Solomon's invitation for me to join Rochdale College of Art would prove a key moment in my life.

I started at art school in September 1975. From day one, I knew this was the place I needed to be – surrounded by kindred spirits, colourful, creative, loud, happy and tactile young people who, without a doubt in my mind, would go on to make the world a better place. The teachers were a revelation. They couldn't have been more different to most of the teachers at school. They would actively embrace, encourage and nurture our strange ways. I was suddenly immersed in an environment where all the things I used to get punished for at school were now treated as positive qualities. Superpowers, even. I felt seen, for the first time.

My first year at Rochdale was mainly taken up with me catching up on some essential O levels I'd need if I was intending to go to university. I'd failed my maths and English exams and so, as tedious and humiliating as it was, a couple of times a week I'd traipse across the third-floor footbridge that connected the art college to the technical college and sit with a bunch of other underachievers who'd also failed the two main subjects in Britain's educational curriculum. Crossing that footbridge felt like a real walk of shame. After five years at grammar school, this bloody loser couldn't even do his sums.

But back in the art college, I quickly embraced the facilities on offer: initially photography, textile design and life drawing. I formed some great friendships within days of starting. There were some real characters there. I'd found my tribe. Alan Wild, a lad from Whitworth, had a brilliant band called Zinc Bath and the Living Dead, whose singer Lambert is still one of my favourite frontmen ever. Brian Lockett, also from Whitworth, was a young man with the wildest imagination. One day, the tutor told him that his project was to do something 'performance related'. Brian went off rock climbing for two days. One of the girls in our class, Bev Hartley, was a beautifully crazy young woman who, on one occasion, created a massive sculpture of a long tunnel, a couple of feet in diameter. On performance day, she turned up with several tins of red paint, stripped to her underwear and replicated a birthing scene in which she was the newborn. She was also from

Whitworth. Maybe the water supply from the nearby Cowm Reservoir had something whacky swimming around in it during the mid-seventies.

Mark Wydler was otherworldly to me. He was the first person I'd ever met whose family (though seemingly financially secure) didn't have a TV in their house. Ironically, Mark was also the first person I'd ever met who'd appeared on TV. A few years earlier, he'd been on *Animal Magic*, where presenter Johnny Morris held court every week with a menagerie of talking animals. Mark was featured on one episode as a child prodigy with an incredible talent for painting wildlife. Collectively, our group of college friends called ourselves Doctor White and the Sanitary Bunch – an imaginary band where Brian Lockett was Doctor White and we were his, assumedly, menstrual entourage. Mark and I became close and formed an imaginary offshoot band called The Sanitarians. A lot of imaginary bands came together in Rochdale College of Art in the mid-1970s. It was that kind of vibe.

In the year above me were two young women I became good friends with: best mates Catherine Fasnacht and Lesley Albiston. They called themselves Catty Da and Lesley Wesley. I became quite obsessed with them and their fantastical world and spent many days under their spell. Their lives revolved around tales of life on board an imaginary sock-shaped spaceship they called the SS *Entersock*. They introduced me to the music of The Sensational Alex Harvey Band, particularly the tracks 'The Faith Healer' and 'Giddy Up a Ding Dong'.

One afternoon, I spotted them leaving college early. 'Where you off to?' I asked.

'We're going to Mr Lowry's for a cup of tea. Fancy coming?'

'Nah, I'm all right'.

How could I have been so stupid? I turned down an invitation to pop round to L S Lowry's for tea. That's the naivety of youth right there.

The soundtrack to that first year at Rochdale art college was the records we played on the cheap portable record player in the middle of our open-plan, communal studio: Steely Dan, The Eagles, Crosby, Stills, Nash & Young, Led Zeppelin. None of which I was particularly into at the time, but all of which take me back to those wondrous days whenever I hear them. I'd grown up obsessed with Elvis, Jerry Lee, Little Richard, Gene Vincent, Eddie Cochran and Bill Haley and I was still into good old-fashioned fifties rock 'n' roll, even well into the 1970s. I'd also come to love some of the glam-rock bands that had a fifties vibe about them: The Rubettes, Showaddywaddy, Mud, The Glitter Band. Bowie was high on my list too. I still hadn't got my head around the fact that this creature from another planet had recorded a version of Chuck Berry's 'Round and Around' for the B-side of 'Drive-In Saturday'.

I went to see Dr Feelgood at the Free Trade Hall in Manchester in November 1975. I'd seen them on TV a few weeks earlier, courtesy of Tony Wilson, who featured them on the 'What's On' section of his *Granada Reports* evening show. Frontman Lee Brilleaux jerked and twitched with a vocal style that looked like he was trying to strangle the microphone to death. He could probably dance like Elvis but chose not to because that's what a weaker man might do. He looked and sounded agitated and really fucking hard. Pop stars on TV never looked like this. The guitarist, Wilko Johnson, wore manic facial expressions, a black suit and black Fender Telecaster, while strutting backwards and forwards at breakneck speed. Backwards and forwards and back again. 'Where the fuck's he going? What's he doing?' I thought to myself. The songs were straight-up, high-tension, full-on, filthy R&B. To me, right there in the middle of the stacked-heel 1970s, it felt like 1950s rock 'n' roll was still very much alive.

One afternoon, early in that first autumn term, one of the tutors, Julian Smith, said he had something to show us. He took us to a small room on the ground floor of the college, near the back door that led out into the yard where I'd park my moped each day by the bins. The room was probably only about 12 feet square, but the ceiling was high enough that a mezzanine level had been installed. Underneath the mezzanine were all sorts of flight cases and bags that contained audio and video-recording equipment. On a table sat a couple of TV monitors and some other bits of fancy-looking tech gear. Video technology was a new thing at this point, even in the educational sector. It would be two or three years until VHS video recorders would be launched onto the domestic market, and even then, affordable to only the wealthiest homes. None of us knew the potential for this new technology.

Up the steps, on the mezzanine level, something mind-blowing awaited: a small, touch-sensitive, two-octave keyboard with a patch-bay module above it. It looked like something from the future. It was the first time I'd seen a synthesiser in real life. I'd seen Brian Eno play a similar instrument (an analogue synth in a wooden case called the VCS3) when Roxy Music appeared on *Top of the Pops* doing 'Virginia Plain' back in 1972. Julian explained to us that we were free to use the audio and video gear whenever we wanted, we just needed to book the video equipment out in advance if we were intending to take it off the premises. Right there and then, in my eyes, Julian Smith became one of the coolest teachers of all time.

The video setup consisted of a huge reel-to-reel videotape machine, which hung by a thick strap over the user's shoulder. The batteries were positioned all around a thick belt, which you wore around your waist like Batman's utility belt. The camera was a huge, chunky thing, the size of a small person, with a heavy umbilical lead connecting it to the reel-to-reel. Still, we couldn't believe how compact and portable it all was!

Alan Wild and I booked the video gear out and headed off into Rochdale to film our first production: me walking around wearing mirrored aviator shades and a PVC biker's jacket, looking cool as fuck to the strains of 'Raunchy' by Bill Justis, a magnificent late-1950s instrumental. We never saved the tapes or mixed them down because there wasn't a format to mix down to, so *Cool Hand Clint* is sadly lost to cinematic history.

One day, a couple of students used the video equipment to film themselves having sex in the shower room attached to our studio. Julian wasn't too chuffed when he found out. The booking-out procedure became a bit more rigorous after that. Even our most liberally minded fine-art tutor, Keith Chadwick, was horrified when he heard what had happened.

Along with photography, the audio-visual and synthesiser mediums became my main artistic focuses. The oil-painting, life-drawing and textile-design classes were all well and good, but I'd found my little piece of heaven. Up a ladder in Rochdale.

5/
'Mobile Disco for Hire'

Towards the end of 1975, me and Kenny and one of his school mates, John Fraine, decided to set up a mobile disco. We each borrowed £100 off our parents and headed to Squire Light and Sound in Manchester, a huge store that specialised in professional mobile disco and lighting equipment. They sold PA systems and all manner of DJ essentials. We spent about £300 on a FAL double record deck console, a small FAL PA, a microphone, a strobe light and a blue 'fuzz' light that looked like it'd been stolen off the roof of a police car. My dad built a pair of big wooden 'traffic light' cabinets fitted with coloured lightbulbs and fluorescent-light starter units that made the bulbs flash randomly. Following a suggestion by John's mum, a lovely Irish woman called Greta, we decided to call ourselves The Royton Interchange Disco Roadshow (catchy, I know) and had some cards printed. We were in business.

Our first paid gig was a wedding reception at the Star Inn, Failsworth, on 2 January 1976. I got drunk on Bacardi and Coke, a fight broke out among the punters, and the best man got his cock out and started pissing on one of the speakers. I phoned my mum from a phone box and begged her to come and get us as quick as possible. The night was a total disaster, but I'd got the DJ bug.

The Royton Interchange Disco Roadshow diary started to fill up with bookings for more weddings, birthday parties and, courtesy of Mrs Fraine, regular Irish nights at the Royton Catholic Club on Broadway, where we'd play a selection of traditional Irish folk tunes as well as the hits of the day. We'd take it in turns throughout the night, one of us playing the records while the other two danced in front of the decks, trying our best to pull off the right dance moves for the record that was playing. Disco, fifties, northern soul, the Twist, the Slosh – almost nothing was off-limits. We stopped short of trying our hand at Irish dancing, though. That wouldn't have been a good look.

At college, we created our own 'uniform'. We'd go to the local Oxfam, Help the Aged or other charity shops in Rochdale and buy second-hand gent's black dinner suits. The kind with satin collars and pocket flaps; sometimes, if you got lucky, with a matching satin stripe down the outside of the trouser leg. We'd then paint the collar and pocket flaps with a white PVA-based paint – also down the middle of the jacket, on the back, a white splatter of the same paint in the style of Jackson Pollock. Worn with a white shirt and black tie and shades, we looked the business.

As 1976 found its feet, a new kind of music started seeping into our lives. A new band from America popped up on our radar, the Ramones, who released their eponymous debut album in April. I don't even think people in Britain were calling it 'punk rock' yet. Someone brought the LP into our art-college studio, and it sat there, on the record player, full volume, on repeat for days on end. Bringing a record into the studio guaranteed its early destruction as our mucky hands would result in the grooves becoming clogged up with paint, clay, glue or whatever other mediums we happened to be working in. Often, we'd have a quick whip round and one of us would nip out to Bradleys Records on Yorkshire Street or Black Sedan on Fleece Street in the hope they might have a new one in stock. If not, we'd place an order for a replacement copy of the vinyl record we'd just killed.

I'd never seen or heard anything like the Ramones before. The music itself had a familiarity about it – rock 'n' roll? Bubble-gum? – but the pace, energy and actual look of the band was all new to me. They were the scruffiest bastards I'd ever seen under the guise of a pop group, and their sound and their image resonated with me immediately. First opportunity I got, I jumped on the number 59 bus up to Oldham in search of some white canvas deck pumps like the ones Johnny Ramone wore on the cover of the album. I couldn't find any on Oldham Market so ended up buying a pair of white leather loafers from Freeman, Hardy & Willis on the High Street. Probably not the most punk pair of shoes I could have bought on the day, but they looked ace with my skinny ripped jeans and cheap plastic biker jacket.

Inspired by the Ramones, I decided to try my hand at songwriting for the first time in my life. I was still 16. I'd always loved music but never tried to learn an instrument. The music teacher at Cardinal Langley, Mr Larkin, would often ridicule me with a stern, 'BOON! THAT'S NOT SINGING! IT'S SHOUTING!!' I'd had similar criticisms at primary school. There seemed to be a pattern. It's fair to say that, during my youth, I didn't have a musical bone in my body. But I really fuckin' loved music and singing. We'd had an old Spanish guitar at home since the early 1970s that no one in the family had taken much time to learn. It had thick 'catgut' strings and none of us really knew how to tune it.

When I decided to start my career as a songwriter that afternoon in 1976, I started by taking all except one string off the guitar. Six was way too many. I left just the bottom 'E' string in place and strummed it like a wild man as I snarled my freshly written compositions into the microphone of my Decca Legato cassette deck. Using a second cassette player that belonged to my mum and dad, I recorded some of the crowd ambience from a live concert album we had at the time and played that in the background, so it sounded like I was doing an actual gig. I still have the recordings. Even though I'm pretending to be doing a live show and generally being an 'angry young punk', you can hear my voice is subdued because I didn't want my mum and dad to hear me through my bedroom door and think I was a nob.

My cassette recorder was my most treasured possession. Our mobile-disco gear was special to me, and already making money, but my cassette machine was like a portal to another world. Mum and Dad had bought it for me a couple of years earlier as a Christmas present. They bought it from a cash and carry in an old cotton mill just off Broadway in Chadderton. My recordings were a mixture of angry songs, braggy songs, a song about a car, 'My 1957', and a song about being in love with television, 'TV Turns Me on'. Over the 50 years since I recorded the tape and proudly poked out the 'erase' tabs with a biro, I've occasionally listened to it. I think the first time I listened back was probably around ten years after I recorded it, maybe sometime in the mid-1980s. I was becoming something of a 'serious' musician by then and I remember being horrified at how shit it sounded and thinking I should probably erase it immediately, or just stamp on it until it shattered and put all the bits in the bin. Pretend it never happened. But, over the years, the level of cringe I've felt whenever I've listened to it has diminished with every listen. If anything, I've become proud of it. A journey of a thousand miles starts with a single step.

Funny to think that, if I'd never have set out on that path, singing quietly in my bedroom with a fake cockney accent, there might never have been a 'This is How it Feels' or 'Saturn 5'. I like to think my songwriting has improved over the years. I feel lucky to be able to write songs. Of all the things I do, it's one of the things I think I do best. That, and singing. I'm known more as a keyboard player, a DJ and a broadcaster – all things I've been relatively successful at throughout my adult life – but it's the songwriting and singing that I've enjoyed the most and which I'm proudest of.

Don't get me wrong, though: I'd never profess to be one of those fortunate souls who were 'born to make music'. I had to work hard to learn how to do it. Even though my earliest songs were things of embarrassment, I'm glad I still have them. Some are in old exercise books or on faded pieces of paper; some exist as scratchy recordings on 50-year-old cassette tapes – but I treasure every one of those early soul-baring offerings. They're where my journey as a songwriter started.

In October 1976 a couple of crucial new punk singles came out. The Damned's 'New Rose' and Eddie and the Hotrods' 'Teenage Depression'. They were both gamechangers. I felt like they spoke directly to me. Back then, the process of acquiring these records could be quite protracted, but it was always worth it. After reading about a new release in the music press or hearing it on John Peel's radio show, I'd get on the bus to Oldham and make my way to one of the record shops, Javelin or Discland, both of which were in the Victorian Arcades, or the Golden Disc at the top of Manchester Street. Over the months, I discovered that the man behind the counter at Discland showed the most empathy to those of us who'd caught the punk bug. Before that, though, the Golden Disc had been my shop of choice when it came to pre-ordering, even though the young woman who worked there showed me total disdain every time I ordered a punk record – all tutting and aggressive breathing. I'd usually have to order the records as the ones I wanted wouldn't generally be stocked. I'd go back home and, over the next few days, receive a phone call or, in many cases, a postcard to say the record had arrived. Then back on the Oldham-bound bus to see the Golden Disc girl, who would put the record in a bag and throw it down on the counter in front of me, all the while staring menacingly at me, without breaking eye contact or even blinking, for the entire duration of the transaction. Take it from one who remembers: the Golden Disc girl was a menace to young punks like me.

I loved my new world at the art college, it was such a different environment to Cardinal Langley. The two experiences could not have been more extreme. Not everyone at college was into peace, patchouli oil and free love though. There was a guy in the year above me during my first year called Gary, who was totally obsessed with Led Zeppelin. He even had a LED ZEP belt buckle that he wore proudly every day. He probably wore it in bed too. With his Led Zep pyjamas, and his Led Zep teddy, which he probably called Ted Zep. The arrival on our shores of this thing called punk rock really rattled Gary's cage. After all, Led Zep stood for everything the punks wanted to destroy. Gary picked up on this from day one when I turned up at college in ripped drainpipe jeans, white loafers, safety pins in my shirt, and the obligatory biker jacket. I'd also cut my own hair, for the first time ever.

Gary: 'What you doin'?'
Me: 'What d'you mean, what am I doin'?'
Gary: 'Why you dressed like that?'
Me: 'Dressed like what?'
Gary: 'Like a scruffy cunt?'
Me: 'I'm a punk rocker.'
Gary: 'You're a what?'
Me: 'A punk rocker.'
Gary: 'I hate punk rock and I fuckin' hate you!'

Because I was the first punk rocker to pop up on Gary's radar, I took the full force of his wrath. At first it was just verbal abuse, but then the occasional 'jovial' strangle-hold or 'matey' dead leg. As the weeks went by, I started to dread hearing the news headlines each morning, because throughout the end of 1976 and into 1977 we were never too far away from another controversial tabloid headline involving the nation's punk rockers and their dirty deeds. On a good punk-news day, I'd get it in the neck off Gary. For every 'Johnny Rotten did this' or 'Captain Sensible did that' story I'd get my ears pulled a little bit harder by Gary the Angry Rocker. I often wonder if Gary's still out there or if he angried himself into an early grave. I also wonder if the Golden Disc girl might have been Gary's sister.

Phil Diggle was also in the year above me at college, but we always got on well. He had this quirky affectation I'd never seen before (and have never seen in anyone since) where, when chatting, he'd waft his right hand aloft as if holding an invisible cigarette. He was a keen smoker, but it was as if, even when not smoking, the muscle memory in his right arm wouldn't allow the limb to just relax and behave like a normal arm. Phil went on to become a very successful and celebrated painter (he doesn't like to be called an artist). I first heard Phil talk about his brother, Steve, in the spring of '76: 'Me bruvvoh's in this really cool band. You need to check 'em out, man! They're called Buzzcocks. You'll fuckin' love 'em, man!'

That summer, the newly formed Buzzcocks put together a now infamous gig at the Lesser Free Trade Hall in Manchester, headlined by the Sex Pistols. It took place on 4 June. I wasn't there. I didn't hear about it until the week after it happened. How could I have missed that one? I know Phil was spreading the word about 'me bruvvoh's band' even back then. Maybe I was too distracted by the invisible-cigarette thing in the moment he invited me to the gig? Maybe I was still too obsessed with my beloved Elvis and Showaddywaddy? Either way, I wasn't at the Lesser Free Trade Hall gig. Famously, there were only a few dozen people at the gig, but those people included young men who would go on to form Joy Division, The Smiths, The Fall and (via the Frantic Elevators) Simply Red. Even though there were only around 40 people in the audience, thousands now claim they were there.*

---

* There's even a book about the gig and the people who were or weren't there, called *I Swear I Was There* by David Nolan.

On Thursday 2 December, 1976, the day after the famous Bill Grundy TV incident, the front pages of every tabloid painted the same picture of the end of civilisation as we knew it. Grundy's interview with the Sex Pistols had descended into absolute chaos, resulting in one of the most iconic music-related TV moments of all time. The news meant every punk rocker in the UK was scanning the press the next day to see where and when they could get to see these boys play live. The Anarchy tour was due to start just a couple of nights later but, after the news broke about the Grundy moment, gigs all over the UK started getting cancelled. Religious leaders, politicians, councillors and other figures of authority up and down the British Isles were simultaneously losing their collective shit. It was a joy to witness.

That's what led us to the Electric Circus on Thursday 9 December, 1976. We were desperate to see the Pistols. We spent the afternoon eagerly getting ourselves ready at college, listening to records, drinking and getting into our outfits for the night. We travelled to Collyhurst on the Number 17 bus wearing our finest, homemade, customised art clobber. We thought we'd be the only people at the gig dressed like us. But when we walked into the venue, we saw dozens of other young people in the uniforms they'd created, crafted from fabric scraps and charity-shop bargains because they couldn't afford to look different in any other way. I felt a sense of unity and of being part of something far bigger than our 'common room/studio' gang from college.

For me and thousands of other kids my age, the weekly music press had become the keystone of our cultural education and enlightenment. I'd digested every word in every vital inch of every page of the music press for the last few years; *NME*, *Sounds* and *Melody Maker* were our bibles.

Now punk was our new religion, and the music journalists were the new apostles. Nick Kent, Charles Shaar Murray, Tony Parsons, Julie Burchill and, slightly later, Paul Morley. The likes of Joe Strummer, Lydon, Devoto and, soon to crash into our lives, Weller, Hugh Cornwell and Mark E Smith, were the new gods on the block.

6/ Booney Takes a Trip

I decided to drop out of college on the night of the Pistols gig at the Electric Circus. Working towards spending the next three years at university didn't seem relevant any more. I knew what I needed to do with my life now. I'd seen my future. There was just one thing that I wanted to do before I left: a college trip to London. It had been organised by the tutors so we could visit London's art galleries and museums and pay homage to some of the world's most loved art pieces. For some of us, though, it was a perfect opportunity to visit what we saw as the more important cultural establishments of the capital.

There were a couple of dozen students on the trip, all eager to escape the dullness of Rochdale, Oldham, Middleton or whichever mill town we happened to be from, even just for a couple of days. I'd only ever been to London once before, when I went to a big karate event at Crystal Palace. On that occasion we only passed through the city, no time for sightseeing, just stolen glimpses of the landmarks through the steamed-up windows of a Yelloway coach after a seven-hour trip south. Most of the students on the 1977 coach trip were up for a bit of the academic stuff, but for some of us it was all about the music. We were desperate to visit these cool places we'd been hearing about. Malcolm McLaren and Vivienne Westwood's clothes shop on King's Road was top of the list. Until December, it had been called Sex. We were all a bit gutted to hear they'd just changed its name to Seditionaries but were still desperate to visit anyway. Also on our wish-list was the brand-new Roxy Club in Covent Garden, where The Damned were due to play on the second night of our trip.

We did a quick turnaround when we got to London. All the lads, 11 in total, checked into our communal dorm room, with steel bunk beds lined up on each side. Those of us that were off on the Seditionaries adventure got into our outfits quickly and gathered downstairs where some of the girls met up with us. I popped into a newsagent's next door and bought a pocket-sized *A–Z* map book and went through it putting rings around the addresses we were heading off to visit. One of the girls needed an eyeliner. I nipped into a small chemist with her, and she picked an eyeliner off the shelf and put it on the counter. The woman serving said, 'Is it for the workhouse, luv?' We were both 17 and she thought we were sex workers. Welcome to London, 1977.

We headed off, *A–Z* in hand, through Hyde Park first, pretending to ride invisible motorbikes, stupid, but giddy with excitement. We caught a tube to Sloane Square. My first ever ride on the Underground. My first time hearing that banshee screech of several tons of steel rattling along at high speed through the tunnels beneath the capital. From Sloane Square, we made a beeline down King's Road in the direction of Seditionaries.

And there it was. The shop that was, pretty much, the centre point of everything we'd read about, talked about, and dreamt about for the last three months. We stood outside taking it all in for a few moments then gingerly stepped inside. The walls were decorated with huge images of bombed-out cities and an upside-down floor-to-ceiling colour picture of Piccadilly Circus. Behind the counter sat a young woman: short blonde hair, mohair 'fishnet' jumper, heavy eye make-up and what looked like a foam neck brace under her chin. I asked her if she'd mind me taking a photograph of her. She obliged and stared wistfully into the middle distance as I pressed the shutter button on my Kodak Instamatic. I think I might have embarrassed her. She asked where we were from. 'Rochdale. Near Manchester.' 'Nice!' she replied, nonchalantly.

We browsed through the clothes, the boots, and the accessories. None of us bought anything. I'm guessing we probably couldn't afford any of it. We were all still living on pocket money from our parents. We'd just have to carry on making our own fashion items when we got back up north.

I took more photographs, thanked the shop assistant and we walked outside onto the bustling King's Road. The weather was glorious, and life couldn't have felt any better. We were in Punk Rock heaven. I realised years later, of course, that the shop assistant I'd photographed was Pamela Rooke, who would go on to find fame as Jordan, one of the first female icons and pin-ups of the punk scene.

We set off back up King's Road, stopping at various clothes shops on the way, including another much-publicised punk hangout, Acme Attractions, and a cool record shop called Rock Dreams. Pink Floyd had released their new album, *Animals*, a few days earlier and the shop window was completely decorated with promotional artwork advertising it. We ended up in Beaufort Market, just off the King's Road, taking in the bondage and mohair vibes and loving our punk life.

Another important entry in our diaries on the London trip was a visit to the only cinema in the country that was screening the horror movie *The Texas Chainsaw Massacre*. The film had been banned in 1975 as soon as the British censors saw it, but we found a small basement cinema just off Piccadilly Circus that was doing late-night screenings. It was a proper gore-fest but none of us seemed too affected or traumatised by it. Safety in numbers, I suppose. We nervously joked and laughed throughout it.

On the afternoon of our second day, we headed to Covent Garden in search of Neal Street, where the Roxy club was located. We wanted to make sure we knew where the venue was so we didn't get lost later, after we'd been for food and drinks. The Damned had only released the one record by this point. When I'd heard the brilliant 'New Rose' for the first time on John Peel's show it had hit me in the heart like a sledgehammer. Two minutes and 42 seconds of sonic perfection; possibly one of the greatest rock 'n' roll songs ever created. The Damned's debut LP was due to be released a week or so after our London trip. They'd taken up something of a residency at the Roxy, playing almost every week during the early part of 1977. We bumped into a couple of punks on the street corner just up from the club and got chatting. One of them asked where we were from.

'Rochdale, near Manchester. Where you from?'

'We're from here, mate! London!'

'Cool! Are you going watching The Damned?'

'We *ARE* the fackin' Damned!'

'No, you're not!'

'Yes, we fackin' are!'

'Give over!!'

'It's true!'

'Prove it, then!' I said.

One of them reached in his pocket, pulled out his driving licence and handed it to me.

'It says Christopher Millar!' I said.

'That's me, Christopher Millar! I'm Rat fackin' Scabies!!'

The other lad explained he was Captain Sensible.

The Roxy was an absolute sweatbox that night. Rammed with young people like us. All pushing and shoving. Some spitting. Kids rolling around on the dirty sticky floor play-fighting in the corners and in front of the bar. The support band on the night were The Adverts, a new band to us. They'd not put any records out yet but would go on to release two genre-defining singles over the coming months with 'One Chord Wonders' and 'Gary Gilmore's Eyes'.

When The Damned came on, we got right to the front. Scabies and Sensible recognised us, and both started grinning. Frontman Dave Vanian looked like the coolest rock star of all time, jet black hair greased back and a silver dagger earring through his right earlobe. He pointed at us, and I grabbed his hand, and held onto it for a very uncool number of seconds too long. I didn't realise what I was doing, I was just so completely spellbound and caught up in the moment. I didn't want it to end.

FACTORY FLOOR

7/
'Once you come in 'ere, you never get out!'

First thing Monday morning, after I got back from London, I went to see my head of year, John Sprakes, and told him I was leaving college to pursue a career in music. He couldn't believe what I was saying at first. He tried persuading me to stay on, but quickly realised it was pointless, that I was absolutely determined to do this, and acknowledged that I should follow my heart. He wished me all the best and I went on my way, ending a chapter of my life that still always fills me with total joy when I think back to it. I *loved* Rochdale College of Art and I loved doing art, but now I had my heart set on another path.

If I was going to make any sort of future for myself in music, the first thing I needed to do was earn some money so I could buy a few musical instruments and equipment. Mum and Dad were still supporting me financially and having some cash coming in meant I wouldn't need to be borrowing cash off them all the time.

We'd sacked off the mobile-disco business by now as Kenny was making good money from his Hawker Siddeley job and my fixation on making music was leading me in a different direction. I could think about nothing else; I was obsessed. The DJing could wait. It was March 1977, and I found a job in the small ads of the *Oldham Evening Chronicle*, as a screen printer in an old mill in Dobcross. I got the job and was told I'd be screen printing thousands of Union Jack flags on bunting, destined to adorn the streets of the UK during the forthcoming Queen's Silver Jubilee celebrations. But the night before I was due to start, the proprietor phoned me to say he'd lost the contract. Fuck.

Mum and Dad suggested I could try to get some work at Stockwell's Sheet Metal, which was just down Springfield Street from our shop. It was a massive warehouse filled with the kind of dangerous, noisy machinery that, at one extreme, could take a man's arm off or, at the other, could crush a man to oblivion. I really didn't fancy working in such a hellhole, but I needed the dosh. I wanted to buy musical instruments, recording gear, microphones, more records, and petrol for my bike. By now, I'd upgraded to a red Suzuki GT500 (LTE 365P), a nippy Japanese two-cylinder, two-stroke machine.

Within days, I found myself kneeling behind a huge guillotine, catching the sheets of metal that would drop in front of me as they were cut to size. I was given protective gloves and ear defenders and advised to buy some steel-toecap boots but, generally, the health and safety was questionable. There were men working there who'd been scarred for life by the merciless raw jagged edges of freshly cut steel. One guy had fingers missing from an accident that happened on Christmas Day, when he was getting paid triple time. The circular saw he was operating, capable of cutting through steel bars up to six inches in diameter, took a couple of his fingers off. He was the only man in the building at the time. The word on the shopfloor was that he bandaged himself up, finished his shift and toddled off home for his Christmas dinner.

The two blokes who operated the guillotine were like Dastardly and Muttley from the TV show *Wacky Races*. They were great to work with, but both had a dark sense of humour. I'd be crouched down on the other side of the brutal thumping monster of a machine, carefully picking up the sheets of oily metal and stacking them on a wooden palette to my side, when half a frog would suddenly appear in front of me, face first. Never smiling. The rest of the poor frog would then pop out with the next revolution of the guillotine's blade. Sometimes it would be parts of dead pigeons found outside the factory and, occasionally, pages from a porn mag. The overhead cranes would constantly be carrying tons of steel sheets above us. Occasionally a load would come adrift and come crashing down. The noise was incredible and would momentarily strike fear through everyone in the warehouse. Then there'd be the sound of a few dozen grown men cheering and clapping.

The de-coiling machine was sent straight from hell itself. The biggest machine in the factory, it unrolled and straightened the huge rolls of sheet steel you still see on the back of big trucks on the motorways. These coils weighed anything between five and ten tons. Sometimes more. The coil was held together by several steel straps and securing clips to hold the straps tight. The uncoiling process would start with the coil being lowered by overhead crane into a pit at one end of the machine. The man in charge, Jimmy Saunders, would then climb into the pit and brace himself with his feet pushing against the coil, and his back against the cast-iron wall of the pit. Sometimes, if the coil was particularly big, his right-hand man, Barry Corry, would climb in and position himself alongside Jimmy. Another one of the team would then lean over, band cutters in hand, and cut each of the straps. Jimmy's job then was to use his entire body to prevent the coil from unwinding before his mates could feed the loose end of the coil into the jaws of the beast.

We'd get our wages on a Friday morning, just before the lunchbreak: a small brown envelope stuffed with your payslip, banknotes and coins. One of the lads at Stockwell's lived near the factory with his wife, who was obviously the one in charge. At the sound of the 12.30 bell, he knew he had exactly half an hour to leg it down the road to his wife, hand his wage over, and quickly empty his bollocks before strutting triumphantly back into work to rapturous applause from his workmates.

The only saving grace about Stockwell's was that the money was great. Especially for a lad my age. I was working long hours and pulling in around 70 quid most weeks (about £400 in today's money), so I was able to look after myself financially. Now I could buy my own insurance for the bike and, for the first time in my life, I was able to give Mum and Dad a bit of 'board' money towards my upkeep. My wage from Stockwell's meant that I could afford to buy records, musical instruments and recording gear, but, for the seven months I worked there, it felt as if serious injury or death was just a second away. The whole experience left me quite depressed, a feeling of profound sadness seeping into my days. One day, I told one of the guys that I was thinking of getting out and finding a different job. Without hesitation, he said, 'You're fucking joking, mate! Once you come in 'ere, you never get out!'

He wasn't joking. But his words made me determined to escape this bedlam. I knew I needed to get the fuck out of there before I was sucked into it for life.

8/
Attack of the Teddy Boys

My first taste of personal 'fame', or at least some minor sort of public recognition, was a letter I wrote to the *Oldham Chronicle* in 1977. It was my response to a scathing letter on the previous week's 'Letters to the Editor' page where a disgruntled reader moaned at length about the scourge of this new disease called 'Punk Rock'. A punk band down south had decided to call themselves the Moors Murderers* and write and release a song called 'Free Hindley'.

They were obviously being deliberately provocative, and it had the desired effect, especially in our part of the world, where the bodies of some of Myra Hindley's and Ian Brady's victims still lay undiscovered on the hills above Oldham – which had caused 'Angry from Abbey Hills' to reach belligerently for their biro and write in to the *Chron*. I didn't for one moment condone the record or the band's name, but in my response to the letter I pointed out and celebrated the positives I saw in the punk movement. The freedom it gave people like me to dress this way, act this way, and do things a bit differently. I signed my letter off with what I thought was a suitable *nom de plume*, 'Future Adult'.

Seeing my words in print gave me a real sense of achievement. Even though only a handful of people in the world knew I was the elusive and enigmatic Future Adult (my mum, dad, Booney and Booney), for the first time in my life I felt a bit famous.

---

* Two members of the Moors Murderers, Steve Strange and Chrissie Hynde, went on to form hugely influential bands (less provocatively named) and write some classic pop singles; Steve with Visage and 'Fade to Grey' and Chrissie with The Pretenders and 'Brass in Pocket', 'Don't Get Me Wrong' and 'I'll Stand By You'.

One evening not long after that, late June 1977, I went to watch Generation X at Rafters on Manchester's Oxford Street. The support band were called Warsaw. They didn't really excite me. To me, there wasn't much to separate them from other local bands. They seemed like they were just finding their feet, finding their sound, and getting used to making the transition from being in the audience to being up there on stage. Generation X, though, blew everyone in the room away.

After the gig, I made my way back through Piccadilly Gardens to catch the last bus back to Oldham. It was a trip I'd taken regularly in recent months after late-night gigs in and around the city, to the Electric Circus, the Mayflower, the Ranch or the Band on the Wall. I can remember the exact spot where it happened that night. I still think about it every time I walk past it in Manchester city centre. Across the street, I saw a couple of Teddy Boys. One of them was linking arms with a woman, who I assumed was his wife or girlfriend. They were all in their thirties or early forties. I thought I recognised the guy with the woman from the Shakin' Stevens and the Sunsets gig I'd been to at the De La Salle College in Middleton in the summer of '76. He had a very recognisable chain around his neck. When he clocked me, a massive look of delight spread across his face. As he grinned, I saw he had no front teeth. He shouted over to me: 'Hey, Tommy! Come here!'

The name 'Tommy' was a reference to the comedy duo Cannon and Ball's recent routine, where Bobby Ball would say he was a punk rocker and start winding Tommy Cannon up with the phrase 'Rock on, Tommy!' 'Tommy' had become a generic put-down for punk rockers in the Manchester Teddy Boy fraternity. Despite my love of punk, its music, fashion, characters and ethos, I was still really into the whole 1950s rock 'n' roll thing and considered myself a Ted at heart. I'd only just turned 18 a few days earlier, not a bad bone in my body. I'd studied karate until recently, but I'd only come out of that phase with party tricks like being able to put my leg behind my head, rather than to channel the spirit of Bruce Lee at the drop of a hat.

When the toothless Ted called me over, I should have immediately turned around and headed for the number 59 and got my arse out of town. This was a time when Teddy Boys famously kicked the shit out of any unfortunate punk who happened to cross their path. The infamous mods and rockers battles had happened just over a decade earlier and had been well documented. The ongoing war in the late 1970s between Teds and punks didn't make the front pages to the same extent but was equally as nasty as what had happened on the beaches of Brighton, Clacton and Margate back in the mid-1960s. Every punk in the UK knew not to approach or get in the way of a Teddy Boy. Especially late on a boozy Saturday night in Manchester.

But part of me was convinced this Ted just wanted to shake hands. Maybe he knew I was a kindred spirit. The presence of an older woman made me, somehow, feel this was all in good faith. I stepped into the gutter and headed over towards him. His gappy smile grew wider as I approached him. He stayed in position, grinning, and released the woman's arm to reach into his pocket. As his hand came flying back out of his pocket, I saw the knuckleduster flash a bright tone of gold in the glow of the Piccadilly streetlight before he smashed it into the top of my forehead, on the right-hand side, just on my hairline. The bleeding was instant and profuse. I heard the woman scream at him. I heard him laugh. Then they were gone.

I was on my hands and knees, blood dripping onto the tarmac, in shock. A few passers-by offered to help as I got to my feet. I made my way to the bus stop just in time for the last bus back to Oldham. At first the driver refused to let me on, I was in such a bad way. Eventually, he realised my predicament and helped me to a seat. No one had ever attacked me with a weapon before. Nobody has since.

This wasn't a case of the Ted wanting to give me a black eye or swollen bollocks. This was a serious attempt at cracking my skull open. You could argue it was attempted murder. Obviously, I didn't report it. I even hid the truth from my mum and dad, telling them I'd managed to bang my head on the ceiling while bouncing down the steps into the underground toilets in Piccadilly Gardens.

For years, I brushed the incident off with boyish bravado as just another one of those 'coming of age' things, or a good example of the old 'I should've known better'. But, as I've got older, and become a parent myself, to five beautiful souls, my thoughts have changed. I often think about that bloke and what he did to me that night. I think about what a disgrace he was, not just to his tribe, but to the woman on his arm and to humanity. To think it's OK to physically attack a young person just because of their love of music or taste in fashion. Pure evil. It's an age-old and primal instinct, that of territorialism and tribal dominance, which I think, sadly, will stay with humans for as long as we're gracing this planet. I guess a man is no man if he doesn't have a beast inside.

9/
Solar Power

I was still catching sheets of metal, manning the guillotine blade, when an old friend of my parents, Mike Milner, came into Stockwell's one afternoon to buy some steel. He was a skilled draughtsman who'd set up his own business. He'd been responsible for building the bunk beds for me and Booney when we were kids. We got chatting and I told him I wasn't happy at Stockwell's. He explained he had a furniture-manufacturing business in Ashton-under-Lyne and I could go and work for him if I wanted. I didn't need asking twice.

I started at Solar Design in late 1977. The business made steel coffee tables and headboards and soon went into producing cheap four-poster beds. Initially, I was working on the shopfloor. I spent my days drilling, sawing, polishing and braising all sizes and shapes of metal. It wasn't exactly the future vision of myself I'd imagined as I stood watching the Sex Pistols a year earlier, but it was an income.

Solar was based in the Guide Bridge Mill on South Street in Ashton-under-Lyne. It was a typical Victorian cotton mill, which had operated as a munitions factory during the Second World War. There were still bullet holes in the basement walls where guns had been tested, and on parts of the exterior brickwork you could still see faint traces of the grey camouflage paint used to disguise the mill from enemy bombers during the war.

A railway line and a canal ran alongside the mill. The railway line wasn't generally used for passenger trains but for less glamourous cargoes of coal, timber, grain and huge tanks of whatever fuels and toxic fluids needed to be distributed across the industrial north. Many communities in and around Oldham and Manchester had acre after acre of red-brick Victorian terraced housing, once homes to tens of thousands of people who worked in the cotton mills. Though I'd grown up nine miles away in Shaw and Heyside, I'd make the eight-mile journey every day, in all weathers, on the Suzuki. I passed red-brick terraces all the way; Guide Bridge very much felt like home.

There were lots of other businesses in the mill: steel fabricators, motor mechanics, metal finishers, a couple of textile companies and Textella, a company that produced prams and baby clothes. The Guide Bridge Mill was a busy place, with dozens of grafters working hard to keep their families warm, fed and in decent clobber.

When Mike's business partner, Ray Hardy, decided to retire from the company, Mike approached me and asked if I'd like to buy shares in the business and become a fellow company director. He explained that my loyalty and good work ethic had inspired him to ask. I didn't know what being a director meant, but I liked the sound of it. I told Mike I'd go home and speak to my mum and dad. I was 19 years old, going on 20. Mum and Dad thought it was a good opportunity, so they lent me some money, I sold some stuff, took out a bank loan for the rest and became Mike's business partner.

Over the next few years, as the 1970s turned into the 1980s, the business expanded, and we took over more and more space in the mill until, eventually, we had most of the ground floor and a unit upstairs too. Sometime later, we took over a few more modern offices on the ground floor of the mill. The first time I entered our newly acquired reception area, I got a pleasant surprise. On the wall facing the entrance, a floor-to-ceiling piece of abstract art was mounted into the expensive wooden surroundings. The nameplate mounted by its side read '*Leaves from a Window* by Susan Bennett'. Sue had been one of my tutors at Rochdale College of Art and I recognised the view in the painting: it was from the life-drawing studio in the college looking out towards a non-descript GPO building on the other side of the street. I'd stood chatting to her as she painted it during my time at college five years earlier. It was an auspicious moment. A lucky sign.

10/ How I Met Elastic Man

The first weekend of October 1977 saw the final two nights of the Electric Circus before its closure and eventual demolition. The local council and fire service had won that particular war. Everyone on the Manchester punk scene was distraught at the news that our cathedral was about to be dismantled.

To mark the occasion, local promoters Richard Boon (no relation) and Alan Robinson put on a gathering of some of the key bands in the scene. They'd been responsible for putting on most of the punk gigs at the venue since the summer of 1976. Buzzcocks, Steel Pulse, The Prefects, John Cooper Clarke, Warsaw, The Worst, Jon the Postman and Howard Devoto's new band Magazine were all booked to provide the entertainment over the weekend.

Warsaw played early in the evening on the Sunday, but I still wasn't really into them. I'd seen them a couple of times now, as support act to other bands: that time at Rafters, and they'd opened up for Buzzcocks and Penetration at the Circus in May. For some reason, they still didn't resonate with me. I wasn't the only one. They were still trying to find their sound. I did like the singer's unusual stage presence, though. He looked like he was in the middle of a severe electrocution mishap involving a wet floor and a dropped hairdryer. Very intense, never cracking a smile, zero banter between songs. I carried a small notebook around at the time and kept a list of the names of the bands I saw, with ticks alongside denoting how many times I'd seen them and a one- or two-word scoring system where 'Ex' meant 'excellent' and so on.

The Damned – Ex / /
Eater – V. Good /
Slaughter & the Dogs – Ex / ('Ex' crossed out and replaced with 'V. Good')

Buzzcocks – V. Good / / / / / ('V. Good' crossed out and replaced with 'Ex')
Victim* – Not Bad /
Warsaw – Poor / /

The Worst were a three-piece outfit and something of an anomaly on the Manchester punk scene. In many ways they were the most authentic punk band in town. They didn't strive for fame, success or financial reward. They just did it for fun. They sounded like they could hardly be arsed even trying to write an actual song. They'd turn up, often unannounced, with the shittest equipment and a Chad Valley drum kit designed for children. On one occasion, on the way to a gig, they found a discarded spare wheel from a car. They brought it along and stuck it in front of the drum kit to stop it sliding around. They were noisy as hell, happy in their heaven, and looked cool as fuck.

Another band on the Sunday-night bill that final weekend at the Circus was The Fall, a band I was aware of but hadn't seen live yet. They'd played at Rafters a couple of weeks earlier, just a few nights after Elvis had died, but I'd got stuck into the Newcastle Brown Ale a bit too early that night, grieving the death of the King, and couldn't remember much about the gig. When The Fall took to the stage on that closing night at the Circus, I remember immediately thinking they didn't look like any of the other bands. The singer wore a red satin shirt, black Sta-press trousers and shiny black leather shoes. He looked like he should have been fronting a cabaret band and knocking out evergreen pop hits by the likes of Neil Diamond or Tony Orlando and Dawn, not an energetic, angular post-punk outfit. He was like no other frontman I'd ever seen. The snarl, the pout, the grin, the clothes, the quirky dance steps. He looked and acted like he did not give a fuck what anyone thought of him. By contrast, the guitarist looked very rock 'n' roll: leather biker jacket, scruffy drainpipe jeans. He could have been a Sex Pistol or one of The Clash. The bass player looked understated and workmanlike, delivering only what was needed and nothing more.

* Victim's 18-year-old drummer, Mike Joyce, would later join The Smiths.

On drums was a young chap with a slight aura of someone deranged. You could see it in his eyes: an unsettling mix of Keith Moon and Charles Manson. On keys, a young woman playing simple nursery-rhyme parts with a minimal amount of dexterity, something that was to inspire me more than I could have known on the night. I stood there spellbound. The Fall weren't like all the others. They instantly became my new favourite band. From that night, I would follow their every move, in the pages of the music press, at any gig I could get to, and on John Peel's radio show.

The Electric Circus reopened for a short time in 1978 as the New Electric Circus, but soon closed again before the demolition teams moved in. A few weeks before it closed for good, a friend of mine from art college, Inga Burrows, introduced me to a friend of hers in the venue one night. Her name was Karen Reed, and she lived with her dad on Broadway in Chadderton, just up the road from the Diggle brothers. She was a hairdresser and had a VW Beetle. Her dad owned a cool Jag that Karen would sometimes drive. We connected straight away. We were soon hanging out regularly, going to gigs and enthusiastically swapping cassette tapes, copying each other's vinyl records and compiling mix tapes. We discovered that her mum and my parents had worked together in the Lilac Mill in Shaw in the late fifties, and it turned out we'd spent a lot of our early years together, as toddlers in the Lilac Mill's nursery. Not that either of us could remember our time as punk-rock seedlings in cotton-mill day care.

Karen had become good friends with The Fall and often helped drive the band and their equipment to gigs. Sometimes in her Beetle, sometimes in her dad's Jag. I was soon invited along with them. I couldn't believe my luck, and my diary quickly filled up with Fall gigs: the Band on the Wall (headlining a Manchester Musicians' Collective event in November); Rafters (supporting Magazine); and the Squat, a popular-but-tired venue on Oxford Road that was part of Manchester University Students' Union.

As I got to know the band's frontman, Mark E Smith, a bit more, I knew I was in the presence of the kind of man you didn't get to meet very often. He was a complete one-off, and his writing was like nothing I'd come across before: intellectual, thought provoking, prophetic and enlightening, while also shocking, throwaway and, at times, impenetrable or nonsensical.

In February 1978 The Fall played Eric's in Liverpool. Karen drove us over there in her Beetle. Eric's was right opposite the site of the old Cavern Club on Mathew Street, which had been demolished and filled in a few years earlier. I just stood outside Eric's looking at the spot where the world's most famous nightclub had stood. There were boards up to keep people out, but I could still see the Cavern's doorstep. 'What a travesty,' I thought to myself. 'How could the people who ran Liverpool let this happen?' This was the birthplace of one of the greatest things to ever happen, not just in their city, but in the world, in the whole of humanity – the Beatles and the Merseybeat scene – and they'd just knocked it down and filled it in. A shopping centre called Cavern Walks was eventually built on the site. Some years later, the town planners realised their mistake and decided to excavate what was left of the original Cavern floorplan, to reopen a new version of the club. A bit tricky, though, when someone's gone and built a big bloody shopping centre in the middle of the dancefloor.

We hung out with the band in the dressing room before and after the gig. Mark was charming, chatty and attentive throughout the night. Martin (Bramah, guitar) oozed rock-star vibes and had an infectious energy. Eric (McGann, aka 'Eric the Ferret'; bass guitar) was quiet and seemed lost in his own world. Karl (Burns, drums) was very sociable and keen to talk, asking how Karen and I knew each other. Una (Baines, keyboards) was a lovely young woman who always seemed far too gentle a soul to be in a band like The Fall. And the omnipresent (at the time) Kay Carroll, Mark's partner and the band's manager, was a friendly but at times fearsome woman who took no prisoners.

During that period, Martin was working on an onstage party trick where he'd stand with his back to the crowd, then bend over backwards, still playing his guitar, until he was looking at the audience upside down. When he eventually pulled it off, it looked stunning. But those first few weeks when he was still trying to master it – falling over, flat on his arse, without missing a note – were amazing to witness. His determination was inspiring.

After their set at Eric's, a couple of local fans came into the dressing room to chat to Mark. It was obvious that they were in awe of him. They hung on his every word, but he was very gracious to them and full of encouragement when they said they'd been in bands together but were now 'in between bands' and 'probably going to start a new band soon'. The lads had quite distinctive hairstyles. One was called Ian and had dark hair and a cheeky little pixie-like face, the other was called Julian and had bleached blond hair and what appeared to be bedroom slippers on. Punk fashion had introduced some wacky stuff to our wardrobes, from safety pins to bondage trousers, but the idea of someone going to a gig in bedroom slippers was a new one!

As time went on, and punk became post-punk, and New Wave, there was great music coming out of Liverpool again. When some of the new Scouse bands started popping up on *Top of the Pops*, I recognised the two young Fall fans who had been in the dressing room at Eric's that night. The one with the cheeky face, Ian, had gone on to form a band called Echo & the Bunnymen, and the one with the bedroom slippers, Julian, was the frontman of The Teardrop Explodes. Two other young souls whose lives, like me, had been changed by punk and The Fall.

Even at such an early stage in their journey, barely a year old at this point and not having released a record, The Fall had an amazing repertoire of songs in their armoury. By far, some of the catchiest songs on the UK's alternative music scene: 'Hey! Fascist', 'Psycho Mafia', 'Bingo-Master's Break-Out!', 'Repetition', 'Mother–Sister!', 'Rebellious Jukebox', 'Industrial Estate'. It felt like I'd found my perfect pop group.

The Fall were the first band in my life to invite me into their dressing room. The first time I was ever 'on the guestlist' was courtesy of The Fall. They showed me behind the curtain, took me through the looking glass. I always felt honoured to be in their company, whether in a sticky venue backroom, the back of a Transit van, or Mr Reed's Jaguar. The Fall played a gig at the Tower Club in Oldham in early 1978, just up the road from where I lived. Una walked around the dressing room offering everyone boiled sweets from a small paper bag she'd brought along. It wasn't exactly the kind of debauched backstage shenanigans you read about in the music press and rock 'n' roll history books, and, to someone else, the world of The Fall might not have felt very glamourous, but I absolutely *loved* it. It was infectious. I felt like I had found the world I wanted to live in.

As they started putting records out, I became more and more obsessed. The *Bingo-Master's Break-Out!* EP was released in August 1978. Three tracks: 'Psycho Mafia', 'Bingo-Master' and, in my opinion, one of the greatest pieces of songwriting of the era, 'Repetition'. That early version of The Fall was a terrific thing to be around. Over the next five decades, the band would see over 60 members go through its doors, but that early line-up was perfection.

My day job at the furniture company saw me driving up and down the country several times each week. I was in charge of the 'assembly and packaging' and 'transport and distribution' departments. I did a lot of driving: delivering all manner of cheap metal four-poster beds, headboards and other furniture to every corner of the UK, in a cool two-litre Ford Transit van (YBA 532Y). The long trips provided a perfect opportunity to digest all the new music that was coming my way. Especially the music of The Fall.

When I wasn't out driving, I'd be working on the shopfloor, attaching brass decorations and castor wheels to tubular-steel bed frames while listening to The Fall. I bought every new record, pored over every word on the sleeves, recorded every Peel Session, learnt every word, and tried my best to emulate Mark's vocal style when singing along.

The corpse of Elvis was still warm in its grave, and when I'd heard the news of his death, I'd been devastated, and yet . . . here I was already pledging my undying love to a new icon. Mark E Smith was a one-off. Not the kind of boy you were ever going to see on *Top of the Pops*.

11/
Factory Opening

Throughout the 1970s Tony Wilson (or Anthony H Wilson, as he sometimes preferred) was one of the main faces of Granada Television, starting as a journalist and rookie TV presenter before eventually becoming an icon of local broadcasting. Most weekday evenings, after delivering the more essential local news stories of the day into our homes, we'd see him execute the most ridiculous and dangerous tasks, simply in the name of good television. He won a warm place in the region's hearts, although, at times, it seemed like someone on Granada TV's production team wanted to see him come a cropper.

Still only in his late twenties, Tony was tall, slim and good-looking, with longer hair than your average TV news reporter. He was always immaculately dressed and obviously a keen music lover as, even when presenting news programmes, he'd manage to shoehorn some music or music reference in there somehow. Eventually, Granada started to give him his own music slots, and that's when the real magic started to happen. First with his little 'What's On' guide on regional teatime news programme *Granada Reports*, then with his own music show *So it Goes*, which aired throughout 1976 and into 1977. In August 1976 Tony became the first person in the world to put the Sex Pistols on TV. To us kids, *So it Goes* was nothing short of a revolution. We'd tune in every week to see the likes of Joy Division, The Jam, Siouxsie and the Banshees and The Clash perform in the Granada studios or at local venues.

By 1977 you'd see Tony out and about at gigs in and around Manchester. Partly because of his earlier slapdash escapades as the hapless travelling reporter for *Granada*, and partly because he came across as extremely well educated, he'd always get a bit of grief from some of the more boisterous gig-goers of the region: 'Wilson, you fuckin' posh get!' 'Wilson, you tool!'

But he always took it completely in his stride. Water off a duck's back. In fact, he seemed to luxuriate in it. Many a time he'd be trying to introduce a band on stage, bigging them up for all the right reasons, and you'd not be able to hear him for chants of, 'Wilson is a dickhead! Wilson is a dickhead! Tra La La La . . .!'

He'd be loving it: 'Yeah. Go on! Fuck off!'

Shaun Ryder says the first time he ever saw Tony Wilson in real life was when he went to see Buzzcocks in 1978, when he was 16. Shaun was with his cousins Matt and Pat and said to them, 'There's that bloke off the telly!' and threw his plastic pint pot at Wilson but missed. If only the teenage Shaun had known then what a massive part Wilson would play in his life later.

In May 1978 Tony and one of his Granada Television associates, the actor Alan Erasmus, launched 'the Factory' band night at the Russell Club in Hulme, an edgy part of town. At the time, the venue was also known as the Caribbean Club and was popular with lovers of reggae music who frequented the place knowing a blind eye would be turned to those having a cheeky spliff.

The building was a weird-shaped, red-brick affair with no windows and the obligatory graffiti. It sat in the shadow of the infamous seven-storey-high Hulme Crescents, the largest public-housing development in the region, and one of the most notorious. The Crescents had seemed like a great idea when Manchester's town planners had approved their construction back in the sixties. Thirteen thousand people occupying three and a half thousand homes, in four huge crescent-shaped tower blocks where the high-level walkways were supposed to be 'streets in the sky'. But only six years after it had been constructed (in 1972), the concrete dream had turned into a dystopian nightmare. Most of the families were long gone, and it appeared that only students, musicians, squatters and drug dealers were content to live there. Scores of people from the Manchester music scene lived there, including A Certain Ratio and people who would go on to make a name for themselves like Mick Hucknall (who apparently slept with an axe by his bed, he was burgled so often), Barry Adamson (soon to join Magazine) and Mike Joyce (later of The Smiths). The Crescents were a failed utopian dream, and the more the estate was neglected by the council and authorities, the more it became a city within a city.

Hulme became a rundown incubator for Manchester's future musicians and dreamers. The Factory immediately felt like a new home for the city's punks, hippies and other music-devoted misfits. Even though the Russell Club itself felt a bit wild, and the ten-minute walk from the city centre was treacherous to say the least, having Tony's name attached gave us a slight sense of security. Hulme was run-down, stark and unwelcoming to outsiders like me, especially at night. Growing up in Oldham, I'd never seen or been anywhere remotely like it. But the pull of the music was always stronger than the fear of physical injury or death.

Warsaw had by now changed their name to Joy Division, and it wasn't just their name that had changed. Over a period of a few months, they shapeshifted from being just another unsigned local band to something that stood apart. They just seemed to get tighter and tighter with every gig they did, and Ian Curtis's stage presence became more and more dynamic. By the end 1978 Joy Division were on my list of favourite bands and, from then on, I'd go to see them whenever I could.* The final time I saw them play live was at the Russell Club in April 1980, Ian's last Manchester gig, just a few weeks before he died.

Over the first few months of the Factory, The Fall, Buzzcocks, The Damned and Joy Division became regular fixtures on the bill, with many upcoming, lesser-known bands always booked to support – the Factory was always about giving a platform to the next generation of music alongside the more established acts.

On one of my first visits to the club, I was in the upstairs bar when a young lad – short, punky, and with a menacing look in his eye – randomly walked over and confronted me: 'Where you from?'

'Oldham.'

'What you doin' here?'

'Watching the bands. Why?'

---

* If you'd told me then that Joy Division's bass player Peter Hook would one day be my best man, and then godfather to one of my sons, it would have blown my young mind!

He put his face right up against mine and snarled, *'Just fuckin' askin''* before walking back over to his mates, laughing.

I was confused. I turned and asked someone who he was.

'That's Fifteen.'

'Is that how old he is?'

'No, that's his name.'

'Why's he called "Fifteen"?'

'Because when he was 15 he stabbed someone.'

The Russell Club was always busy with young, probably underage, punks. I'm guessing the door policy was bit lax. Given the place's large West Indian clientele, reggae music provided the constant aural backdrop. In later years the likes of Dennis Brown and Gregory Isaacs would perform there.

I saw Suicide at one of the Factory nights in July 1978. Joy Division were the main support band. I'd fallen in love with Suicide's debut album when it came out at the end of 1977. They were unlike any other act of the time. Just the two of them, Alan Vega on vocals and Martin Rev on organ, synths and sound effects. They were true pioneers of electronic rock music.

To me, Suicide's music was fifties rock 'n' roll set against a soundscape of melancholy but distorted, transistorised keyboard sounds, courtesy of Martin Rev's Farfisa organ and effects units. The melodies were catchy and quaint. Somewhere in the mix was a drum machine rattling out its dirty metronomic rhythms. Tracks like 'Ghost Rider' and 'Rocket USA' had an immediacy that I found infectious. The album had some exquisite moments too, like 'Cheree'. But there were plenty of elements that were dark and disturbing, particularly 'Frankie Teardrop', which tells the story of a young father who loses the plot one day, walks out of his job, goes home and kills his wife and baby. I'd never heard such a brutal and graphic depiction of murder and suicide on a record, and I don't mind admitting that the first few listens, with Alan Vega's blood-chilling screams, left me feeling shocked and disorientated.

Soon after Joy Division's set, Alan Vega appeared on the dancefloor and was immediately surrounded by fans. He signed autographs and chatted enthusiastically with those who approached him. It was hard to imagine him being the same person who'd made me fully shit in my pants the first time I heard 'Frankie Teardrop'. He seemed so kind and gentle – smiling, shaking hands, and politely accepting sweaty hugs. This all changed when he took to the stage. They looked iconic, Martin Rev stood behind his Farfisa, wrap-around shades as big as welding goggles and a 'Don't fuck with me!' facial expression. Alan Vega, now totally in Frankie Teardrop mode, 30 seconds into the first song, smacked himself in the face with the microphone.

'What the fuck just happened?' I thought.

He did it again a few seconds later. There was blood trickling down his face. He kept doing it. There was an Iggy Pop-feel to his stage presence and an Elvis vibe to his vocal, thanks to the loud slap-back echo on the mic, but I'd never seen anything like this. The set was only short, half an hour at most, but Alan attacked his own face constantly throughout the performance. It was scary as fuck.

Slaughter and the Dogs were a band from Wythenshawe, a massive council estate on the outskirts of Manchester. It's an understatement to say they had a rough and ready reputation. They were one of Manchester's first punk bands – arguably, the first. They'd formed in 1975 and had opened for the Sex Pistols on their second visit to the Lesser Free Trade Hall in July 1976. I'd seen them a couple of times at the Electric Circus and once supporting X-Ray Specs at Belle Vue. By mid-1978 they'd signed to Decca Records and released their debut album *Do it Dog Style*. By the time the Factory opened, the album's opening track 'Where Have All the Boot Boys Gone' was something of a local punk anthem. Over the next few months, they played the Factory that often they felt like the house band. Singer Wayne Barrett was a great frontman, full of energy, angst and passion. He'd often walk on stage wearing a mortarboard hat and cape, looking like he'd just graduated from the University of Insanity. With the first beats of the opening song, he'd rip off the cape and with a furious headbutt motion, release the ton of talcum powder he'd emptied onto the top of the hat before stepping on stage. Those of us at the front would spend much of the gig choking on talc as he threw it about like a priest splattering holy water across the sick.

The Human League played the Russell Club in November 1978, supported by the Gang of Four from Leeds. The Human League were still a four-piece, with Phil Oakey on vocals, Ian Craig Marsh and Martyn Ware on keyboards and Adrian Wright looking after projectors and visuals. They stood in Perspex booths as they played. 'Very Kraftwerk,' I thought to myself. They also played a haunting cover of the Walker Brothers' 'You've Lost That Loving Feeling'.

The Gang of Four had just released their first single, 'Damaged Goods', a few weeks earlier. They'd recorded it at Cargo Studios in Rochdale, where I would record my own first ever record a decade later. 'Damaged Goods' was a brilliant track with a syncopated feel to the rhythm and guitars so sharp it threatened to slice your speaker cones at any moment. The rush I felt when I first heard John Peel play 'Damaged Goods' is still there whenever I hear it.

Inspired by the success of the nights at the Russell Club, the Factory team decided to put out a compilation record of some of the artists that had featured there. Joy Division, the Durutti Column and John Dowie were booked into Cargo Studios in Rochdale. Sheffield band Cabaret Voltaire recorded a couple of tracks at their own Western Works studio. The record, *A Factory Sample*, was released in January 1979 as a double seven-inch vinyl package with two tracks by each of the bands and three by 'alt comedy musician' John Dowie. The poster for the opening night of the Factory at the Russell Club, designed by Peter Saville, had been given the catalogue number 'FAC-1'. *A Factory Sampler* EP was given the catalogue number 'FAC-2', and Factory Records was born.

At one of the early Factory nights me and my old art-college mate Mark Wydler bumped into Tony Wilson outside the venue. We were in awe and slightly nervous as we got talking to the great man. He asked our names.

'I'm Mark.'

'And what do you do, Mark?'

'I'm an art student.'

'And what's your name, young man?'

'Clint Boon.'

'And what do you do, Clint Boon?'

'I was at art college, but I dropped out.'

Without missing a beat, Tony announced, 'Fuckin' hell! If there's one thing worse than a fuckin' art student, it's a failed fuckin' art student!' and walked off into the venue.

At moments like that, you could really see why people thought Tony was a twat.

12/ The Groover

When you're a teenager, your whole life can change completely in the space of a year. Around the same time I started going to the Factory, I started to explore other venues in and around Manchester city centre. Rafters was one of the first places I started to frequent, sometimes two or three times a week. They had a great DJ there and they would put a lot of great bands on too. I got on nodding terms with the DJ, and I'd regularly chat with him, asking him about the records he was playing and the bands that were playing. One night, when I was at the back of the room near the bar having a pint of Newcastle Brown, he put a record on that startled me. I only heard the intro, the first verse and the chorus before I picked up my drink and walked across to the DJ booth to ask him what it was. As I approached the booth, he was talking to a bloke who smiled and walked away as I arrived. I said to the DJ, 'Who's this track by?'

He nodded at the guy who was walking away: 'It's his band, they're called Magazine and it's their debut single, "Shot By Both Sides".' I remember the incident so clearly. The DJ was Rob Gretton, and the guy walking away was the bass player on the record, Barry Adamson. Howard Devoto had left Buzzcocks and started a new band called Magazine. Having loved Buzzcocks it was no surprise I also loved Magazine. 'Shot By Both Sides' came from a political argument between Devoto and his girlfriend, when she said to him, 'You'll end up shot by both sides.' It featured a brilliant guitar riff that Pete Shelley had come up with while Devoto was still with Buzzcocks. A few months later Shelley used the same riff on the Buzzcocks song 'Lipstick'. It was an early indication to me that band line-ups are not always set in stone.

Rob Gretton had made a name for himself as a DJ and would soon become manager of Joy Division. Rafters was a seminal venue: I saw bands like X-Ray

Specs and Sham 69 there. During that period, at every gig Sham did around the UK there'd be a fight and inevitably there was one that night at Rafters. At first it was fine, then frontman Jimmy Percy said something like, 'Right, we've got a load of skins here, and a load of punks there. We're not going to be fighting, are we?' And suddenly everybody started fighting. Sham 69 gigs were always a bit edgy. Rafters was such an important cultural venue for Manchester. It's now a 24-hour Tesco Metro. At the exact spot that was the entrance to Rafters now sits a cash machine. That's progress for you.

One of the other places we discovered was Pips. You couldn't really avoid Pips if you were on the punk scene – it was the first club in Manchester I was aware of that would play the kind of records we were buying. They had several different spaces, including a Bowie room and a Roxy room. We also went to a place called the Ranch on Dale Street, which was owned by the drag artist Foo Foo Lammar, who was a local celebrity around Manchester. I think he was the first drag artist I'd ever seen in the flesh. You didn't get many around Oldham in the sixties and seventies. Frank Pearson, the man who created Foo Foo, was a real character, and was friends with some of the Manchester United players, so they'd sometimes end up in there for a late drink too. He already had a couple of other venues and, in opening the Ranch, created a place where people like us could hang out and feel safe. Frank was a pioneer of the drag scene, a prolific charity fundraiser and a friend of the city's punks. There was always a fabulous mix of people in there. They also had these tall bar stools in the Ranch that had actual leather saddles that you had to straddle, if you wanted to sit on them.

There were parts of Manchester where you had to watch your back, especially as a punk walking about town. Some of us did do that thing occasionally, where you'd turn your jacket inside out, so all the safety pins, badges and paraphernalia were on the inside and not visible. You'd have to do that now and again to attract less attention on the walk across town, or on the bus home, especially if you were on your own. I was more wary after the attack by the toothless Teddy Boy with the knuckleduster, but on the whole I didn't feel that threatened. The naivety of youth, maybe. You're bulletproof when you're young. I was never a hard lad, I was always more of a lover than a fighter, but I had done karate for years, until I was 15, and got to quite a decent level.

I was nimble and quick on my feet, and, I think, subconsciously that made me more relaxed when I was out in town. When I think back to those times, I don't remember ever being particularly scared going in to Manchester; I just remember being excited. Sometimes on my own, sometimes with Mark Wydler, jumping off the bus in Piccadilly, then bouncing down the street, jibbering excitedly at each other, thrilled that we were going to see The Adverts or The Dammed, or whoever was playing that night. It felt like Manchester, and the world, was opening itself up to me, and I couldn't get enough of it. I was in. My world had changed completely in the space of a year.

There was also the Mayflower, where on one visit I saw the amazing all-female punk band The Slits, who were superb. It seemed brazen for a band of girls to be doing the punk thing as, apart from Siouxsie and Poly Styrene, it seemed like the whole scene was quite male dominated.

The Mayflower was just down the road from the Belle Vue, which always held a big place in my heart. It still does. It was one of the most magical places on Earth. I still drive up Hyde Road, past where Belle Vue was, several times a week, and it still gives me goosebumps every time. It's hard to believe such a place existed in east Manchester. If I tell my kids about it now, they think I'm making it up. Belle Vue was a magical urban wonderland to me. Its full name was Belle Vue Zoological Gardens, and it originally opened in 1836. By the start of the 20th century, it boasted one of the biggest urban zoos in the world, and an amusement park. It was like Disneyland in east Manchester a hundred years before Walt Disney had his idea. They had ballrooms and concert halls, and it was home to the world-famous Hallé orchestra for a while. When I was a kid, we even went there for our 'holidays'. Because Mum and Dad had the corner shop to run and couldn't afford to close it, we'd just go to Belle Vue for day trips, because it was near and fairly cheap. To us kids, Belle Vue was heaven. I mean, it had giraffes, elephants *and* a big dipper, all next to each other. It even had a little recording booth where you could put some coins in a slot and record yourself singing, which was cut onto a seven-inch vinyl single in real time as you stood there. What more could a kid from Oldham want?

Jimi Hendrix, The Who, Nat King Cole, the Rolling Stones, Leonard Cohen, Johnny Cash and Led Zeppelin all played at Belle Vue back in the day, and they also filmed scenes from *That'll Be the Day* and *Stardust* – the rock 'n' roll coming-of-age films from 1973 and 1974, which were hugely influential to kids of my generation – there. Shaun Ryder says he sneaked into a cinema in Salford to see *Stardust* as a 12-year-old, and that's what first made him want to be a singer. Years later, Shaun even used a couple of lines from *Stardust* for the Happy Mondays song 'Wrote for Luck' – the bit where David Essex is in his castle and Adam Faith comes to see him and says, 'You're wet,' and David replies, 'Yeah, but I'm getting drier.'

So, when punk bands started to play Belle Vue, it was extra magical for me, with all the evocative memories I had from going there as a kid. The zoo had long gone, but some of the kids still behaved like animals. Funnily enough, the worst behaved were the teenybopper fans of the Bay City Rollers, who managed to kick all the glass doors in at the front of the venue in 1975.

I'd see a lot of the same people at gigs around Manchester. It was a tight-knit community. Most of the venues were quite small and intimate, so even if you didn't know people by name, you'd recognise the same faces and let on to some of them. One of the great things about Manchester is that it's a perfectly sized city to cultivate a healthy music scene. It's big enough to support a strong, vibrant music community, but small enough for you to feel a part of it, to meet like-minded people and find your tribe. That's how Bernard Sumner and Peter Hook first noticed Ian Curtis: before they were in a band or even talked to him, they just knew him as the guy they'd see at gigs around Manchester in a donkey jacket with the word 'HATE' painted on the back. The three of them got chatting one night and decided to form a band. That band would become Joy Division and would make a massive impact on British culture before going on to become the equally monumental New Order. But whatever the evolution, you can trace it all back to this tiny, close-knit scene, where people had the space to stand out and be noticed.

I saw Ian in that same donkey jacket. It really did make him stand out. It was quite a look: the fact that the rest of his outfit had nothing particularly 'punky' about it; the cheapest coat available to people like us, yet with the boldest, one syllable, anti-everything statement scrawled across the back.

I was still knocking about with Mark at the time. Later, he would move to Cheltenham and became the artist-in-residence at a bird sanctuary. Before that, though, we had a lot of our punk and early post-punk adventures together in the late 1970s. We always used to see this one particular lad, at gigs in Manchester, who was always on his own. He always wore a biker jacket and was quiet and unassuming, but obviously really loved his music. He'd do this little dance on his own, like his own take on 'the Twist', his own understated groove; not trying to look cool or show off, just him in his own world, enjoying the music. We nicknamed him 'the Groover'. I found out many years later his name is Dave. I still see him out and about in Manchester now, 50 years later! He comes to watch me DJ, always on his own, still wearing a biker jacket and still doing the same dance. I don't even think he remembers me from the punk days. He's still the Groover to me. He doesn't know that's my nickname for him. If I see him on the dancefloor when I'm DJing, I'll leave the DJ booth, walk over to him and give him a big fucking hug. Bless him. I still don't know anything about him. But, fair play to him, he's still grooving, half a century later. Every city and every scene need their own Groovers. Not everyone can be on stage in the spotlight and not everyone can be in the band or be the DJ. People like the Groover are just as important, in their own way, in supporting and sustaining a scene. Most of the venues I've mentioned are long gone, lots of them decades ago, and Manchester is a completely different city to the place it was 50 years ago. But me and the Groover have survived it all. I'm still on the decks, and he's still down there on the dancefloor, in his own little world – the Groover.

13/
A Little Help from My Friend

The furniture company continued to thrive and expand. We rebranded ourselves as Solar Metal Industries and invested more money in the company. We took out a massive loan with a London-based bank, the Commercial Bank of the Near East, the only bank willing to loan us the amount of money we wanted to inject. Our range of products expanded to include hospital furniture for export to Africa, and low-budget reproduction antique furniture imported from Taiwan. As the business expanded, my mum came to work for us, managing the office and looking after most of our admin. Soon after, my brother Booney and, eventually, my dad, also came to work on the shopfloor. It was a proper family affair. At the end of my time at art college, I'd started seeing Alison Sutcliffe, one of the students I'd met there. She eventually went to continue her art studies at Cardiff University, and we separated soon after. Recently, I'd met a girl from Royton called Debbie Black on the biker scene. She and her previous boyfriend, a biker called Mark Beckley, had split up and she'd stayed part of the gang. At first it was me just letting her ride on the back of my Suzuki so she could still hang out with us, but after a few weeks, we started seeing each other. One of the other bikers I met around that time was Dave Bradbury, who did the best wheelies of all time and could even get his mum's Mini Metro MG onto two wheels when driving in fast, tight circles. We became friends for life and, at the time of writing, Dave travels with the Inspirals selling our merch. He doesn't need the money; he just loves the band and the people he meets along the way.

After a while, Solar caught the attention of a businessman from Liverpool. His name was Clive, and he wanted to invest in Solar Metal Industries. The deal went through quickly, and he became a business partner and fellow director. Clive was a lovely bloke with a gentle soul. I was still in my early twenties while

Clive was well into his forties. I'd been starting to do a bit of work with some of the bands I'd met around town, driving them to gigs in the company van and recording their live sets onto a portable cassette system I'd put together. By the time I met Clive, I'd bought a Tascam four-track recorder and was able to record decent-quality multi-track demo tapes for bands in their practice rooms (Aldo in Arcadia, Dysrhythm) or the local church (the Dead Heroes, the Tubigrip People). Clive seemed interested to know more about this side of my life. One day, he asked how much I charged the bands to record them.

'Two pounds an hour, Clive.'

He laughed out loud: 'Clint, you should be charging much more than that!'

'What does he know!' I thought to myself.

I'd be copying cassette tapes of the bands on a cassette-duplication system I'd set up under my desk in the office. The bands would then sell the tapes to their mates. Sometimes, I'd post tapes off to promoters, venues, journalists or record labels to try and help the bands along. In between my duties with Solar, I'd often be on the phone, trying to book gigs for the bands.

For the first couple of months, Clive would only drive over from Liverpool to visit the office once a week, so we didn't really get to know each other too well. But as time went on, he came in more often and we spent more time together, at our desks. He'd be on the phones, plugging away at our business, and I'd be copying tapes while going about my other tasks. He'd often come looking for me out in the factory: 'The cassette machine just switched off, Clint. Time for another tape, I think!' As if everything depended on me getting the next tape in position immediately.

One day, early in our relationship, he said to me, 'Clint, I've had a bit of experience in the music industry, and I've got a few contacts. Let me know if I can ever help . . .'

I was intrigued, as Clive was a modest chap and not the kind to brag. 'Who do you know then, Clive? What have you done . . . in the industry, like?'

He seemed a bit flustered and started to blush slightly. I started to think I'd put him on the spot, and he was making it up.

'Well, my brother . . . used to manage a few acts and I'm still in touch with some of them.'

'Anyone I've heard of?'

'Well, er, my brother used to manage . . . erm . . . the Beatles.'

'Fuckin' hell, Clint, you absolute bellend!' I thought to myself. 'He's from Liverpool and his surname is Epstein . . . you idiot! How could you not have figured that one out?!'

Clive's older brother was Brian Epstein, the man who brought the Beatles to the attention of the world. Because of the way Brian had set up his management business, Clive had inherited the job of managing the Beatles after Brian's death in 1967. Eventually, the Beatles would set up Apple Records and take on Alan Klein as their new manager. I knew Brian's music journey had started when he persuaded his parents to help him set up a little record shop. Unbeknown to me, the Epstein family had originally made their name as the biggest name in the furniture industry in Liverpool. After Alan Klein had taken over managing the Beatles, Clive had returned to his family roots in the furniture trade, which is how he wound up working with me in a mill in Ashton.

Recently, I came across a 1967 news article from the *Daily Mirror* about Clive taking over managing the Beatles after Brian's death, with a quote from Paul McCartney saying, 'Clive is not only a good replacement but is an ideal man for the job.'

This unassuming man, who had been kindly showing interest in the little local bands I was recording demos for, had once managed the biggest and most loved band of all time! But that was the measure of the man. Clive was one of the humblest human beings I ever met. I loved him. One afternoon, he brought his mum, Queenie, to the mill. She was charming and seemed delighted with Clive's new business venture. It felt like our own version of a royal visit. You were never too far away from a celebrity phone call when Clive was around. The phone would go in our office. If Mum was out, I'd answer it: 'Hello, Solar Metal Industries . . . Clive? Yep, he's here. Who should I say is calling, please? OK, Cilla? Yep . . . Clive, it's Cilla Black.'

On another occasion: 'Hello? Yep, he's just walked in. Who should I say is calling? Gerry . . . OK, won't be a sec . . . Clive, Gerry Marsden's on the phone.'

My favourite ever one was: 'Hello? Clive, yep, he's here. Who is it, please? Ken? OK . . . Clive, it's Ken Dodd for you!'

14/
The Haçienda Must Be Built

By early 1982 Factory Records had achieved significant commercial success with Joy Division and then New Order, whose debut album *Movement* had been well received by fans and critics after its release at the end of '81. There was no bigger champion of Manchester and its music than Rob Gretton, and he suggested the idea of Factory opening its own nightclub: somewhere the musicians, misfits and miscreants of the city could hang out. If we thought it was going to be anything like their previous gaff, the Russell Club, we couldn't have been more wrong. We knew New Order had been to New York and worked with the legendary electro producer Arthur Baker, which seemed like another world to us kids from Oldham in overcoats, skinny jeans and winklepickers. What we didn't know is that they'd been hanging out in all the legendary New York clubs like Paradise Garage and Danceteria, and wanted to bring a bit of New York back to Manchester. Rob Gretton thought Manchester should have its own Paradise Garage and persuaded New Order and Factory to give it a shot.

Tony Wilson, as understated as ever, felt they had a duty to build a cathedral to pop music's zeitgeist. They brought in interior designer Ben Kelly, who came up with a spectacular and groundbreaking industrial design. The name came from Wilson's fascination with Situationism, particularly Ivan Chtcheglov's *Formulary for a New Urbanism*, and the idea that behaviour is shaped by environment, not personality. Wilson loved the idea that you could build a place that changed how people acted, simply by existing. Chtcheglov had written, 'The haçienda must be built.' So they built it and gave it that name.

Unfortunately, early 1980s Manchester wasn't quite ready for the Haçienda. I started going to the Haçienda the week it opened in May 1982. I already knew the building on Whitworth Street, as it had previously been the showroom for a boat manufacturer called International Marine, with motorboats, dinghies and small yachts on display in the windows. There was something incongruous about a yacht showroom just on the edge of a rainy northern industrial city centre, 50 miles from the nearest sea. I've always believed it even had a deep indoor pool into which the vessel you fancied could be hoisted to give you the complete seafaring experience. This part of the building would later become the Gay Traitor Bar. I might have imagined this, but the idea has lived happily in my head since the day the Haçienda opened.

It seems fitting that the Haçienda sat only a couple of hundred yards from the exact spot where the Romans set up camp around 1900 years earlier. They built a fort and christened the region 'Mamucium' because the terrain, a gently sloping hill at the side of a river, made some Roman bloke think of a mammary gland. Yes, strange things happen to a man's mind when he's been away from home for a long time. Over the years, Mamucium became Mancunium, and eventually, Manchester. Today, that part of town is known as Castlefield.

My earliest memories of the Haçienda are of a large, hard, empty, cold and uninviting space, with a poor sound system and bad acoustics. In those early months, it never seemed busy. Me and Debbie always seemed to arrive unfashionably early and find ourselves the only ones in there, shivering, with our coats fully buttoned up and often wearing scarves. The sound, whether from the bands playing or the DJ on duty, just bounced around the room, accentuated and amplified by the dozens of hard, flat surfaces that made up the place. The benches were hard, too. Not a scatter cushion in sight. Nothing about the Haçienda, in 1982, hinted at what was to come. 'Who have you built this for?' one journalist asked Wilson. 'We've built it for the kids,' he replied. 'Have you seen the kids?' asked the journalist, incredulously. 'They're walking around in grey overcoats; they don't want a New York nightclub.'

There's a scene in the Michael Winterbottom film *24 Hour Party People* where Tony Wilson, played by Steve Coogan,* is watching Vini Reilly play

* A casting memorably described by Peter Hook as 'Manchester's biggest twat, played by the second biggest'.

one night at the Haçienda. Tony is portrayed as being one of only a handful of people in the venue as he stands on the dancefloor applauding. I have a distinct memory of seeing that exact same situation on more than one occasion in those early Haçienda days.

Tony and Rob brought in Mike Pickering* to book the artists and DJs for the club and, as time went on, the venue became a stop-off point for some of the coolest bands in the UK. Echo and the Bunnymen, The Cure, The Smiths, The Fall and Simple Minds all graced the stage at some point. Obviously, New Order were a regular turn as well, being co-owners, especially at times when the venue was struggling for cashflow.

The Haçienda soon started to gain a better reputation: no longer a barren architectural folly, more a stylish place to go for the best gigs and the best club nights. You could even get great-quality food while you were enjoying the music. This was unheard of in a venue like that at the time. Sound-absorbing curtains were fitted up in the higher parts of the room, and the sonics improved immediately. International acts like The Residents, Gil Scott-Heron, Lee 'Scratch' Perry, Johnny Thunders, the Birthday Party, Run D.M.C. and Einstürzende Neubauten all did shows at the Haçienda over the next couple of years. Famously, Madonna played her first ever British show at the Haçienda, albeit miming to two of her tunes for a filming of *The Tube*, one night in January of 1984.

Through his friendship with Buzzcocks guitarist Steve Diggle, Tony Wilson got to know Steve's brother, Phil, who had been at Rochdale College of Art with me. Wilson became a big fan of Phil's paintings and bought a couple of his works and had them mounted on the walls of the Haçienda. So impressed was Wilson with Phil's talent that he declared him 'a Rolf Harris for the New Age'! I'm not sure that testimonial still sits on Phil's CV.

* Mike Pickering would go on to record the first British acid-house record, 'Cariño', under the name T-Coy, then later form the massive band M-People (the M stands for Manchester).

15/ These Charming Men

On 31 May 1983 John Peel played a session by a new Manchester band. Peel admitted on air that it was his producer John Walters who'd tipped him off about them. Their debut single, 'Hand in Glove', was causing waves of excitement, particularly in Manchester, where their off-centre vibe set them apart from everything else that was going on. Their eccentric and charismatic frontman had an unconventional vocal style, which only added to the buzz around them.

The band were called The Smiths. The choice of name alone was mind-blowing to me, simply because it was probably the most un-rock 'n' roll band name of all time. Most bands were still trying to come up with unique and out-there names, but The Smiths had gone for the most common surname in the English language. No one else was making music like this. The Fall were about to release their new single 'The Man Whose Head Expanded' and New Order's 'Blue Monday' was enjoying its twelfth week in the top 50, but these three bands were connected by geography and nothing more. It's hard to comprehend three bands from the same city and similar backgrounds having such disparate styles.

Irene Cara's 'Flashdance' was a new entry in the singles chart, Manchester United's 'Glory, Glory, Man United' was hovering just outside the top 10, and The Police's 'Every Breath You Take' sat smugly at number 1. Tears for Fears, Ultravox, The Human League, Big Country, The Style Council and Fun Boy Three were all flying the flag for decent music in the hit parade, but no one was taking lyrical liberties like Mr Steven Patrick Morrissey of Stretford, with his odes to mammary glands, vicars wearing tutus, and the sun shining out of people's bottoms.

This was not rock 'n' roll as we knew it. It was an absolute breath of fresh air. So were the band. Johnny Marr had a unique guitar-playing style: a jangly sound full of inventive melodies, catchy hooks, arpeggio riffs and unusual chord progressions. To me, it was miles ahead of the stuff any of his peers were coming out with. Behind Morrissey and Marr was the tight-as-fuck rhythm section of Andy Rourke and Mike Joyce. Andy's melodic and funky bass combined with Mike's pristine drumming made them the best 'engine room' in town. Mike had previously been in Manchester band The Hoax and, of course, Northern Irish punks (and adopted Mancs) Victim.

I first met Johnny Marr before he formed The Smiths, when he was still a young lad working at X Clothes in Manchester. The shop was next door to another clothes shop, called Crazy Face, which was owned by Joe Moss, who went on to manage The Smiths. Johnny was known as 'Johnny X Clothes' and, even then, there was something really striking about this stylish young teen with tight jeans and big hair. He had a punky attitude but was charming and attentive at the same time. Even though he was still only about 18, he seemed really cool and connected. He would turn out to be one of the most celebrated and distinctive guitarists of his generation. He was still only 19 when he met Morrissey and put together The Smiths. Their rise was so meteoric and they were so prolific that people forget they were only together for five years. Johnny was still only 24 when they split up! Imagine changing the face of guitar music before you reached the age of 24. I don't think I've ever met anyone with a bad word to say about Johnny; he's considered to be one of the nicest people in the music industry.

I didn't realise it at the time, but I would cross paths with each of The Smiths in one way or another over the coming decades.

16/
Keys to the World

As a teenager obsessed with music, fuelled by the rush punk had given me, I started scouring junk shops for old tape recorders, microphones, drum machines, effects pedals and anything I could use to make sounds. I even had a couple of 8-track cartridge players, the predecessor to cassette tapes, the ones you'd see mounted in the dashboards of cars in the 1960s and 1970s. The tapes inside the cartridges were basically really long loops. I'd take the cartridge shell apart, take the tape out, make a short loop and reassemble it all to create various strange effects; just short chunks of sound, repeating over and over again. By 1979 I had a car battery in my bedroom to power them, and it stunk. It *really* stunk: battery acid smells like the worst farts imaginable. My dad would come into my room in the morning with a brew and a bowl of Kellogg's for me: 'What's that bloody stink? Smells like a pig's arse!'

'What? I can't smell owt!' I'd reply, knowing full well it was the car battery under my bed, gently breathing its hydrogen sulphate into the room.

I started picking up old keyboards and some of the new, more affordable electronic keyboards that were coming onto the market. The Casio VL-Tone was quite notable: a weird little monophonic thing (it only played one note at once, no chords) with a built-in drum machine. Check out 'Da Da Da' by weird German outfit Trio, or The Fall's 'The Man Whose Head Expanded' to hear it in action. Mine cost £29 from Makro cash and carry in Eccles. It even had a built-in electronic calculator. What more could a young man want? I lent it to one of the young lads I worked with in the mill one weekend. He took it home on the Friday night and his brother accidentally set fire to the house on the Saturday night. He came home from the pub, a bit tipsy, put the chip pan on, went into the lounge to watch TV, fell asleep, and the next thing, there's firemen everywhere. My mate brought the melted Casio blob back into work on the Monday: 'Booney! Look at this wot ar kid did!'

Thankfully, no one was injured in the blaze. Their mum wasn't too chuffed, though. 'Ar kid' did the same thing again a fortnight later.

The only short-lived period of piano tuition I ever had (apart from those casual school lunchtime sessions with my mate Stephen Buckley) was back in the late seventies, with an old bloke up Ripponden Road in Oldham. It was fuckin' dreary. He insisted on teaching me shit like 'It's a Long Way to Tipperary' and 'When the Saints Go Marching in'. At the end of my second visit, he said, 'Next week, "She'll Be Coming Round the Mountain"!'

'No, she fuckin' won't!' I thought to myself, and never went back.

One day in 1983 I was reading the small ads in the back of one of the weekly music papers when I saw an advert for a used Vox Continental electric organ. It was only a hundred quid. I'd wanted one for ages, since I'd fallen in love with tunes like '96 Tears' by ? & the Mysterians and 'Light My Fire' by The Doors.

I rang the bloke. He was called Nick and lived in Peckham in south London. He said he'd just sold the Vox. I was a bit cheesed off but then he said, 'I've got something else you might fancy.'

'What is it?'

He explained he had another 1960s electric organ, similar to the Vox but made in Italy. A 1966 Farfisa Compact Duo, in mint condition.

'What does it sound like?' I asked.

'Have you heard Pink Floyd's early stuff?'

Yep, I told him I was a Floyd fan.

'First album, *Piper at the Gates of Dawn* – and the singles "See Emily Play" and "Arnold Layne": Floyd used a Farfisa on all those tracks. The flutes, the oboes, all those sounds – that's the Farfisa Compact Duo!' He told me to look at the photo on the back of Floyd's *Ummagumma* album. I pulled it out, and there's Floyd with all their gear laid out on a big runway in front of their tour trucks. Right in the middle of the photograph is the Farfisa Compact Duo. The guy wanted a hundred quid for it. I rang him back and said I'd have it.

The Farfisa Compact Duo was the synthesiser of its age. In the late 1960s it cost £350. You could buy a small house in Oldham back then for that!

(Although the average price for a house in Britain was around £3,500.) Imagine spending the cost of a house on a musical instrument?! That's how revolutionary this instrument was – and that's why Floyd had one.

I sent a mate of mine down in his wagon to get it, a bloke called Xenon from Rochdale. He used to do a lot of deliveries for Solar. I stuck £100 in his hand and said, 'There's the address, pick it up for me after your London drop tomorrow. Look after it!' Two days later, he pulled up outside the mill, opened the roller shutter on the back of his truck, and there it was, strapped to the floor.

That Farfisa is probably the single most important purchase I've made in my life (alongside the £1.50 I paid to see the Sex Pistols in 1976). For the next ten years that same Farfisa came with me to every corner of the world and never let me down. I plugged in the machine, and it showed me the world.

THE NORTH WILL RISE AGAIN

17/
Eighties Industrial Psychedelia

Towards the end of 1982 I began to hear about a new, happening band from Oldham called Wheatstone's Bridge. Their name kept cropping up in the *Oldham Chronicle*'s music page, courtesy of their music writer, John McDonough. Debbie's sister, Keely, had also been raving about them for weeks, telling me they were a great covers band with a few of their own tunes mixed into the set. They were doing a Saturday-night residency at the Miners Arms on George Street in Oldham, so I decided to check them out.

The Miners was a small pub with the band room on the right as you walked in, and the taproom on the left. That night, the band room was rammed with young people, and as soon as the band started playing, everyone was up dancing, standing on benches and tables to get a better view. They played a groovy selection of sixties and seventies standards, including songs by The Kinks, The Animals, Jimi Hendrix, the Beatles and the Stones. The frontman, Malik Green, had a wild, magnetic stage presence and the look and guitar style of a young Hendrix. Whoever invented the Afghan coat must have had Malik in mind. Also on guitar, a young chap called Kev McGladdery, and on bass, Howard Tompkinson.

Howard was a cheerful hippy type who would dress most days in a boho shirt and ripped, faded, flared jeans. Howard, like Malik, loved a spliff. The catchphrase I remember most from 1983 was 'Skin up, 'edders!' where the term ''edders' referred to any 'heads' in the room who happened to have a block of cannabis and some Rizlas close to hand.

The drummer was another young lad from Oldham called Chris Goodwin. He was an excellent drummer but looked like he'd stumbled into the wrong band, his hair and fashion style making him look more like a Perry boy than a rocker.

I fell in love with the band on the spot. Malik had a flat in Royton with his girlfriend, Loz, which became party central for the rest of 1983. We started to spend a lot of time together: I drove them everywhere, recorded every gig they did and, on occasion, would look after their live sound. After shortening their name to 'The Bridge' they eventually became 'The Exit'. I would go on to help them organise and promote gigs, even though I never actually considered myself to be a real manager and never took any money for it. In those days, in the sweaty pubs of Oldham in the early 1980s, any local band would let you 'manage' them if you had any one of two things: a rehearsal space, or a van. I had both.

The first time we met, Chris told me most of his mates called him 'Spud'. I became close to all the band members, but in Spud I found a kindred spirit. He had a wicked sense of humour and great taste in music.

Spud kept telling me about a mate of his from Failsworth who I needed to meet. They'd been mates for a while, having shared adventures in everything from discovering new music to football hooliganism. They both followed Manchester United. One night in the Miners, Spud introduced us: 'Clint, this is my mate I've been telling you about: Mani . . . Mani, this is Clint.'

I was struck immediately by this lad Mani's spirit. He was genuine and down to earth, funny as fuck and mischievous; the sort of kid who seemed to light up any room he was in, just an infectious presence. Mani was a scooter boy and football casual and, like Spud and me, had a total passion for music. He told me his story over a pint. His full name was Gary 'Mani' Mounfield, and when he was born, in 1962, he was so premature and underdeveloped that at first no one expected him to make it through the night. Mani's dad, Colin, was the head chef at Café Monico on Union Street in Oldham, and was well known and respected around town. The restaurant belonged to the Berni Inn company and was considered by most Oldhamers to be quite 'high end'. Colin was friends with George Best and had become one of Man United's 'go-to' caterers. Mani's mum was a sweet Irish woman called Anne.

Me, Spud and Mani got on great from minute one, and we decided that night at the Miners to start making music together. Our first session together was on Sunday 5 February, 1984, at the Guide Bridge Mill. It seemed like the perfect place for it. Loads of space, no one working, and well away from any neighbours. We set up on the shopfloor, next to a forklift truck and stacks of flatpack four-poster beds awaiting dispatch: Spud on drums and occasional vocals, Mani switching between guitar and bass, and me on vocals and keyboards. There was no plan. We started off jamming a rickety version of Joy Division's 'Decades', then a sped-up version of 'Ghost Rider' by Suicide. Other songs in our ramshackle and spontaneous repertoire that day included: Suicide's 'Frankie Teardrop'; New Order's 'Blue Monday' and 'Age of Consent'; The Fall's 'English Scheme'; The Stranglers' 'Down in the Sewer'; Echo and the Bunnymen's 'The Killing Moon'; and 'Police and Thieves' by Junior Murvin/The Clash.

It wasn't unusual for bands back then to see members jumping off and joining other bands – all in good faith and never with any acrimony.

Spud left Malik's band soon after and a lad called Batch took over on the drums. Batch was a dynamite musician, the nearest human equivalent to Animal, the manic drummer from The Muppets.

By the second session at the mill, we were playing around with some of our own ideas. Influenced by the likes of Einstürzende Neubauten and Tools You Can Trust, we'd record lots of industrial sounds as well as the more conventional stuff. We'd make sounds with whatever machinery was lying around. There'd be a lot of glass being smashed, things getting drilled, angle grinders going off, sparks everywhere; me with safety goggles on, microphone in hand. On one occasion, I drove the forklift truck over a microphone that I'd laid down on the stone floor. The last thing that mic ever recorded was its own final moments. 'Quite a work of art,' I thought at the time. We came up with a new genre to describe our music – 'Eighties Industrial Psychedelia' – and started calling ourselves 'The Mill' and then 't'Mill' to make it a bit more northern.

In the summer of '84, Mani mentioned that he had a couple of mates who fancied coming to the mill and maybe jamming with us. One was a singer, the other a guitarist. There was a suggestion that we could maybe form a group together. Me and Spud were up for it and told Mani to get his mates to come down. We were still setting up and playing out on the shopfloor at this point. As the two lads entered through the little wooden door, I was smashing some milk bottles into a dustbin with a mic suspended inside it. We'd heard the Velvet Underground do it on their track 'European Son' (although apparently that was a chair knocking a glass over accidentally) and wanted to get a similar sound. I took off my goggles and gloves and walked over to greet the lads: 'Hi, I'm Clint.'

'Hi, I'm Ian and this is Andy.'

The two lads were Ian Brown and Andy Couzens. Andy had driven them both to the mill in his gorgeous red 1955 Chevrolet. He had a rockabilly vibe about him, and his guitar matched the look. Ian told me he'd originally met Mani through the scooter scene. The way Mani told it, his north Manchester scooter boys had run into some bother with some National Front hooligans, so they teamed up with Ian's scooter lot from south Manchester to sort them out. Mani had also played in a short-lived band with Andy called The Fireside Chaps, then The Waterfront.

We plugged Andy's amp in. He fired it up, plugged in his guitar and struck out some glorious big major chords – probably the most 'in tune' music that had ever been made in that room! I gave Ian the mic and we all started playing. I'd like to say that in that moment the clouds above Ashton-under-Lyne parted, sunbeams radiated through the walls and into the room, heavenly angels sung the most glorious of hallelujahs and the forklift truck started whirling around in a total state of nirvana. But, unfortunately, it all sounded a bit shit.

Bands are all about the chemistry and the skills of the individual members, and we hadn't found the right combo on that occasion. We exchanged pleasantries and said our goodbyes. Giggling to myself, I put my safety goggles back on, grabbed another milk bottle and headed back to the dustbin. Ian and Andy went off and formed a more conventional band than the one we had in mind and, unbeknown to any of us, our paths were destined to cross many times in the future.

Throughout the rest of 1984, me, Mani and Spud spent every available Sunday in the Guide Bridge Mill getting up to all sorts of sonic nonsense. I'd pick Spud up from his parents' house at the top of Ashton Road in Oldham, then head down Manchester Road to Failsworth to pick up Mani from his parents' house on Lord Lane. On our way to Guide Bridge, we'd cut through Daisy Nook, a beautiful, idyllic green oasis cut into a valley between Ashton and Failsworth.

I eventually took over the company's boardroom, a small office space that hardly ever got used. I converted it into a makeshift recording space where we could spend our weekends recording and then leave our gear set up ready for our next visit.

We recorded every session onto stereo cassette tapes. With the Tascam 234 'Portastudio' I'd bought, I was also able to do multitrack recordings. I treated myself to a Promark MX3 eight-channel mixing console. We carried on with our Sunday sessions right through 1984 and into 1985. We even did a session on Christmas Day 1984. The first proper demo tape we recorded was a selection of songs that we called 'Sounds Awreet to Me'. That had become a bit of a catchphrase during our sessions. I'd record something, play it back and say, 'Sounds awreet to me!' Later, we put together a second collection of tunes and called it 'Mynstrels in Lullaby Land'. On the 'Sounds Awreet' demo, we came up with the idea of taking one of the tracks – 'Set Fire to the Wick of a New Day' – and just playing the entire thing backwards to create a completely different track.* The sound of the reverse vocals inspired its title, 'Russian Mill Workers' Song'. Another of our songs, 'Mind Train', started with Mani saying, 'Destination central brain, via your cerebellum!', followed by the sound of one of us farting into the mic (with backwards echo for added psychedelic vibes) and on into a very trippy piece of sixties-inspired pop.

My Polaroid camera had a big button on the front rather than on the top, like most other cameras. It had no shutter timer, though, so taking photos of

---

* A trick The Stone Roses would use several times a few years later, most notably on their debut album, where 'Don't Stop' is the previous track, 'Waterfall', played backwards, with a few extra embellishments.

ourselves was a bit tricky. Because there was usually just the three of us in the room, the only way I could get us all in the photo was to place the camera on a shelf, against a wall and push a long stick against the trigger button. I'm not saying I invented the 'selfie stick' back in 1984, but I came close!

T'Mill was never going to be anything more than a studio project, really. We never planned on doing gigs. I mean, how do you get a forklift truck on your average 'rock 'n' roll venue stage? Plus, all that broken glass would have been a health and safety nightmare.

We did occasionally gig as the rhythm section in a band called The Hungry Socks, another Oldham outfit whose frontman Martin Swinburne (aka Swinny) was a local legend and whose repertoire included such self-penned classics as 'Nelson's Eyeball' and 'Henry's Tash' and a cover of 'Psycho' by The Sonics.

Over subsequent months, and with the help of my dad, I took over and converted the two empty offices on either side of the main studio room and created a three-room setup. The middle room (the first one I'd converted) became the 'control room' with a 'live room' on either side. It gave us more space, made sound separation easier and helped me establish a small side business, where bands could come to record cheap demos or rehearse.

On one occasion, while Dad was busy putting sound-insulation sheets behind the plasterboard of one of the rooms, I placed a cassette tape of some of t'Mill's songs into the cavity with a note explaining what it was. Thirty years later, someone pulled the wall down, found the tape and contacted me to say they'd found it. Nice little time-capsule story.

An important part of our Sundays at the mill was the obligatory stop-off at 'our chippy' on Crowhill Road in Ashton on the way home. I can't remember its actual name, it was probably 'Crowhill Chippy', or something equally imaginative, but it was a cornerstone of our weekends; we were just a trio of hungry and excitable Manc scallies with the happiest of grins, a couple of screwed-up fivers and coat pockets full of C90 dreams.

Nowadays, 'our chippy' is probably called 'Crowhill Cod', decorated and branded in the standard 21st-century British chip-shop livery of cool whites and vibrant deep navy blues. No such Hockney-esque vibes in Tameside's fast-food establishments back in 1984 – just a murky grease-fest with the occasional scruffy rat scurrying across the pavement outside, much like us, looking for something to eat before heading off home for the night.

We'd park my silver Opel Manta Berlinetta (A391 GBU) outside and march in like men on a mission. 'All right, mate! How's business been in our chippy this week?' Mani would ask.

'Really good, boss. We've made some decent wedge!' the chippy owner would reply, always happy to humour his last customers of the weekend.

Mine was always, 'Puddin', chips, peas 'n' gravy, please, brother . . . and a can of Coke.' The famous Holland's Steak & Kidney Pudding had been a staple part of every typical northerner's diet for well over a hundred years by that time. Even today, it's still seen as an evergreen culinary classic in these parts (unless you're a vegetarian, of course). The nimble slap of a chippy worker's fingers on the tinfoil shell of an upturned Holland's pudding is a sound I'll always relish. 'Naughty pudding!' I still say to myself every time I hear that sound. I'll occasionally step out of my comfort zone and go for the curry instead of the gravy. Occasionally, if I'm in a rush, on the move, or not wanting to make a mess down the front of my outfit, I'll get sausage and chips. But, more often than not, the good old faithful 'stodge special' does the trick.

'What d'you fancy, boys? I'll treat ya!' I'd ask Mani and Spud.

'Chips, peas 'n' gravy, please, mate,' Spud would say.

'Meat 'n' potato growler 'n' chips for me, Booney!' Mani would reply.

We'd pile back into my Manta, eat our scran, then head off through Daisy Nook in the direction of Mani's house. At night, the narrow country lanes and farm pathways were a haven for courting couples who, for whatever reason, needed to have sex in their cars. One of our favourite pastimes was to drive slowly alongside the parked cars with our lights out and surprise them with the flash of the Polaroid camera stuck up against their window, then drive off quickly. Occasionally, we'd get a great arse shot, but it wasn't about getting a decent photo, it was about seeing the panic on people's faces when they thought their game might be up. Some of the facial expressions we captured were priceless.

Alongside a good chippy tea, we also enjoyed a decent donner kebab – Al Fayyaz on Union Street in Oldham was our favourite kebab shop – chased down by a nice cold can of Coke, resulting in the kind of heroic belch that only that kebab–Coke combination can foster. If we found ourselves in Manchester and needing a 'K', we'd head for the legendary Topkapi on Quay Street, directly opposite the Gallery.

Me, Mani and Spud went to a lot of gigs at the Gallery, as it was the busiest venue of its size in Manchester at the time, and open seven nights a week. Every local band played there, or wanted to play there. Occasionally, an upcoming international act would pop in: Bad Brains and R.E.M., to name just a couple. As with the punk venues from a few years earlier, the between-bands soundtrack was an important part of the night. The venue owner, Omar, seemed to have the phone numbers of all the best DJs in town. The weekly Saturday-night soul-and-funk disco was one of the key nights in the city for fans of black music. I feel like I first heard electro and the embryonic seeds of house music in the Gallery, rather than a year or two later at the Haçienda.

I had two bar stools in my studio at the mill. They were samples given to Solar by one of our suppliers. When you sat on them, a bit of air would blow out from a small hole under the seat, which made a sound like a pan pipe. It coined the phrase 'Pan pipes of the Andes!' which we'd all say in unison every time one of us sat down on one of the stools. For years, me, Spud and Mani would still use the phrase every single time we spoke. Every conversation would be signed off with 'pan pipes!' or, in more modern times, '#panpipes'. Those Sundays at the mill were some of the happiest days of my life. Proper 'salad days'. I know Mani and Spud treasured them too. The last text I ever got from Mani, before he passed away, he signed off with, 'Pan pipes of the Andes!'

18/ The Bowlhead

As a kid, having a cool hairstyle wasn't really that important. It just didn't matter. Every few weeks we'd be packed off to Joe Waring, the local barber, nicknamed the Butcher of Shaw, and he'd shear us to a frog's bollock of our lousy scalps, leaving us looking like pre-pubescent conscripts. If you had an empathetic parent, you might be lucky enough to escape with a 'short back and sides', a national favourite through the sixties and seventies. Often, though, Mum would simply take her kitchen scissors to our hair to save a few shillings and the wrath of the Butcher of Shaw.

Our lives changed overnight when K-tel launched their Hair Magician styling device, which was basically just a razor blade mounted inside a cheap plastic comb. Dragging it through a wincing child's mop, in a jagged motion, removed sizeable chunks of hair in just a couple of tugs. The school playgrounds of the north became awash with spiky-haired, bald-patched, scabby victims of these unforgiving weapons. It looked like we'd suffered some sort of follicle-related pandemic. Around the same time, Ronco launched their Trimcomb, a more compact but equally brutal piece of kit. Joe Waring's days were numbered.

It was only when I reached 11 or 12 that I started looking in the mirror for any other reason than to brush my teeth or squeeze the ubiquitous blackhead. Glam rock had hit the nation in a big way and boys were starting to wear their hair longer. I followed the trend, growing my hair down to my collar, but rarely any further. Most of my mates were doing the same. Even at Cardinal Langley, the boys were allowed to sport longer hairstyles if they wanted.

By 1974, with the spirit of the 1950s still pumping through my skinny pale frame, I was doing my best to wear my hair in a quiff, sometimes resorting to using my dad's Brylcreem to keep the thing in shape. I've always had fine hair, which often ignores what I'm trying to make it do. Entering the world of mopeds and crash helmets in 1975 put paid to any further plans I had of looking like a Teddy Boy. I was at art college now. I tried my best, but whenever I took the helmet off, I'd look more like Hitler than Elvis. On top of that, the Brylcreem was making the fabric inside the helmet greasy and stinking like a wet dog. A new approach was needed.

Punk came along at exactly the right moment. Through 1976, myself and thousands of other kids throughout the country were desperately digging out those old Trimcombs, Hair Magicians, thinning scissors and whatever else we could find to cut our own hair. We worked hard on looking poor, poorly and neglected. This look served me well until the early eighties, when I became a company director in the furniture business and decided it was time to smarten myself up a bit. I went back to a more slicked-back sort of style and grew a moustache. I figured the tache might make me look a bit older and wiser when holding business meetings or negotiating with salesmen and the like. Maybe people would take me more seriously. In my head, I was channelling Midge Ure, but more often people would say I looked like local comic hero Bobby Ball.

Another new approach was needed. As I got more and more into psychedelic music and fashion in the early eighties, I started to contemplate the 'bowlhead' as an option. It wasn't a popular hairstyle at the time. Far from it. Many of the older bands in my record collection had members with bowlheads – Jefferson Airplane, the Ramones, The Byrds, The Seeds – but you'd rarely see a bowlhead on *Top of the Pops* in 1984, and you certainly didn't see any on the streets of Oldham or Manchester.

Brian Jones of the Rolling Stones had one of *the* great bowlheads of all time, but he'd been dead for 14 years by 1984. In the early years of The Stranglers, keyboardist Dave Greenfield was often 'with bowl', and occasionally 'with tache' at the same time, but, by now, he'd grown his hair long and had a centre parting.

'Time to give it a go!' I thought to myself.

Actress Joanna Lumley famously had an iconic bowlhead back in the seventies when she played Purdey in *The New Avengers* TV show, and the *Beano* character Bully Beef was an early ambassador for the bowl, but I hoped their names wouldn't come up too often as I set off on my new chapter.

My friend Karen, who used to take me to The Fall gigs, had married a lad from Failsworth, Carl Drinkwater, and they were living on Huddersfield Road in Oldham. She was still a hairdresser, and every few weeks me and Debbie would go to see her and she'd give us a tidy-up while we drank wine, played records and put the world to rights. By the spring of '85 I'd grown my hair quite long, ready for the big occasion. I went to Karen's and explained what I wanted.

'You want what?'

'A bowlhead.'

'A bowlhead?!!'

'Yeah, a bowlhead.'

'What, like Bully Beef?'

'No. Like Johnny or Dee Dee from the Ramones, or Brian Jones from the Rolling Stones!'

Karen did a great job. My new hairdo looked amazing. I knew it would be a head-turner when I next went down to Oldham Market or Woolworths. At the same time, I knew I'd get grief. I wasn't arsed, though. I didn't know any other blokes who had a haircut like this. A few older women around Heyside had vaguely similar haircuts, but for a youngish lad like me, it wasn't the done thing.

It wasn't just my hairstyle that changed either. My music taste was moving on too. Punk music had arrived on the scene hand in hand with reggae in the late seventies and, by '85, I was still listening to the likes of Dillinger, Matumbi and Lee Scratch Perry constantly. Dub reggae was a big thing for me during this time, but I was also becoming more and more obsessed with sixties garage and psychedelic records. Me and Spud were inseparable, even though we weren't really playing together with Mani as t'Mill any more. Mani had got himself a proper job as a lighting technician at the Opera House in Manchester, so we weren't seeing as much of him, and Spud had joined a new band from Oldham called T'Challa Grid, which I ended up managing. We started DJing together and got ourselves a weekly Sunday-night slot at the Grey Horse in Oldham. We called the night 'Take a Back Trip Thru Time Zones Yet to Come!'. I found a beautiful picture of the Grey Horse from the 1930s when it was first renovated in an art-deco style and turned it into a psychedelic artwork to advertise the night. We played a lot of the music we'd listened to and tried to emulate with t'Mill at our Back Trip Time Zone night, but we were also into a lot of new music. We were playing records by current bands from the States, the Dream Syndicate, R.E.M., Rain Parade, the Three O' Clock and other bands that would soon be referred to as the 'Paisley Underground'. We were mixing all this up with leftfield sixties psychedelia and mad stuff like the theme tunes from *Zorba the Greek* and *Doctor Who*. It was a real mix of influences and showed where our heads were at. The night became really popular. With it being a Sunday night, it wasn't like everyone was coming out to dance all night or get hammered, it was more like the cool place to hang out in Oldham if you were into alternative music and wanted to meet like-minded heads.

I'd spent about ten years as a motorcyclist, graduating from my Fantic Caballero moped to the Suzuki GT500 and then on to a Honda Gold Wing (XRJ 999S), but my passion for music had now become stronger than my desire to be a biker. I sold my Gold Wing motorbike in 1985 to buy some more much-needed recording equipment for my studio in the Mill. I loved that bike, but I had music to make and bands to help. It would be the last motorbike I'd ever own, but music was everything I needed now.

My dress sense was also kind of taking a Back Trip Thru Time Zones Yet to Come. I was now mostly wearing tight white jeans, winklepicker ankle boots and a silk neck scarf, which, together with my new bowlhead, created what I thought was a cool late-sixties California throwback look. Initially, I kept the tache, growing the sides around the edge of my mouth and down to my jawline. I felt like Captain Beefheart or Charles Bronson, but the reaction on the street wasn't quite as appreciative. I'd often get shouts of 'Fuckin' porn star!' or 'Look at you, you big puff!' as I walked past the lads who hung out in the doorway of the NatWest bank at the traffic lights in Royton most nights. But it didn't bother me. I felt I needed to be as different as possible to everyone around me, regardless of how much stick I might get. I was just a young music lover who wanted to look and feel distinct and individual. I had no idea then that my new haircut would, in the eyes of many people, define me for the rest of my life.

19/
Blue Mondays

By the mid-1980s New Order were gods in Manchester. As a band and as individuals. Not only had they reinvented themselves after Joy Division to become a second ground-breaking band – a feat almost unheard of – they'd also started the reinvention of Manchester as a city. Despite their status, you would still see Bernard and Hooky around Manchester (Stephen and Gillian were a bit more elusive). Hooky was New Order's man about town and was always very engaging but would often take the piss.

'What's goin' on with your hair?!'

'It's a bowlhead innit!' I replied.

'You look like Joanna fuckin' Lumley!'

Hooky seemed to be omnipresent in the live-music venues and nightclubs of Manchester. You'd spot him propping up the bar at gigs, usually surrounded by a bunch of excited young lads talking about football or sticking demo cassette tapes into his pocket. Or he'd be nipping in and out of the better-quality clothes shops of the city centre on a Saturday afternoon, always seeming perfectly down to earth and with time for anyone who wanted to chat with him.

To me, the likes of Hooky and Steve Diggle from Buzzcocks were authentic rock stars who still had their feet firmly on the ground. Real men of the people. I saw Steve on *Top of the Pops* on a Thursday night in September '78 doing 'Ever Fallen in Love' then, two days later, he was sifting through the record racks in the Virgin shop on Lever Street in Manchester, happily chatting to anyone who approached him. No hiding behind minders or blacked-out car windows; none of that, 'Sorry, mate, not when I'm out with the family!' Lisa Stansfield was like that too, a few years later. She had massive success with her singles in the late 1980s and early 1990s and became a huge pop star all over the world, but you'd still see her and her best mate skipping between the clothes rails in the Arndale Centre or giggling their way around Affleck's Palace.

I saw an article in the *NME* about New Order, with a photo of Hooky at the wheel of some kind of vehicle, held in position by a heavy-duty seatbelt harness. It looked like some kind of racing car, but the caption read: 'Peter Hook at the wheel of the New Order tour bus.' I believed it. 'This bloke's a fuckin' legend!' I thought to myself. I'd occasionally join that gaggle of young men bending Hooky's ear at the bar of the Boardwalk, the Haçienda or the International. Around that time, I'd usually be with Spud, Debbie, Mani, a couple of Mani's mates, Lee Butterworth and Paul 'Baz' Bowers and a few others from the Oldham and Failsworth crowd. Hooky was always affable, engaging and supportive. Even to weird-looking upstarts like us, doing our best to look and sound like the Velvets or The Seeds.

At the end of January 1985 New Order had played two consecutive nights of gigs: one at King George's Hall in Blackburn, then Tiffany's in Leeds, and we'd decided to go to both nights. I drove us over in my Opel Manta; me, Spud, Mani, Lee and Debbie. I noticed on the posters that the support at the Blackburn gig was a band called Blue in Heaven; at the Leeds gig, a band called Happy Mondays. I hadn't heard either name before, and, at first, I presumed it was New Order and Factory having a bit of cheeky fun with some wordplay: 'Happy in Heaven' and 'Blue Monday', with the support band being some sort of tribute act or art troupe. I was completely wrong. Blue in Heaven were a pop-rock band from Ireland, and Happy Mondays were a band from Salford who were about to crash into my life.

On that second night, in Leeds, the Happy Mondays stumbled on stage looking like a gang of scallies hanging around at a bus stop waiting to mug someone. When they started playing, they were wonderfully shambolic. The songs sounded like they were going to fall apart at any minute but somehow hung together. They were so unique: the way they looked, the way they sounded, and the way they looked like they didn't know where they were, or what the fuck was happening. They went straight to the top of our list of favourite new bands.

I got to see the Mondays play live on a couple more dates, then one night that summer I heard them on the radio for the first time, when Tony the Greek (aka Tony Michaelides) played one of their tracks on his Sunday-night show on Piccadilly Radio. It was like no recorded music I'd heard before. The track was called 'Delightful'. It had a spirit and a vibe that was uplifting, uninhibited and slightly psychedelic; a wobbly sort of punk-funk that sounded like it might grind to a spectacular halt at any moment. Shaun Ryder later said that in the early days of the Mondays, if they came up with something that sounded like the Beatles, the Stones or The Velvet Underground they would ditch it immediately. Which is such a simple thing to say, but it speaks volumes about them as a band. That was their accidental genius. Every other band would love it if they came up with something that sounded like the Velvets or the Stones.

I'd go and see them live as often as I could and, every time, they blew me away. You couldn't take your eyes off them. A few weeks after 'Delightful' (aka *The Forty-Five EP*) was released, the Mondays played the Haçienda. Unbeknown to the audience, Shaun had taken some LSD beforehand and, not wanting the audience to look at him during the gig, he persuaded his best mate to get up on stage and dance with the band. Bez, who had also taken acid with Shaun, climbed up on stage looking more like some kind of alien life form than a human being; a skeletal figure, eyes on stalks, and angular movements. He casually picked up some maracas, started to dance and, in a single moment, the world changed.

20/
Roses Start to Bloom

By the start of 1985 I was getting more and more well known for my work with bands in and around Oldham. I was recording demo sessions almost every weekend and bands were hiring my rehearsal room at the mill most nights. On top of that, I'd be at most of the gigs in town, delivering the bands' gear in my van, helping set up the PA, and often recording the gig.

One of the bands I started recording demos for were Asia Fields, an Edwyn Collins/Orange Juice-inspired bunch with funky Latin undertones; Oldham's answer to A Certain Ratio. Their singer, Graham Maley, was a brilliant songwriter. His father was a printer, and Graham held huge disdain for Robert Maxwell because of what he'd done to the workforce of his printing empire. Maxwell's embezzlement meant that, ultimately, thousands of his workers never got the pensions they were due, including Graham's dad. He wrote a song called 'Miss Maxwell', in which he addresses Robert Maxwell's daughter on the subject of her family's unimaginable wealth compared to the dire situation he saw his own father in:* *'Flowers in her hair, blood is crawling in the clothes she wears/On the day that you get wise, I'll be the flag-waver in your eyes.'* Just one small example of the kind of art that was being created in the back streets, bedrooms and broken-down mills of Oldham in 1985.

The *Oldham Chronicle* came to interview me one week for their music page. That was quite a big deal, as none of our family had ever been in the *Oldham Chron'* before, unless it was in the births and deaths section. It was also the

---

* Obviously, he had no idea at that stage about what would be revealed decades later, about Maxwell's daughter, Ghislaine, and her relationship with the paedophile Jeffrey Epstein.

first proper interview I'd ever done. My focus was still on helping bands out, while learning the trade at the same time. In the article, I was quoted as saying, 'I want to build an empire in Oldham!' I got a bit carried away with the glamour of being interviewed by the *Chron*, as if I was the north's answer to Berry Gordy, or something. Never mind Motown, welcome to Milltown!

One day not long after that, I was walking through Rochdale town centre when I bumped into Andy McVittie, a bass player I knew who'd done some gigs with The Hungry Socks. He started telling me about this new band he'd heard about and wrote their name down on a piece of paper. He added a phone number for a guy called Howard Jones who was looking after them: 'Give him a ring. You might be able to do summat together.'

The band were called The Stone Roses. Howard was part of the Haçienda's management team and well connected on the Manchester scene. Andy's scribble on the scrap of people was the first time I'd seen the words 'The Stone Roses' written down. I spoke to Spud a couple of days later and he told me that the two lads that Mani had brought up to jam with us at the mill a few months earlier, Ian and Andy, were in the band; Ian on vocals, Andy on guitar.

I went to see them at the International in May, and they were ace. They still had a harder, rocky, slightly goth element to their sound, but there was also a nice psychedelic vibe going on, probably because of the way they looked. This was the first time I saw Ian performing as a frontman; he was quite animated onstage. It wasn't what I expected at all from my experience of meeting him back in the mill. He wasn't a polished performer, as such, but he was a unique frontman: he would step off the stage, still singing, and wander into the audience and get right up in the faces of lads in the crowd. It looked quite confrontational, but he did it with this air of indifference, like he really didn't give a fuck.

Soon after the International gig, I heard about a cool party that was coming up in July in Manchester. One of the lads on the scene, Steve 'Adj' Atherton, was putting together a 'secret' gig called The Flower Show in an empty warehouse space next to Manchester's Piccadilly station. The Stone Roses were going to play, and there'd be a makeshift bar and DJs playing all through the night. It all sounded a bit dodgy, maybe slightly illegal, but we all fancied it. I was absolutely gutted when I realised I'd be away on holiday in Spain with

Debbie on the date of the gig. When I got back, Spud was raving about the band's set and the event in general. It sounded like the kind of 'happening' that the likes of Pink Floyd and the Soft Machine played in London in the late sixties. The Roses didn't go on until 1.30am and the party went on until 5am. The Flower Show was Manchester's first ever warehouse party and is seen by many today as a predecessor to the rave scene's warehouse parties and illegal all-nighters.

Over the coming months, it was rumoured that the Roses adopted guerrilla tactics to make sure everyone got to know their name. One morning, Mancunians woke up to find the band had graffitied their name on walls all around town. The *Manchester Evening News* ran a news story about it, criticising them for vandalism.

I saw the Roses play a couple more times through '85, including an electric show at the Haçienda where they were supported by another one of my favourite bands from the time, The Playn Jayn. In November, I managed to land T'Challa Grid the support slot for the Roses at Manchester University. We turned up in the afternoon at the soundcheck to find their drummer, Reni, cycling around inside the empty venue on his BMX, listening to rock music on his Walkman and singing along loudly as he pedalled his bike in circles on the dancefloor. What a voice.

That was also the first time I got to properly meet the band's bass player, Pete Garner, and their guitarist John Squire, who were both quiet lads – in John's case, quite introverted. Even back then, it was obvious John was a brilliant guitarist. Andy Couzens was still in the band at this stage, and we had a bit of a giggle about our wacky jam session at the mill the year before. It was clear that Ian and Reni were the big characters in the band. Watching them soundcheck that afternoon left me and the T'Challa Grid boys gobsmacked.

Ian was still honing his frontman act. His hair was cut really short, and he was still wearing paisley shirts tucked nicely into his straight-leg jeans – proper mod-looking, and still with this air of casual confrontation. Seeing him in action that night was spellbinding. You could feel every girl in the crowd was drawn to him. I wouldn't say they adored him yet, but they were certainly distracted. Their boyfriends weren't quite sure how to react to his confidence, but he had their full attention too.

Ian later told a story about how he was at a party at a girlfriend's flat in Hulme in the early eighties, when someone brought the legendary 1960s soul singer Geno Washington back to the party after he'd played a gig in Manchester that night. Ian got talking to him. Geno had met some of the greatest musicians of all time, he knew what it took to be a star, and something struck him about this young Mancunian, his confidence and the way he carried himself. 'You're a star, you should be in a band,' he told the young Ian Brown. Now he was, and he was slowly finding his feet as one of the most charismatic and influential frontmen of his generation, right there in front of our eyes.

21/ His Name Was Joe

While I was working at the mill, I got to know a local character who used to spend his days pushing this big old wooden cart around the area. He would collect bits of scrap metal, stack it up on his cart, then take off to the local scrap yard in exchange for a few coins, which was how he scraped together a living. When I first met him, he had an old donkey that pulled the cart, but, after the donkey's sad demise, he decided to push the cart around manually – at that stage he was still a strapping middle-aged chap. His name was Joe. He was the first homeless person I ever knew. Back then the world still referred to homeless people like him as 'tramps', 'vagrants' or 'dossers' – but to me he was always Joe.

Our company was located on the ground floor of the mill, and the big steel roller-shutter door at the back was wide open most days, partly to help the ventilation, partly to give us a sense of day and of the real world ticking by outside. Joe would always stop by and pop his head in. We'd stand and chat. He'd blag cigarettes off the lads on the shopfloor, who would always be more than happy to oblige. Joe was a likeable chap. He'd tell us stories about his past. How he'd fought in the war, and how, more recently, he'd lost some toes to frostbite. He was well liked in the neighbourhood. You'd see kids on South Street winding him up sometimes, but he'd go along with it, just having a laugh, getting on with his day. You could tell he had a strong spirit and a good soul. We'd give him offcuts of tubular steel and bits of metal to take away and weigh in for cash. That, and whatever social benefits he got, seemed to keep him content and on the move.

Joe spent most nights in a homeless hostel, not far from the elegant and opulent-looking Twelve Apostles building in Trafalgar Square in Ashton. The building had been constructed in 1881 for the managers of the nearby Oxford

Mill. As Joe got older, he got weaker. He'd been a strong healthy bloke when I'd first met him in 1979 but, by 1984, he was losing his weight and his strength. He had to get rid of his cart, as he didn't have the strength to push it any more, which meant he couldn't earn that extra bit of cash he needed. But he would still come round to chat, borrow a cigarette, and check in on us. Joe knew I was into music and that I had a little studio in the mill. He'd see me coming and going with music equipment, amps, guitars, flight cases, and escorting bands in for rehearsals or recordings.

Sometime in 1985, I decided to write a song about him. I'd still never made a record back then and didn't have any way of releasing anything. I just thought it'd be nice to write a song, record it on cassette, then play it to him and say, 'Here y'are, mate. I wrote this for you.' I finished writing the song while I was away on holiday and planned to record it as soon as I got back. I thought the lyrics captured his spirit perfectly: his resilience, his character, and his past. I remember thinking, 'Joe's gonna love this!'

Sadly, I came back from holiday and went into work on the Monday morning to hear the news that Joe had died while I was away. They'd found his body on a small piece of land just up the street from the mill. He'd collapsed and died of hypothermia during the night. I was absolutely gutted, but I completed the song anyway and put it on a shelf. The organ riff and the rhythm of the chord sequence was inspired by The Fall track 'New Face in Hell'. It's a real shame that Joe never got to hear his song. I can just imagine him smiling as he listened to it, cigarette in hand.

22/
Garage Bands in Transit Vans

I got a phone call from Spud in March 1986. He told me he'd been doing some drumming with a band who needed a demo tape recording. They'd heard some of my T'Challa Grid recordings and were impressed by them. I was to expect a call from their guitarist, a lad called Graham Lambert. The band were called 'Inspiral Carpets'. 'What a fuckin' great name!' I said to Spud.

They'd been going a little while but weren't as active on the local gig scene as the likes of Athol K, The Jonah, The Tubigrip People and T'Challa Grid, all regulars in the *Oldham Chronicle*'s weekly gig guide. The name Inspiral Carpets reminded me of some of my favourite sixties psychedelic outfits, The Chocolate Watch Band, The 13th Floor Elevators, The Doors and, more recently, The Dukes of Stratosphere and The Three O'Clock. 'Inspiral Carpets!' I thought, 'I fancy a bit of that!'

When Graham called, we chatted for ages about our favourite garage and psyche bands from the sixties through to the eighties, and the Oldham music scene. He was slightly younger than me, but it was immediately obvious we were going to get on and that we had a mutual obsession for music. Graham told me the Inspirals' history. He and his good mate, Stephen Holt, had started the band a few years earlier, and had a few name changes before settling on Inspiral Carpets. They were originally known as The Furs, as they were both massive fans of The Psychedelic Furs. They were a four-piece band who'd already gone through several bass players* and a few drummers, with Spud being the current one.

---

* Fun fact: Mark Jordon, a member of an early Inspiral Carpets line-up, went on to play PC Phil Bellamy in the popular television soap opera *Heartbeat*.

When Graham and I met up, we hit it off right away. We were from similar backgrounds, both from very working-class families. It turned out our parents' paths had crossed in the past. Graham's mum grew up on a farm in Shaw, right next to the allotment behind Lilac Mill, where Marie and Cyril Boon did the deckchair trick back in 1958.

Graham walked with a limp due to a medical issue he had when he was 15 – one of his thigh bones had become severely damaged after a football injury. He spent a year in hospital and was left with one leg shorter than the other. Despite the limp, he was one of the fittest and most sporty blokes I'd ever met, a keen swimmer and cyclist who would seize every opportunity to play football, cricket or whatever else was on offer. Graham would later claim that when we first met, I was wearing a cravat. I contest this, your honour. It was a scarf. A thin cotton burgundy number with a fine white polka-dot print. No fancy knot or cravat ring to be seen. Just a scarf, tied like a scarf, and casually tucked into the top of my shirt. I felt it complemented my bowlhead haircut, white jeans and purple suede winklepicker ankle boots. I was still living my 'Oldham meets Haight-Ashbury' dream, man! I'd found the boots in Makro sometime in 1984, on sale for £3, so I bought two pairs. I wore nothing else on my feet but those purple suede winklepickers for the next five years.

We organised a date to record the Inspirals' demo session: Sunday 16 March, 1986. The band arrived in the morning and started setting up. The singer, Ste, was a tall bloke with a gentle nature. Given the band's revolving door of drummers and bass players at the time, on that day it was Tony Welsh on bass, a quirky Oldham lad with a unique playing style, and Spud on the drum stool. They were all very much in the same musical mindset as me – stick to the basics, just give the song what it needs, don't be fuckin' about with over-the-top embellishments: 'We're not Dire Straits, lads!'

My 'talkback' system was a cheap battery-operated baby-monitor intercom from Maplin's. When the time came to record, I pushed the button on the baby monitor and shouted, 'Right, lads, go for it!' And away they went. Ste had a great vocal style, loud and firm. Equal parts deadpan and passionate. The voice of a mill-town generation. Very punk. He looked great too, iconic and not too full-on with his frontman presence; more Ian McCulloch than Iggy Pop. Graham's guitarwork sounded like a million insects crawling across the microphone and into the ether. Occasionally, Graham would do some vocals. I liked the way he sounded and would have liked him to do more. The Inspirals were probably the most 'punk' band I'd had in the mill.

As I sat there at my small mixing desk, the band playing away in the next room, I was hypnotised by the noise and the energy. I couldn't see them as there was no window between the rooms. Using my tried and tested (very lo-fi) four-track bouncing tricks, we rattled through the recording in no time at all. We recorded five songs: 'Slow Suicide', 'Oh Lord, Let Me Go', 'Thinking of You/You're Gonna Miss Me', 'A Memory' and 'Just Out of Reach'.

We were all in a similar frame of mind in terms of what we wanted to get down on tape, aware that none of us was a world-class musician (or in my case, producer), and all still learning our respective crafts, trying our hardest to get the best results possible with the very limited finances we had between us. But what we did have was a common drive and self-belief. It didn't matter that some of the other bands I'd recorded recently, like All Fall Down, The Vicar's Grip, The Dead Heroes or The Exit, had arguably more accomplished musicians in their ranks. It didn't matter that there were other recording studios in the suburbs – like Parish Bowman in Middleton, Cavalier in Stockport and Pennine Sound in Oldham – that were able to deliver far better-quality recordings than mine. What mattered more was that we were all singing from the same hymn sheet. And the song on the page was probably 'What Goes On' by the Velvets.

The band loved the results of the recording session. They called the demo tape *Songs of Shallow Intensity*. That evening, I wrote in my diary:

> Recording went well. Very 'garage band'. They were happy and paid up. May remix in my own time. Really enjoyed it . . .

I didn't realise it at the time, but some important seeds were being sown. Seeds from which my entire future would grow.

Early one Sunday morning in the summer of '86 I got an unexpected call from Graham asking if there was any chance I could pick their gear up from the mill in the Transit van and get it to the Red Barn restaurant in Chadderton. As always, I was happy to oblige. The Inspirals had been invited to play at a Piccadilly Radio roadshow in the car park of the Red Barn. Andy Crane was the host and celebrity DJ for the day. He was just making the transition from being a radio presenter for Manchester's Piccadilly Radio to hosting a show from a broom cupboard for Children's BBC television.

I dropped the gear in the car park at the Red Barn. The band sat on the amps waiting for whoever was playing drums that day to arrive. The *Spinal Tap* effect meant Spud had left the Inspirals by then. Me and him had recently recorded a couple of tracks under the name 'The Golden Voice of Joe' and were planning on putting a cassette out. We got the idea for the name from an A-board outside the City Road Inn, opposite the Haçienda, one afternoon. It read: 'TONIGHT! THE GOLDEN VOICE OF JOE!!' On the day of the Red Barn gig, we'd planned a trip into Rochdale to do some photographs. The war memorial opposite Rochdale Town Hall had the words 'For Evermore' carved into it and we thought it would be a nice image for the inlay card of our tape. Debbie took some black-and-white photos of us in front of the monument, then we set off back to the Red Barn to watch the Inspirals.

When we got back, the band were still sat with their gear exactly where we'd left them in the corner of the car park. There was still no sign of the drummer, but there was a young red-haired kid sat next to them on a BMX bike. While they'd been waiting a local chap called Dougie had stopped to chat and asked what was going on. The band had explained their drummer hadn't turned up. 'My son's a drummer and we live just over there,' he'd said, before rushing home and arriving back a few minutes later with a car full of drums and his little lad peddling behind eagerly clutching a pair of drumsticks.

Unfortunately, by the time 'lad and dad' got back, the event organisers had decided that, due to timing issues, the band's live set needed to be pulled. Graham and Ste really liked the kid's vibe and, as it looked like they were now without a drummer again, invited him to a rehearsal at the mill a couple of nights later. The youngster grinned and eagerly accepted the offer. It was Sunday 1 June, 1986. The lad's name was Craig Douglas Gill, he was 14, and his life's path had just changed in ways none of us could ever have imagined.

A few months later I recorded the Inspirals at a gig at the Hurricane Club in Oldham. Thursday 11 September: the line-up was The Parade, Inspiral Carpets and T'Challa Grid headlining. It felt like a real event. The Hurricane Club had belonged to the snooker legend Alex 'Hurricane' Higgins, who had converted it into a snooker club many years earlier. By now, it was a live-music venue hosting local cabaret acts and upcoming bands from all over the north-west. That weekend, me and Debbie went on holiday to Greece, and I took a stack of cassette tapes, a small ghetto-blaster and my Walkman with me. I spent most of the holiday listening to the various Inspiral Carpets tapes rather than the tapes of other bands. I became obsessed with them. Their sound and vibe had completely got into my head.

A couple of weeks after we got back from holiday, the Inspirals were booked into the mill for another couple of evening rehearsal sessions. They had a gig coming up in early November at the Mare & Foal on Primrose Bank in Oldham and needed to run through their set. I had a conversation with Graham that night and said, 'I've been thinking. What do you reckon about us dragging my Farfisa into the room and seeing how it sounds if I play along with you lot tomorrow night?'

I'd been mulling it over: in my mind, the combination of their full-on psyche/garage/punk and my definitive sixties-sounding transistor organ could create a sonic mix along the lines of ? & The Mysterians, The Seeds, the Velvets and a current act of the mid-1980s that we all loved, The Prisoners. Graham was up for trying it out and Ste was cool with it. I don't think they even asked poor Craig.

On Tuesday 21 October, 1986, we carried my Farfisa organ into the live room at Guide Bridge and I plugged it into my amp. Craig looked confused but, being only 14 and relatively new to the band, I'm guessing he didn't feel qualified to question what was going on. We started playing. I was familiar with the songs, having lived with them for the last few months, and I'd worked out some simple melodies that sounded perfect in the moment. It worked. The Inspiral Carpets' sound was born that night on the ground floor of a cotton mill somewhere in the grim north.

There was never a proper sit-down discussion as to whether or not I was now in the band. It just felt like it was the right thing to do. We pretty much just got on with being a five-piece. Decades later, if he ever got pissed off with me, Craig would often joke, 'I've still not been asked if it's OK if Clint joins the band!'

23/ Moo!

It was a Monday night, 3 November 1986. The band had already done a gig at the Mare & Foal pub in Oldham back in April as a four-piece, with Tony Welsh on bass and Spud on drums. Now they were back as a five-piece, this time with Craig on drums, Mark Hughes on bass and a new addition on keyboards – me. I'd given Craig the nickname 'Noddy' by now on account of the way his head wobbled when he played the drums. The Mare & Foal was a big, detached pub that had local bands on quite regularly, but there wasn't a proper stage – more of a small, raised seating area – and we had to clear the tables and chairs away to set up on the carpet. About 40 people turned up: mostly mates and members of other bands like the lads from The Dead Heroes, The Tubigrip People, The Zodiacs, or other groups that I'd been recording at the time. There were also a handful of people you'd always see from around town, who'd turn up at any gig in Oldham, as well as a few non-plussed regulars at the bar.

I felt brilliant during the gig. It felt like we were the coolest band in town. There were no clichés, or rock-star posturing. We just got on with it, workman-like. I was wearing my usual white jeans and winklepickers. I placed my thermos flask of coffee on the floor to the side – just in case I fancied a brew during the set. I always liked a pint of lager, but, being the van driver, I had to take it easy.

When we finished our set and the applause from the small crowd died down, I heard Craig laughing behind me: 'That sounded fuckin' brilliant, Clint!' Graham came over to me as I started switching my gear off: 'Whaddya reckon? Did you enjoy it?'

'I loved it, mate!' I replied.

'It sounded great!' he said.

'Yeah, I thought so too. I really think we've got something here!' I was knelt on the carpet folding the legs of the Farfisa into their compartment on the underside of the instrument. People were coming over from the bar telling me how great it sounded, and the band all seem chuffed with how well it had gone.

'Should we start loading the van, Clint?' asked Ste.

'Yeah, I'll bring it round to the side door.'

I was just a bloke packing away the tools of his trade on a pub floor in Oldham, but inside I felt like I was one step closer to being a rock 'n' roll star! Sometimes in life, something just clicks and feels right. It could be a new job, a new girlfriend, a new club you've discovered or, in my case, a band you've joined almost by accident. It just felt right. Within a few rehearsals, I was writing songs, contributing and playing a big part in shaping the actual sound of the group. We had a very industrious approach. Live wise, I think we carried a lot of the spirit of The Fall or the Spacemen 3 – bands that never had to try hard to be cool. I suddenly felt this is where I was meant to be. It was almost like everything that I had been doing was leading up to this.

Over the next few Inspirals gigs, I started to introduce a basic lightshow. I had hundreds of slides (photographic transparencies) thanks to a friend of a friend who worked as a driver for a photo-lab supply company. He'd nick films from the warehouse, and I'd buy them off him for a quid each – slide films (where the developing process was included in the price by sending off the film in a yellow 'postage paid' envelope) and Polaroid films, where the photograph developed in front of your eyes a minute or so after popping out of the camera. Because the films were so cheap, I could afford to take loads of photos without worrying about the cost. I'd buy 50 films at a time and get 36 photos out of a slide film and 8 out of each Polaroid cartridge.

I was staying over at Debbie's parents' house a lot, and their back garden looked out over a big field that was usually full of cattle. The cows would often stick their heads over the fence, trying to nibble the Black family's shrubs, or just being nosey. Except when we had barbeques. Then they'd be over at the other side of the field, probably thinking, 'Have you seen what they're doing over there? Out of order!' Sometimes they'd watch me out of the corners of their eyes, as if they were thinking, 'Ere'ya, he's here again. That pillock with his bloody camera. Oldham's answer to David Bailey!'

I spent a lot of time stood at that fence with my camera, a Chinon CM-1, watching the cows and snapping away. Over the space of a couple of years, I amassed a stack of high-quality photographs of bemused cows going about their daily business – really beautiful creatures in super close-up detail. Admittedly, I also accumulated dozens of photographs of cows and bulls pissing, shitting and shagging each other.

I started setting up domestic slide projectors and pop-up projection screens around the stage at Inspirals gigs, using bedsheets for extra projection coverage. I'd buy the projectors cheap from a large high-street store in Oldham, which had become an outlet for soiled, faulty, slightly damaged or 'end of range' electrical goods. I never found out why the Oldham branch was chosen to be the damaged electrical goods dumping ground of the north. Maybe that branch had far less chance of being sued if some daft bugger from Oldham ended up getting electrocuted – less so than our wealthier counterparts over the border in Cheshire. Either way, I'd be in there every weekend getting my hands on cassette decks, tuners, speakers and whatever else would help me on my way.

I bought a couple of cheap 'par can'-type spotlights, which sat on the floor of the stage and, when we had a gig coming up, I'd hire a strobe light, oil-light projector and a bubble machine from a shop in Shaw that hired out PA systems and funky lights. During Inspirals gigs, I'd operate the entire lightshow from the stage while playing the organ and singing backing vocals. My dad built me a 'control unit' out of a wooden case made from a section of an old bed headboard he and Mum had recently binned off. He mounted eight domestic 13-amp plug sockets on it, each with an on/off switch. It became known as 'the Bird House', because that's what it looked like. It sat to my left for every gig during my first year or so with the band. I was gutted when we eventually lost the Bird House. It got left behind at a gig somewhere back in the chaotic and shambolic late 1980s. It served us well, though, and was a stepping stone to us having one of the most talked-about lightshows and visual experiences of the time. Unsigned bands never had this sort of lightshow. We were Manchester's answer to Pink Floyd. Manc Floyd!

Each of the slide projectors held a magazine that would carry around 50 transparencies, and they'd be rattling away behind us at gigs, the photos randomly changing. Many of the slides were from collections I'd found in junk shops, with names like 'Niagara Falls', 'Times Square at Night' and 'Man on the Moon'. I included a couple of other photos I'd taken, one showing my dad with a massive wound on his head, and one showing Debbie's cat, Henry, eating a pigeon he'd just killed.

The scores of cow images popping up every few seconds led to our fans starting to 'Moo!' during the gigs. At first, we weren't sure if the crowd were booing or mooing. One of the first tracks I wrote for the Inspirals was about those cows in the field in Royton. It's called 'Theme from Cow' and it was my way of explaining the cow theme that runs through our work. It's written from the cow's point of view: '*The field is green/So serene/You point your camera at me/ Cow theme.*' It says it all, really. Just some herbert from Oldham with a Chinon and a bunch of knock-off film.

Over the New Year period of 1986 into 1987, we recorded another five-song session. It became known as the *Waiting for Ours* demo tape. We recorded five songs, 'Garage Full of Flowers', 'Give Me Less Time', 'Beautiful Face', 'You're Gonna Miss Me' and 'Slow Suicide'. These were the first recordings where I got to play the Farfisa with the band. We gave 'Garage Full of Flowers' to Dave Haslam, a well-respected Manchester-based music journalist, who was also a DJ at the Haçienda and shared an office with The Bodines manager, Nathan McGough. Dave had a fantastic fanzine called *Debris* and Issue 14 (40p) had Bob Dylan on the front cover and our free 7-inch flexi-disc, the first ever Inspiral Carpets record. Both Dave and Nathan became close friends and big supporters of the band.

I had a couple of songs that I'd written before joining the band, 'Whiskey' and 'Joe', which were soon brought into the set, and I got busy writing more. From then on, things started to happen quickly, albeit with small steps, but always in the right direction. Our audiences started to grow. The reviews got better and better. Graham was getting more and more phone calls. Or, should

I say, his mum and dad were, as he still lived at home with them, and it was their number printed on all our publicity material and some of our gig flyers. The Lambert family phone started to ring at all hours of the day and night, much to the chagrin of Graham's parents, Cliff and Jean (aka 'Christ, Jean!', one of Cliff's more well-worn catchphrases): people wanting to buy tapes, wanting to book us for gigs, fanzine writers wanting to interview us.

In keeping with my sixties psychedelic fashion sense, I'd bought a cheap gold pocket watch on a chain, which I attached to a belt strap on my jeans, with the watch tucked in my pocket. One night during a rehearsal session, knowing Craig was a massive Public Enemy fan, I put the watch around my neck and said to Craig, 'Look Noddy! Flavor Flav!!' He pissed himself laughing before replying, 'That actually looks really good! You should keep it there.' I would wear the pocket watch that way constantly, until a few years later when I bought a more expensive version.

People were starting to get the Inspirals bug. For years, we'd been seeing a lad from the Tameside area bootlegging all the best gigs in Manchester. He'd stand there proudly with his portable cassette recorder in one hand and a compact stereo microphone held high in the other. His name was Alex 'Stash' Staszko and none of the bands minded his audacity. It was like they all knew he was documenting these special moments in time and turned a blind eye. When Stash started turning up and recording our gigs, we felt it was yet another sign that we were doing something right.

It was an exciting time. I'd suddenly be getting stopped in the street by people who recognised me from a gig and wanted to chat – sometimes in Oldham town centre, sometimes in Manchester. Those were nice moments when you'd spent all your life dreaming about them.

24/
Sun Sets on the Day Job

While the Inspirals were starting to do well, my day job was about to go down the shitter. Business had slowed, and Solar Metal Industries was struggling to pay its bills and bank repayments. Cash flow was always a big problem in a world were some of our debtors were given up to three months to pay but our creditors were far more ruthless. In hindsight, we'd probably expanded too quickly and bitten off more than we could chew. I still can't believe that we went from making steel headboards and coffee tables to furnishing entire hospitals in Africa in the space of a couple of years. On top of this, my obsession with music meant that my mind was never fully focused on Solar. Like most businesses going bust, it happened slowly, and then very quickly. The company went into liquidation and, because I was a director, I was personally liable for a percentage of the debt to the Commercial Bank of the Near East. I'd understood the risk I was taking when I joined the company, as did my fellow directors. Not all businesses survive. Collectively, myself and my business partners decided it was best to throw the towel in. I was still only 26, but I was left with a huge debt around my neck. My parents were worried for me, as any parent would be if their son or daughter suddenly found themselves in this much debt. The band were also quite worried about my financial situation. To have a mate that was owing all this money was quite a notable thing at the time. Graham, in particular, seemed very concerned about me and my wellbeing. He knew I was constantly getting letters from the bank.

I managed to buy the company's transit van for £500 from the receiver, and that was a lifesaver. Four or five businesses rose out of the ashes of Solar, all based in the Guide Bridge Mill, and they were all using me as a delivery driver, so I at least had some income. Keeping hold of the van was also really important for the Inspirals, as we used it to get around to all our gigs. I also managed to keep hold of the rehearsal space in the mill, as I just rented it back from a guy called Alan Hepworth, a businessman who had a photography and hi-fi shop in Ashton town centre. He took over Solar's unit on the ground floor of the mill and carried on in the business of steel fabrication and epoxy powder coating.

Somehow, I managed to stay off the dole. I was still quite young, and I was living most of the time at the Blacks' or my Mum and Dad's house, so I didn't have to pay rent or a mortgage. I manged to scrape through. If that had happened to me in my forties when I was married with kids, I don't know how I'd have got through it, but when you're young you can bounce back from almost anything. It wasn't easy, though, and it took me years to pay the debt off. Mum and Dad were really good about it. I'd worked pretty much full time since I'd left college and always paid them rent or board. Their approach was: 'If you're earning money, pay us some board; but if you're struggling, then it's cool.'

That said, I'm not sure my parents thought there was a solid future in the Inspirals. 'Are ye still messin' about wi those 'erberts from Chadderton?' Dad would ask. 'When're ye goin' to get a proper job?' He was joking, obviously. I think the way my parents raised us as kids was quite liberal in a lot of ways, considering their backgrounds. I knew they just wanted us to be happy and follow our dreams.

In April 1987 Happy Mondays' debut album *Squirrel and G-Man Twenty Four Hour Party People Plastic Face Carnt Smile (White Out)* came out on Factory Records. I loved it from my first listen. It was produced by John Cale from The Velvet Underground, which in itself was a massive thing. 'Fuckin' 'ell! Imagine recording your album with one of the Velvets!?' we all thought. We later found out it wasn't quite as debauched as that sounds. The Mondays themselves were excited at the idea they'd be able to hang out and share a few spliffs and tales with one of their heroes, but were shocked to find out on day one of recording that Cale was recently sober. His biggest indulgence during the album sessions was the bag of satsumas he kept to hand.

John Cale is a classically trained musician and was dumbfounded and intrigued by the Mondays' unorthodox approach to music and their instruments. When Mark Day first started playing guitar in the studio, Cale was transfixed by his playing and came out from behind the mixing desk into the live room to get a closer look at Mark and his playing. He'd never heard a sound quite like it: 'Can I ask, where did you get those chords from?'

'Er, Marks and Sparks, I think,' replied Day.

'Not yer keks, Mark,' shouted Shaun Ryder. 'He means your fuckin' guitar chords!'

CLINT BOON ARCHIVE

Me and Alan Wild being iconic. Rochdale College of Art, 1976.
'I wanna be a rock star! Wanna go places!'

RON KIRWIN

The Sanitary Bunch. Rochdale College of Art, 1976. (L–R) Martyn Reed, Ryan Baptiste (front), Rod Holt (back), Mark Wydler, Brian Lockett, me (in shades), Alan Wild (front), Lydia Solomon (back), Brian Millar.

OLDHAM CHRONICLE

The Inspirals in the *Oldham Chronicle* photo studio, 1988. (L–R) Me, Stephen Holt, Dave Swift, Craig Gill, Graham Lambert.

CLINT BOON ARCHIVE

Is this what Morrissey saw somewhere on the Pennines on a cold dark night in 1989?

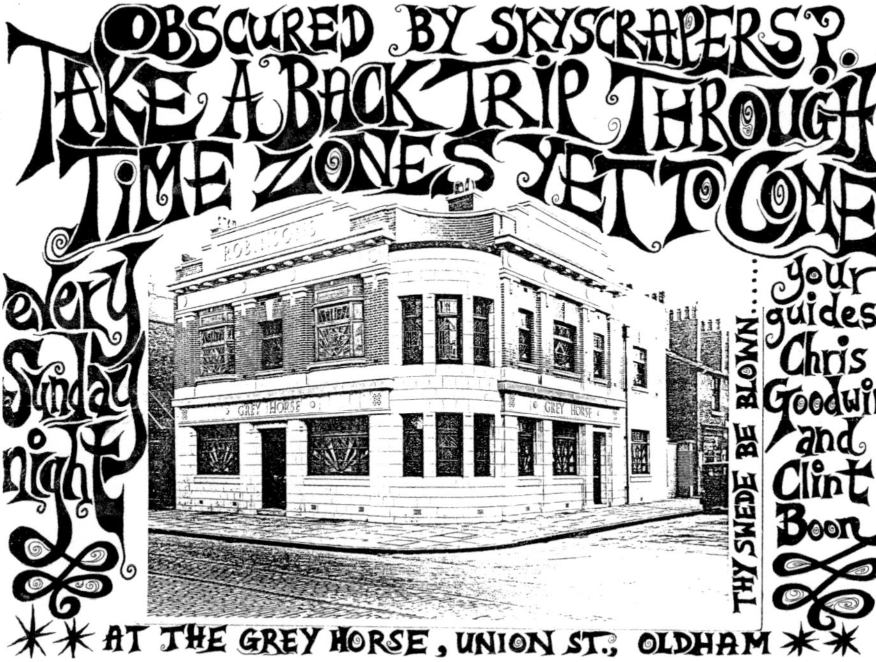

CLINT BOON ARCHIVE

The poster I made for our weekly disco in Oldham. The Grey Horse was an art-deco-era pub. By 1984, it was surrounded by office blocks, hence the 'skyscraper' reference.

© AJ BARRATT

The Inspirals sign to Mute, January 1990. (L–R) Craig, Graham, Tom, Martyn, me. I quickly drew a fake cheque for the *NME* photo. People really believed we'd signed for a million quid!

© P R BROWNRIDGE

Inspiral Tap! We had a cow brought to the venue before the soundcheck. Like you do. G-Mex, Manchester, Saturday 21 July 1990.

CLINT BOON ARCHIVE

Me and Noel doing a radio interview in the USA, 1991. It wasn't unusual for Noel to join us for promo. Sometimes, if we couldn't be arsed, he'd do phone interviews pretending to be one of us.

© TOM HOWARD

The Clint Boon Experience!, 1999. (L–R) Richard 'Stubbsy' Stubbs, Matt Hayden, me, Tony 'Papa T' Thompson, Kathryn 'Sista-Stubbs' Stubbs. Some of the greatest musicians I've ever worked with.

CLINT BOON ARCHIVE

Me and Shaun on one of our regular DJ excursions. Somewhere in the northeast, 2003.

© MATT SQUIRE

Organ-surfing in Shaw Quarry, Lancashire, 1999.

Wreckage of the Clint Boon Experience! tour bus, April 1999. Two band members, Kathryn and Tony, were thrown onto the motorway as the bus rolled over. I was the driver.

CLINT BOON ARCHIVE

CLINT BOON ARCHIVE

Look at this couple of troublemakers! Mani and Craig at mine and Charlie's wedding, Sunday 18 September 2005. Each of them did DJ sets for us. Still can't believe they're both gone.

25/ Inspiral Tap

By the time I joined the Inspirals, they were already on their tenth bass player. In the movie *Spinal Tap*, the fictitious band had over a dozen drummers pass through their ranks who would all come to untimely and messy endings, spontaneous combustion and choking on vomit being just two examples.

Some of the Inspirals' ex-bass players (even Mani played bass with them for one night) had only been invited along for the odd rehearsal or pub gig in those very early fledgling days in the earlier eighties. It's an understatement to say the Inspirals' line-up was very fluid back then.

When I joined the band, Tony Walsh had just left, to be replaced on bass by a friend of his called Mark Hughes, who lived with his partner, Viv, in a pretty little cottage in one of the nicer parts of Oldham. Mark was a good bass player and a great bloke who loved red wine and used garlic in his cooking. Stuff like this was fairly new to me as I couldn't stomach either. Mark was always good company and me, Debbie and him spent a lot of time together. The three of us would go off on road trips to exotic places like Blackpool or the Beatles Museum in Liverpool. The problem was, Mark just didn't seem as committed to the band as the rest of us. He was deep a thinker and, more so than us lot, always had an eye on the world of politics. It seemed as if life under the Thatcher government and the state of the country in general had left him with an air of pessimism. Whenever we'd discuss trying to get a gig in London, or dream about the day we might get played on John Peel's show, Mark would start shaking his head and laughing as if it was a ludicrous notion: 'London?! You're never going to get a gig in *London*! You're dreaming!'

We all liked him, and he looked great on stage, but if you're going to make it as a band you need everyone pulling in the same direction, and everyone believing you are going to make it. If you don't believe in yourselves, how can you expect anyone else to believe in you? We decided that we had to part ways, and in March '87 me and Graham drove up to his house and explained to him why the band would be carrying on without him. He took the news on the chin, made us a brew and wished us well.

In those early years, our focus and commitment to making the band succeed was intense. We were going to make it work at all costs and by any means necessary. Along the way, we were going to have to make choices that would surprise or upset people, but we knew our potential. We believed in this amazing thing we had. All these years later, that commitment and drive is still there.

I didn't see Mark again for about another 20 years. He walked into South Nightclub one Saturday night during one of my weekly DJ sets. I spotted him as soon as he came down the stairs and walked straight across the floor towards the DJ booth: 'All right, Mark,' I said. 'How you doin'?'

'Not very well, actually!'

'Why? What's up?'

'I'm not very happy about the way I've been written out of the history of the Inspiral Carpets!' he announced, then turned and walked straight out of the building and off into the night.

Well, here you go, Mark! You're back in our history now!

A few nights after our trip to Mark's house, a guitarist we knew called Mike, from the Ashton-under-Lyne band All Fall Down, brought a lad called Scott Carey down to the Grey Horse for our Back Trip Time Zone night. Mike introduced us to Scott as he knew we needed a bassist. I liked Scott and got on with him straight away, so arranged for him to come to our rehearsal the following night.

26/ Sent to Us from Heaven

In May 1987 The Stone Roses released their second single, 'Sally Cinnamon', on FM-Revolver, which felt like a real gamechanger. When I first heard it played, it took me by surprise, as the sound was a lot softer and more melodic than I'd got used to from the Roses. Their previous material like 'So Young', 'Tell Me' and their live shows in general had a much harder sound and a slightly rocky edge. 'Sally Cinnamon' was softer, more upbeat, while still skipping along. It sounded like a shaft of sunlight breaking through the permanent rain clouds above Manchester. They were obviously listening to the same bands as me, Spud, Mani and the Inspirals. Bands like R.E.M., the Rain Parade, the Dream Syndicate, the Three O'Clock and modern British bands like The Prisoners. It felt like it had more in common with the Paisley Underground than the gothic sounds of Joy Division or Echo and the Bunnymen. But it also sounded fresh, new and optimistic. The Roses had taken a huge step forward, were full of confidence and were well on their way to finding their sound. A sound that spoke directly to a lot of young Mancunians; lads like Noel Gallagher, who later said that hearing 'Sally Cinnamon' was the first time he realised he might be able to write songs.

The single entered the UK indie chart. Which made what happened next even more surprising. A couple of months later, I went down to the Boardwalk one Friday night. A lot of Manchester bands rehearsed in the basement there: the Mondays and ACR had their own rooms there, and a lot of band members would hang out upstairs in the venue after or between rehearsals. It was kind of a social club for Mancunian musicians at the time.

Thanks to Boardwalk owner Colin Sinclair's fondness for the Inspirals we became something of a resident support band at the venue for a while, warming up for any indie types who might be passing through. Over the years, the Inspirals would hold the record for playing at the Boardwalk more times than any other band. We'd also recently had our first national press: a live review of us playing the Boardwalk by Bob Stanley.*

This particular Friday night, I was in the Boardwalk with Graham. I don't think there were any bands playing. Ian Brown and John Squire were sat at a table looking a bit glum. Even though the Roses were pulling decent crowds and had a real buzz about them in Manchester, and we all loved what they were doing, there was no real sign of anything spectacular happening to them yet. Ian told me that their bass player Pete Garner was leaving, and they needed a replacement as soon as possible. I started laughing and said, 'Don't mention it to Scott! He'd be well up for it but we need him!' I knew Scott was a massive Roses fan. I reckon there were two bands Scott would have happily jumped ship for: the Bunnymen and the Roses.

I told Ian I'd have a think about possible replacements. At this point, the job could've gone to anyone with the right look, the right attitude and a bass guitar in Manchester that weekend. But the next day, Saturday afternoon, I was walking down Oldham Street and bumped into Greg Mounfield, Mani's little brother. Straight away, it hit me. I thought 'Fuckin' 'ell, of course . . . Mani!! He'd be the perfect bass player for the Roses!' I hadn't seen Mani for a while, but Greg told me, 'He's not playing much these days, he's still busy doing the lights at the Opera House and the Palace.'

I told him to get hold of Mani asap and tell him the Roses needed a bass player. On the Sunday night, I got a call from Mani to say he was now a Stone Rose and cheers for wording Greg up. It was written in the stars. Some things are just meant to be.

The Inspirals actually supported The Stone Roses at their first gig with Mani in the line-up, at the International in November 1987. It would be Scott's last appearance with us. After the gig, Reni invited everyone to a party back at his gaff. We decided not to go, because we had a post-show

---

* We became friendly with Bob Stanley, who we nicknamed 'Little Bob'. He would later go on to found St Etienne, a great band, which surprised me at first, as he never talked about being in a band when we first knew him.

routine where we'd all go back to the mill to unload the van together and put the gear back in the studio. On this night, though, Scott decided he wasn't missing the party at Reni's and disappeared there instead, leaving the rest of us to drive back to Ashton and unload without him. I think it was on that journey, in my Transit van, that someone suggested if Scott wanted to put partying first, then we should start looking for bass player number 12. Aren't bands fickle sometimes!

As for Mani, you could tell straight away that the chemistry was right with him, Ian, John and Reni. He just slotted right in. Sometimes it's just obvious when a band finds its classic line-up – we were still looking for ours. It was beautiful watching the Roses blossom after Mani joined them. As Ian said himself, Mani was the final piece in the jigsaw, and after he slotted into place they became the great band they had always threatened to be.

We, however, had to find yet another bass player. And, ironically, Mani wasn't available.

27/
'Clint, is this a fuckin' joke??'

At the end of 1987, while everyone else was out partying for New Year, the Inspirals hunkered down at the mill. Ste had suggested we bring his mate Dave Swift in on bass. Swifty was ace, seldom taking his coat off in rehearsals, always smiling to himself and with a proper dry, Inspiral sense of humour. He fitted in perfectly. We were increasingly driven and keen to keep the momentum up, so we decided to get our live set down onto a tape that we could send out to potential promoters to give them an idea of how our live gig might sound and why they should book us. Over the New Year period of 1987 into 1988 we did a three-day recording session at the mill. We chose 11 songs and spent the first two days recording, and the third day mixing the tracks. One of the tracks we recorded was my song 'Joe'. To make it a bit punchier, and stop it being too long, I binned off some lyrics. After we recorded the shortened version, I got Craig to read the omitted lyrics over the bridges in his cool Manc drawl. It made the track sound even more like a Fall tune.

Although the recordings were never intended to be an album as such, I knew during the session that we were capturing a very special moment in the band's story. On New Year's Day, towards the end of the mix session, I took a moment and sat down in the corner and wrote several pages of thoughts.

Over time, this session become known as the *Dung 4* session. We didn't end up using the tape as a demo at the time and didn't really consider releasing it in any way. Things were happening fast, and it was starting to feel like we wouldn't be needing demo tapes for much longer. We felt it was only a matter of time before we'd get a record deal and be able to record our debut album in a professional studio. The *Dung 4* recordings were put on a shelf and forgotten about.

Just a few weeks after the *Dung 4* session, I received the news that Clive Epstein had passed away. He'd suffered a heart attack while on a skiing holiday with his wife, Barbara. He was just 51 years old. I was gutted for his mum, Queenie, Barbara and their children, Henry and Joanne. I managed to stay in touch with Henry for a few years and was pleased to see him eventually become a musician. I've always felt a real sadness that Clive never got to see the success I was about to have with the Inspirals. I can just imagine his beaming smile on the day when I would hand him a copy of our first record or tell him we were going to be on the TV.

The Inspirals had become one of *the* Manchester bands to watch, according to the music press. Things were getting wild. More and more, it seemed to be my name getting mentioned in the reviews. They talked about my organ sound, my haircut and my name (many assuming it was a stage name). Those who didn't know any better would assume I was the frontman when reading our press. I never tried to suggest that was the case or encourage it. Luckily, the rest of the band seemed to take all this in their stride.

We formed friendships with some of the movers and shakers on the Manchester scene, including Nathan McGough, manager of one of our favourite bands. The Bodines, total music-press 'darlings' at the time, had just signed a record deal with Magnet so were now a 'professional' band. Nathan invited us to visit their rehearsal room in Glossop one afternoon, a sleepy little village where the Manchester sprawl ends and the Peak District begins. The Bodines rehearsed in another old, stone two-storey mill, this one on the main road that cuts through Glossop and becomes the Snake Pass just a couple of hundred yards up the hill. We couldn't quite believe we were there, seeing this band rehearse during the day. We all still had full-time jobs, so most of our band action was at night. The idea of a band doing this through the afternoon, as their 'day job', seemed like a real luxury and a sign of success. Nathan and The Bodines took us under their collective wings, and we did a couple of gigs with them, one being our first ever London gig, at a venue called Portlands on Euston Road.

I decided to build a huge cow's head to use as a stage prop at our gigs, fabricated from tubular metal and whatever else I could get my hands on.

The former foreman of Solar, Larry Carty, had set up a new steel-fabrication company called Triform elsewhere in the Guide Bridge Mill. I was doing a lot of driving for him at the time. He gave me total access to use all his tools and machines to create my work of art. I got busy, first by building the tubular-steel cow 'skull', then covering it entirely in a fluffy white fabric that I blagged off Textella, the pram and baby-goods business based upstairs in the mill. The cow's head was huge, over six foot high, big enough for a person to stand inside and operate. It had green headlights for eyes and a smoke machine in its nose. The smoke blew out through its nostrils while its massive ears wiggled like an actual cow, operated by levers that I welded onto the inside of each ear. I spent ages building it and the end result was, hands down, one of the finest things I've ever created in my time on Earth.

Mike West was the frontman of upcoming Manchester band The Man from Delmonte, one of the more colourful and upbeat bands on the scene at the time. He was also a journalist whose reviews and articles would often appear in the music press. On one occasion, he came to visit the Inspirals at the mill to interview us for the *NME*. The piece he wrote read, 'If you meet a Capri boy with a pear-shaped nose and a fruit-bowl haircut, follow him. He will lead you to a bed frame factory in East Manchester, where the fumes are toxic and the employees have mutated into beer-monsters. There, in a back room, you will find a Guernsey cow as big as a Buddha, with spotlight eyes and a polyester hide. It is a parody of a Motorhead stage prop built, with a loving care verging on bestiality, by the INSPIRAL CARPETS.'

Mike's article couldn't have captured the moment more accurately (apart from the fact he thought my Opel Manta was a Ford Capri). Sadly, the giant cow's head only had one outing, when Nathan and The Bodines offered us the support slot at their gig at the Main Debating Hall* in Manchester University. It was a big stage. Led Zep, Pink Floyd and Hendrix had all played there back in the day. I borrowed Larry's long wheelbase Mercedes van for the night, as the cow's head was way too big to fit in my Transit. When we arrived at the venue, I went and found Nathan as I thought I'd better check with him

* Now called Academy 2.

first about using the cow's head during our set. Also, I'd need a hand getting it up the stairs as it was too big to get in the lift. He seemed enthusiastic if a little confused, and was keen to see it before we brought it into the university. We walked down the stairs together and out into the loading bay behind the venue. When I opened the van doors, Nathan went silent. After a few seconds, he turned to me and said in his soft Scouse tone, 'Clint, is this a fuckin' joke??'

I explained I was totally serious and stressed to him that the cow's head wouldn't affect the changeover time or The Bodines show too much.

'Clint, there's no way you're putting that fucking thing on my stage! You're a fuckin' madman!'

I could tell by his body language as he walked back into the venue that he was serious. I left the cow's head in the van, and sadly it never got to play live with us. I stored it at the mill for as long as I could, but it eventually ended up in someone's backyard in Stalybridge, slowly rusting and dreaming of what might have been.

28/ The Baldricks

Come the spring of 1988 there was a noticeable vibe happening around Manchester. A real buzz. You could sense it. There was something in the air, a scene was developing. The music was changing, the way we dressed was evolving, and it felt like everything was coming together. One of the first magazines to try to capture what was happening was the style mag *i-D*. They wanted to do an article on this new scene that was happening in Manchester that didn't have a tag or a name yet. They rallied the troops and got a bunch of us to meet outside the Boardwalk in March 1988 to do a group photoshoot. There was me, Graham and Craig from the Inspirals, Shaun Ryder, Martin Prendergast, a DJ at the Haçienda who was also known as Little Martin, and Stephen 'Cressa' Cresser, who was a face around town and a good mate of Shaun and the Mondays. Cressa would end up being The Stone Roses' answer to Bez, a kind of vibesmaster who would dance behind John Squire's amps while simultaneously switching the patches on John's effects unit. It wasn't just musicians and DJs outside the Boardwalk that day, some were just other cool-looking characters from the city: Paul the Hat, who sold hats in Affleck's Palace, Lee Daly and Al Smith; most of them wore great gear and had unusual haircuts. Several of the crew had already been to photographer Ian Tilton's place in Chorlton-cum-Hardy to do some portraits and top-quality studio shots. I think the idea of the shoot at the Boardwalk was probably to get some shots of these northern scallywags in their natural habitat, skulking around in the back streets of Manchester. Inspired by one of the main characters in the TV show *Blackadder*, someone coined the term 'the Baldricks' to describe this new movement, although we'd never used that term to describe ourselves.

When the piece came out in the April issue of *i-D* there was a double-page feature on 'the Baldricks', describing them as a 'surreal youth cult roaming the Haçienda'. The main photo showed four of the lads wearing flares and big outdoor jackets, and the article said they were defined by 'a love of sixties psychedelia and acid that had instinctively drawn them to house music'. It explained that their lineage was drawn from Perry boys, casuals and scallies. The *i-D* piece went on to say that the Baldricks had initiated the return of the flared trouser in 1984 '. . . or 1983 if you lived in Oldham and Salford'. It was the country's first glimpse of what became known as the 'baggy' look. Shaun Ryder was quoted as saying, 'It's just a way of life.'

As we were milling around outside the Boardwalk that day of the photoshoot, New Order's Bernard Sumner pulled up in his red convertible Mercedes SL with the top down. I'd met him briefly a couple of times previously but didn't really know him enough to talk to yet. Although none of us would show it, we were all a bit excited to see him there. It was Bernard fuckin' Sumner. He nodded and said, 'All right, lads!' and disappeared into the venue, I assumed to meet A Certain Ratio, who were rehearsing in the basement (he produced some of their music, as well as being label mates on Factory). After Bernard went inside, I reached into his car, ejected the cassette tape from his player (Sharon Redd), and replaced it with a tape of some of our tracks before we snuck off, grinning like brazen scamps.

Later that night, we went down to the International 1 to watch a gig and when we walked in, we saw Bernard stood at the bar. We went over, and I said to him, 'All right, Barney, did you listen to our tape?'

'Yeah, you cheeky cunts! You sound just like the fuckin' Stranglers!'

We couldn't have been more chuffed.

29/ Jamming with James

Not long after the Baldricks issue of *i-D* came out, we were included on a compilation tape called *Manchester: North of England*. Curated by Sarah Champion and put together by *City Life** and Bop cassettes, it was a snapshot of the scene that was developing in Manchester. They included the version of 'Joe' that I'd recorded at the mill during our *Dung 4* session. The Stone Roses and Happy Mondays weren't included (maybe they declined), but there were 14 bands in total, included James, The Waltones, The Man from Delmonte, The Railway Children, Johnny Dangerously (John Bramwell, a great singer-songwriter who would later form the seminal band I Am Kloot), The Milltown Brothers (a cool band from Burnley), Dub Sex and a few others. On the front cover was a photo of a Morrissey lookalike, wearing a t-shirt that said 'MANCHESTER – BORN IN THE NORTH, RETURN TO THE NORTH, EXIST IN THE NORTH, DIE IN THE NORTH'.

The tape was well received, and a couple of weeks after it came out I got a call from Tim Booth of James. I'd never met him in person and I didn't know how he'd got my number, but I was a huge fan of the band. They were well established in Manchester way before any of us 'Madchester' upstarts appeared on the scene. They'd originally signed to Factory in 1983 and released a couple of EPs with them before leaving to sign for Sire records. Tim had heard 'Joe' and explained James were thinking of expanding their four-piece line-up and wanted to experiment with bringing other instruments into the mix. They wanted to see how their music would sound with things like brass, strings and, in my case, keyboards. I told the rest of the

---

* Manchester's answer to *Time Out*.

Inspirals what was going on. I didn't think it was an invitation to join James and, in my mind, it was no threat to the great chemistry the Inspirals had. I met Tim in his management's office on Princess Street before he took me for a ride around the city in his car (a very modest hatchback). During the ride, Tim put a cassette into the tape player: 'Clint, would you like to hear our new album?'

'Yes please, mate. I'd love to hear it!'

Tim played me a pre-release tape of their forthcoming *Strip-mine*. I took the tape home and knocked up some keyboard parts and then did a couple of sessions with James at their rehearsal room on the top floor of the Beehive Mill in Ancoats. The room was directly below the square brick structure that juts out from the roof with the words 'Sankeys Soap'* emblazoned boldly for all to see from miles around.

I decided to take my Vox Continental organ to jam with James rather than my Farfisa. By this point, playing the Farfisa with another band might have felt like some sort of musical infidelity, as it was becoming something of a trademark sound for the Inspirals. On my first visit, James' drummer, Gav Whelan, spent most of the afternoon hanging upside down in the doorway like a bat. He'd just bought some of those weird 'inversion' boots with hooks on the shins, where you dangle yourself, head-down, from an iron bar mounted above the doorway. Something to do with improving your posture. I remember thinking that having all your blood running to your head for half an hour can't be a good thing. In November of that year, Gav and Tim got into a fight on stage during a gig, which led to him being kicked out of the band. Personally, I'd blame whoever invented those stupid boots for Gav's demise.

One of the other bands on the *Manchester: North of England* compilation were The Waltones. They were a cool jangly guitar band from Manchester

---

* Beehive Mill was another former industrial workplace that became home to lots of creatives. Five years later, Andy Spiro and Rupert Campbell would open a seminal nightclub called Sankeys Soap, named after the cleansing manufacturer. Sankeys Soap was the first home to the legendary Manchester club night Bugged Out!

who featured Mark Collins on guitar (he'd later join The Charlatans) and had already had a minor indie hit with their third single, 'Spell it Out'. We knew them from the Manchester scene, and as they were about to record their debut album, *Deepest*, they asked if I'd be up for playing keyboards on a few tracks. It was only a few days' work in a studio down on the south coast, and I played keyboards on about half a dozen tracks. Unfortunately for them, the album's release was delayed for almost a year, and by the time it came out they'd lost some of their momentum. They would regroup as Candlestick Park sometime later but never really enjoyed the success they deserved.

Through The Waltones, I met their manager Anthony Boggiano, who was already aware of the Inspirals, and made it clear he was keen to start managing us as well if we wanted him to. The rest of the band met him and got on with him OK, and we all liked the fact that he seemed ambitious and keen to make something of himself. We agreed to take him on board as our manager. Anthony was part of the Boggiano family, one of the famous Italian ice-cream families of Manchester. In the 19th century a lot of Italian immigrants had settled in Manchester during the Industrial Revolution. So many of them settled in a part of Ancoats that the area became known as 'Little Italy'. They brought their culture and cuisine with them, not least ice cream, and there were several Italian families in Ancoats that made a name for themselves with their ice-cream dynasties. It's a little-known fact that the ice-cream cone was invented* in Little Italy in Manchester. But what impressed us most about Anthony was not his ice-cream connections, more the fact that he still had a day job hiring out audio and visual equipment from a company called HSS in Manchester. This meant he could arrange cheap, or even free, hire of equipment for the Inspirals. It also meant we had access to the best projection equipment available. Our lightshow expanded tenfold overnight. We decided very early on in our relationship with Anthony that he should be called 'Binsy', simply as an immature reference to the fact that he wore spectacles. As far back as the Ice Age, glasses have been referred to

* By the Mancunian Italian immigrant Antonio Valvona, who patented a 'cup-shaped waffle iron for baking biscuit-cups for ice cream' in 1901.

as 'bins' in the north of England. The addition of the surname 'Smith' just made it even funnier. Oh, how we laughed!

I got a call one afternoon from Martin Coogan. Martin had been in the year below me at Cardinal Langley, but I didn't really get to know him until he was the frontman of a cool band from Middleton called Judge Happiness. He sung and played guitar and had a real Bowie vibe going on. I saw them do a gig one night at the Hurricane Club in Oldham and overheard a group of girls at the bar: 'Fuckin' 'ell! Fit or what!!'; 'I'd shag that!'

I was at home in Heyside when he called. I'd given him my number a few months earlier at a Judge Happiness gig. By this point they'd changed the band's name to The Mock Turtles. They were in the process of recording some tracks for their *Pomona* EP, which would come out in February 1987 on the Imaginary Records label.

'Clint, is there any chance we could borrow your Vox Continental for a session we're doing in Suite 16?' Martin asked.

'Yeah, man. When do you need it?'

'Well, we're in here now, recording a couple of tracks. We should be done in a couple of hours.'

I loaded the organ into my car and headed over to Suite 16 in Rochdale, which was only ten minutes' drive from our house. The band greeted me at the door and helped me get the organ, the stand and a bag of cables up the stairs and into the studio. I set the organ up on its stand, attached the volume pedal, plugged it in and fired it up. The band stood around listening as I tried to play The Animals' 'House of the Rising Sun', a Vox Continental classic. After about 30 seconds of showing everyone present how my name should probably never be mentioned in the same sentence as Alan Price, I left them to it.

A few hours later, I got a call from their drummer Steve Cowen: the organ was ready for picking up. When I got there, Martin looked dishevelled, and in a state of shock: 'Fuckin' 'ell, Clint. I nearly died!'

'Y'all right, Martin? What's up?'

'It nearly killed me, Clint!' He seemed really shaken up. 'I saw me life go past 'n' everythin'!'

Eventually, he explained that, after I'd left the studio, he'd gone over to look at the organ, and noticed an exposed fuse on the back near the jack-lead socket. Instinctively, he touched the fuse and got the biggest electric shock he'd ever experienced. Steve went on to describe how, in the moment Martin was getting electrocuted, his body levitated 'vertically *and* horizontally' and shot across the room before landing with a thud on his back on the sticky carpet. For a few seconds, everyone thought he was dead: 'He just took off . . . like he was jet propelled! He flew through the air and landed on his back groaning,' said Steve. 'We all tried to show concern but were all laughing too much to help!'

When I'd set the organ up, I hadn't realised the fuse cover had fallen off on the journey. I found it in my car on the way home. Fittingly, the track they were working on was called 'The Waning Moon', which is where, for a few moments, it looked like Martin* might be heading.

After my Vox Continental sessions with James, where I managed not to electrocute any of them, they did subsequently bring in keyboards, brass and strings to create their defining sound. To this day, they're one of my favourite bands and have given us some classic and timeless records. I do think if I'd gone along to those sessions in a different mindset, super keen to be a member of James, they might've have suggested bringing me in full-time, and my story might have panned out in a different way. But my heart was already set on taking the Inspiral thing all the way.

* Martin later bought a recording studio in Cheetham Hill, which became the Inspirals' base for a couple of years. 'Can U Dig It?' is still one of the most played singles of the era. Surreal to think that, if Martin had touched my dodgy organ for just another second or two that afternoon, it might never have existed.

30/ Rave On

By the summer of 1988 the secret was out. What had started as a little scene under the balcony in the Haçienda, powered by Happy Mondays and their wider crew, had swept through the whole club. It was the perfect storm: house music played by DJs like Mike Pickering and Graeme Park, coupled with the effects of ecstasy that was now widely available (and affordable). The DJ booth was up on the balcony, with a commanding view over the club, and, from up there, Mike Pickering said that he could almost see ecstasy sweep across the club like a tidal wave. It changed everything. The Haçienda was nothing like the cold, empty venue it had been for those first couple of years: it was now packed most nights, steam rising from the bodies.

Overnight, the club became the epicentre of the world. There were huge lines around the block. People would wait for an hour or more to get in, and the queues got so long that someone started a fanzine specifically for the Haçienda queue, called *Freaky Dancing*, after the early Happy Mondays single. People would buy the fanzine to read while standing around waiting to get in.

Inside the club, you'd see different football factions and Mancs and Scousers dancing side by side. That would never have happened previously. I remember going to see R.E.M. in the mid-1980s in Liverpool with Mani and Spud, and having to keep quiet so none of the Scousers clocked there were Mancs in their midst. But now the same lads who, a year ago, would have been downing pints and looking for trouble, were downing half an ecstasy – and the only thing they were looking for was the perfect beat, hands in their air, all 'loved-up'. It really was a social revolution. The other thing about it was that everyone who had their own personal epiphany wanted to spread the word and evangelise about the acid-house revolution.

There were several alcoves at the back of the room underneath the balcony in the Haçienda, and you needed to be aware which alcove 'belonged' to who. The Mondays and their entourage had the last one on the left, near the bar, and that was always the busiest. I always got on great with all of the Mondays, but it's fair to say that some of their wider social circle were a bit rum. I still hadn't sampled ecstasy at this stage – I was a bit late to the party and usually driving. Or should I say, I was early to the party, but late at getting stuck into the buffet – then one night in the Haç, I was sat in the Mondays' alcove and saw a lad smoking heroin. It wasn't one of the band members (although Shaun would later talk openly about his struggles with heroin), but this lad was just sat there openly chasing the dragon in the shadows, zero fucks given. I was shocked. Heroin had been a problem in the city since the early eighties, and some estates and towns in the north had been hit heavily by it, but growing up in Shaw and Oldham I'd never really come across it before. Seeing it with my own eyes felt heavy. It was a sobering moment.

For the most part, though, the mood in the club was upbeat – euphoric. By the time the new Wednesday 'Hot' night started, with Mike Pickering and Jon Dasilva on the decks, the roof had lifted right off the Haçienda. If there were 2,000 people in there, 1,800 would be off their tits. Obviously, the ecstasy played a huge part in the transition of the place. It intensified the experience and meant the crowds were open and responsive to new music and sounds. Dave Haslam, another one of the resident DJs, said the crowds were so excitable at points that he felt like he could have played a recording of a Hoover and 2,000 people would have screamed with joy and waved their arms in the air. Anyone who has done any DJing knows that most of the time you're faced with a crowd waiting to be entertained, and it's your job to get them going. Dave said that during that era in the Haçienda it was almost the opposite, that he was faced with 2,000 baying punters on the verge of such euphoria that their heads were almost exploding. He said he felt like he had to almost hold them back a bit, it was like trying to guide wild horses.

On 30 May 1988 The Stone Roses played an 'Anti-Clause 28' benefit gig with James at the International 2. It felt like everyone on the Manchester music scene was there. That gig was hugely influential in lots of ways. It was the night The Stone Roses really hammered home to a few hundred Mancs what a great band they'd become. The addition of Mani had really taken them to another level. The mood was euphoric that night. Ian Brown walked on stage ringing an old bell, and it felt symbolic. Like he was ringing out the old, ringing in the new. '*The past was yours, but the future's mine,*' he sang. Graham was at the front of the balcony, recording the gig on his portable cassette recorder, as he often did. A young scally came up to him and started chatting. He said his name was Noel. He asked if he could get a copy of the tape of the gig and started talking about other Manchester bands who were breaking through at the time. He asked Graham if he liked the Inspiral Carpets, and Graham explained he was one of them!

Graham agreed to do a copy of the tape and post it to him. When Graham told me about the encounter later, it reminded me of my similar encounter with The Damned outside the Roxy Club in London all those years before. It wouldn't be the last we heard of Noel Gallagher from Burnage.

31/
Plane Crash

The Inspirals' first recording session in a 'professional' studio, one that wasn't my own low-budget studio at the mill, was at a place called the Kitchen, in one of the Hulme Crescents, not far from where the Factory nights had started at the Russell Club. Hulme was now even more lawless than it had been in those days. In the mid-1980s Manchester City Council had decided the whole area needed demolishing, but they couldn't afford to do that, so they basically gave up on Hulme and simply stopped charging anyone rent. The huge housing estate became one huge dystopian squat, a post-apocalyptic *Blade Runner* free-party scene. Completely wild, as if some huge social experiment had gone badly wrong – but somehow wonderfully right. The promise of free rent was a magnet for musicians, creatives, artists and all those living alternative lives on the margins of society. DIY gig venues and studios sprung up; even an art-house cinema. Word was that the poet and musician Ed Barton had knocked two flats through and built himself a giant throne in the middle. Even Nico from The Velvet Underground, who was like royalty to us, the mythical *femme fatale*, ended up spending time in Hulme. She was in a bad way at the time, with a well-documented drug habit, and when she came up from London to do a gig at Rafters in the early eighties, she just stayed on in Manchester for most of the decade, seemingly appreciating both the cheap heroin and bohemian vibe.*

There was an inspiring, febrile creative atmosphere about Hulme, but it was still rough as well. I wouldn't say you were taking your life in your hands

---

* Nico eventually left Manchester for Ibiza, and sadly died in 1988 of a cerebral haemorrhage while riding her bike. She was only 49. In 2019 the Manchester International Festival celebrated her with *The Nico Project*, a theatrical tribute to her 1968 solo album *The Marble Index*, starring Maxine Peake.

going there, but there was a very real danger of being mugged, and everyone was always getting broken into. Mark Kermode, now one of the country's foremost cinema critics, was living in Hulme and just starting out on his career, writing reviews for *City Life* magazine. He got so fed up with being broken into that he installed a security door on his flat, only for someone to take it off its hinges and carry it away.

Hulme even had its own sound, led by artists like the brilliant Ruthless Rap Assassins,* whose debut *Killer Album* was described by *The Face* as 'the first and the greatest rap record Britain ever produced'. Also in residence in the Crescents was Gerald Simpson, a young 19-year-old lad who moved on from being an early member of 808 State to go solo as A Guy Called Gerald and produce the seminal 'Voodoo Ray', a record that would become the soundtrack to all the partying and shenanigans at the Haçienda in the summer of 1989.

The studio was called the Kitchen because it was *literally* a kitchen. A lad called Jamie Nicholson, who lived in Charles Barry Crescent,† had built it in what had been his own kitchen. It was a bit ramshackle, but way more professional than my setup at the mill. It felt like another step forward for us, actually paying to record in somebody else's studio. We weren't totally happy with the results of the session, though, so it never got released. A short while later, Jamie knocked through the wall of his flat into the empty one next door, because he needed some extra space. That's what people did in Hulme. Dystopian open-plan living.

After it expanded, the Kitchen soon became the go-to place for after-hours partying. The Haçienda and other clubs in the city centre still only had 2am licences and, considering how refreshed, wired and excitable a lot of the punters were when they spilled out onto the streets, there was a huge demand for

---

* Kermit (Paul Leveridge) from Ruthless Rap Assassins had previously been in the Haçienda's breakdance crew Broken Glass, and would later form Black Grape with Shaun Ryder.

† The four Hulme crescents were all named after distinguished architects – Robert Adam, Charles Barry, John Nash, William Kent – a bit ironic considering they became viewed as an urban-planning disaster.

after-party venues. In the Kitchen you could buy beer, spirits, weed, Es and acid, and parties would sometimes go on for days.

The Kitchen is frequently credited as being one of the most important addresses during the birth of acid house. Another similar late-night venue soon opened in Hulme called Epping Walk (so named because it was on Epping Walk; people in Hulme were obviously too busy partying to think of complicated names).

Through my friend Mark Hodkinson of The Monkey Run (another band I'd recorded at the mill) we were introduced to Dave Fielding of The Chameleons. Mark was a journalist for the *Oldham Chron'* and had recently taken over writing the music page.* He'd heard our music and liked what we were doing. Mark brought Dave to the mill one night to meet us. Dave offered to produce a recording session for us. He was a brilliant guitarist. His work with The Chameleons remains some of the greatest music ever recorded by a British band. Dave had seen the highs and lows of the music industry in his years with the band. By now, they'd split up. He also had a stack of experience in the recording studio, having worked in some of the best in the country. Me and the Inspirals would sit in awe listening to tales of his time with The Chameleons; about waking up on their sleeper bus not knowing where he was, and stepping out – hungover, dressed head to toe in black, wearing a trenchcoat – into the blazing sunshine of a beach in St Tropez. As we chatted, we realised that Dave's mum had been a dinner lady for the entire five years I'd spent at Cardinal Langley: the famous Mrs Fielding. It was all the serendipity we needed to believe that this was to be a fruitful working relationship.

We booked a session at Suite 16 in Rochdale, a studio that had previously been called Cargo. The likes of The Fall, Joy Division, Orchestral Manoeuvres in the Dark and the Gang of Four had recorded some of their earliest and

---

* Mark later started Pomona PR, who did the press for lots of Manchester bands, then started a publishing company called Pomona Books. He also became a columnist for *The Times* and has written fantastic non-fiction books about football and music, as well as several great novels.

finest work at Cargo. It was the studio which, alongside Strawberry Studios in Stockport, every Manc band used when they could afford it. It was also the studio where, according to legend, Joy Division drummer Stephen Morris got left behind one night, still obediently drumming out on the roof, as ordered by producer Martin Hannett as he and the band locked up for the night and headed off home. Even if that story was totally fabricated, the truth to us was that Joy Division's DNA would still be crawling around in the threadbare weft of Cargo's dirty carpets. For his payment, Dave asked for, 'Sixty quid 'n' a block of draw.'

We recorded the tracks through the day and on into the night. Back then, most commercial recording studios offered a cheaper 'lockout' deal whereby, if you could find yourself a recording engineer, you could use the studio through the night and save a lot of money. I think our session cost three hundred quid, plus Dave's 60 quid and the 'block of draw'. We recorded four songs: 'Keep the Circle Around', 'Theme from Cow', 'Seeds of Doubt' and 'Garage Full of Flowers'. With the addition of the version of '96 Tears' that we'd recorded at the mill, this would become the *Plane Crash* EP.

When we came out of the studio, the sun was coming up. We were tired but elated. This was the rock 'n' roll lifestyle we'd dreamt of all our lives. We weren't in sunny St Tropez – we were still in dusty Rochdale – but, in that moment, we were happy with our lot in life.

Dave enthusiastically sent the recordings to his close friend Dave Gedge, lead singer of The Wedding Present, who immediately offered us the support slot on their forthcoming Scottish tour. We got to play Glasgow's Barrowlands for the first time.

Graham had been helping a friend of the Inspirals, Debbie Reid, to decorate her new office. Debbie was omnipresent on the Manchester music scene, writing about bands and gigs for various fanzines. We all liked her a lot, but her credibility went through the roof when we heard that she'd managed to get hold of Syd Barrett's address and made her way to Cambridge on her own to knock on his door. Apparently, he opened the door, chatted to her for a short while before saying goodbye, gently closing the door, and returning to his lonely sanctuary. It turned out Debbie was sharing her new office with

Paula Greenwood, who ran Playtime Records. Graham, paintbrush in hand, met Paula and they got chatting. She agreed to put out our *Plane Crash* EP on the spot.

The reviews were great and local radio started to play the lead track, 'Keep the Circle Around'. Some of the most respected broadcasters in Manchester got behind it, including Pete Mitchell, Mike Sweeney, Terry Christian, Phil Korbel and Liz Kershaw. Then came the blessing from John Peel, which meant everything to us, as we'd grown up listening to his show. On Wednesday 6 July, 1988, the day Peel received a promo copy of the *Plane Crash* EP, he opened his show with 'Keep the Circle Around' and immediately offered us a Peel Session. We became his favourite new band, and his enthusiasm meant every major record label in the country suddenly wanted the Inspirals. Everything sped up, and it felt like our future was being laid out before our eyes. All our dreams were beginning to come true.

We booked into Out of the Blue Studios in Ancoats to record our next EP in September 1988. The studio was owned and operated by Nick Garside and his business partner Adam Lesser. Nick was one of the go-to recording engineers for Manchester bands, working with the likes of James, The Railway Children, Vini Reilly and The Man from Delmonte, while Adam involved himself mainly with the city's nascent dance-music scene. Out of the Blue was situated on the first floor of a four-storey red-brick building on Blossom Street, only a couple of streets away from where I'd jammed with James in the Beehive Mill.

Ancoats in the late 1980s was completely unrecognisable to the place it is today. Back then it was still an industrial wasteland. Historically, Ancoats had been the heart of the Industrial Revolution, Manchester being the first industrial city in the world. When the Rochdale Canal opened in 1804, huge mills sprung up and dominated the area, along with cheap housing for the mass influx of workers, including Italian immigrants like our manager Anthony's ancestors the Boggianos. By 1815 Ancoats was one of most densely populated areas of Manchester, but also one of the poorest. L S Lowry would frequent the area in his day job as a rent collector, and painted some of his most famous pieces there. In 1978, when I was over on the other side of town heading to the Factory to see bands like Joy Division and Suicide, Ancoats was namechecked in the Lowry-inspired number 1 single 'Matchstalk Men and Matchstalk Cats and Dogs', by Brian and Michael. Morrissey later made a playful reference to the area when the backing vocals on 'Bigmouth Strikes Again' were credited on the sleeve to a mysterious 'Ann Coates'.

By the time we were recording there in the late 1980s, Ancoats still hadn't recovered from the industrial slump of the 1930s, half a century previously, and the slum clearances of the 1960s had left behind areas of barren wasteland. There were no shops, and only a couple of pubs, frequented mainly by old men with not much money in their pockets. You couldn't even buy a pint of milk round there. When the nightclub Sankeys Soap opened in 1994, Ancoats was still such a dystopian landscape that when they booked Derrick May, the DJ from Detroit, a city that was, at the time, famously derelict, he got out of the car when he arrived, looked around in shock, and said, 'This place is more fucked up than Detroit!'

The transformation in the 30 years since we recorded there has been incredible. The mills have been converted into fancy loft apartments, one of which sold for over a million quid recently, and there's even a Michelin-starred restaurant. If you'd have told me that in 1988, I would've thought you'd lost the plot.

On the ground floor, directly below the studio, was an electro-plating company whose services involved using huge vats of ammonia and other substances to chrome plate and brass plate various metal contraptions. The intense stench generated by the chemicals meant that often the studio upstairs stunk like a septic tank. To add to the pungent mix, Nick's dog, a spaniel called Max, would spend his days stretched out under the mixing desk, farting his way through doggy dreams while occasionally shooting his duff across the rug. It all helped to give Out of the Blue its own unique odour. They should have renamed it 'Out of the Brown'. The studios have long since gone, but the building, which has been extensively renovated, still stands.

As a studio, Out of the Blue was well equipped and relatively affordable. It had a two-inch 16-track tape machine and half-inch reel-to-reel stereo mastering. It also had a DAT (Digital Audio Tape) recorder, which was the industry-standard, cutting-edge mastering machine at the time. A large pair of stereo monitor speakers in wooden cabinets were mounted quite low down on either side of the control-room window. The one on the right was situated close enough to the door to guarantee guests at least one substantial head wound on every visit.

Nick was a nice chap and great to work with. Being the studios co-owner, he knew the gear inside out and was able to get great results in a short time frame. The studio had a huge plate-reverb unit in a massive wooden box, which sounded incredible, but most of the effects Nick used on our session were courtesy of digital rack-mounted units. We recorded four songs, which would eventually be released as the *Trainsurfing* EP – 'Butterfly', 'Causeway', 'You Can't Take the Truth', 'Greek Wedding Song'. We loved being at Out of the Blue, even though that part of Ancoats was a bit of a shit hole. The only thing that mattered to us, though, was we had another EP of great material recorded. I was absolutely buzzing. Life was great.

32/
We Lost Our Voice

Things were going great for us as a band. I really felt like we were on our way. Which made it even more of a shock when Ste decided to leave. He broke the news to us during rehearsals one night at the mill in October 1988. It was a decision brought on by various circumstances, as far as I can recall. He was about to get married and needed the kind of financial security his day job offered and singing with Inspiral Carpets didn't. Despite all the good things that were happening around us, we were still making zero money. Our gig fees were barely covering the costs of our fuel and sandwiches.

I've only realised in recent years that Ste's feelings about the band changed during the period after I joined. As things started to become a bit of a rollercoaster ride, as our popularity started to explode – as everything suddenly became all about bowlhead haircuts, the 'fairground' organ sound and bewildered cows staring into the camera lens – it was over for him. Ste fancied life as the frontman of a more traditional kind of indie band like The Bodines, The Mighty Lemon Drops or The Railway Children. The Inspirals were changing rapidly into the kind of band Ste hadn't really set out to be a part of. To be honest, even I felt a bit like, with the Inspirals, the circus was coming to town. And I know I was the main reason for that change in the dynamic of the band.

Being a very close friend of Ste's, our bassist, Swifty, followed his lead and left a few days later. They would soon set up a new band together called The Rainkings. Ste nobly offered to do the last couple of Inspiral gigs that were already in our diary.

In a matter of weeks, we'd lost two crucial members of the band. Bands rarely survive something like that. Losing a guitarist, a drummer or, even, dare I say it, an organ player, were never seen as career-wrecking moments in bands' journeys. But the frontman and the bassist – at the same time!

Despite our huge loss, we knew we'd get sorted one way or another. Maybe it's a working-class thing? Maybe a Manchester thing? I'd like to say it may have been the folly of youth, but I was getting on for 30 by then. Our first back-up plan was for me to take over on vocals and play the basslines on the bass pedals that came with the Farfisa. I'd never used them before. We tried it in rehearsals, but it was fuckin' hard. I was like a bowlheaded octopus, all four limbs thrashing, flailing and kicking while I'm trying to hold a tune and read the lyrics from a notebook on a music stand. It was obvious we'd need an actual singer and bassist sooner rather than later.

When Martyn Walsh, bass player with Ashton based hip-hop/electro band The Next Step heard about our plight, he immediately offered his services but, initially, we were reluctant to take him on. We weren't convinced his look would suit the Inspirals. Martyn was a lovely chap with good sense of humour, and was a decent bass player, but he wore his baseball cap sideways, and his bass guitar was bright pink. Call us fickle and shallow, but that's where our heads were at.

A couple of weeks later, at the end of November, me and Graham went to see psychedelic shoegazers Loop at Manchester University. Martyn was also at the gig and he literally followed us around the venue all night begging us to let him audition. The bugger was relentless. He followed us to the bar, into the crowd, into the bogs. That's how much he wanted to join the band. By the end of the night, we succumbed: 'All right, you bloody pain in th'arse! Come and rehearse with us on Monday night.' He did, and it worked. Martyn got the gig. But the pink bass had to go.

Martyn always had a 'cheeky little scamp' vibe about him. He still does, some of the time. He's very intelligent, eloquent and really clued up on topics as diverse as Depeche Mode B-sides and aircraft seating configurations. We christened him 'Bungle' soon after he joined the Inspirals, after the character in the British kids TV show *Rainbow,* who had a similar-shaped head. It was only a few weeks after that we realised that we'd got the characters mixed up and the one that looked like Martyn was actually called 'Zippy'. But it was too late, the name had already stuck. To this day, he's still 'Bung' to me or, occasionally, 'Bung-a-delic'.

During one particular interview, back in the late eighties, Bung somehow managed to make a bad impression on a journalist. She went away and wrote, 'The bass player, Martyn, has the charisma of an earthworm.' I still believe he should consider using that as his epitaph: 'Martyn "Bungle" Walsh. The charisma of an earthworm.'

Martyn became bass player number 13. Unlucky for some but, for us, the right man for the job. Ste's final gig with the Inspirals, and Martyn's first, was on Thursday 15 December, 1988, at the Cricketers on Kennington Oval in London. The venue was situated right next to the famous Oval cricket ground and was well established on the city's live-music scene, particularly for new and 'upcoming' bands. The support band was a new upcoming band called Jesus Jones, who hadn't yet released a record. The crowd that night was minimal, to say the least: maybe around 40 people. It wasn't exactly a glorious exit for Ste, but we drove home, thanked him for helping us out and went our separate ways. I had no idea, when Ste got out of the van that night, that I wouldn't see him for another 23 years.

33/
The Boy from Burnage

Just before Christmas 1988 we found ourselves in the peculiar position of being one of the most talked-about new bands in the UK, but without a singer. John Peel was raving about us on his BBC Radio One evening show, and his listeners voted 'Keep the Circle Around' as their eleventh-favourite tune in his 1988 'Festive 50', which was a huge deal. Our second EP, *Trainsurfing*, was in the can and ready to go, we had 5,000 copies pressed up on 12-inch vinyl. Everything was looking great, apart from the fact that we didn't have a lead singer and the bloke singing on the new record wasn't the bloke who'd be singing at our gigs. We needed to find our new frontman.

Six nights after Ste's last gig, on Wednesday 21 December, 1988, we gathered at the mill to audition a fan of ours for the lead-singer role in the Inspirals.

Noel, the young lad from Burnage who Graham had met at The Stone Roses gig, had sent word, via Craig, that he'd like to audition for the job of frontman in our garage band. Noel had been a fan for some time. Not just a fan of ours, but of all the other cool stuff that was going on in the city. After Graham had first met him at the Roses gig, we'd got to know him better as he started coming to more and more of our gigs. Noel had a job working as a watchman in the British Gas storage yard at the top of Little Peter Street, just a stone's throw from the Boardwalk in one direction and the Haçienda the other way. His working day mainly involved sitting in a little shed on the site, making sure deliveries came and went safely, and that no one tried nicking the tons of gravel, sand or underground piping that lay around the place. After a few days, when he realised hardly anyone came into the yard, Noel started taking his guitar into the shed with him each day.

We all thought Noel auditioning was a funny idea, as we'd never heard him sing, but we all liked him so thought we should give him a shot. He already knew a lot of the words to the songs, but some were recent additions to the set, so he wasn't as familiar with them. I handed him the lyrics for the song called 'Whiskey', which I'd written for t'Mill back in 1984 and had recently brought to the Inspirals. It was written as a 'snapshot' of Oldham's nightlife back then, about some of the dickheads who used to frequent the town's pubs and clubs. We used to use the phrase 'beer monsters' to describe them. The song was written from the point of view of a beer monster on an average night out.

Whose round is it next, boys?
Do you think we make enough noise?
Let's try wake the dead.
Let's get whiskey in our heads!

Let's get some skirt.
Go out and get hurt.
Cause a fight and wreck the night.
I know a cop and we'll be all right!

Noel only got part way through the song before cracking up laughing and saying, 'Who the fuck wrote this load of shit?!'

'Er, it's one of mine, Noel,' I said.

'It's a bit fuckin' sexist, innit?!' he replied.

Noel's performance was great, and he could sing well, but we didn't think his voice suited the Inspirals' sound. Ste had a big voice, which had become one of our trademarks, and we felt we needed someone with similar lungs. On another night, we auditioned a good friend of ours called John Matthews. He'd been in a band from Shaw that I'd recorded at the mill. They were called Turning Blue and had a dreamy R.E.M. quality about their sound. John's vocal style was entrancing. As with Noel, though, John's voice was a bit too gentle for what we were looking for. John would go on to form a band called The High, with Spud on drums, Simon Davies on bass and Stone Roses founder member Andy Couzens on guitar (that's right, the lad with the red Chevvy, who came to the mill in '84 with his mate Ian to form a supergroup!). Even though we didn't think Noel's voice was right for the job, we did love his personality and spirit. Within a few weeks, we'd given him a job as our roadie and full-time general helper.

One afternoon, I nipped into Ashton Office Supplies, a big shop just around the corner from the mill, and bought a small red hardback notebook. On the front, I wrote 'Setting Up' in black marker pen, and on the back, with the book now upside down, 'Packing Up'. This would become Noel's bible over the coming months as he learnt how to set up our gear at gigs and then pack it all away at the end of the night. I wrote lots of notes and drew diagrams showing how to wire everything up, and Noel added his own instructions to help him along. From then on, he was with us pretty much every day for the next four years. It's a real cliché in the world of pop music, but, after a few months, Noel felt like another member of our band.

After he became part of the Inspirals' family, Noel would regularly bring along his little brother, Liam, and their mates, Tony, Guigsy and Bonehead, to hang out at our gigs or help us out when we needed more hands-on deck. I have a vivid memory of Liam in our dressing room at one of our Boardwalk gigs in early 1989. He was a quiet lad and really polite, squatting on the floor in the corner rather than taking up one of our seats. He didn't ask for a drink but accepted as soon as I offered him one. He sat there watching us and taking it all in. In that moment I saw myself in The Fall's dressing room a decade earlier. They were all good lads, and, in a few years, they'd start a band of their own.

34/
The Other Side of Midnight

After Noel's audition, we carried on in our search for a new frontman. It seemed like a mountainous task. A short time before Ste had left the band, Craig and Noel had bumped into Tony Wilson at a house party in Manchester. They got talking to him and the conversation turned to the Inspirals. Without any prompting, Tony said, 'I like what I've heard of you guys, come on *The Other Side of Midnight*, if you like?'

The Other Side of Midnight was an ultra-cool Sunday-night music- and arts-based TV show that was a platform for everything Tony loved, including new music. The Stone Roses had made their debut TV appearance on the same show two weeks earlier, where they performed 'Waterfall', and the Mondays had turned in an incredible bit of TV with their live and chaotic rendition of 'Performance'. For that studio recording, Shaun and Bez had performed on ecstasy, bringing freaky dancing slap bang into the middle of unsuspecting living rooms across the northwest. Anyone who knew the score was tuning into Tony's show every Sunday night, hanging on every word and every note of music.

We had a date pencilled in our diary for the recording, but when it became clear that we wouldn't have a singer in place in time for the filming, we thought we'd better let Tony know. We called him up and explained we were still without a frontman, but he wasn't bothered in the slightest, and just said, 'No problem! Do it anyway! Just come on and do an instrumental.'

This was Anthony H Wilson as I will always remember him. He did things his way. He did things other people in his position would never do. No other TV presenter or producer in the world would have given such important and significant screen time to a garage band from Oldham who were struggling to find a singer.

Our debut appearance on *The Other Side of Midnight* was transmitted at the end of January, 1989. We chose to do an instrumental of 'Directing Traffic', one of our most psychedelic and Doors-esque tunes. I brought a couple of our slide projectors along and set them up among the TV cameras and studio lights, and another mate of ours brought along a couple of Super 8 cine projectors. As always, to the right of my Chelsea boots stood my trusty thermos, filled with the obligatory strong coffee (white, no sugar). When we'd finished setting our gear up in the studio, Tony walked over to me, still quietly rehearsing his scripted introduction to himself under his breath. He stopped by my Farfisa and touched it lightly on top: 'So, Mr Clint Boon, tell me about this wonderful machine of yours?'

Tony had this unique way of simultaneously making you feel at ease but also utterly aware you were speaking to Tony Wilson from the telly.

'It's a Farfisa Compact Duo, Tony,' I said. 'Made in Italy in the mid-1960s. Only cost me hundred quid. Gorgeous, innit!'

'It certainly is. I've heard that sound on the *Nuggets* albums. Did The Doors use the same organ?'

'Yes, Tony. Ray Manzarek had a Farfisa, but his main keyboard with The Doors was a Vox Continental.'

'Well, it's an extraordinary sound and I love it! Keep up the great work, young man!'

With the swivel of an expensive leather shoe and the swish of his smart black Yohji Yamamoto suit, Tony glided back to his cue point and addressed camera number one, 'And now . . . from Oldham, *Inspiral Carpets* . . .'

As a nod to our cow-themed slideshow, and the fact that our fans were now mooing incessantly at our gigs, I'd made myself a bespoke t-shirt especially for the TV appearance. I bought a plain black t-shirt and two tubes of Puffy paint, one green, one red, and decorated the shirt with a cartoon image of a cow with spirally eyes and stuck the word 'moo!' next to it. The paint was designed to puff up slightly when exposed to the heat of an electric iron. I wore the t-shirt for our performance, and the world's first ever Inspiral Carpets cow shirt was born and televised across the northwest of England.

At the end of our performance, the lights came up, Tony stepped out in front of us and said, 'Thank you very much, gentlemen. Inspiral Carpets "Directing Traffic". They're looking for a new singer, but doing all right in the meantime.' Which was, pretty much, exactly how we were feeling at the time. We're doing all right. We'll get through this.

Our appearance on *The Other Side of Midnight* made the buzz around the Inspirals even bigger. At this point, we were still intending to put the *Trainsurfing* EP out on Playtime Records. We were holding out for a new frontman before we put the record out; someone who could convincingly take over from where Ste left off. We needed someone with a strong voice. Loud and commanding. Ideally, good-looking too.

We'd become aware of a singer in one of the other bands on Playtime. They'd done a Peel Session a few months earlier and had a single out called 'Jayne'. The first time I heard it, I was bowled over. The vocal style was exactly what we needed. The band was called Too Much Texas and the singer was called Tom Hingley. We'd also seen them live as they'd supported us at a couple of gigs a few months earlier, so we knew they were a decent bunch. We got hold of Tom's phone number and gave him a call. He said he'd love to audition for us but was adamant he should tell the rest of his bandmates first, which we thought was admirable. A few days later, he came to the mill for a run-through of our songs. He sung well, looked good and was confident and quite animated with his performance – a great showman with a stunning voice. We knew on the spot he was the right man for the job. We suggested he lose the slicked-back hair, grow a fringe and not jump about as much. He laughed and accepted the job. We'd found our singer. It felt like we were back on track.

I think the combination of all our tastes and influences made our sound unique and stand out from the crowd. In Tom, we now had a voice that was unlike the rest of the Manc frontmen. Graham brought the garage and punk with his guitar technique. In Craig and Martyn we had a couple of young lads eagerly consuming all the new hip-hop and house music that was freefalling into our world. I had one foot planted firmly in the psychedelic sixties and the other in the weird and wonderful world of the bands like Can, Faust and The Fall. In the relative simplicity of the music we created, there was a purity.

Some of our favourite bands from the late eighties, like Birdland and Zodiac Mindwarp and the Love Reaction, didn't enjoy the mainstream success and longevity that we did because they were stylistically and musically too easy to pigeonhole. If the Inspirals had been five lads with bowlheads and pointed purple boots, we probably wouldn't have made it into the nineties. To me, all this meant we had the perfect recipe. The way we looked and the way we sounded. We were as contemporary as we were retro. We were equal parts garage and pop. We didn't realise it at the time, but we were poised to take our idiosyncratic sonic mix right into the pop charts.

35/ On a Hillside, Desolate

One dark evening in early 1989 we were returning from supporting James at a gig in Sheffield, making our way across the bleak Pennine moors. It was a clear night but totally black, with just a hint of moonlight. As usual, we were giddy and a bit pissed up, getting up to all sorts of laddish nonsense in the back of the Salford Van Hire Ford Transit minibus.

The moors can be a scary place late at night. Not somewhere you'd want to break down. There's lots of legends and ghost stories to do with that bleak and scary locale. We pulled over right up on the tops, so a couple of us could take a leak. I noticed that by the roadside, every 30 yards or so, there were mounds of soil, as if some sort of groundwork had been going on. I had an idea. We told our driver to drive off down the road and come back for us in about five or ten minutes. Off he drove away into the distance.

My idea was that by standing in a crucifix pose on top of these mounds at such an ungodly hour in this desolate part of the planet, we'd put the total shits up whichever unfortunate driver would be the next to come along. We took our positions, me on the first mound, Craig a bit further down the road, then another Inspiral and roadie beyond that. I still had the trademark bowlhead hairdo, but after a sweaty gig it would often turn from its pristine blown-under look to a shaggy, almost Neanderthal-man sort of thing. I also still dressed exclusively in white jeans (always carrying at least one spare pair with me) and on this occasion wore a short white denim jacket with no shirt underneath. I climbed a mound and stood there in the dark giggling to myself, waiting for the first car to come along. Headlights appeared. I stood there like Jesus. Arms out. Head to one side. Looking a bit gutted. Like you do when you've been nailed to a cross. The car approached, slowed down a bit . . . then immediately accelerated and leathered it in the direction of Manchester.

I could see Craig, on the next mound further down the road, pissing himself laughing as the car shot past him. Two or three more cars went past, slowing only slightly, before accelerating away, until one slowed down and I distinctly remember, as they pulled pretty much alongside me, bending from my crucifix pose and leaning down and reaching out towards the car, snarling like a wild animal. At which point, the car was gone, screeching away like the Road Runner running away from the Wile E Coyote.

Reading this, you're probably thinking, 'What a complete dickhead.' And I accept that. I take it on the chin. It was a proper bell-end thing to do. Which is why I've never talked about it in public before. We never really mentioned that night again, until nearly a quarter of a century later, in 2013, when Craig rang me one afternoon: 'Have you read Morrissey's book?'

Morrissey had just published his long-awaited autobiography. 'Not yet, why?'

'Er . . . I think yer in it!'

I was surprised to hear that, as I've never had the pleasure of meeting Morrissey, although Graham tells me that the three of us – me, Morrissey and Graham – once chatted while watching James from a stairwell at the side of the stage at the Free Trade Hall.

But that wasn't the moment in his book. In his memoir *Autobiography* (Penguin Classics, 2013), Morrissey recounts a tale of a car journey he and some friends took over the Pennines, one dark evening in 1989. He describes how they encountered '. . . a figure, standing upright and then throwing his arms towards our lights in a terrifying and unspeakably forlorn plea for our attention . . . this wretched vision of sallow cheeks and matted shoulder-length hair . . . a short coat that was open to expose the white of his chest . . . the boy threw out his arms in a forsaken Christ-like appeal.'

'Wretched'? 'Sallow'? 'Matted hair'? You cheeky bugger, Moz! I thought I looked cool as fuck!

36/ Sackville

Soon after Tom joined, the Inspirals set up office on Sackville Street in what, at the time, was Manchester's red-light district. These days, Sackville Street is part of the 'Gay Village' and completely unrecognisable: a beautiful part of town, aesthetically and in spirit. But back then it was dodgy. You only went there for three things: sex, drugs or (as in our case) because the rent was dirt cheap.

Tom's girlfriend, Alison, was in the clothing business and had a unit on the second floor of a grand-looking Victorian building at 42–44 Sackville Street. Her company was called Baylis & Knight and some of her pieces were starting to become popular with the city's music community. Alison kindly let us build an office in the corner of her space. Immediately above us, on the third floor, was the studio and office of the era-defining artist team Central Station Design, who were responsible for all the Happy Mondays' artwork. Central Station was brothers Matt and Pat Carroll and Karen Jackson. Matt and Pat were cousins of Shaun and Paul Ryder and equally as colourful and chaotic.

The Inspirals office window overlooked Sackville Street and Canal Street, with the Rembrandt pub standing on the opposite corner of the junction from our building. Directly below our window was the Rochdale Canal, famous for swallowing up the occasional late-night reveller or, on frequent occasions, people not under the influence of drink or drugs but seemingly targeted by muggers. Many such unfortunate souls have lost their lives in the canal's deep and unforgiving waters over the years. That stretch of canal would make headline news around the world some years later when numerous stories of an elusive serial killer, 'the Manchester Pusher', started to populate the pages of the UK's tabloids. To this day, it's never been proven whether the Pusher was real or a myth, but, sadly, people still meet their fate in the canal.

We had some bad news when Playtime's distribution company, Red Rhino, went out of business just a few days before we were due to press the green button on the *Trainsurfing* EP. Red Rhino's closure left Playtime and lots of other small record labels in the lurch financially and logistically. We waited for a few weeks for Paula to find a new distribution company for her label, but not much progress was being made. She was holding out for a distribution company that would take on her whole roster, but no one was forthcoming. At the same time, everybody wanted to help put our record out. We made the decision to jump ship as we wanted to make the most of the momentum we had. Paula's important part in the Inspirals' story can't be emphasised enough. In helping us make the *Plane Crash* EP she enabled us create one of the most talked-about and sought-after records of its time.

Now that we had some money coming in, through the ever-increasing t-shirt sales, we decided to set up our own record label. Our idea was to keep the momentum we had and bide our time until we could find a record deal with, hopefully, a major label. We decided on the name Cow Records. Bit of a no-brainer, really. Initially, we wanted to use 'Moo' as the prefix on our catalogue numbers: Moo1, Moo2 and so on. But then Manchester-based folk hero Mike Harding (aka The Rochdale Cowboy) got in touch and explained that we couldn't use 'Moo' because that was his prefix for his Moonraker label recordings. We decided that Mr Harding was a mardy bum and that we should use 'Dung' as our catalogue prefix instead, which is why, to this day, Inspiral Carpets records each have a 'Dung' number. Thank the Rochdale Cowboy for that. I reckon he did us a big favour there, to be honest. The *Trainsurfing* EP was eventually released in March 1989 to more rave reviews from the music press. John Peel's love of the band was bringing us lots of positive attention and gave us immeasurable levels of kudos. Major labels started to sniff around – it felt like we were back on track.

For our next single, 'Joe', we decided to bring in 808 State to help on the production: true pioneers of the acid-house sound in the UK, they'd just released their debut album *Newbuild*. In the next couple of years, indie dance collaborations would become a big thing, but, to my knowledge, this was one of the first times it had been tried. Martin Price of 808 State also partly owned Eastern Bloc, an amazing record shop in Manchester, and an independent record label called Creed. Martin introduced us to the distribution company that he worked with, Nine Mile, and we were back in action. For the recording of the 'Joe' single, we set up camp in Square One Studios in Bury. This is where I met Stephen Boyce-Buckley for the first time since we'd been at school together in the early seventies. It's also where I first met Rowetta. She was a regular visitor to Square One, laying down backing vocals for various acts, often with Denise Johnson, another incredible Manchester-based vocalist. For our 'Joe' session, 808's Graham Massey would oversee the main part of the sound engineering and production.

Martin Price was a real character. I remember being surprised to see him dancing in the studio while we worked on 'Joe' because, back then, blokes didn't really dance on their own. Unless it was in the Haçienda with a couple of pills down their neck. Dancing was still considered something you did with your girlfriend. Martin was going for it: stood up, arms out, having his own little rave right there in front of the mixing desk. 'Y'all right, Martin?' I asked.

'Yeah, man!'

'What're ye doin'?'

'I'm ravin', man! It's a fuckin' tune this! Can you feel it? Get on yer feet!'

'Nah, I'm all right!'

We were all made up with the final recorded version of 'Joe'. It felt like a big step forward for us. It was wonderful to see this little song I'd written a few years previously about a guy I knew with not a penny to his name transform into one of the cornerstones of our set. It's still one of our biggest songs today. Music is such a powerful thing: it's truly magical when the spirit of something or someone can live on in a song. It's hard to believe it's 40 years now since Joe died, but I think it would bring a real smile to his face if he knew that kids that weren't even born until long after he passed away are still singing his name at gigs: '*Because I'm Joe, the street lamp is my home/from place to place I like to roam/the cold wind blows right through my bones.'* God bless you, mate.

I'd often sit on the windowsill of our Sackville Street office gazing out and watching Manchester go about its business: miscreants plying their trade on the streets directly below; sex workers leaning into the passenger windows of slow-moving cars, trying to negotiate a deal; rent boys strutting stealth-like, in and out of the Rembrandt and off in the direction of Piccadilly Gardens or the Arndale Shopping Centre with rolled-up newspaper in hand. Everyone on Sackville Street in 1989 looked like they were on a mission. The Inspirals certainly were. Graham had a brown Ford Cortina Mark 4 (NNA 886W) and we'd cruise around town at night, going to see bands, sorting out gigs for ourselves, flyposting and generally having adventures. Like young men in rock 'n' roll bands always have done, ever since bands and cars were invented.

The people I met and the things I saw on this street inspired me to write the song 'Sackville'. The area was a popular stomping ground for the city's sex workers. The girls would be working, day and night. We'd often chat to them and have a laugh as they sat smoking on the doorsteps of our office building. They'd make fun of our clothes and tell us to get proper haircuts. We'd give them a bit of banter back and tell them to get proper jobs. 'Lads, fuck off, you're scaring me customers away!' If they saw us flyposting, they'd take the piss: *'Inspiral Carpets??* No one's gonna come to your gig with a fuckin' silly name like that!'

They were real characters. It was a dark and dangerous world, and these strong, animated women were right at the heart of it. I felt like we had things in common. We were all from similar backgrounds: we grew up in the same towns supporting the same football teams and listening to the same records on the radio. We were all hoping for better things.

Then one night one of the girls was murdered. It wasn't someone we knew personally, but it still felt close to home. It made the national news. When I heard about it I felt the need to capture the moment. Within hours I was writing, scribbling my thoughts down. As a songwriter, sometimes, it's all you can do, pick up a pen and get those feelings down on paper.

Laughing with your sisters in the rain
Dancing on a kerb stone
When last you saw her
But when the trick goes wrong
there's no one there to help her
There's not a thing that I
Can do about it
I guess I'll just go home and write a song about it

I wanted to paint a picture of that world on that day: a melancholy snapshot of a dark and dangerous world with these women '*stronger than a man could ever be*'. I wanted the Farfisa part in the verse to have a cold industrial feel – the vibe of some of the acid rhythms I was hearing in the clubs around town. I played the verses with no vibrato, so the organ sounded raw, cutting and brutal. Then I wanted the chorus to be uplifting, heavenly and gospel-like, with my backing vocal weaving up and around Tom's epic lead vocal. Craig came up with a perfect drum pattern, stomping out a similar rhythm to the organ riff. Martyn did the same, laying down a bassline as dirty as the gutters on the street in the song. 'Sackville' went on to become a crowd favourite in our live set. The audiences always do that 'radio gaga' clapping thing in time with the drum beat.

In the spring of 1989, we let Tony Wilson know we'd found our new frontman and he invited us back onto his show again. Our performance of 'Sackville' on *The Other Side of Midnight* went out on Sunday 19 June, six months after our 'Directing Traffic' appearance. Tony introduced us by saying, 'How could we not have them back when they found a lead singer through a special dating service that we operate here at *The Other Side of Midnight*?'

As with our first performance on the show, it was a great bit of television. It felt like we were still, somehow, out on a limb doing our own strange little thing, and we liked that. And now we had a singer with a massive voice. Tom was never 'classically trained' but he had a voice that was equal parts rock singer, crooner and choirboy, setting us, quite spectacularly, apart from our contemporaries.

On 1 April 1990 a riot broke out at Manchester's Strangeways Prison, just a few minutes' walk across the city from Sackville Street. Several prison officers and prisoners were hurt, and a load of inmates managed to get onto the roof. They spent the next few days up there, throwing roof tiles down onto the courtyard and shouting profanities for all the world's media to enjoy in real time. In one famous TV clip, a prisoner is seen emerging from the eaves and through the broken slates early in the morning, climbing to his feet and greeting the assembled masses and the world's cameras with a proud 'Good morning, Manchester!'

We thought it'd be fitting to mark the moment by doing a photoshoot on the roof of our building on Sackville Street. We climbed through a small door and out onto the slates where we posed precariously while our friend Paul Brownridge took a series of ultracool shots.

I saw one of the Sackville girls again a couple of years later. The band had made a bit of money in the meantime, been on the television quite a lot, and I'd bought myself a fancy little British sports car, a TVR Tasmin (CEY 406X) – the only sports car ever made in Blackpool. It was a weird-looking vehicle that turned heads every time I drove it. It looked a bit like the DeLorean in *Back to the Future* and cost me ten thousand quid from a second-hand garage in Oldham. I had it resprayed in a gorgeous black-and-grey metal-flake paint job. It looked the bollocks, but it had some proper peculiar technical issues. The driver's side pop-up headlamp would regularly go rogue and start randomly popping up and down, like it was winking at all passers-by, until I pulled over and restarted the car. One day, I was at a red light near Piccadilly Station with my windows down. One of the old girls was walking past. She spotted me, bent down, looked in the passenger window, and shouted, 'Clint Boon! Get a proper fuckin' car!'

37/ Cool as Fuck

We were starting to build a solid fanbase, and after I wore my original handmade cow t-shirt on *The Other Side of Midnight* fans started asking for them at gigs. At first, I made a couple by hand, but when more and more people kept enquiring about them, we decided we'd knock some proper ones up and see how they sold.

I'd met a young lad at the Boardwalk called Liam Walsh. He was at art college and was printing t-shirts for friends, so I asked him if he could print some 'Cool as Fuck' t-shirts for us. The Boardwalk owner, Colin Sinclair, also managed The Railway Children, a cool, summery, guitar pop band from Wigan who the music press were hailing as the saviours of music and life as we know it. Colin's dad, Donald, had helped Colin buy the venue and was very supportive of his son's business, always knocking about, busy doing anything DIY related. Liam had been helping Donald print Railway Children t-shirts on a screen-printing carousel and dryer that Donald had built. Eventually, Liam bought the printing gear off Donald and set up his own printing business, SWAG in Sackville Street. From there, he continued printing our t-shirts. All the Inspirals hit it off with Liam from day one. He was bubbly, sociable and gave off great energy. Eventually, he would become the Inspirals' merch seller and travel the world with us. This young lad climbing on the tour bus every night, after a gig, with a big smile and a black bin bag full of cash.

Within a couple of weeks of getting Liam involved, we were struggling to keep up with demand. We were making more money from t-shirts than we were from gigs or record sales. Our Sackville Street office was full of boxes of t-shirts, and Noel would spend half his day dealing with all the orders that came in. The Inspirals' cow t-shirt and the alternative 'Cool as Fuck' version, with a cow wearing shades and smoking a spliff, became a crucial feature of the Manchester scene. You'd see people wearing them at almost every gig you went to, not just ours. I couldn't walk down Oldham Street without seeing at least half a dozen. We expanded the range of designs and sold tens of thousands of the things. For a while we became more famous for our t-shirts than anything else. The press said we sold more shirts than records. When the Harlem Globetrotters came on tour to Manchester, they all bought 'Cool as Fuck' t-shirts to take back to the States. By accident, we'd stumbled across a huge revenue stream: t-shirts funded the band until we signed our first proper record deal. Other bands started to come to us for advice on where they could get their t-shirts printed and how best to shift them.

Over the next couple of years, we released more cow-based t-shirt designs, including the 'Multi-Moo!', which was a shirt with loads of cow logos across it, and the 'Mega Moo!', where I drew one big cow cartoon that spilled off the edge of the shirt and onto the sleeves. We even did a 'Mini-Moo!' version for babies and toddlers.

The 'Cool as Fuck' shirt is probably one of the only band t-shirts in Britain that led to people getting arrested for wearing it. At the time, bands didn't tend to put the word 'fuck' on t-shirts. Sometimes, the hapless offender would just get a stern, 'You'd better turn that inside out, sunshine!' from the neighbourhood cop, but occasionally the nasty garment would be confiscated and taken away to be destroyed. One unfortunate fan was stopped in the street by a police officer who arrested him for breaching obscenity laws. The story was picked up first by the music press and then by the tabloids. The fan ended up in court and, if I remember correctly, we paid his fine and sent him a new shirt.

38/
Viva La's and Mondays

In June 1989 we got our first gig abroad, in València, on a mini-festival bill with Happy Mondays, The La's, from Liverpool, and a band from Brighton called The Popguns. We were buzzing to be playing our first gig abroad, and to be playing with the Mondays again. We were also huge fans of The La's. Their early recordings were the soundtrack to our trips around the UK, a La's demo cassette constantly pumping out Mersey magic from the dashboard – 'Timeless Melody' left the five of us in a reverential silence every time we listened to it. The festival was called 'La Conjura De Las Danzas', and was curated by Jorge Albi, who was Spain's answer to John Peel, and had a radio show of the same name. When we arrived, València was in the middle of a heatwave – over 100 degrees Fahrenheit was just a bit warm for a bunch of lads from Oldham. (Or Salford or Liverpool.) The venue we were playing was a weird two-storey building that seemed to double as a brothel. We were all in shared rooms, almost dormitories, which were basic, to say the least.

My standout memory of the trip is of hanging out on a large balcony on the roof of the venue with The La's late at night, and every one of them had an acoustic guitar, even the drummer. They were all great musicians and had beautiful voices – even their roadie. They were insanely melodic and quite cosmic, in that inimitable Scouse way. They were such impressive musicians when they were jamming they'd be playing a Beatles song and then segue into an Everly Brothers track, complete with all the harmonies weaving in and out of each other, and then into 'Timeless Melody'. It was a mind-blowing thing to witness close-up. When you're right in the thick of a bunch of musicians who are so in tune with each other, harmonising and strumming away together, just breathing music from every pore, it's an almost spiritual experience. I can picture them on that rooftop now, the constant whiff of weed hanging in the air around them, the innocent pure joy from jamming together. Frontman Lee Mavers had a dreaminess about him; he was constantly smiling and seemingly happy. He would become quite intense when it came to chatting about music. I felt we really connected. He had a warm aura and a gentle soul, and I felt like he liked the Inspirals.

The Mondays had got there the night before and had already had a wild night out. Shaun said Jeff Barrett, who did press for Factory and the Mondays at the time (and would later go on to start Heavenly Records) had scored some mescaline and gave some to the Mondays, who'd never had it before. Shaun was on E and mescalin and partied all night before falling asleep on the beach with their tour manager Anthony 'Muzzer' Murray. They were so wasted they lay there on the beach, asleep, all morning and afternoon, in the blistering sun. They woke up horrifically sunburnt, especially Shaun, who had to go to hospital. They weren't on stage until 5am; Shaun scored some heroin to help him deal with the pain of the sunburn. Years later he said it might actually have been that incident that was the spark that put him on the road to a serious heroin habit.

But you know what? Despite all that, and even Gaz Whelan falling off his drum stool during their set, the Mondays were still sensational. They always were. You just couldn't take your eyes off them.

39/ Life's What You Make it

People often underestimate the role the Inspirals played in laying down the foundations of what became Madchester. John Robb once wrote that the Inspirals were 'the first band to break out of the city's next wave of bands after the Smiths' and I don't think that's too far from the truth. From early 1987, we kept ourselves busy gigging up and down the UK and writing and recording new tunes at every opportunity. Through 1989, we were banging out singles every two months and had recorded our third Peel Session by the end of the year. We were early purveyors of the idea that 'Manchester bands are coming back'. We were the preachers stood on upturned beer crates telling our stories of life in the north.

We had a decent amount of money in the bank through t-shirt sales; we had a lot of record companies sniffing around us, indies and majors; and we were ready to make our debut album. We'd seen other British bands sign big record deals with major labels only for the relationship to get a bit strained once the label realised they were only going to sell tens or, if they were lucky, hundreds of thousands of units, rather than the millions that could be shifted by the likes of Elton John or Jacko. That's when the label's A&R team would usually start trying to persuade the band to 'be a bit more pop!' or 'lose the goofy-looking fat kid on bass'. To us, it seemed obvious to get as far along the road as possible before getting involved with a bigger label. We decided to pay for the recording of the album ourselves, which would put us in a much stronger position when we did eventually come to negotiate a deal. It also meant nobody from the record company would be able to interfere with the recording. We knew what we wanted the album to sound like, and we had enough studio experience by then to make it happen. We knew we could record it in Out of the Blue in Manchester – we trusted Nick there – which also meant we could stay at home, so there were no hotel or transport costs. It sounded like a no-brainer. We paid for the recording of the album entirely with the profits from our cassette and t-shirt sales. We didn't do the final mixes at Out of the Blue as we wanted to get enough money together to finish the album at Square One, which had more 'high-end' equipment but was more expensive. At the end of the Out of the Blue sessions, Nick ran off monitor mixes of all the tracks that we could start playing to people.

We had meetings with most of the major record labels, including CBS, Warner Bros. and RCA. We enjoyed all the attention but were constantly questioning if getting into bed with a major label was the right move for us. The big turning point came when we were invited to meet Daniel Miller, head of Mute Records. A radio plugger we'd been using, Nicki Kefalas, knew Daniel and, as a favour to her, he'd offered to give us any advice we needed. Within a few days we found ourselves down in London waiting to meet Daniel in the modest boardroom of Mute Records. We sat there having a giggle about the table, which appeared to be some sort of door, propped up by piles of boxes containing records, magazines and other record-label paraphernalia. After a while, Daniel walked in, sat down and said to us, 'So . . . you want to throw it all away, do you?'

'Sorry?'

'You want to throw it all away?'

'What do you mean?'

'You've put all this hard work in for years, building up a solid fanbase, and a good set of songs, and now you want to throw it all away by signing to a major label?'

That completely threw us. Daniel explained how he thought it would be a disaster if we signed to a major record label, how they would mismanage our career and we would be dropped before we knew it. He explained how Mute was more geared to giving artists the artistic freedom they needed. Nicki had already stressed that this meeting wouldn't be about Daniel wanting to sign us, and even we couldn't imagine ourselves on a roster that included such a mad cross-section of acts as Laibach, Erasure and Nick Cave and the Bad Seeds, but he was speaking our language and addressing the reservations we already had about the majors. We left Daniel with a tape of the rough mixes of all the tracks we intended to use on our album.

The next day, we got a call from Nicki: 'Daniel wants to meet you guys again as soon as possible.'

Daniel loved the tape and wanted to talk to us about working with Mute. The diversity of Mute's stable of acts was one of the things that swung it for us. Their acts also included Depeche Mode, Diamanda Galás, Mark Stewart and the Maffia and Einstürzende Neubauten (the only band I've ever seen live who had more power tools than B&Q). If they were going to let bands as eclectic as that make the records they were making, we'd probably be left to create the music we wanted to make.

We headed off to London again and signed on the dotted line. Rumours at the time were that we'd signed for a million quid. That was because, on the day of us signing, the *NME* sent journalist Steve Lamacq and photographer A J Barratt along to record the occasion. I picked up a dummy album cover that was lying around, opened it up and, on the blank side, drew a fake million-pound cheque with a marker pen. The picture got published and everyone thought we'd got a million-pound advance. What actually happened was this: Mute would obviously pay for the recording, manufacture, promotion and distribution of our records for the next four or five years. When it came to our living costs, we calculated how much we'd need by starting with a figure of £70 a week, the basic amount each band member needed to get by on. Multiply that by six (Binsy was cut in as a sixth member rather than the traditional management split of 20 per cent), times it by 52, and stick a bit on for the taxman. That's year one sorted. Up it a bit for year two, and so on. If things go well, bang us a Brucie Bonus on top. Quite a modest sum of money, really. We were happy, Mute were happy.

On the day we signed the record deal, Depeche Mode frontman Dave Gahan popped into Mute's office to say hi. At that point, Depeche Mode were one of the biggest bands in the world. Arguably, *the* biggest band in the world. They were selling out 60,000-capacity baseball stadiums all over the USA and were massive in every single country on the planet. They also had a reputation for being the biggest party animals in the world. But when we met

Dave Gahan in the Mute Records building on Harrow Road, he was charming, eloquent and seemed genuinely excited about his new labelmates: 'Welcome to the Mute family, you guys. You're going to love working with the team here. They've helped us achieve great things – without them we'd be nothing. Let us know if we can be of any assistance to you . . .' A true ambassador for Mute Records, and extremely sober. The exact opposite of the state he would be in the next time our paths crossed.

MADCHESTER, SO MUCH TO ANSWER FOR

40/ Halcyon Daze

By the summer of 1989 things had gone crazy in Manchester. It felt like the city was the centre of the world. John Squire from the Roses summed it up when he said, 'It all came together – the people I was hanging about with, the clothes we were wearing, the records we were buying, the drugs we were doing.'

The Stone Roses debut album came out in May '89, and although it was more of a slow burner than an instant success, it felt like every cool kid in the country had it. 'It takes people time to fall in love with you,' Ian Brown explained in an early television interview, with inimitable composed self-belief, 'but it's inevitable.'

Everywhere you went in Manchester, you'd hear it being played. They released 'She Bangs the Drums' as a single in July '89 then played a huge statement gig in August at Blackpool Empress Ballroom to 4,000 people. It felt like half of Manchester was in Blackpool that day, all along the seafront were gangs of kids in Roses, Mondays and Inspirals t-shirts.

The lemons on the cover of John's artwork for *The Stone Roses* were a reference to the Paris riots of 1968, when students used lemons to counteract the effects of tear gas, and to anyone in Manchester at the time it felt like we were having our own revolution right here. The music press was really talking up the Manchester scene – not only the bands and the Haçienda, but the record shops and places like Affleck's Palace – and everyone wanted a bit of it. Applications to Manchester University and Manchester Poly went through the roof. As much as we all benefited from everyone talking about Manchester, none of it would have happened without the actual music being so great. It felt like all the key bands were hitting their stride at the same time. Neil Tennant of the Pet Shop Boys coined the term 'imperial phase' to describe that period when a band or artist reaches their commercial and creative peak simultaneously, like the Pet Shop Boys did with four number 1s in a row: 'West End Girls', 'It's a Sin', 'Always on My Mind' and 'Heart'. We weren't having number 1s (although we did get to number 1 in the 'alternative chart' several times), but it felt like the Roses, the Mondays and the Inspirals were all having their own little imperial phase from 1989 into 1990. We had a run of four great singles – 'Joe', 'Find Out Why', 'Move' and 'This is How it Feels' – each of which sold more and charted higher than the previous one. The Mondays released two remixes of 'W.F.L' ('Wrote for Luck') by Paul Oakenfold and Vince Clarke, with a video shot in Legends nightclub that really captured the mood of the times. It was possibly the first time an authentic rave vibe was captured on film. It was so authentic that Shaun Ryder later admitted the band were all on ecstasy during the shoot, and had made sure lots of the extras were as well. You can tell. The video was shot by the Bailey Brothers, who Shaun credits as coming up with the term 'Madchester'. Factory loved the tag, and decided to roll with it, naming the next Mondays single the *Madchester Rave On* EP. Factory took over an old two-storey red-brick building on the corner of Princess Street and Charles Street and completely plastered the outside of the building with big posters of Central Station's Madchester logo. The press lapped it up; Kevin Cummins photographed Shaun and Tony Wilson in front of the Madchester poster, and the *NME* put it on the front cover. Nobody had really used the term in Manchester up till then, but the tag seemed to sum up the mood of the times. Everything had gone a bit mad. Living in Manchester was like living in a cartoon; the city had completely rediscovered its swagger.

We released our 'Move' single on 6 November 1989. We knew that if it entered the Top 40 we'd be the first Madchester band to appear on *Top of the Pops*. The amount of excitement around the band in the media convinced us we were in with a good chance. Sadly, 'Move' only entered the charts at 49, so we just missed out. The following week, the Roses released 'Fools Gold' and the Mondays released their *Madchester Rave On* EP, which had 'Hallelujah' as its lead track. They entered the charts at number 8 and 19 respectively, so both bands appeared on the same episode of *Top of the Pops* on 13 November

1989, taking Madchester into the front rooms of the nation. It was an episode that went down in musical history. Mark Day from the Mondays was still a postman at the time and had to get back from recording *Top of the Pops* in London the same night so he could do his round the next morning. He gave it up after that, though. The next week, 808 State were on *Top of the Pops* with 'Pacific State'. Andy and Darren from the band had still been working as roofers only weeks before. Andy said that when he got back from London, his mum said to him, 'What are you lot doing on *Top of the Pops*!??'

While we would've loved to have been the first Madchester band on the show, we couldn't have been more chuffed for the Roses, the Mondays, 808 State and Manchester in general. In a matter of weeks Manchester became the most talked-about city in the UK and, for the first time, not because of its football. The music me and my mates were making was starting to resonate with people right across the planet. I was confident that our turn would be next, and our next single would get us on *Toppy*.

Wherever you were in the city, you'd hear the same records playing out loudly and proudly from open bedroom windows in Stretford, cars on Deansgate, the stalls in Affleck's, and every shop whose staff knew the score. The Roses, the Mondays, the Inspirals, 808 State and James were everywhere. We were in the ether. Also on repeat were De La Soul's *3 Feet High and Rising* and the Pixies' *Doolittle*, two stunning albums, both released earlier in the year – all of this punctuated with the pulse and ethereal voice of Gerald Simpson's 'Voodoo Ray'. What a time to be alive and what a time to be in Manchester.

We were on the cusp of a new decade, and the future suddenly looked bright. 'The idea of the city as an attractive vibrant place to be begins with rock 'n' roll,' Tony Wilson once explained, at length (the only way he knew!). 'Why is that even more true in cities like Manchester? When it comes to popular culture, you're talking world, global level.'

'Manchester reinvented itself,' Oscar-winning film director Danny Boyle, also a Manc (he's from Bury), later reflected. 'It didn't wait for a leader to do that for it. In fact, it took the lack of interest that was clearly shown to it by Margaret Thatcher's premiership as the signal to do things for itself. There are some great northern cities that aren't beholden to anyone. And no matter how bad it gets they will always regenerate themselves.'

Whenever I was in town and not on tour, I'd walk along Oldham Street every Saturday afternoon, soaking it all up. I loved it. There was such a buzz about the place. Everyone was bouncing along the street. I'd pop into Affleck's Palace's psychedelic rabbit warren of clothes shops, record shops, tattooists and poster shops, like Tom Bloxham's Splash. Also on Oldham Street, Factory Records had just opened Dry Bar, which made the road even more of a destination once Dry became the main hangout in that part of town for musicians, DJs and everyone involved in the scene. There was a payphone on the wall just inside the front door and some bands would use it to phone their record companies or set up gigs. I bet it could tell some stories, that phone: the amount of drugs that must have been ordered and called in on it every day. If Greater Manchester Dibble ever tapped that phone, they'd have got a nice surprise. I never saw any trouble in Dry Bar, the vibe was always great, but you would occasionally hear about it getting 'a bit moody in there last night!'

If I think about those afternoons on Oldham Street, way before it was called the 'Northern Quarter', it was never raining. The sun was always blazing, everyone was smiling, and the music was loud and groovy. I know in real life that's not how it would've been, but that's the image my mind has decided to leave me with.

As our popularity began to grow, we started being given free clothes by all sorts of brands, including Sonneti, Joe Bloggs and JD Sports. We were introduced to Joe Bloggs by a young lad called Karl Campbell who worked for Bloggs owner Shami Ahmed. Karl'd persuaded a few of the other Manchester bands to wear Bloggs pieces. They couldn't give us clothes fast enough: jeans, t-shirts, sweatshirts, hoodies, the lot. We lapped it up. There's photos of us from late '89 and early '90 where we're dressed head to toe in Bloggs gear. Their showroom was right next to Strangeways prison, and we'd be down there every week getting 'Bloggsed-Up'. I think the Mondays must have had a bit more wedge coming in at that point because they gave Joe Bloggs a swerve in favour of more upmarket brands like Armani.

The JD Sports 'sponsorship deal' didn't go too well. It all started fine:

'Come to our store in the Arndale Centre and pick anything you want?'

'What, anything?'

'Yep. Supermarket Sweep!'

We were down there like a shot. I picked a nice Reebok shell suit, a few pairs of British Knights trainers and some Adidas tops. We all gathered our swag and took it to the counter.

'OK, lads. Leave it with us for a few days, we'll get it branded up.'

'You'll what?'

'Get it branded up. Y'know, with our logo?'

At the start of the nineties JD Sports' logo looked like some sort of ripped ticket stub with a big 'JD' on it. Ugly. Like some work-experience kid had knocked it together. We went back, as instructed, two days later. They'd ironed these logos all over our gear, even the trainers. To add insult to injury, they wanted the money shot: 'All right, lads, slip into your gear while we get a photo.'

Reluctantly, we slipped off into the cubicles and got changed, thinking the photo would just be used in *JD Staff Monthly* or some other publication we'd never get to see.

Within days, the 'bigger than life-size' photograph of us in our free outfits was plastered across the windows of JD's Arndale store.

Leo B Stanley, who owned the clothes shop Identity, was a real character and a key protagonist in fuelling the scene. His shop was on the ground floor of Affleck's. It couldn't have been situated in a better spot in terms of visibility and passing trade. He was at the epicentre of Madchester. Leo was an east Manchester lad who fully embraced the whole scene and started printing a t-shirt which, like our Cool as Fuck shirt, soon became a ubiquitous part of the moment. In an interview for the *Guardian*, he remembered, 'One night after the Haçienda I couldn't sleep,' he said (I wonder why?!), 'so I picked up the Bible and read: "On the sixth day, God created Man . . ." and wrote down in my Filofax: "On the sixth day, God created MANchester."' From the moment he first printed that slogan on a t-shirt, people went mad for them. I blagged one off him and wore it proudly (along with a black-and-gold Malcolm X-inspired

'By Any Means Necessary' shirt). 'That t-shirt went mental,' remembers Leo. 'We couldn't print them fast enough. Someone sent me a photograph from a French magazine, of Jean Paul Gaultier and Madonna at a party, both wearing "On the Sixth Day, God Created MANchester" t-shirts.'

If people mention Madchester to me now, that's what I think of, that's the time I'm taken back to: just buzzing around Oldham Street and hanging out, bumping into other bands in Dry Bar, getting stopped on the street for a few autographs. Everyone was so optimistic, and everything seemed perfect. Our city was the centre of the world. Ian Brown summed it up when he once said that all Manchester needed was a beach.

Oldham Street in 1989 was to me what I imagined Haight-Ashbury had been like in 1967. They were halcyon days. Wordsworth once wrote, 'Bliss it was in that dawn to be alive, but to be young was very heaven.' He was talking about the French Revolution, but that's how we all felt in the Madchester years. It was an incredible feeling to be right at the heart of that beautiful hurricane of love and energy. For me, it was a time of sunshine, colour, peace and profound contentment.

41/
The Second Wave

The first time I heard The Charlatans was in Eastern Bloc Records on Oldham Street in the winter of '89. Their debut single 'Indian Rope' seemed to be playing on repeat in the shop for several consecutive weekends leading up to Christmas. It was still only a white label at this point, but the staff were raving about this 'cool new band from Northwich'. Martin Price, who'd co-produced 'Joe' with us, would be behind the counter doing his trademark rave-boy dance steps in his high-top sneakers.

Like the Inspirals, The Charlatans' spiritual roots lay firmly in the UK's retro garage-band scene of the mid-1980s, where acts like The Prisoners, The Mighty Caesars and The Sid Presley Experience had many of us wanting to never grow old. The Charlatans' bassist, Martin Blunt, had previously been a member of a group called Makin' Time, who we'd crossed paths with on some of our trips out of town. Makin' Time had also had a strong mod 1960s organ vibe, courtesy of keyboardist Fay Hallam. Those of us who knew our sixties psychedelic music knew the name 'The Charlatans' might cause problems for these new kids on the block further down the line, given the notable American band from the late sixties also called The Charlatans. Their eponymous debut album, a mix of guitar-based R&B, garage rock and jug-band music sat in many a northern English boy's record collection at the back end of the eighties. But these new guys sounded nothing like their namesakes from across the Atlantic – they were equal parts Stone Roses and the Spencer Davis Group. The Charlatans' sound resonated with me immediately: there hadn't been many bands in recent years who'd stuck the keys so high in the mix. And the fact that this was an actual Hammond B3 organ made things even more authentic and relevant. No quick-fix, cheap-shit, synth-organ replicant for these boys. I needed to hear more.

The Charlatans' music would soon become a permanent fixture on Manchester's radio airwaves. Even though they were essentially a midlands-based band, with a frontman, Tim Burgess, who resided in the Cheshire town of Northwich, the city immediately took them to its bosom. Tim having been born in Salford was all we needed to claim them as one of our own.

By February 1990 'Indian Rope' was out in the world and would soon be in everyone's record rack. In the summer of 1990 The Charlatans' second single, 'The Only One I Know', smashed into the Top 10, and they were away. For a period of 18 months to two years it felt like the charts were never far away from the next Inspirals or Charlatans single. Dreamy, psychedelic garage music was officially back in the mainstream. It wasn't long before we'd be bumping into The Charlatans regularly – mainly at gigs and music-industry events, or sometimes in the office of Red Alert PR, who were promoting a lot of the new records coming out of Manchester.

I liked Tim from the moment I first met him. He had beautiful looks, a cheeky smile, and the gentlest soul. Keyboardist Rob Collins was a quiet young man and a great musician. Whenever we met, we would dive into deep discussions about organs, synths and our mutual dismay over keyboard players who chose to stand up while performing, something that never sat well with people like us. All the great keyboard players sat down while playing their instruments, people like Ray Manzarek, Alan Price and John Cale. The likes of Dave Greenfield, Rick Wakeman and Keith Emerson were spared our scorn for simply being phenomenal musicians.

Rob tragically died in a car crash in Monmouth while The Charlatans were recording their fifth album *Tellin' Stories* in 1996, only two weeks before the band were due to support Oasis at Knebworth. A scooter was auctioned off in the VIP backstage area at Knebworth and the proceeds went to Rob's family. Martin Duffy from Primal Scream stepped in and played Rob's parts. Shortly after that, they recruited Tony Rogers, and they're still going strong and making sweet psychedelic music to this day.

Over the years, I've often heard a tale that Tim Burgess was one of the people who auditioned to be our singer after Ste left in 1988. I knew Tim hadn't actually auditioned with us, but while I was writing this book he explained to me what happened. At the time, he was singing with a band called The Electric Crayons, and he heard we were looking for a new singer. He was about to contact us and ask if he could come up to the mill to audition when, on the Mancunian grapevine, he picked up that we'd found a new singer in Tom. Another one of those sliding-doors moments. We might have ended up with Tim instead of Tom. But it worked out well for all of us, and Tim found himself the frontman of another great keyboard-led group. One day, not long after he'd joined The Charlatans, Tim was walking down Market Street in Manchester when he bumped into Mani, who he'd met previously at a Roses gig. When he told him he'd joined a band called The Charlatans, Mani just gave him a great big bear hug and said, 'Welcome to the brotherhood!'

The Charlatans were the first of the next wave of Manchester bands coming through. The entire scene could not have been any more colourful. Intastella had formed out of the ashes of a four-piece guitar band from Stockport called Laugh, who'd been together since the mid-1980s and had done a couple of sessions for John Peel. Laugh were the first Manchester guitar band that I knew who started experimenting with samplers. The Inspirals were big fans of theirs and we'd visited them at Suite 16 studios in Rochdale, ahead of recording our *Plane Crash* EP. The Laugh boys had been sat around this cream-coloured, rack-mounted machine with a TV monitor and keyboard attached – the Akai S900 sampler, which hadn't been on the market for long. Until now, such equipment had been the exclusive domain of electronic and dance-music producers. 'What you doin' with that?' I asked.

'Just playing around with some new sounds,' said Martin Mittler, who was Laugh's bassist.

'We're thinking of changing direction a bit,' said frontman Martin Wright.

In 1989, Laugh enlisted a beautiful scenester called Stella Grundy to front the group, and they became Intastella. Their cover of Frankie Valli's 'The Night' remains one of the most significant and exciting releases of the time and brought them the mainstream attention that they'd missed out on with Laugh.

Northside brought the party, the energy and the youthful exuberance with tunes like 'Shall We Take a Trip?' and 'Take Five'. Their singer, Warren

'Dermo' Dermody, seemed like the little brother of all of us – proper cheeky fucker at times, but ultra-loveable.

The New Fast Automatic Daffodils brought yet another seminal piece to our aural jigsaw with 'Big', a hypnotic and seductive six minutes of electro pop that sounds as contemporary today as it did back then (the Jon Dasilva remix became a big hit at the Haçienda).

Then one night I bumped into Scott Carey in the Boardwalk. I'd not seen much of him since his time with the Inspirals. 'Clint, I've started a new band!' he told me with glee.

'Cool! What are you called?'

'You'll like this . . . PARIS ANGELS!!'

The name brought an air of exotic sophistication to the table, but when I heard their music . . . fuck me! They were good. Again, as with Intastella and the New Fads, the new technology was upfront: the sequencers, synths and electronic beats. Their debut single 'Perfume' still sounds great today and remains a permanent feature of my DJ sets.

It's hard to describe how much of a sensation World of Twist were when we first saw and heard them. They were a crazy, psychedelic, krautrock pop group who had upped roots from their native Sheffield and moved over the Snake Pass to reside in a Manchester postcode. Their frontman, Tony Ogden, was a one-off. He had elements of Cliff Richard, Mark E Smith and Elvis to his look and his vibe in general. Their stage show was the ultimate celebration of cabaret. Not so much your usual rock 'n' roll setup, more a mix of fancy-dress hire, junk-shop trash and TV game shows. Their gig at the Ritz in Manchester in December 1990, with Intastella supporting, remains one of the most memorable I've ever witnessed. The band came on stage and broke into a cool instrumental piece for a couple of minutes, before Tony came out from the side of the stage, completely wrapped in aluminium cooking foil. He looked like something from a cannibal's Christmas dinner. When he arrived at the mic stand, he ripped the lot off and got on with the business of being one of the greatest frontpeople Manchester ever saw. Throughout the gig, small volcanoes smoked, giant clam shells yawned, and a huge plywood *Generation Game*-type wheel rotated as if there was about to be some sort of glitzy tombola. Legend has it that Jarvis Cocker caught an earlier incarnation of World of Twist and took some of their essence into his Pulp stage presence. I know for a fact that The Clint Boon Experience!, eight years after that Ritz gig, were heavily inspired by what I saw that night. Both Noel and Liam Gallagher were huge fans of World of Twist and, years later, after Oasis split and Liam formed a new band called Beady Eye, they recorded a fantastic version of World of Twist's 'Sons of the Stage'.

The whole scene was full of beautiful people. I don't remember there being any bad eggs in our circle. The kind of bloke who, when you see him walking down the street, you think, 'Ey up! Here comes cunty bollocks!' They were all good souls. It was as if some sort of loved-up ark full of chosen people had landed, bang in the middle of Piccadilly Gardens.

42/ This is How it Feels

When I write a song, I write as if it might be the last song I'll ever write. (That's what I assume most songwriters do.) The song by which I may be judged more than any other. Not only because it's me opening my soul right at that very moment, but because it's the most recent work I've created in the fifty-odd years or so since I started writing. I've seen some of my songs go on to have spectacular and breathtakingly wonderful lives, while others, some of which I consider to be my greatest, have been heard by no more than a handful of people. Others will possibly never see the light of day. I try to write in a photographic style. I try to paint a picture of the person, the object, the moment I'm describing, or the emotion I want to share. I try to avoid clichés or well-worn phrases. Wherever possible, I'll find my own set of words to describe the scene rather than just reaching for the standard 'off the shelf' way of saying something. I'm a big believer in the listener putting their own personal interpretations into songs, but I don't mind telling the actual stories of how these songs came to life.

Most people, listening to 'This is How it Feels', assume the final line in the chorus is: '*This is how it feels when your world means nothing at all*'. The lyric I wrote was actually '*. . . when your* word *means nothing at all*'. This tale may surprise some people. It's a story I've never told publicly and its one that comes from a place of sadness and guilt. 'This is How it Feels' is by far our biggest song, and one of the most recognised songs in the UK – partly because it's something of an evergreen radio classic, and partly because it's been adopted by football fans across the country (fans of several teams have used variations of the chorus to taunt their rivals). It's also probably true to say, though, that many of those people singing it in the nation's football stadiums on a weekly basis don't even know it's a song by a band called Inspiral Carpets.

June 1989. Our minibus arrived in another coastal town that they forgot to close down. The gig the night before had been another blinder. We were playing better than ever and enjoying our ascent from playing smoky pubs in Oldham to touring the universities and bigger venues on the national circuit. But something different had happened the night before. A young woman came into the dressing room just before we went on stage. She and I chatted and arranged to carry on our conversation over a drink after the show. Soon after the gig, I crept out of the venue, met up with her and disappeared into the seaside mist along the promenade.

It was the first time I'd been unfaithful to Debbie. The guilt hit me hard. Family and relationships had always meant everything to me. I'd always been loyal to her, and now this. Such powerful feelings. I didn't share what had happened with the band. I certainly didn't want to tell them how bad I was feeling. As any young man in a British pop group from the late 1980s will tell you, you'd get the piss well and truly ripped out of you if you started whimpering on about feeling guilty after a one-night stand – or any other sensitive subject, for that matter. Young men in bands can be brutal with each other at times, and back then we were no different.

How did I feel at that moment in time? I felt lonely. I felt small. I felt like my word meant nothing at all. I decided to put my feelings into a song. Even if only as a way of offloading some of the guilt. How could I put these emotions into a song without telling the real story of what had happened? I put it all into a fictitious tale, a 'kitchen sink' drama, where the mother of the family has had an affair with a local boy. On the surface, she's happily married with kids. No one knows about the affair. She doesn't want to leave her husband. She knows she's made a mistake and won't commit to any further romance with the boy. He's taken his own life because he wanted more. It's the day of the funeral. *'Black car drives through the town/Some guy from the top estate/Seems they found him under a train.'* She wants to be at the funeral but obviously can't. The dad and kids haven't got a clue why she's down. *'Husband don't know what he's done/Kids don't know what's wrong with Mum/She can't say, they can't see/Putting it down to another bad day.'* It's the mum in the song whose word means nothing at all. But, in reality, it was me who was questioning if my word meant anything at all any more.

'This is How it Feels' was only ever intended to be a way of me getting some of the guilt out. A sort of exorcism. Instead, it took on a life all of its own.

43/
Top of the Pops

One night in late 1989 my dad picked up the *Oldham Chronicle* and opened it to show me an article he'd just read about a new Manchester band: 'Look at this, Clint! Says 'ere they're gonna be reet famous!'

I leant in and saw the black-and-white photograph of a bunch of young lads smiling joyously at the camera. 'What they called?'

'Take That!' said Cyril. 'One of 'ems from Oldham! They do all the dancing too!'

I sensed he might have been having a bit of a dig about the fact that these young upstarts could hit the big time before the Inspirals. And they could dance. 'Dad, mark my words,' I said. 'Our next single will get us on *Top of the Pops*! As for that bunch of losers, they're going nowhere. That'll be the last you'll ever see of 'em!'

We had 'This is How it Feels' earmarked as the next single, and this time we absolutely knew we'd have a hit. Mute suggested we make a little change to the single version and change the line '*Seems they found him under a train/And yet he had it all on a plate*' to something else. They thought the '*under a train*' might be a bit graphic for daytime radio and *Top of the Pops* (if we made it on there). We didn't have a problem with that, and I changed it to '*Left a note for a local girl/And yet he had it all on a plate*'. Same storyline, softer imagery. We released the single in early March 1990 and it entered the singles chart at number 22. We were going to be on *Top of the Pops*!

In 1990 I saw all my ambitions coming to fruition. But doing *Top of the Pops* for the first time sat on its own, really – appearing on *Top of the Pops* was the moment that spoke to your friends and family more than any other. Even Mum and Dad watched *Top of the Pops* and knew how important it was. At the start of the nineties it was still a huge national institution.

Even though appearing on *Toppy* was every young British music lover's dream back in the 20th century, the experience on set, in the actual studio, was far from glamorous. For the artists, it meant a full day of rehearsing, not just for the benefit of the band, but for the camera operators, the lighting technicians and a whole community of people working behind the scenes. While we all relished every minute we spent in the BBC Television Centre, by around 3pm the novelty had usually subsided. The studio audiences had it even tougher, watching pop stars go through every emotion – joy, boredom, anger, aloofness, petulance and giddiness – often in a state of inebriation or under the influence of drugs. On top of all this, you'd see members of the BBC floor crew using actual wooden sticks to direct and corral confused punters around the studio, making sure they were in position when the next act appeared on the second or third stage. This gave the viewer the impression that a couple of hundred kids were in the studio, when, in actual fact, 40 or 50 eager music lovers, prodded and cajoled into position, resulted in the same effect. The stages were quite small too, so there was not much space to move around. The BBC's lighting effects, smoke and mirrors all helped to make the audience look something bigger than just a small huddle of people.

The excitement would always return as we were told to get in position for the actual performance. But that first time for us, performing 'This is How it Feels' to the nation, was a profoundly special moment in time – three or four minutes to be witnessed by 11 million people that might possibly change our lives. I wore a beautiful Jean Paul Gaultier cardigan with a gold lamé front. Only two had been brought into Manchester, courtesy of Richard Creme at L'Homme, Manchester's finest gentleman's outfitters. Morrissey bought the other one. I wore white jeans, high-top British Knights trainers in black and white and the obligatory pocket watch.

We were ready to go. Some of the audience were looking at us in a 'Who the fuck are this lot?' sort of way. Others seemed genuinely excited to be part of the moment. Tom looked a bit nervous. 'Are you OK, Tom?' I asked.

'Yes, thanks. Feeling really good. I'm actually really excited!'

I smiled over at Graham: 'We've done it, man! Fuckin' *Top of the* fuckin' *Pops*!'

We were all elated. The anticipation was like nothing I'd ever felt. We were introduced by Simon Mayo, who talked about how it was proving a great year for Oldham: 'OK, success city of 1990 is Oldham! There's Oldham Celtic in the basketball, Oldham rugby club, Oldham Athletic in the football and, oh yes, at number 22 . . . Inspiral Carpets!'

The backing track kicked in and the cameraman zoomed in on me, as I mimed to the intro on my old trusty Farfisa.* So, 'This is how it feels to play *Top of the Pops*,' I thought. It was a surreal moment to be there in the *Top of the Pops* studio after watching it every week since I was a young lad. The red lights on top of the cameras flickered into life. The backing track started. This was a full mime performance – the BBC's way of making sure the nation's front rooms weren't swamped with half an hour of out-of-tune cack every Thursday night. I felt goosebumps the size of the Pennines all over my body. I thought about all my heroes who I'd seen on this show throughout my life. Bowie, Roxy, The Stranglers, Showaddywaddy, Dusty, Lulu, even the likes of Elvis and Chuck Berry had appeared on it, albeit, in Elvis's case, with gig footage recorded on the other side of the Atlantic.

The men with the long sticks encouraged the crowd to act excited and animated. They happily obliged. If anything, they overdid it. The cacophony of screams, whistles and shouts gave the impression we were performing in the middle of the world's worst-ever fairground disaster. But we were blissful in our moment. This was our time. The country had been gently introduced to our music through the radio, and to our antics via the music press, but this was the most important British music television show of all time, and the cameras were well and truly in our face. I looked over and caught Martyn's eye and smiled as I remembered that night at the Loop gig in Manchester: 'Clint, please let me join your band!' I thought about those finite points in time where your life's path can change in an instant – me seeing the Pistols in '76, or getting the call from Graham ten years later about recording a demo tape; Craig

---

* I later got a second Farfisa organ that was a bit battered, which I used for the occasional TV appearance. I used it on *Top of the Pops* in 1991 and Noel forgot to put it back in the van afterwards. Never to be seen again.

sat on his BMX in the Red Barn car park that Sunday afternoon; Peel playing a song called 'Jayne' sung by a young chap called Tom. Then, the final bars of the song and it was all over. The audience applauded and cheered as the camera panned to Simon Mayo, who said, 'I'm telling you, that's an inspirational song, that's Inspiral Carpets . . .' We'd finished the performance. Within moments, the crowd were being herded across the studio to be mentally scarred for the rest of their days by a video playback of the new Jive Bunny single, which had hopped into the charts at number 4.

Primal Scream had performed just before us with a brilliant version of their new single 'Loaded'. It was great to be on the same episode of *Toppy* as the Primals, as I'd followed them since the mid-eighties. I first saw them at the Haçienda in 1985 when they played with fellow Creation bands The Weather Prophets and Meat Whiplash. In June '86 we'd piled into the Opel Manta one night to drive over to Leeds where the Primals and Pop Will Eat Itself played at a venue called the Pub with no Name.* During the Primals' set, someone had shouted something derogatory at their frontman Bobby Gillespie, to which he casually responded down the mic with one of the best heckler put-downs ever: 'Underachiever.'

I'd met Bobby a few times through Factory PR man, Jeff Barrett. Jeff had known Bobby since his days working for Alan McGee at Creation Records. Bobby would often be hanging out in Jeff's office on Clerkenwell Road in Farringdon. In fact, it was Jeff who had first suggested that the Primals get Andrew Weatherall to remix their track 'I'm Losing More Than I'll Ever Have'. This move had resulted in 'Loaded', a record that, in my opinion, was a true piece of art and made a lot of us rethink the concept of what makes a great pop single.

After the *Top of the Pops* recording was over, we went to the bar for a drink and eventually headed to the reception area of Television Centre to wait for our lift back to the hotel. We were tired, slightly drunk, but in great spirits. We knew this was a massive milestone and we felt like we'd really achieved something special. As we sat waiting in the plush BBC reception, Bobby

* Which later became the Duchess of York.

strutted past us on his way to his cab. He was dressed head to toe in black leather and, with his long dark hair, had the look and aura of a young Jim Morrison. He waved and wished us well, 'See you later, guys. Good luck!' He was still looking at us and smiling as he walked straight into the plate-glass door. Ouch! In my mind, he slid down to the floor like a scene from *Tom and Jerry*, the leather of his outfit squeaking loudly against the glass as he fell. In real life, though, he probably just styled it out casually and went on his way – because he's Bobby Gillespie and he's cooler than fuck.

After that first *Top of the Pops* appearance, everything went up a gear. To the man in the street, being on the show was the ultimate measure of success for any band or artist. It didn't matter if you only had 50 quid in the bank or if you had to go back to work at the local scrapyard the next day. Those few minutes on the BBC, in that time slot on a Thursday night, meant you'd made the big time. We felt the effects immediately, not just from our parents, who were all very vocal about the pride they felt, but from our contemporaries and the people of Manchester in general. Even if you didn't like the Inspirals' look or sound, you couldn't help but feel excited for us. My mum and dad were over the moon. So were Booney and Booney. For the next few weeks, the joy I could sense when I walked in the room or spoke to them on the phone was overwhelming. 'I'm dead proud of you, Booney!' Lynda would tell me at every opportunity. 'What's it like bein' a pop star, Booney?' Craig would ask, with a massive grin on his face. 'You've bloody cracked it, lad, aven't ye?!' said Dad, as Mum beamed by his side. 'Your nana's proper chuffed too, y'know, Clint?' pointed out Mum. 'She can't believe it!'

On my travels, I'd always phone home for a catch up with them. It felt like they were along for the ride too. As a family, we'd sat together for years watching *Top of the Pops* through some iconic music chapters – the swinging sixties, glam, punk, New Wave and, more recently, hip-hop and acid house. Like for millions of other British music lovers, it was *our* show.

It was quite unreal seeing this sad little song that I'd written in a dark and sombre headspace become a new anthem for the baggy masses. The funny thing was: the fans' parents loved it too. No one even knew what had inspired me to write the song, but everyone picked up on the relatable family-based storyline and the notion of feeling really fucking lonely. The fact is, everyone in the world knows what loneliness feels like. It's a universal emotion. You can be stood on the terraces of Old Trafford with 40,000 other Mancunians on a Saturday afternoon but, because of what life has sent your way, still feel like the loneliest person on the planet. Or sat on Market Street with a dirty paper cup, hoping for some empathetic soul to share some coin. I helped conceive and bring 'This is How it Feels' into the world. I often think of it as a child, heading off into the world, spreading its message, helping people feel part of something bigger. It's grown up now, but it still phones home every day.

After signing to Mute, we reconvened in Square One Studios in Bury to finish and mix our debut album. We'd paid for the recordings that we'd done at Out of the Blue Studios, but Mute paid for the mixing sessions. We decided on the name *Life* and it entered the UK album chart at number 2, which seems almost more remarkable now than it did at the time. We were disappointed not to reach number 1 – but being kept off the top by *The Best of the Carpenters* was OK for me. I've always loved The Carpenters. Getting to number 2 was a huge thing at the time. The Stone Roses' debut had come out the year before and got to number 5; the Mondays' debut hadn't made the chart, and their second album *Bummed* got to 59 (although their next album would get to number 3).

But the biggest achievement for me was that we'd self-funded an album purely by selling cassette tapes, t-shirts, hats and frisbees with my silly doodle of a cow on, recorded it on a back street in Manchester, and reached the upper echelons of the charts. I was on top of the world. Life, and *Life*, could not be better.

44/
23 New Mount Street

After Noel came working for the Inspirals, his younger brother, Liam, took over his old British Gas job. It was Liam's turn to sit in the little shed, halfway between the Haçienda and the Boardwalk. There was only room for one man in that shed: one man, one chair, a shelf with a small ghetto-blaster on it, and a Roses poster on the wall. Liam was only 18 then, and he was obsessed with The Stone Roses – he had been since he saw them at the International 2 in the summer of 1988. That night had changed his life.

One day in 1990 the Inspirals had to do a photoshoot for *Melody Maker* in Manchester city centre, and the photographer asked us if we had any ideas for a location for the shoot. We'd seen these huge yellow pipes in Liam's yard, and thought they would make an unusual, striking background for some cool pics, so we suggested that as a location, and the photographer was into the idea. We went down to Liam's yard. He was in his shed, as usual, listening to the Roses' album. It was the only cassette tape he had in there. He just sat there in his shed, playing it over and over and over again. All day, every day.

We set about climbing the pipes for the photographer and posing like boys in Manchester bands did back then: arms stretched out, mouths slightly ajar; a bit gormless looking, really, but everyone was doing it so we went with the flow. After a while, we thought it'd be funny to throw stones at Liam's shed while he was in it. Big white British Gas stones started landing heavily on his roof. Liam poked his head out of his shed door: 'Fuck off, you dickheads!!' And again. Another massive white stone . . . BANG! 'OI!! Pack it in, you nobheads!' The photographer found it hilarious. If only he'd known that the pissed-off kid in that shed would soon become the greatest rock 'n' roll singer of his generation.

We saw a lot of Liam and the rest of his mates around that time. Paul 'Bonehead' Arthurs was a plasterer by trade and had an old Austin A40 that he'd drive around with all his plastering paraphernalia in the boot. When Noel needed a lift moving the Inspirals' equipment about, he'd often recruit Liam and Bonehead to help out. Bonehead was the only one who could drive, so he'd be the one who'd go to Salford Van Hire to rent a van for us.

Bonehead was a great plasterer, one of the best. He did a load of plastering for our guitarist Graham, and it was spot on. Right smooth. Bonehead and his wife Kate had an impressive house in Didsbury, which he'd done up himself. It was so nice that they decided to shoot the cover of *Definitely Maybe* in Bonehead's front room. He still does the odd bit of plastering to this day. He doesn't need the money, obviously – he's minted. He must just enjoy doing it. Last time I saw him I mentioned I was doing my house up, and he asked if I needed any plastering work doing.

As the Inspirals got busier and busier, we needed a bigger office. We'd outgrown Sackville Street. We moved across town to an area called Angel Meadow and took some space in a building that became one of the creative powerhouses of the Manchester music scene: 23 New Mount Street, a large five-storey building originally built in the late 1800s as the home of the Co-operative Printing Society. It had recently been converted into a multi-occupancy workspace by an enterprising chap called John Lancaster. It was now home to dozens of the city's seedling creative businesses: designers, bands, DJs, management companies, record labels, t-shirt manufacturers, clothes-makers and a handful of small recording studios. Our office was at the back of the building on the ground floor in what was once the loading bay and had a grandiose-looking glass ceiling – through the day, the room was bathed in natural light. It was quite an opulent space from which to carry on with our quest for world domination.

Anthony was in his element in our new gaff. He was the calm and collected leader we needed at a time when we were smack bang in the middle of all that wonderful chaos between 1989 and 1991. Some days we'd be bending his ear, wanting to know every minute detail of the business; other days we'd be giddier than The Monkees, getting up to all sorts of frivolous nonsense in the office while he beavered away at his desk. He was unflappable. He never once tried to get involved with our writing and, on creative issues, just left us to do our thing. He helped us get the right record deal and publishing deal and put together a great team of agents and pluggers to make it all happen. He represented us perfectly throughout that period.

Places like 23 New Mount Street were a relatively new concept in the city: lots of small units available at affordable rent and situated just a few minutes' walk from the city centre. He might have been a successful property developer, but John Lancaster, like myself and many of my contemporaries, had been inspired by the spirit of punk, not being afraid to go against the grain or do things differently to what was expected of us. Manchester was still very much a city in flux, ripe for change and for being redrawn. While some of us were building musical blocks, some were taking over the old mills and repurposing them, taking the bricks and mortar of the world's first industrial city and turning them into something for the world's first post-industrial city.

Just behind the building lay a large area of land paved with hundreds of gravestones. The area was known as St Michael's Flags, after a church that had once stood nearby. We'd often take a football out onto the flags for a kickabout to break up the day. Sometimes we'd sit out there doing interviews with the music press and media. Occasionally, we'd do a photoshoot or film some video footage. Angel Meadow was once one of the most densely populated districts of Manchester – and the final resting place of tens of thousands of the poorest people of the city. The death rate among the city's poor in the late-eighteenth and early nineteenth centuries was phenomenal. To the civic leaders, the burial pits and mass graves at Angel Meadow were the most effective and hygienic way of disposing of the dead. In 1844 Friedrich Engels famously christened this part of Manchester 'Hell upon Earth'. Things were looking a bit brighter by the time the Inspirals moved in.

Liam Walsh moved into 23 New Mount Street around the same time as us, setting up a graphic-design business, designing and printing flyers for club nights and stationery for various music-industry clients. He was still designing t-shirts but had moved away from the printing side of things. He didn't like the mess. He became a regular visitor to the Cow Records office – part of the furniture. He would go on to become part of the Red Alert team.

Everyone in the building was helping each other out, cross-pollenating like a bunch of proverbial Manchester bees.

In the basement of New Mount Street was another screen-printing company called Notorious, which was owned by a chap called Cliff Saffer. We started using him soon after we moved into the place. When we first met him, he worked alone, but as our t-shirt empire continued to grow, Cliff couldn't cope with the demand, so he brought in a young woman called Penny Campbell to help out. They were glad of the trade, and we were glad to be in the same building as it meant we could communicate with them quickly and keep our t-shirt business running smoothly. Bands were still coming to us for advice on how to get their shirts printed and onto people's chests. We were happy to oblige. Cliff and Penny made so much money from printing Inspirals merch, that they were able to upgrade their machines to the extent that they could now print on black t-shirts. That was considered very high-tech back then.

We'd started putting 'Moosletters' – a folded A4 sheet printed on both sides, featuring my handwritten notes and drawings – inside the sleeve of every single we released. We'd use a Moosletter to give our fans all the latest band gossip, forthcoming tour dates and any other news. It also acted as a mail-order form for our merchandise. Noel and Debbie would be kept busy packing t-shirts and posting them off to all corners of the globe. It was a common sight to see Noel shuffling through 23 New Mount Street's reception, heading off to Affleck's Palace and various Manchester record shops with a couple of bin bags full of Inspirals t-shirts over his shoulder. Between his time working in our Sackville Street office and our office in New Mount Street, Noel probably got more steps in than at any other point of his life: 'Noel, Piccadilly Records have run out of black medium Cool as Fucks. Can you sort it, mate?!'

'Just finishin' this spliff then I'm on it!'

'Noel, Penny just phoned. There's a box of Mega Moo shirts to bring up from Notorious.'

'Just skinnin' up then I'll nip down for 'em!'

Simon Moran was just beginning to make a name for himself as SJM Concerts and was based in New Mount Street too. SJM would go on to become one of the biggest and greatest concert promoters in Britain. Early in 1990, Happy Mondays announced they were playing G-Mex*, which was a big statement. G-Mex was the biggest venue in the city at the time, with a capacity of around 11,000. We were impressed. But it wasn't Simon Moran or a normal concert promoter putting on the gig, it was two local blaggers who had a better idea than anyone of how big the band were becoming. Jimmy Muffin and Johnny the Hat were originally bootleggers who sold snide t-shirts outside Mondays gigs. Nathan McGough, who we'd got to know well since his time managing the Bodines, was now managing the Mondays. Nathan and the band invited Jimmy and Johnny to become the band's official merch people in exchange for 50 per cent of the takings. It was Jimmy and Johnny who took a punt on putting the Mondays on at G-Mex through their Night-time Promotions company. One afternoon, Nathan phoned our office to ask if we would like to support them at the G-Mex gig. We were flattered to be asked, but at that stage we didn't want to be the support band for one of our peers. 'What shall I say?' asked Anthony, with his hand over the phone receiver.

'Tell him we'll do it if I can bring the giant cow's head!' I shouted, laughing with the lads.

Eventually, we told Anthony to decline Nathan's offer as 'We're going to headline G-Mex ourselves soon!' which was quite a ballsy call in hindsight, but that's the kind of self-belief we had.

A couple of young DJs called Ed and Tom also had a small studio in New Mount Street. They'd both come to Manchester University as students and made the city their home. They were DJing around Manchester in the smaller bars and club nights and had set up a residency at the Swinging Sporran, which was one of the city's favourite student bars. They built their New Mount Street studio so they could record their own backing tracks for mixing into their DJ sets. At the time, they called themselves The Dust Brothers, but they would eventually head south and, unlike the Charlatans, decided to change their

* G-Mex was short for Greater Manchester Exhibition Centre. Snappy! In 2007, it was renamed Manchester Central Convention Complex, but these days everyone just calls it 'Manchester Central'.

name to avoid any conflict with an American act with the same name. Ed and Tom became The Chemical Brothers.

Alison Martin and Sue McDermott had set up a music PR company called Red Alert in the building – in an office right next to the reception area. Alison had been responsible for helping the Inspirals get some of our first ever radio exposure, when she'd worked on Phil Korbel's *Meltdown* show on BBC Radio Manchester. The Red Alert office became something of a hub where bands hung out to chat: upcoming and established artists would be coming and going every day and Alison would often phone our office: 'Clint, the lads from Definition of Sound are in the office, would you like to come and meet them?' . . . 'The Ruthless Rap Assassins want to say hi to you and the boys Clint' . . . 'Fancy a quick brew with The Charlatans?'

New Mount Street's crowning glory, up on the third floor, was Sunset Radio. Sunset was a pioneering radio station created by the highly regarded local broadcaster Mike Shaft. Mike had made Manchester his home after leaving his native Grenada in the late 1960s to work at Piccadilly Radio then, later, the BBC. From as far back as 1984 Mike had been campaigning for a different kind of radio station to be established in the UK. 'Specialist' or 'minority' stations were the norm in the States, but Britain didn't have a dedicated black-music radio station at that point. Mike's original vision was of building the UK's first 'ethnic radio station'. He wanted to see a 'third tier' network of radio stations that would operate alongside the BBC and commercial stations. Pirate radio had been busily simmering away in the UK for many years and, in some parts, served the local community in a way that mainstream radio never could. But Mike wanted to create something more permanent. After years of raising awareness and petitioning the radio industry, Mike saw his dream come true. Britain's first ever community-based radio station was born right there in 23 New Mount Street in 1989. Throughout the day, Sunset transmitted an eclectic mix of black music and dance music; in the evenings, a more diverse programming schedule was aired. Everyone was talking about this new station. As Sunset found its feet, a cool mix of programmes started to appear in its scheduling. Haçienda DJs Dave Rofe and Pete Robinson had a show, as did Terry Christian. Alongside shows aimed at Afro-Caribbean,

Chinese, Ukrainian and Asian listeners, would sit hip-hop, jazz and house-music shows. Hewan Clarke, Richard Searling, Greg Edwards all took turns to serenade the listeners with their favourite records of all time on Sunset Radio.

808 State also started a weekly Tuesday-night show on Sunset, which was like no radio we'd heard before. I'd followed 808 main man Graham Massey since I'd first heard one of his previous bands, Biting Tongues, in the early eighties. They released a fantastic track called 'Compressor' on Factory Records in 1987. Graham was a multi-instrumentalist; a quiet bloke who always had an air of contentment and a smile on his face. The story goes that all four members of 808 were due to do the radio show together but, during the first show, Graham and Martin Price realised the two young lads who'd only recently joined 808 State were in their element behind the mic. Graham's young partners in crime, Darren Partington and Andy Barker, had started out as 'the Spinmasters', a DJing duo from Ancoats, who first DJ'd at their local Salvation Army when they were still at school. The Spinmasters had joined 808 as the whole acid-house thing started to take off, and both oozed Mancunian charm and were brilliantly funny. The radio show they did on Sunset was equal parts educational, carefree, hilarious and euphoric; an evening of cutting-edge dance music, bonkers Manc humour, unorthodox presenter styles, 'shouts goin' out' and a 'listeners' problems' section.

Another room in 23 New Mount Street was home to two young music producers, Suddi Raval and Jonathan Donaghy, who called themselves 'Together'. They'd had a hit single with 'Hardcore Uproar', inspired by the huge raves in Blackburn, which got into the Top 20 in 1990. Suddi was from Tameside, and I'd run into him daily in different parts of the building. He told me that he always found Noel a bit grumpy when he bumped into him getting a brew in the café at New Mount Street, but then not everyone was as constantly 'up' as Suddi! He was always darting around the place, full of energy, buzzing about his latest musical masterpiece. Jonathan had originally come up with the name 'The Jam Factory' for their act, taking the piss out of Suddi, who worked in the Robertson's jam factory in Droylsden. Suddi hated that, and when 808 State wanted to play the first recording of 'Hardcore Uproar' on Sunset Radio, they had to come up with an alternative name on the spot.

Right there and then they chose 'Together'. Tragically, Jon died in a motorbike accident in Ibiza in 1991.

I loved 23 New Mount Street. It reminded me of Rochdale art college. I felt like we were among kindred spirits who were all part of this amazing scene, which was changing the face of music and Manchester. It felt as if there wasn't a better place on the planet to be doing what we were doing.

45/
The 8:15 from Manchester

By the spring of 1990 even Saturday-morning kids' TV shows were jumping on the Manchester bandwagon. Or, in this case, the Manchester train. We were approached by the BBC to see if we would be interested in supplying the theme tune for a new Saturday-morning show called *The 8:15 from Manchester*. It was the BBC's summer replacement for *Going Live,* and was named after the 8.15am train from Manchester Piccadilly to London Euston. Don't ask me why. Maybe a BBC commissioner had to get that train one morning when they were struggling to come up with a title and thought, 'Fuck! That'll do!' Or perhaps they just wanted something with Manchester in the title. It felt like everyone was looking for a Manchester angle on anything at the time.

By this point the Inspirals were in and out of Manchester's BBC and Granada studios on almost a weekly basis, doing interviews, promo and sessions; it was just part of our busy itinerary. The BBC was still based on Oxford Road in the city centre at the time. At some point, the question about the theme tune came up. We were bang up for it, but we were so busy that we didn't have time to write and record something new from scratch. To keep things quick and simple, we decided to offer a reworking of a song we'd already recorded. We hastily amended the words to our recent single 'Find Out Why' and totally nailed it. The show's producers loved it. The show was presented by Ross King and Charlotte Hindle and had features like 'It's Tough at the Top', a snakes & ladders game where contestants tried to win without landing on a 'snake' and sliding down into a pool of gunge.

They did a feature on us in the first ever episode. They filmed us in the studio working on the theme song, with me and Tom doing the new vocals. Then back to our office, where I demonstrated how to draw the Inspirals' cow. After that, they took us outside and filmed us walking casually through the back streets of the area. This was just a few months before the area was rechristened the 'Gay Village'. It was still one of Manchester's most well-known 'red-light' districts at the time. Fortunately, none of the girls or rent boys were around that day to heckle us. That would've made uncomfortable viewing for the kids watching at home: 'Get a proper fuckin' haircut!'; 'Get a proper fuckin' job!'

Back in the office, they made us do this cheesy thing were Tom and I put our hands together and, as we pulled our hands apart, a pre-recorded video appeared. But that's what kids' TV is all about. We knew it when we agreed to do it, and we were cool with it.

Noel was with us that day, watching everything. He found it all a bit cheesy and was totally unimpressed that we were doing kids' TV. We just saw it as a bit of fun and free publicity, but I don't think it will shock anyone that Noel could be quite outspoken at times. 'If I ever have a band,' he said to me, shaking his head, 'you won't see me doin' shit like this!'

We also appeared on another popular Saturday-morning kids' TV show, *Wac '90,* with Michaela Strachan and Tommy Boyd as the presenters. The show felt a bit grittier than some of the other kids' TV shows – we all knew Michaela from *The Hitman and Her,* which she co-presented with British music mogul Pete Waterman. It was a show that everybody would put on when they got home from the pub or club.

Our appearance on *Wac '90* was broadcast live but started off with us miming to our single 'Move', with the studio completely flooded with dry ice. It looked like the smoke machine's 'on–off' switch must've been knackered as the smoke just kept churning out. They positioned 20 or so kids around us and had them dancing while we played. They'd been shown how to dance in a sixties psychedelic style by the floor manager. They looked like they were off their tits, and the smoke meant a couple of them had to leave the set coughing their guts up. Proper bonkers – not the kind of TV you'd see today.

After 'Move', we took our places on the couch with the kids sitting all around us while we did the interview, which consisted of loads of 'What's your biggest ambition?'-type questions. Michaela surprised me by having my mum live on the phone. They handed me a 'phone' to use, but it was actually just a plastic dinosaur, while my mum's voice was coming over the speakers in the studio.

I was holding a small prehistoric model to me head, saying 'Yeah, hello, Mum!'

I could see to my side they had a little TV screen with my mum's picture on.

'Have you got clean underpants on?' she asked.

'Yeah, Mum!'

'I've washed your others. D'you want to come and pick 'em up?'

Maybe Noel had the right idea, after all.

46/
Manchester Takes LA

In the summer of 1990, Anthony told us Mute wanted us to go to America to promote the *Life* album. I couldn't believe it! I'd dreamt all my life of visiting the USA and here I was going out there, not as a holidaymaker but as a relatively successful musician. Fuck it, I'll say it . . . a POP STAR! By means of a celebration, we all went out and bought matching Samsonite suitcases with pop-out handles, combination locks and two little wheels at the back. Rock 'n' roll!

It would be a short promo trip, not a full-on tour, as such, just half a dozen key cities. We flew from city to city and used limos and people carriers to get us from hotels to gigs to radio stations and anywhere else we needed to be. We played LA, San Francisco, New York, Boston, Washington DC and over the border to Toronto. As well as the live shows, we were taken to visit cool record shops and various record-company offices for labels that wanted to sign us. We were like kids in the proverbial candy shop. We couldn't believe we'd made it this far.

The trip started in LA. The Mondays were in town at the same time recording their third album, *Pills 'n' Thrills and Bellyaches*. There was also a big Haçienda club event happening downtown the same night as our gig. It felt like Manchester was taking over LA. Well, it did to us, anyway! Terry Christian and a TV crew were in town grabbing content for a new music-based TV show that Terry had co-created and was about to launch in the UK. It was called *The Word*. The trip gave Terry and his team a great opportunity to capture footage of a load of Mancs swanning around the City of Angels like they owned the place. Terry met us at our hotel in the afternoon and we all jumped in a limo to go and do some shooting. We cruised down Sunset Strip, soaking up the cool California vibes. What a feeling.

We stopped at a red light and an open-top jeep pulled up alongside us. We recognised the driver: 'Fuck me! It's Jeff Goldblum!'

For four lads from Oldham and their mate from Oxford, who'd only been in the USA for a matter of minutes, this was the stuff of dreams. That night, we were booked to play at the Roxy on Sunset. It was my thirty-first birthday and I was as happy as a pig in shit.

While we were in the States, Mute wanted us to meet some of the record labels out there. They were hoping we could help them secure a 'label deal' where the entire Mute roster could be signed to an American label. There were more than a few suitors; it seemed every US label wanted their own Manchester band. The most bizarre meeting was with David Geffen, the multimillionaire music mogul who owned the record label he named after himself. I mean, come on! What kind of man names a record label after himself?!* As we sat in his luxurious office on Sunset Boulevard, just down the road from the Roxy Club, Craig decided it was the perfect opportunity to take his trainers off and start picking at his athlete's foot infestation. Graham asked Mr Geffen what he thought about the Inspirals' music and if he was coming to our gig that night. 'I don't go to gigs,' he replied. 'I have people who do that for me.'

Suffice to say we didn't sign to Geffen. We ended up signing with Elektra, who had also signed the Mondays in the US, which we were all really happy about. Another plus point was that Elektra was home to the back catalogues of some of our favourite bands, including The Stooges, Love, MC5 and The Doors.

When we got to Boston, the Pixies turned up at the gig to watch us. We chatted with them at the back of the venue next to the sound desk while the support band played. I couldn't believe they'd come to see us, but they told us they were really into the Inspirals. I remember telling Frank Black that *Doolittle* was one of Manchester's most loved albums at the time.

Every couple of days, I'd send my Grandma Scarsbrook a postcard giving her a full update of what cities we'd visited and what sights I'd seen.

---

* In 1999 I set up my own record label, Booney Tunes. I take it back, Mr Geffen. Booney Tunes made a bit less money than your label.

In New York, we played at the Marquee, a cool venue with a small aircraft stuck in the roof as if it had run out of fuel just short of LaGuardia Airport. The venue was just around the corner from the Chelsea Hotel. That afternoon at the Marquee we got a call from Depeche Mode. They were in the middle of their 'World Violation Tour': 'We've got a night off in New York tonight, we're coming to see you guys!' We were obviously made up to hear this and looking forward to hanging out with them. Their album *Violator* was in the Top 10 of the American Billboard charts. The gig went great, and the crowd were totally loving it – until near the end. We knew the exact moment the Depeche boys arrived. It started like a ripple effect: first people at the back of the room started turning round and looking away from us then, within seconds, like a weird reverse Mexican Wave, the entire audience had their backs to us. 'Hey, look over there, dude! It's Depeche Mode!'; 'You guys rock!!!' etc. I think we even finished our set a bit earlier because no one seemed that bothered about us once Depeche were in the room. We came off stage and sat in the dressing room, slightly deflated. About a minute later, the dressing-room door flew open and Dave Gahan came piling in, totally bladdered, fell over the coffee table flat on his face, muttered some profanity, then lost consciousness face down on the floor. I thought, 'Is this the same bloke who was so polite and warm when he greeted us that day at Mute?' The rest of Depeche came into the dressing room, very apologetic, and started trying to wake Dave up. Martin Gore was saying, 'Wake up, Dave. Don't die, man . . . we're flying to Canada tomorrow!'

Luckily, they did wake him up, because by the end of that tour Depeche had played to 1.2 million people. They were the biggest band in the world. I managed to catch them later that year at one of their Dodger Stadium gigs in LA. Electronic were supporting them. I saw Electronic's recent collaborator, Neil Tennant, in the hotel lobby on the afternoon of the gig, walked over to him and introduced myself, 'Hi, Neil. Clint Boon, Inspiral Carpets. Big fan!'

'How lovely to meet you, Clint. Big fan too!'

We chatted for a couple of minutes. 'Looking forward to tonight, brother?' I asked him.

'Oh yes, absolutely!' he said. 'Johnny will be down in a minute.'

A few minutes later, Johnny Marr stepped out of the lift. He recognised me straight away, even though we'd only ever met in passing back in Manchester. I told him I'd be at the gig, and he said to make sure I came backstage afterwards. The gig was one of the greatest I've ever been to. Depeche were at the peak of their powers. The audience were amazing too. Dodger Stadium has two tiers of seats all around – in one section, three. After Electronic's set, while the crowd were waiting for Depeche Mode, I witnessed the biggest food fight I've ever seen as thousands of people around the stadium started launching food, paper cups, plastic drinks holders and anything that wasn't secured down – all in good humour and nothing that could take your eye out; far better than the coins, darts and pints of warm piss favoured by British audiences over the decades.

Before the gig, I'd gone backstage where I bumped into Johnny again. While we were chatting, Bernard Sumner came over and introduced himself. A few minutes later a good-looking bloke with long hair appeared beside us smiling. Johnny gave him a hug and turned to me, 'Clint, have you ever met Billy Duffy?'

Billy Duffy was the lead guitarist of The Cult, and he and Johnny had been at school together as kids back in Manchester. Two of the greatest guitarists of their generation in the same classroom in Wythenshawe. It seemed like wherever you went in the world in 1990, Manchester vibes were always in the area.*

---

* Shout goin' out to Alfonso 'Fonzo' Buller, who passed away while I was writing this book. Fonzo was the ultimate Manchester party vibes master. He grew up in the city and started a sound system called MVITA (Manchester Vibes in the Area) back in the eighties. The man oozed peace, love and understanding. His spirit and his mantra will stay with the city for eternity.

47/ Cool as Milk

In the Chinese calendar, 1990 was the year of the horse, but in the Mancunian calendar, it definitely felt like it was the year of the cow. Whole swathes of the city, and the country, had caught mad cow disease. The cow logo, which I'd started as a bit of a joke, was now everywhere: on the t-shirts of tens of thousands of kids on streets up and down the country, particularly in Manchester. We were struggling to keep up with demand at times.

Someone at Mute came up with the idea of advertising the album and our forthcoming G-Mex gig on milk bottles. Most people still got their milk delivered daily to their doorstep by their milkman, and businesses that wanted to advertise their products could pay the Milk Marketing Board a chunk of money to put their advert on the side of thousands of milk bottles. The thinking was: it would be a great PR stunt to have 10,000 milk bottles printed up with our artwork and the caption 'COOL AS MILK!' before being circulated around the doorsteps of Mancunia. I loved the idea! It was far more inventive than taking adverts out in the *NME* and the *Manchester Evening News*, and it seemed to chime with the Inspirals' off-the-wall image.

The milk bottles looked amazing, and soon people all over Manchester were pouring milk over their morning cornflakes from an Inspirals milk bottle. The fans loved it. Cool as . . . Unfortunately for the Milk Marketing Board, the Inspirals milk bottles were a bit too cool. Usually, empty milk bottles would be returned, washed, stripped of the old advertisement and then recirculated. What the Milk Marketing Board didn't bank on was the Inspirals milk bottles immediately becoming collector's items for Manchester music fans. That was 10,000 bottles they never got back.

In 1990 G-Mex was the largest indoor venue in Manchester. It could accommodate a standing audience of around 11,000, but it was usually played by huge pop acts like INXS or Mariah Carey. The Mondays had played it earlier in the year, of course. Before that, the only gig that I'd been to at G-Mex was the Festival of the Tenth Summer in 1986, when New Order and The Smiths topped a big bill to celebrate the tenth anniversary of punk coming to Manchester. The idea that the Inspirals could possibly sell it out was amazing.

The room was vast. In an earlier life, it had been Manchester's biggest railway station, Manchester Central, built in the late 1800s then left derelict after its closure in 1969. The paved concourse at the front of the building was situated on the exact spot where the Peterloo Massacre had taken place in 1819. And it was in this building that, in 1965, a storage locker was forced opened to reveal evidence that led to the arrests of Ian Brady and Myra Hindley. The Smiths also undertook one of their most iconic photoshoots within its walls, draping themselves lazily around the abandoned structure one afternoon in 1983.

Back in early 1990, when we'd turned down the chance to support the Mondays at G-Mex, we weren't sure if we could pull off a headline gig there. But just a few months later it was happening. Our show was on Saturday 21 July, 1990. Two nights earlier, we'd played the SEC in Glasgow. In true rock-star fashion, we had two limousines waiting at the bottom of the stage ramp inside the arena to whisk us back home the moment we stepped off stage after the encore. We were driven straight to the Midland Hotel in Manchester so we could get a good night's sleep before a day of pre-production in G-Mex. The sense of occasion in the Inspirals' camp was immense. This was our biggest gig so far. It would be filmed by a multi-camera crew and screened by Granada Television a few weeks later. Our hotel rooms overlooked G-Mex and we had a bird's eye view of the front of the venue.

We'd asked The La's to support us. We'd been huge fans ever since we played with them in Valencia and had become obsessed with a pre-release cassette of their debut album. Their music was incredible – as with the Inspirals, retro, but totally 'now'. I thought 'Timeless Melody' was aptly titled – it was one of the greatest songs I'd ever heard. On the afternoon of the gig, a couple of cars parked behind the venue in the backstage area were broken into. The finger of suspicion from quite a few of the Manchester crew was automatically pointed at the Scousers in our midst, The La's and their crew, who thankfully laughed off all accusations and got on with the job in hand.

Throughout the day, we could see masses of fans arriving from every direction – herds of cow t-shirts, mainly 'Cool as Fuck', but a lot of generic cow-design shirts for those who didn't want to risk getting arrested. Also on display were scores of t-shirts bearing the logos of the other happening bands of the day: the Roses, the Mondays, The Charlatans and James.

Someone had the bright idea of bringing an actual cow to G-Mex for a photo opportunity. A bloke pulled up outside the front of the venue around 4pm, ushered a fully grown dairy cow out of the trailer and down the ramp and onto the concourse. The photos of the Inspirals posing alongside a gaggle of excited fans and a confused-looking cow show the extent some bands will go to in the name of entertainment and publicity. It was one of our more *Spinal Tap* moments but, on that weekend, we couldn't care less – we felt like we owned Manchester!

We had a backstage VIP area where our families and friends could meet up with us before and after the show. My mum and dad were overwhelmed with the size of the event. They'd never questioned my determination to make things work with the band. They'd never tried to persuade me to try other career options. Even when my dad used to say, 'When are ye goin' te get a proper job?' we always knew he didn't mean it. Anyway, I'd already had proper jobs, and we both knew that wasn't my world. At that moment, standing with my parents backstage, with 11,000 young people waiting to hear our songs, some of which I'd written years earlier in the bedroom of my mum and dad's house in Heyside, the three of us knew it had all been worth it.

As we walked out on stage, I could see my mum and dad in the VIP seating area in the stands over to my left. They were both standing up, clapping and cheering. It was one of the proudest moments of my life. I got quite emotional but held it together. The G-Mex gig was undoubtedly one of our finest moments. We were at the top of our game that night. We'd just done a headline tour of the UK to promote the *Life* album and we were on fire. We played great and looked cool as fuck. There wasn't much chit-chat between songs, just banging out the tunes and taking it all in. I felt a sense of total serenity throughout the set. I could feel the 'Inspiral Orb' above us. It's something I've always felt during our gigs over the years: an invisible, electrifying force that starts to spin slowly like a small planet when the five of us step out on stage together. It watches over us, guides us and adds to our chemistry. It's the spirit of all the bands that ever inspired us, the people we've lost along the way, members past and present, and all the energy and emotion the five of us spent getting to this point in time. All our dreams. I'm sure many other musicians, performers and artists, spiritual or not, experience a similar sense of energy as they go about creating their art. But, for me, it's the orb.

I'd bought another Farfisa Compact Duo on my travels to take on the road as a spare. It would usually stay in the back of the truck until such time as we might need it. For the first time, I set up both organs, just in case I had any problems with my main one. I'd recently bought an Ensoniq VFX SD synth, a state-of-the-art keyboard 'workstation' made in the USA. The piano, brass, string and synth sounds were mind-blowing, and it meant I had access to perfect samples of any musical instrument that ever existed. The Farfisa, though, would always remain at the centre of my sonic spectrum. The VFX sat on top of my main Farfisa, and to my left I set up the back-up organ with my trusty Logan String Melody on top of it. The Logan had served me well as my second keyboard until now, but my inner Rick Wakeman needed something more than the clunky analogue strings emulator the Logan could offer.

Noel had moved over to being the drum roadie at this point. I brought in a chap called Ian Hargreaves to help set the keys up and look after things during the set. Mark Coyle looked after Graham and Martyn's gear while Dian Barton and Ed Hallam from the legendary Oz PA company looked after the front-of-house sound and monitors respectively. Oz himself oversaw the whole thing like a good foreman, keeping spirits high and insisting on being referred to as 'Man at Bus Stop' on the closing credits of the film.

As always, we brought along our famous visuals, which included 14 or so Kodak Carousel projectors randomly casting images of astronauts, Daleks, *Sunday Sport* front pages and various roadkill onto a huge screen behind us. And lots of cows, obviously. All projected blazingly, courtesy of our lightning man, Loucas Athienites.

We invited the Haverettes, an all-girl marching troupe from Hornchurch, to join us on stage for 'She Comes in the Fall'. They'd appeared with us in the video for the single. They travelled to Manchester in a coach. There was about 25 of them. The song started – the military-style drumming intro – with them out of sight behind the stage. As we started to play, the girls, led by a baton-twirling majorette, marched out to the sound of 11,000 screaming Mancs who'd never seen anything like it at a gig. Especially a gig by a garage band from Oldham. You could see the fear in the eyes of some of the girls. They'd never experienced anything like it either. As the song progressed, they marched off and back behind the screen. Towards the end of the song, they came marching out again, still drumming. But this time, there were fewer of them. We found out later that some of the girls had fainted after their first walk on due to the shock of what they'd just witnessed.

Local shirt designer Simon Foster had been making all my shirts in recent months. He had a place in 23 New Mount Street, which was where I'd got to know him. I wanted something extra cool for the G-Mex gig. He produced a spectacular tracksuit. We had the fabric imported from Italy – black velour with brightly coloured graffiti artwork. Baggy as fuck. I wore it only on that one occasion. The obligatory pocket watch hung around my neck, and a pair of blue suede British Knights completed the look. Ten years later, I would give the pocket watch to Travis frontman Fran Healy as a gift. The tracksuit is a masterpiece of tailoring and remains in my wardrobe. Whenever I see it, I'm transported back to that night in July 1990 when everything and anything seemed possible.

One of my most treasured photographs is one taken backstage at G-Mex that night. I'm deep in conversation with Lee Mavers, who's sat on my left. To Lee's left is Noel, sucking on a cigarette. To me, it perfectly captures one of the most special parts of my life.

As we finished the set, we knew we'd pulled off the biggest gig of our lives. As I got up to leave the stage, I leant into my mic and said to the crowd, 'Top that!'

48/
'Ah! Mr Craven!'

The Inspirals had started attracting a few celebrity fans, including a couple of cricket players and some footballers. Graham, who was a sports fanatic, especially football and cricket, had got to meet them on his travels and would always invite them to our gigs or whatever recording studio we might be working in. The Chelsea player Graeme Le Saux was a regular at our gigs for a while, as was cricketer Graeme 'Foxy' Fowler, and some other sportsmen not called Graeme, including various Oldham Athletic players.

But one of the more unlikely celebrity guests at Inspiral shows was the famous children's television presenter John Craven, who started coming to our gigs in 1989 because his daughter, Vicky, was a massive fan. She was only around 16 at the time, so whenever we were in their neck of the woods – Norwich, or somewhere in East Anglia – John would bring Vicky along and chaperone her for the evening.

John was one of the most famous faces on TV at the time, thanks to *John Craven's Newsround*, which several generations of British kids had grown up with throughout the seventies and eighties. John was one of those 'guiding light' characters you'd see on TV but never expect to meet in real life. His easy presenting style had a way of making you feel safe: 'Everything's gonna be OK . . . despite the horrific news story I've just told you about . . . Massive earthquake wipes out half of South America, but it's all right . . . this class of eight-year-olds in Leamington Spa have built a massive replica of the Space Shuttle using nothing but lolly sticks . . . Someone tried to assassinate the Pope yesterday; but now . . . a panda that talks!'

By 1990 his TV show *Countryfile* was one of the most popular TV shows on British television. He always wore mad jumpers too. That was something else he was famous for. He was funny on *Countryfile*; he presented it with two other people, a bloke and a woman. The other two would get all the tough jobs like 'This farm's riddled with foot-and-mouth disease, all these cattle are about to get slaughtered . . .' or hanging off a cliff on a piece of rope talking about people nicking eagles' eggs, while John would be at a real-ale festival, necking pints of beer and dancing, meat pie in hand, with some Morris dancers. Or you'd see him lording it up on some old steam train.

The first time we met John Craven, we were doing a gig in Norwich. We knew Vicky was coming as she was on our guestlist as 'Vicky Craven + 1'. What we didn't know at that stage was who her +1 was. We were chilling out in the dressing room after the soundcheck with our crew, drinking beer and eating nuts and snacks from our rider. Noel, as usual, was in the process of building a massive spliff – building great spliffs was one of Noel's super-powers. That, and getting the venue's luggers to do all the hard work. Even in the hustle and bustle of a gig day – with all the heat and chaos of setting things up, breaking things down, changing guitar strings and pushing over-zealous fans off stage – Noel would never break a sweat. He was unflappable. And he built great spliffs.

So, Noel's Norwich super spliff was fully assembled and ready for action. Just as he got his lighter out to spark it up there was a knock on the dressing-room door. In walked Vicky Craven, followed by her dad, everyone's favourite TV presenter, Mr John Craven, OBE. At which point Noel, spliff held aloft, came out with one of my favourite quotes of all time: 'Ah! Mr Craven . . . fancy a suck on this?'

Mr Craven smiled and gallantly declined.

49/
Can This Get Any Bigger?

After years of grafting every single day to make your band succeed, scratching around in the dirt to survive, chasing that elusive dream, it's incredible to wake up one day and realise you've done it. Your records are in the charts, your songs are on the radio, the man on the street knows your name and there's more money in your bank account than you could ever have imagined.

That was us in the second half of 1990. On top of the Mute deal, we were raking it in with our t-shirt sales and we'd signed a massive publishing deal with Chrysalis Music. We went to London to shake on it and pick up the cheque for the first part of the advance. On the train back to Manchester, I walked up and down the aisle, Red Stripe in hand, wafting the Chrysalis cheque above my head and saying loudly, 'Would anybody like to hold a quarter of a million quid?' Several passengers took me up on the offer.

Craig bought himself a detached house in Chadderton, just a couple of hundred yards from where he'd first stumbled across the Inspirals in the Red Barn car park in 1986, when he was 14. Here he was, four years later, just 18 years old and living the dream. Craig was always quite calm about his success, never the type to brag or punch the air and shout 'Go on lads! Get in there!'. Despite his age, he had the air of someone far older. I always saw him as the best musician in the band. He mastered the drums at an early age and just got better over time. Me, Graham and Martyn had to work a bit harder at learning our instruments. Craig would soon meet Rose, the love of his life. She was from Manchester but was working as a nanny in New York around the time they met. She soon moved back to Manchester to live with this remarkable young man.

Martyn bought a property in Denton and set up home with his girlfriend Joanne. Martyn had a loveable and childlike persona, which he never lost, even through those mad years when it felt like we were on our way to ruling the world. His dad, Mel, was a builder who often worked with Billy Duffy's dad, who was also a builder. This was to be a big talking point when we met up with Billy backstage at a Cult gig at the River Plate Stadium in Argentina.

Graham bought a house in Moston with his girlfriend, Karen. He was as chuffed as any of us that we'd finally made it, but he didn't drop the baton once when it came to keeping things moving in the right direction. He was always the motivator, always the first one out of bed, and always the one to astound us with his surreal ways, which ranged from playing 'imaginary cricket' to vowing to never talk while driving over the flyover section of the Mancunian Way and (in October 1980), vowing to never eat chocolate ever again.

Tom was from a more academic background than the rest of us and had moved from his home in Abingdon, near Oxford, to Manchester for a place at the University. He read constantly and was very eloquent, and his impressive vocabulary would have us reaching for the dictionary on a daily basis. When the money came in, Tom and his partner, Alison, splashed out on a gorgeous convertible Mercedes sports car.

I bought some ridiculously expensive Cazal sunglasses with lizard skin on the frames, and a new Opel Manta GTE Exclusive in a dark blue metal flake finish (D84 ONA). I was still living most of the time with Debbie at her parents' place, so house-hunting wasn't a big priority yet.

When we were asked to headline Reading Festival in 1990, it felt like another giant step for the band. The year was just getting crazier and crazier – we barely had time to catch our breath. Reading was our first ever festival headline. There were two major British festivals at the time, Reading and Glastonbury. Reading wasn't just one of the biggest festivals in the UK, but in the world. It was held in high esteem by every pop or rock musician on the planet. The year before, New Order had headlined, at a time when we didn't even have a record deal. Fast forward a year, and now we were headlining, above others on the bill who we'd looked up to and who had influenced us to start our band. Happy Mondays had headlined Glastonbury a couple of months previously; now we were headlining Reading. Manchester was ruling the festival world as well as everything else.

There were plenty of wild stories circulating about what the Mondays had got up to at Glastonbury. They included their trip down in a double-decker tour bus where the driver had crashed into a tree, which came through the windscreen. They also brought a large menagerie of scallies with them, and a colour photocopier that some of their entourage used to make copies of backstage passes to sell onsite. Full marks for enterprise, although I'm not sure the Glastonbury organisers were quite as impressed. Rumour has it that, after the Mondays headlined Glastonbury, Michael Eavis and his team decided it was time to up their security across the whole site for future festivals.

We arrived at Reading in the afternoon and checked into the Caversham Hotel, which is where a lot of the bands playing the festival stay. We took over an entire floor for our band and crew. We felt like the kings of the Caversham. Because the Inspirals t-shirts were so popular we were getting increasingly targeted by bootlegging gangs selling fakes outside our gigs. Anthony had decided to tackle the issue by employing a couple of ex-coppers from a security firm to seize the counterfeit t-shirts. Normally, we would turn a blind eye to a few bootleg shirts being sold outside a gig, but by the time we did Reading the bootleggers were operating on an industrial scale and we all felt we should do something about it – our t-shirt and merch business was still one of our main income streams.

Anthony's ex-feds ended up seizing so many t-shirts that we had a room in the hotel full of them. We even ended up with stacks of other bands' snide t-shirts. I can't remember what happened to them, but I think if they were half-decent quality, we probably sold them on ourselves. Our Reading bootlegger raids would backfire on us a couple of weeks later, when me and Graham went down to a gig at the International 2 in Manchester. Some of the same bootleggers that Binsy Smith and his henchmen had targeted at Reading, and a couple of ticket touts, were working outside the venue. They spotted me and Graham and started threatening us loudly before chasing us off down the road back towards Graham's car. I guess bootleggers are just grafters too at the end of the day, and we're all just blagging our way through life in our own way.

Headlining the Reading Festival on Saturday 25 August, 1990 was one of the most thrilling moments of my life. We played the main stage on the Saturday night – and our performance was perfect. We added a few surprises into the show. We'd raised an eyebrow at the vast fee we were to receive for headlining, which I think was £40,000 – way more than we'd been paid for any gig before, so we decided to spend a big chunk of it on putting on an extra-special show. We decided to set off a few grands' worth of fireworks during the first song, which we thought would be a nice touch and a bit different, as it's usually the end of the gig when the fireworks go off. We hired a pantomime-cow outfit from a local fancy-dress shop, which was a bit cheaper than the fireworks. There's been some debate over the years about who was inside the pantomime cow. As far as I remember, one of the occupants was, indeed, Noel Gallagher.

'Ere'ya, Noel, get in this and walk round on stage a bit.'

'Do I have to?'

'Yeah!'

'OK, fuck it . . . zip me in!'

As we ended the gig, our special-effects people made it snow. This completely blew the minds of several thousand attendees who were 'under the influence' in one way or another. All in all, it was a definite pinnacle of our career. We'd bought a massive top-of-the-range video camera especially for Reading, to record the gig. Someone left it at the hotel, so we didn't manage to film the show. But at least I can remember most of it. Shaun Ryder says he has no memory of playing Glastonbury. He knows it happened, and his mum had a picture of him on the Pyramid Stage on her kitchen wall for years. He just has no memory of it.

We made a few thousand new fans that night in Reading. People who'd never really got what we were all about were suddenly raving about us. It was another one of our proudest moments, real testament to all the graft me and my mates had put in over all those years since we first got together in the mill. I remember standing on the stage next to my Farfisa at the end of our set, 50,000 people applauding, and thinking to myself, 'Fuck me! Can this get any bigger?'

50/ 'Clint, Shaun's got a knife!'

The Inspirals had supported the Mondays at the Boardwalk in late January 1987. The spiritual connection between us and them started at those early gigs. I remember being stood at the side of the stage in a narrow corridor at the Boardwalk, chatting to their guitarist Mark Day and thinking what a cracking bloke he was. Same with Shaun and Gaz. Gaz was always very lucid and had a bubbly, energetic charm – and great hair. Shaun was very sociable but a bit more distant than the others, like he'd just that second woken up from a long sleep. Shaun's brother, Paul, seemed the serious one, the chap who was holding things together but, again, was, very personable. And there was keyboardist PD: quiet and lovely, always with a gentle smile on his face and, if anything, looking slightly lost in his crazy world.

Bez was, and still is, a total enigma. I know we're all unique in our own ways, but occasionally in life you'll meet someone who seems like they could've been sent here from another world – just like the scene in *24 Hour Party People* where the flying saucer drops Bez off in a street in Little Hulton. These souls are different.

One day in 1990 I got a phone call from my friend, the journalist, musician and author John Robb, asking if I'd contribute to a piece he was writing for *Sounds*. It was a double-page spread about the Mondays. He knew I was a fan. Everyone did. Me and the Inspirals were singing their praises and dropping their name at every opportunity. By now, Rowetta had joined the Mondays and they were even more of a force of nature with her on board. As with the rest of the Mondays, Rowetta was great to be around; she had an energy that was infectious and a voice that was unbeatable.

John Robb was an early supporter and a keen fan of the Inspirals – someone I would always trust as a journo. I sat at home talking to him on the phone about the Mondays for a good half an hour. I told him everything I loved about the band: their uniqueness, their punk-funk sound, their attitude and their look. I told him how much I loved the characters and the chaos. When the article was published the following week, they lifted out one of my quotes in large type – a pull quote – something along the lines of, 'The Mondays are the real spirit of the street'.

Over the next couple of days I heard on the grapevine that Shaun wasn't happy about the article, or some of the things I'd said in it. I called the Factory Records office and got through to the Mondays' manager, Nathan, and asked him what was going on. 'I don't know, Clint, mate,' he replied. 'It's just Shaun being paranoid. He's totally got the wrong end of the stick. Don't worry about it.'

James were the latest Manchester band to play G-Mex, at the end of that year. I was out of town, so I missed the gig. When I got back to Manchester, a very close friend who'd been at the gig told me he'd bumped into Shaun, who was off his nut and a bit agitated. Shaun was asking where I was. My mate told him he had no idea. Apparently, Shaun said, 'If you see him, tell him I'm looking for him and I've got a knife!'

Even at the time this didn't sound like Shaun; I'm guessing he was just having a bad episode that night, or my mate had taken what he said too seriously, because when I saw Shaun soon after, he seemed absolutely fine and with no particular axe to grind. Or, thankfully, no particular knife to stab me with. I mentioned this to Shaun recently, while I was writing this book. He doesn't remember the occasion and said, 'Clint, mate, I've never carried a knife in my life!'

One night back in 1990 he was in Dry Bar with some of the Mondays and Martyn and Craig having the crack when one of the Mondays asked, 'Why does Clint do all the interviews?'

'Cos we don't want girls camping in our front gardens when we're famous!'

Next thing we know, Shaun was interviewed in *Vox* magazine, talking about the Dry Bar conversation and said, 'Inspiral Carpets. They're just nobheads, man. Clueless nobheads!' Which we found funny. It was one of *the* great Madchester put-downs. Whatever was going on between us and the Mondays, we continued to look up to them and, whenever we met, there were no problems. In fact, for a period in the early nineties, when things were going great for both of us, whenever we released a single Shaun would send us a fax from the Factory offices saying, 'Good luck with the new single, Carpet-heads!' – or similar positive messages.

Maybe it was Nathan exercising a bit of damage limitation. Either way, all these years later, me, Shaun and the rest of the Mondays are still good friends. Still here sharing stages well into our sixties.

With a bit of distance and hindsight it's easy to see that some of those music publications back then really did try to stir up aggro between the bands. It makes for better copy, more sales. It wasn't necessarily the writer doing the dirty work, sometimes the editorial staff would stick the boot in. They had too much power. In the nineties a paper like the *NME*, *Melody Maker* or *Sounds* could totally halt a new band's ascent in a single issue with a few snidey comments. Richard Ashcroft summed it up perfectly in a radio interview I heard him do recently when he described the music journalists of the nineties as being that generation's trolls, just sniping away at people like us all the time, trying to destroy us while we went about creating our art. Back when The Verve started out, one of the music papers had christened Ashcroft 'Mad Richard', so he knew what he was talking about.

That said, I must admit, occasionally when looking through old press cuttings, I do come across articles where I'm mouthing off about other bands and artists of the day. It was the norm. I recently found an old press cutting from that time, where I was shocked to read myself calling Bobby Gillespie a 'cunt'. I've no idea why. I've always been a big fan of Bobby and never had a negative thought about the man. We made our *Top of the Pops* debuts on the same episode, and we've remained friends throughout our careers. He's a fellow indie-pop time traveller who's always a pleasure to be in the company of. I can only think I was probably trying to get a reaction out of the journalist. That's how it was back then. Pissed-up rock 'n' roll stars winding each other up in the weekly music papers. In other interviews I might be having a go at Black Box or Rozalla for no other reason than they were Top 5, while our new single had crashed into the Top 68. When I read back through some of those old press interviews, I honestly don't know where our heads were at. Maybe it was the alcohol? Maybe the drugs.? The dosh in our bank accounts? The free clothes, free records, free love? Or maybe the fact that things were going great for us today, and we were all a bit worried it might end tomorrow. I think it's fair to say that a whole community of musicians were slightly losing the plot a bit right there and then.

Some of the older heads in the Manchester music scene, who'd been around long enough to see how things work, made some sage comments around the end of 1990. Bernard Sumner told the *NME*: 'Every movement is false in some degree, and every movement explodes eventually. It starts as a social thing, really. I'd hate to come from Manchester next year. I think people are already sick of hearing about it.'

The BBC ran a special programme on the Manchester music scene, in which Martin Price from 808 State warned, 'There's a backlash to come. All the journalists that have built this up will try to knock it down – you know that's gonna come next. It kind of saddens me that you've not seen the true picture of what Manchester's like. It's kind of being misrepresented, as if Manchester is all about scallies and flared jeans, which is not really what it's about at all. It's about the spirit of the people . . . to be a northerner.'

'Yeah, the famous *NME* backlash, it's scheduled to start around any moment now,' Danny Kelly, then *NME* deputy editor, told the BBC sarcastically. 'In people's minds, they think we build people up then smash them down, but I think it's an exaggerated notion. It doesn't happen like that.'

Hmmm. We'll see.

51/
'You'll get nowhere with a name like Oasis!'

Any possible backlash, though, couldn't have been further from our minds. We were enjoying our moment as much as anyone. In 1991 the Inspirals needed to shoot a video for our new single 'Caravan'. We all loved the stunning video for Depeche Mode's 'Personal Jesus', directed by Anton Corbijn and filmed in the Tabernas Desert in Almería, Spain. Due to its arid landscape, numerous spaghetti westerns were filmed in Almería back in the fifties and sixties; *Lawrence of Arabia* and *A Fistful of Dollars* were shot there, and even parts of *Cleopatra*, starring Elizabeth Taylor, the first film I ever saw in a cinema. Mute were happy with the idea and funded the cost of the shoot in Almería, which featured me driving a vintage VW Camper.

The day after we filmed the 'Caravan' video in Spain we flew out to the States to start a five-week tour. We were to do the entire trip on one of the Florida Coach company's state-of-the-art sleeper buses. Our gig in Dallas was at a venue called Trees in the Deep Ellum part of town. That was the night I met a young woman called Meg Sheehan. She hadn't been to our gig and wasn't familiar with the Inspirals, but had gone to the venue after her shift working at a local restaurant, to meet a friend of hers called Jack. We chatted for a while and I asked for her phone number before getting back on the bus and leaving for the next stop on the tour. I kept in touch with Meg for the rest of the trip and we met up again when she flew out to the last date on the tour, which was in Atlanta.

A few days after I got back to Manchester, I told Debbie I'd met someone else on the American tour and wanted to end our relationship. She was devastated but seemed to accept that our relationship had run it's course. We'd done some house-hunting over the years but we'd never really committed to anything. We'd never planned on getting married or having children.

We remained friends, and I explained to the rest of the band that I wanted Debbie to carry on working for us. She'd been a big part of the Inspirals' team, all the way back to those first demo-tape recording sessions at the mill. She'd supported me through every crazy life choice I'd made since the night we'd started going out together back in 1978. I spent a few weeks living in the Britannia Hotel in Manchester, before moving back in with my mum and dad. I was back in my old bedroom and looking out for a house to buy.

When we were on tour with the Inspirals, sometimes for weeks on end, we'd all phone home every few days, or at least once a week, to check in with our families. There were no mobile phones, no text messages or email, and hotel phones were expensive. It would be normal to make 'reverse charge' calls or, as they were called in the States, 'call collect'. One day during our European tour in the summer of 1991 Noel rang his mum, Peggy, to reassure her he was healthy, alive and not in prison. 'How's Liam?' he asked.

'He's gone out, rehearsing.'

'Rehearsing what?'

'He's in a band?'

'A band?!'

'He's a singer.'

'Liam's a singer???!' Noel couldn't believe what Peggy was saying. I was just as surprised when Noel told us what he'd just heard. I had no idea Liam was a singer, although he had always looked cool as fuck, so it did kind of make sense. But Liam had always been quite shy when he was around us, when he'd tagged along with Noel and helped with our gear and sat in the corner of our dressing room waiting politely to be offered a drink. I couldn't quite imagine him as a frontman, commanding the stage and an audience.

Liam's band were called The Rain. Once we were back in Manchester we went to see them at the Boardwalk, and I stood with Noel in the audience of 30 or so people. The band were loud, that was my first impression. Really loud.

Liam looked cool on stage. His vocals weren't quite there, but he had a real presence. I was impressed. So was Noel, even if he wasn't going to come right out and admit it to his little brother straight away. Walking back to Noel's flat in India House* later that night, with his girlfriend Louise and their friend Alison Bell from Red Alert, Noel told them he was thinking about joining Liam's band. He didn't even have a guitar strap at that point, as he'd never played guitar standing up before.

He told us that he was joining The Rain too, and that they were going to change the band name. We knew there was a band called Sister Rain in Middleton, but Noel reckoned there'd be other bands called Rain or something similar, especially in the wet northwest. One afternoon a few days later Noel was in the office: 'Clint. I've got the new name for the band.'

'Go on?' I said.

'Oasis!'

'That's a rubbish name, you can't call your band "Oasis",' I told Noel with an air of disappointment. 'Plus, there'll be loads of other bands called Oasis, especially if you get to America. You'll end up having to call yourselves Oasis UK. It's a terrible name. You'll get nowhere with a name like that!'

But Noel was adamant: 'We're sticking with Oasis.'

A couple of weeks later we went to see the band's first gig with Noel. The crowd was only slightly bigger than at The Rain gig. They only did four songs, one of which seemed to go on for about four hours. All the Inspirals were there, and we were absolutely buzzing for Noel. We all knew this was exactly where he'd wanted to be since the night he auditioned for us three years earlier. Penny Anderson, a music journalist who was friends with Noel and Louise, and a neighbour of theirs in India House, was also there and wrote a short paragraph about them in her column in the *Manchester*

* India House is a Grade II listed textile warehouse, which was converted into housing-association flats in 1989. Noel and Louise lived in Flat 47, and were one of the first to move in. Noel later said, 'India House is ground zero in the story of my musical life! I moved into a flat there with my then girlfriend in 1989, broke and bored. By the time I left in 1993 I'd joined my little brother's band and had written "Live Forever" and "Rock 'n' Roll Star!"'

Evening News the next week. 'Oasis will go places' read the prophetic headline. 'They sound different from all the rest,' Penny wrote, and described an audience 'full of local pop luminaries' – which I think meant me and the Inspirals! – 'They're much harder, rougher and, erm . . . madder, but not so much as to preclude commercial success. People are already predicting they could be the next big thing to come out of Manchester. Let's hope it's a prediction and not a curse.'

It certainly didn't turn out to be a curse. I liked Oasis as soon as I heard them. They had the energy and attitude of many of the punk bands that had changed my life almost two decades earlier. At first, I wasn't blown away with Noel's songwriting. Songs like 'Columbia' were catchy as fuck but, lyrically, just seemed to have a throwaway vibe. It was only much later, when I started to hear tracks like 'Live Forever' and 'Slide Away' that I started to realise something wondrous was happening. These were songs that people could live by. The audacity Noel had to write the lyric '*Tonight, I'm a rock 'n' roll star!*' was awesome. By the end of the first chorus of that song, Noel had described everything that people like me had aspired to be since our childhoods. It reminded me of something I'd written in one of my diaries back in November 1976, while I was still at Rochdale art college:

> I wanna be a Rock Star, wanna go places
> Stand on the stage, see all the faces

When Noel wrote 'Live Forever' he said he knew enough about music to know that it was something special. When he took it into the Oasis rehearsal rooms at the Boardwalk, Bonehead refused to believe that Noel had written it at first. He was quickly becoming a great songwriter. Noel would be proved right. They would get somewhere with a name like Oasis. But not for a while yet.

As for the Inspirals, we were still enjoying the ride. We were in our own little bubble when we were away recording or on tour for weeks, even months, on end. We were oblivious to the fact that back home in Manchester the clouds were gathering and the mood was starting to change.

DRAGGING ME DOWN

52/
Factory Closing

We were on tour in November 1992 when we heard the news that Factory Records had finally gone under. Our tour manager at the time, Jane Roberts, was going out with Hooky, so probably had inside info through him about what was happening at Factory, and she was the one that broke the news to us. It was devasting. We were all gutted. It was no secret that Factory had been in financial trouble for a while, and everyone knew that they had been hoping new albums from Happy Mondays and New Order, their two main bands, would get them out of the hole. Instead, the Mondays' infamous *Yes Please!* recording sessions in Barbados, and New Order's £400,000 bill for recording their album *Republic*, pushed the label into massive financial difficulties. Factory had been hoping to do a deal with London Records that would allow the label to continue. In Factory's early days, Anthony Wilson would often opt for a casual 'verbal agreement' arrangement with his artists, rather than a legally binding contract. At the eleventh hour of negotiations with Factory, London realised that, due to this approach, Factory didn't even own New Order's back catalogue; New Order owned it. London pulled out of the deal and New Order signed directly to London. All hope had faded for Factory and the company was officially declared bankrupt.

It almost felt like there had been a death in the family. The fact that we'd recently gone through an acrimonious split with our manager Anthony 'Binsy Smith' Boggiano only added to our despondency. The Manchester music scene was so-close knit at the time, it really felt like we were all in it together. In my mind we were an extended family of a few dozen creative people that were all closely linked and co-dependent in some way. All the bands, DJs, record labels and venues were connected – one big, at times dysfunctional family who were all inspiring each other, supporting each other, collaborating with each other and achieving great things. Of course, there was some rivalry and a few squabbles now and again, like most families, but for the most part I generally didn't feel any friction between the bands or the businesses. It was always quite harmonious in my mind.

Just like me, the guys who started Factory and the lads that became Joy Division and New Order had all been first inspired by seeing the Sex Pistols in 1976. For all of us that was the spark, the Big Bang. Factory had gone on to redefine, reinvent and reinvigorate the city. First with the Russell Club, then Factory Records and the Haçienda. The mission statement of the Haçienda said they wanted to restore 'a sense of place'. Factory had done all that and more. They had restored a self-belief in Manchester and Mancunians that would go on to power the regeneration of the whole city.

I was a proud holder of a Haçienda membership card. I'd bought the records and followed the bands. Our stories were intertwined. When Tony Wilson had put our band on *The Other Side of Midnight* before we even had a record deal he'd expressed some interest in us joining Factory. Early on, there'd been some vague discussion about that as a possibility. But, even as an unsigned band, we weren't sure it was the right label for us. Don't get me wrong, we all *loved* Factory, and the bands on Factory, but I'm not talking about the music – more the way it was run as a business. Or the way it wasn't run as a business. We could see the disorder at Factory, even then, and we weren't sure we wanted that chaos in our lives. Factory was groundbreaking but it was also, at times, anarchic and shambolic. It sometimes seemed more like an art or social experiment than a serious business. I think we were always quite industrious as a band. We'd all had 'proper' jobs working in factories and the like, doing the nine-to-five grind to get your little pay packet at the end of the week. That had instilled a strong work ethic in us. We didn't treat the Inspirals as a laugh – it was a serious business and our escape from those mundane jobs. We always grafted hard for the band, that's how we'd been brought up. So as much as we loved Factory, their approach didn't seem to match ours. Joining a label like Mute seemed a better fit for us.

We were never 24-Hour Party People as such, and we were probably slightly less unhinged than some of our Manc contemporaries. We were maybe seven-hour party people. Eight on a good night. We'd always put a shift in before we started partying and then, no matter what happened that night, we'd be up and back at the coalface putting in another shift the next day. Of course, we still had moments when we went for it, especially on tour, but we also had that in-built mentality and belief that you need to work hard to get results.

Some people blamed the Mondays for the demise of Factory, which I know pisses Shaun off as he says it was because the label was mismanaged. The tales of them recording their final album *Yes Please!* in Barbados and how out of control they were there are legendary. At one point Shaun even sold a sun lounger from the recording studio to get more drugs. Chris and Tina Frantz from Talking Heads had produced the album and were shocked by the debauchery of the Mondays. Tina came out with a great line about them. She said Talking Heads had started out in New York in the seventies, when it was a dangerous place to live, surrounded by freaks and weirdos and people who lived life on the edge, but most of them were just playing at it, really – working with Happy Mondays was the first time she had met people who had no idea where the edge was. Nobody would have said that about the Inspirals. We knew where the edge was.

I'm with Shaun. I don't think you can blame the Mondays, or New Order, or any of the bands for demise of Factory. It was the chaos behind the scenes that did it, the lack of contracts, the high cost but under-performing projects, and Rob Gretton's unorthodox financial management. When the film *24 Hour Party People* came out a decade later, starring Steve Coogan as Tony Wilson, it was only loosely based around the truth, but what it did capture was the colour and the chaos around Factory and the madness of the times. You can pull the film apart and point out all the inaccuracies and contradictions, but the essence of the overall anarchic spirit of that group of brilliant people, the label, those bands, is bottled perfectly. As Tony Wilson said, 'Some people make history, other people make money.'

Alan Erasmus had first come up with the name 'Factory' because they were sick of seeing signs everywhere around Manchester, in the 1970s post-industrial slump, saying 'factory closing', and he thought, 'Wouldn't it be great to have a Factory opening?' Now, 15 years later, their own Factory was closing. It was all over. There was a mood change in the city. Only a couple of years earlier, it had felt like anything was possible. We'd gone from black and white to glorious psychedelic technicolour in the space of a few months. But now, for the first time, it felt like there were dark clouds forming over our utopia. We were all waking up to the realisation that it wasn't going to be 1990 for ever. The times were a-changin', and not necessarily for the better. Even the drugs were changing. Where there had been ecstasy and light, now there was cocaine and moodiness. To some degree, it felt like there was a loss of innocence and optimism. It all added to the disillusion we felt after our fallout with our own manager. Factory going down seemed to reflect what was happening across the city. The party was over, and it felt like the hangover was starting to kick in.

53/
Bon Voyage, Mr G!

Noel had now been in Oasis for over a year, and they were getting more and more gigs in and around Manchester. I went to see them a couple of times at the Boardwalk, and then in Middleton in north Manchester when they supported Hooky's band, Revenge, at the Hippodrome. I'd recently given Noel my Vox AC30 amp, and he used it that night. Oasis were still finding their feet as a band but getting better and better with each gig. Noel was clearly becoming more confident as a songwriter. He was also adapting to writing songs for a band, as opposed to just writing for himself, in his bedroom.

We'd bump into Oasis in the Boardwalk, as they'd now taken on a rehearsal room in the basement, and we were rehearsing on the top floor. One weekend, I lent Noel my Ensoniq synth when they wanted to record some tracks in Out of the Blue for a demo. One of the tracks, 'Better Let You Know', was their interpretation of the rave track 'Feel the Groove' by Belgian Eurodance group Cartouche. That might seem strange to some people, but Noel always had far more eclectic tastes than people later assumed. He was a regular at the Haçienda and places like the Kitchen and the Thunderdome.* Noel was the one who introduced the Inspirals to The KLF's *Chill Out* album on our first big tour of America. I don't remember Noel going on about the Beatles so much back then, not as much as he and Liam would later, although they did have a *Magical Mystery Tour* poster on the wall of their rehearsal room in the Boardwalk.

One of the big things they had going for them when they played live was the huge sound they got. First of all, they were a five-piece, and having Bonehead on second guitar really helped them create that big sound. But the other secret

---

* A north Manchester club that even Shaun Ryder described as 'a bit moody'!

weapon they had was that Noel had brought in Mark Coyle, who he'd met while they were both working for the Inspirals. With the Inspirals, Noel and Mark would set up our gear, tune the guitars, check everything was working and be around for the soundcheck, after which they'd often sit jamming together on the stage in between the soundcheck and doors opening. Between them, thanks to those years working with us lot, Mark and Noel had a lot of experience. Mark was also a sound engineer, sometimes looking after our monitor mixes, sometimes doing the front-of-house sound.

When Noel joined Oasis, he brought in Mark to be their soundman. Mark helped Noel and the band create this huge wall of sound, even when they were just playing the Boardwalk, or small venues to a couple of dozen people. But no matter how big or small the crowd, there was always a cocksure self-belief to them – especially Liam and Noel. Liam quickly assumed a nonchalant stage presence that clearly owed a lot to his hero Ian Brown, but Liam made it his own. He would stare the audience out, daring them not to fall in love. He had this doe-eyed look that would occasionally give you glimpses of tenderness, a glimpse behind the bravado, a glimpse of that shy kid that had hung out in the Inspirals' dressing rooms only a year previously.

Once Noel had written some of those classic early songs, you could tell that, in their minds, their dreams were increasingly real. Liam, still a teenager, would sing to the sparse audience with every ounce of his breath and spirit about being a rock 'n' roll star. Some of the audience would snigger to their mates. But he was becoming one.

After our winter tour of Europe in 1992, we decided to make a few changes in the Inspirals' camp, and after a band conversation, we decided it was the right time to let Noel and Mark go.

During the European tour, it became obvious they'd both lost their enthusiasm for working with us. It didn't help that they ran out of drugs partway through and couldn't source any more. I didn't know it at the time, but the two of them would take my Farfisa apart and stash their drugs inside while we were on tour, in case we were ever stopped by the authorities or when crossing borders. I remember taking a picture of the two of them in a dressing room on that final tour, and they were both gutted about the absence of drugs. I'd taken hundreds of photos of them during our years together but, on this occasion, they were almost scowling, and I clearly remember thinking, as I looked at their faces through the viewfinder on my camera, 'I've lost them.'

Noel was always great company – funny as fuck, fun to be around – and had been a great sounding board, as he was astute and had good musical taste. Even he would admit he was never the hardest-working roadie in the world, but he always made it clear how much he loved the job and how much he appreciated us giving him the break. His focus now, though, was obviously on Oasis, not the Inspirals. It was time for him to go out and do his own thing. I wouldn't say we sacked him, more that it became apparent that it was time for us to go our separate ways.

One weekday afternoon we went down to the basement of the Boardwalk to break the news to Noel. He was on his own, sat on his amp, strumming his guitar. He seemed surprised to see us. For some reason, I found myself being the one to deliver the bad news: 'Look, Noel, we're making a few changes, and we've decided we won't be taking you on the American tour.' I think Noel half knew it was coming – he wasn't stupid. 'We know you've lost your enthusiasm for working with us and that you want to get on with your own thing.' I tried to soften the blow by saying, 'If there's anything we can do to help you out with your band let us know.'

Noel looked glum, still sat on his amp, but managed to say, with a sense of dark humour and a slight grin, 'You bunch of cunts . . .'

One thing we did do, as a gesture, was give Noel £2,000 (about £5,000 in today's money) as a thank you for the past four years, which he obviously appreciated. That money would pay for their rehearsal-room hire and any equipment they might need while they tried to get themselves a record deal. I went on to make various calls to A&R people, radio presenters and other people in the industry that I thought needed to know about and support Noel's new band. I wanted to help him, as we really had been through a lot together.

It was sad to part ways with Noel, as he'd been with us since we were an unsigned band and was a big part of our story. He witnessed our whole journey first hand. As well as being with us in rehearsal and recording sessions, we'd also let him sit in on band meetings and record-company meetings. No part of our business was out of bounds for him. Occasionally, he'd even jump on the phone pretending to be one of us for an interview if we were late into the office or couldn't be arsed. He had all that knowledge from nearly four years of working with us and had learnt from our mistakes as well as our good decisions, which was invaluable experience to take with him into Oasis. Many unsigned bands would sign the first contract that was put in front them and come to regret it. Noel was less likely to do anything like that after everything he'd learnt with the Inspirals. He had soaked it up like a sponge. It meant that he wasn't surprised by anything. 'I'd been in airport lounges,' he said later, 'so I wasn't blown away by the fact there were free crisps, while all the rest of the band were running around going. "*There's free crisps!!!*" I would just be like, "There's free biscuits as well, you know." ' It was no surprise to me when I heard that his nickname in the Oasis camp became 'the Chief'. It wasn't just that he wrote the songs, it was because he knew how everything worked.

What happened next, as Oasis went stratospheric, is history. But what *didn't* happen is mad to think about, too. None of us will ever know what might have been if we'd taken Noel on as our frontman back in 1988. It's surreal to imagine that, in a parallel world, songs like 'Don't Look Back in Anger' or 'Wonderwall' might have been Inspiral Carpets' songs . . .

54/ Mancs in Space

Meg and I married in 1992 at Rochdale Town Hall, and Graham was on duty as my best man. Our first child, Harley Luv, was born in March 1993 in Birch Hill Hospital in Rochdale. Two years later, January 1995, her brother Max Presley arrived. Having babies in my life was a beautiful thing and something I'd always wanted. Meg was a fantastic mother, and her family couldn't have been any more supportive. Her mother, Doña, worked for American Airlines so she, Meg's dad Dave and brother David Ryan would jump on planes whenever they could to come and spend time with us and help out with childcare.

On one of our visits to Dallas, in late '93, we drove down to Houston where Meg's dad, a restaurant manager by trade, was overseeing the opening of a new eatery. While we were in Houston, we took the opportunity to visit the Johnson Space Center. It was a place I'd never in my wildest dreams imagined I'd ever get the chance to visit. Like most kids growing up in the 1960s I was completely obsessed with the space race and the Apollo missions. It was an incredible time to be alive. It seemed like almost every month there was another *Saturn V* rocket being launched from Cape Kennedy into space, trying to reach the Moon. They just kept going up. I didn't know it at the time, but it was part of John F Kennedy's long-term project started in May 1961: 'By the end of this decade . . . I want an American chap walking on the moon.' Or words to that effect. I bet the NASA scientists crapped themselves when they heard that: 'What did he just say?'

'He wants us to put a man on the moon?!'

'Fuckin' 'ell! We'd better get busy!'

Through the rest of the decade, through every minute of every mission, me and a couple of million other British kids would be glued to our black-and-white television sets watching those fuzzy little images, where you couldn't always see what was going on but you got the feeling something exceptionally cool was happening. My dad would tell me, 'Watch these fellahs! They're gonna change the world, this lot. No one's ever done owt like this. Pioneers!'

I had a telescope on a tripod by my bed focused constantly on the night sky. Mum and Dad bought it because they knew I had a fascination with space. No one really knew what'd happen when man actually did get to walk on the Moon. I think most of us thought he'd just sink into the Moon dust or float off into some sort of eternal lunar orbit. Like a David Bowie song. Watching those space trips was one of the happiest times of my childhood.

So it was incredible, 30 years later, to be standing next to one of *the* actual space rockets I used to watch as a nipper. I was gobsmacked. I could hardly talk. I just kept swearing under my breath as I looked up at it, 'Fuckin' hell!' The pure size of the thing was overwhelming: the full rocket, all its stages completely restored, reassembled and laid out, horizontally, in a field in Texas. To me, it was as magical as any of the Seven Wonders of the World. It really was the greatest sight I'd ever seen. Even now, I'm struggling to describe its incredible beauty. As a symbol of what mankind can achieve, it was unbeatable. I knew, as I stood there next to the *Saturn V* space rocket, that a song would be popping along very soon.

I started putting pen to paper on the flight back to Manchester. By the time I landed, the song was complete. I knew even before I played the track to the Inspirals that it would end up being a single. It had all our trademarks: a quirky hook, and that cool sixties garage-pop vibe that the Inspirals do so well, even if I say so myself. I based the chord sequence around one of my favourite garage records from the sixties, '96 Tears' by ? and The Mysterians, from Michigan.

As well as the actual 'Saturn 5' spacecraft, my song also focused on another unforgettable image of 1960s America, the assassination of John F Kennedy, the thirty-fifth President of the USA. The line '*the lady crying by his side is the most beautiful woman alive*' is a reference to his wife, Jackie Kennedy.

Mute Records loved the song and gave us a £30,000 budget to be able to fly back to Houston to film a promo. We worked with a brilliant director called John Hillcoat, who helped get all these ambitious ideas into the video. John had previously worked with Depeche Mode and Nick Cave and went on to become a successful film director with his breakthrough film *The Road*, an adaptation of Cormac McCarthy's book of the same name.

I spent an hour on the phone to John one night explaining our ideas. In the video, we would play five NASA employees: astronauts by day but by night in a band called 'The Saturn 5'. Thankfully, and perhaps a little surprisingly, NASA were happy to fully co-operate with this little band with strange haircuts from some place they'd never heard of called Oldham. NASA helped us make a classic pop video. They gave us full access to the Johnson Space Center's tourist museum and some of the other facilities on the site. They even let us start filming two hours before the tourists were let in. Talk about a dream come true. There's a great bit in a TV interview that I did while filming the video. Because we were in astronaut overalls with official embroidered NASA crew patches, some of the tourists thought we were real astronauts and came over wanting to have their photos taken with us and asking us questions about the Moon and space travel in general. They must have been curious as to why there were so many Mancunian astronauts on duty that day.

Zoe Ball and a TV crew flew out to film a feature about us making the video for a TV show called *The O-Zone*. We were all a bit in awe of the fact that TV personality Johnny Ball's daughter would be joining us on the trip. Zoe had only been in TV for a year or so, and just as a kids' TV presenter. Part of us filming the video involved us driving around Houston in a Mustang at night. It was quite surreal to find myself driving around this futuristic city on the other side of the world in one of the most iconic cars ever built. We drove out to a huge industrial complex outside of the city, some sort of oil refinery with smoke and steam billowing out of hundreds of steel pipes. It felt like something straight out of a science fiction film. I was absolutely buzzing my tits off, until a member of the local crew said, 'Welcome to the most polluted place on the surface of planet Earth!'

Impending death by chemical poisoning aside, it was one of the highlights of my life. Not just to a 34-year-old pop musician who'd visited the Johnson Space Center in 1993, but for that little kid in Oldham who spent most of the 1960s and early 1970s glued to a monochrome TV set.

55/
I Want You

During our time in 23 New Mount Street, I'd often bump into Mark E Smith in the reception area. The Fall had set up office in the same building. He'd always let on and stop for a chat. I'd not really spent any time in his company since I was a teenager and hung around the band's dressing rooms for those early Fall gigs.

He knew I was now in the Inspirals and was always very complimentary about our music, which obviously meant a lot to me. He liked to mention bands like The Seeds and Sam the Sham and the Pharaohs whenever we talked, explaining that a lot of his favourite bands were from the sixties garage movement. Whenever I spoke to him, I was still quite awestruck. He was still my hero. I tried hard not to show it, though, always doing my best to act cool and unfazed.

In late 1993 we went into Parr Street Studios in Liverpool to record our fourth studio album. We'd recorded our previous album, *Revenge of the Goldfish,* there and loved the experience and the results. We didn't know it at the time, but we would end up calling this album *Devil Hopping*, after our producer Pascal Gabriel's amusing pronunciation of the word 'developing'. His Belgian accent often created much hilarity among us. 'This song is devil hopping quite well now, I think.' We'd be on the floor rolling about.

At the time, it was still the trend for bands like ours to release remixes of each single, on various formats, the week after the definitive version, to capitalise on unit sales and gain a higher place in the charts. It often felt like we were rinsing our loyal fanbase a bit too much for loose change, and we were getting a bit jaded with the whole concept of remixes. We'd managed to get some fantastic remixes done in the early days as we knew some future star remix producers among the nascent dance-music scene. Justin Robertson,

808 State, Fortran 5, Forgemasters and Paul van Dyk all produced some of their earliest remixes for the Inspirals. Not all our remixes were well received by the band, though. On one memorable occasion, we paid Rebel MC a nice wedge to do a remix of our 'She Comes in the Fall' single. When it came back, we were stunned to hear it. We were expecting something a bit different but to us it was pretty much an instrumental version of his hit single 'Street Tuff' with a few bits of vocals by me and Tom from our multitrack dubbed over it. 'Street Tuff in the Fall'. We didn't release it.

By '93 we thought we'd try something different. We came up with idea of collaborating with some of our favourite artists to rework some of the new tracks, to make cool alternative versions to use as B-sides, rather than just another 'Balearic' remix. The first three names that came up were Peter Hook, Mark E Smith and Basil Clarke. Basil was the singer in one of our favourite Manchester bands, Yargo, a soul, funk and jazz outfit whose debut album *Bodybeat* was a massive influence on us all. It was because of Chris Nagle's production work on the *Bodybeat* album that we asked him to produce our second album, *The Beast Inside*.

The Fall were out on tour, but I managed to get the number for the hotel Mark was staying in that night. I phoned the hotel, got put through to Mark's room and he answered in his unmistakable tone: 'All right, Clint? What can I do for you, cock?'* We exchanged pleasantries, and I started to explain our idea to him: 'What we want to do, Mark, is alternative versions of a couple of new tracks, with our favourite artists guesting on them, and we'd bloody love it if you could do some guest vocals.'

'Sounds great, Clint. Send me the mixes and I'll have a listen.'

I told him that we thought he'd sound great singing 'I Want You', a song Martyn had written recently, which we'd earmarked as a potential single, but to give the rest of the tracks a listen and get back to us with his thoughts. We sent a cassette of the rough mixes over to him, and I soon got a call back from him: 'Clint, it's Mark. Yep, I'm well up for doing "I Want You".'

'That's great, Mark! Amazin'!'

---

* 'Cock' is an affectionate term used by some Mancs for a friend: 'All right, cock?'

'And I'll have a go at that "Sputnik" one as well!'

' "Sputnik"? Not sure which one you mean, Mark?'

'That space one – "Sputnik Five".'

'Er, OK, Mark!'

Cut to a cold Friday night in Liverpool in the spring of 1994. We'd finished working on the album tracks for the week, with Pascal and Clif Norrell, our engineer for the sessions. Clif lived in Los Angeles, and Pascal had suggested bringing him over to work with us after hearing his work with R.E.M. on their *Automatic for the People* album. We were huge R.E.M. fans, so didn't need any persuading. Pascal wanted to just focus on the album, so he wasn't too arsed about working on the extra tracks. He'd left the studio to head off home to his family in London for the weekend. Clif, however, was staying in the residential rooms above Parr Street for the duration of the sessions, as nipping home to California for the weekend wouldn't be practical, and he was happy to stick around and help us get the Mark E Smith performance on tape.

Mark was coming over from his house in Prestwich, and we told him to get to Parr Street for about 5pm. Six pm came and went. Seven pm came and went. Still no sign of Mark. At 8pm we were still waiting. Just after 9pm, the studio door burst open, and Mark stood there with a carrier bag in each hand. 'All right, Clint! You got sixty quid for the taxi, cock?'

Sixty pounds was a lot of money in those days. We'd not discussed transport with him ahead of the session but assumed he'd get a lift over to Liverpool from one of his mates. We scraped some cash together and I went outside to pay the taxi driver.

We decided to do 'I Want You' first, then 'Saturn 5' if we had time. As we were getting the microphone set up, Mark disappeared into a small storage room just off the control room, where the cleaner kept her mop and bucket. He seemed more animated when he emerged and looked at Tom: 'You back, Tom? Yeah? You back?'

Tom looked confused.

'You back, Tom?'

'What do you mean, Mark?'

'You back, Tom? Yeah? You back?'

'I've not been anywhere, Mark . . .'

We chaperoned Mark into the live room where Pascal's treasured vintage valve microphone was placed securely on a stand behind a protective 'pop shield' just on the other side of the control-room window. I positioned myself at the mixing desk, by Clif's side, A4 notepad and pen in hand. 'Right, Mark, ready when you are,' said Clif.

Mark looked through the window at Tom, sitting on the other side of Clif: 'You back, Tom? Yeah? You back?'

'What the fuck is he goin' on about?' I said as I pushed the talkback button on the desk: 'Mark, what do you mean, "You back, Tom"?'

The chorus lyrics to the song on Mark's lyric sheet were, *'I want you. Right now, and for ever . . .'* Mark was basically asking if it was OK if he sang, *'I want you BACK!'*

We told him it was fine, and Clif hit the 'Record' button. The two-inch tape started rolling. When the music kicked in, Mark snarled into the mic, *'There are already illness rumours circulating around/I think you should remember whose side you are on . . . No one said it was gonna be easy . . . A pain to tease, the barrier's broken . . .'*

At this moment, for some reason, Mark smacked the pop shield – designed to prevent the delicate components inside the mic from damage through excessive volume – across the room and grabbed Pascal's £4,000 microphone, Elvis style, and screamed into it: *'. . . AAAAAND CLIMB ONBOARD A KNUCKLE RIDE!!'* Then the microphone died. Clif stopped the tape machine, the colour drained from his face.

'Everythin' all right, fellahs? I reckon that was a good take!' said Mark, still holding the mic.

'Erm, give us a minute, Mark.'

Clif explained that it was normal for expensive studio mics like this to pack up if any moisture got onto the internal components. We were in no doubt, at this stage, that the inner workings of Pascal's mic must have been totally drenched by Mark E Smith's finest saliva. We gave it a few minutes to dry out, reassembled the pop shield, and started again. Mark's performance was erratic and inconsistent, but classic Mark, working and weaving around Tom's vocal, which was already on tape. As always with Mark, none of the takes were the same. We recorded six tracks of him singing, some of it ad-libbed, most of it from the lyrics he'd scribbled when he came out of the cupboard earlier. I logged all the parts of his various takes onto the notepad and realised there and then that the 'cut and paste' process was going to be a big task. But I knew we had everything we needed.

We put the kettle on and had a short break while Clif got the 'Saturn 5' tape in position, still worrying about how we could explain to Pascal about the microphone incident. Mark disappeared into the cupboard again. He emerged grinning, 20 minutes later, carrier bag in hand: 'Right, c'mon, lads, let's get a fuckin' move on!'

We went through the same process as 'I Want You', recording five or six tracks of Mark's unique, train-of-thought ramblings. Not only did he get the word 'Sputnik' into his performance but he also managed to sneak in a subtle mention of the Telstar satellite that had inspired Joe Meek to record one of my favourite records of all time, 'Telstar' by the Tornados. That same record had been one of my main inspirations when writing 'Saturn 5'.

Again, we had what we needed. We had some real magic in the can. Presumably, somewhere in Pascal Gabriel's fine collection of vintage microphones, still sits a healthy gloop of Mark E Smith's DNA should family, friends, or the scientific community ever decide to clone the great man.

As part of the promotion for our 'I Want You' single, Mark agreed to help us out with a couple of press interviews in Manchester and a videoshoot at the Brixton Academy in London. On the afternoon of the Manchester session, I picked Mark up to drive into Manchester, where we had a room booked in the Palace Hotel for one of the interviews. I had one-year-old Harley in the back of the car, strapped into her car seat. She looked confused when this strange man with a wonky face and a lit cigarette in his mouth climbed into my car.

'Who's this then?' he asked loudly, looking over his shoulder.

'That's Harley Boon!'

Mark leant over, blew out a big cloud of smoke, pointed his cigarette at her face, ash dropping on to her lap, and snarled, 'Uncle Mark's gonna get ya!!'

I thought, 'Fuck me! That nappy's gonna need changin'!'

56/ Devil Hopping

After Mark E Smith, Hooky was next on our collaboration wish list. We'd got to know Hooky over the previous couple of years when his girlfriend at the time, Jane, was our tour manager. We explained the idea to him on the phone, and Hooky was up for it straight away. We booked a session at his Suite 16 recording studio in Rochdale, which had previously been Cargo Studios. This was the same studio where Hooky and Joy Division had made some of their earliest recordings. Hooky liked the studio so much he bought it in 1984 and changed its name to Suite 16. It was also the building in which we'd recorded our debut single 'Keep the Circle Around' with Dave Fielding from The Chameleons four years earlier, so we all had history with the place.

Usually with the Inspirals, whoever had a song idea would bring a set of lyrics, chord progression and basic melody to the rehearsal room or studio and we'd work on it collectively from there. We were never the kind of band who were good at jamming or improvising, so this way of working saved us a lot of time. It was never an issue as, after all, it was the simplicity and the punk vibe of our style that was bringing great results. We knew our strengths and our weaknesses. We weren't Dire Straits or Led Zeppelin. We were Oldham's version of The Velvet Underground. T'Velvets, if you like!

Occasionally, we'd completely craft a track in the studio. Almost like an artist with a blank canvas, experimenting with the colours on his palette, throwing a bit of paint around, scratching at it; turn it upside down, burn it, bend all the rules, ignore everything you learnt at school or college. Sometimes, just one or two of us would pop into the studio and do bit of work on such a track. It's how we created some of our finest pieces, albeit usually for B-sides of singles: 'Skidoo', 'Boomerang' and 'It's Only a Paper Moon'.

'Theme from Devil Hopping' was put together in this way. We all felt it would be the perfect track for Hooky to put some of his trademark bass sounds on. Before Pete got to the studio, we'd created a backing track with a stunning ambience: a slow menacing thing of beauty. Martyn put down a simple, gently pulsating bassline over a steamy percussive rhythm, courtesy of Craig, which occasionally picked up in an almost Phil Collins style.

I laid down a track using a cool, slowly phased ambient-pad preset on my Ensoniq synth. One of my favourite sounds. And the ubiquitous Farfisa interludes obviously (oboe setting). I added a track of slowed-down whale song from the four-track cassette deck I used for all our onstage sound effects. I added some birdsong, the sound of a clock ticking, and a recording of a drunk man singing. Graham's guitar was on point, measured and economical, Tom's vocal, as always, pristine in its tone. Tom wrote the lyrics for this one – surreal and serene at the same time. He always had a great vocabulary, but a lot of the time I didn't know what his songs were about. He and Graham had an ambiguous way of writing – quite a non-figurative or abstract approach – which allowed the listener to put their own meanings to the lyrics. My songs were generally a bit more literal.

I added a double-tracked backing vocal over certain parts of the track. All we needed now was the Hookmeister to work his magic. Seeing Peter Hook strap his bass on to play on one of our tracks was one of our proudest moments – one of those beautiful instances that you don't ever contemplate when you buy your first guitar or start your first band in your garage. At the start of our journey, we all dream about making a record, doing *Top of the Pops*, or getting on planes to do gigs in other countries. But when your heroes want to make music with you, it's something else. I'd followed this bloke since I first saw him at the Electric Circus in 1977 with Warsaw.

He played his bass part on 'Theme from Devil Hopping' with his guitar strap a bit shorter than usual, so his bass was a bit higher up than we were used to seeing. It wasn't swinging around his ankles in his usual style. There he stood. This icon, this Manc Viking, playing on our track, in the same room where he'd recorded 'Atmosphere' 15 years earlier.

CLINT BOON ARCHIVE

Part of my first 'home studio' set-up in my bedroom at 15 Polperro Close, Heyside, 1983. That Tascam 234 (under my record deck) changed my life. Don't I look proud!

CLINT BOON ARCHIVE

Seditionaries, 430 King's Road, Chelsea, February 1977. The girl behind the counter let me take her photograph. Her name was Pamela Rooke. She would find punk fame as 'Jordan'.

T'Mill, 1984. Me, Mani and Spud working hard on some new tunes at the Guide Bridge Mill in Ashton-under-Lyne. Beautiful memories of happy days.

CLINT BOON ARCHIVE

'ALL GAFFERS WANT SAFE WORKERS!' The Inspirals in the Solar Metal Industries factory. Guide Bridge Mill, 30 December 1986. (L–R) Ste, Mark Hughes, me, Graham, Craig.

© P R BROWNRIDGE

On the corner of Sackville Street and Canal Street, 1990. (L–R) Graham, Martyn, Tom, me, Craig. In the background is 42–44 Sackville Street. Our office was on the second floor, just out of shot.

CLINT BOON ARCHIVE

Noel couldn't come with us on our first trip to Argentina in 1991. As a treat, we brought him back an Argentina 'away kit' football shirt. He put it on in the office as soon as we gave it to him.

CLINT BOON ARCHIVE

Me, Graham and Noel hiding from the 'floor assistant/runner' at *Top of the Pops*. We knew she'd be coming to get us for the filming at any minute. Oh, how we laughed!

CLINT BOON ARCHIVE

Me and Lee Mavers backstage at G-Mex, 21 July 1990. We first met on a venue rooftop in Valencia a year earlier and got on well from minute one. I was completely in awe of the La's. Still am.

ALISON BELL

(L–R) John Bramwell (I Am Kloot), Graham, Caroline Aherne and me in Dublin, 1991. John and Caroline were hosting a new TV show. It was one of Caroline's first outings as Mrs Merton.

ALISON HOWE

Me and my daughter, Harley Luv, with John Peel at the Reading Festival, 1995. John was genuinely upset about the Inspirals' recent split. 'I really can't understand why this keeps happening to bands like yours!'

CLINT BOON ARCHIVE

Me and Shaun backstage at the *Engie Benjy* stage show at the Manchester Opera House, 2004. 'Jollop! It's yer party!'

CLINT BOON ARCHIVE

Hooky fixing my tie just before I married Charlie on 18 September 2005. This was taken in the Slug & Lettuce in Albert Square, Manchester, where we had pre-service drinks. We got married in Manchester Town Hall.

CLINT BOON ARCHIVE

Just me getting a shoulder massage from one of my all-time heroes! Me and Mark E. Smith, Brixton Academy, 1994. During a break while filming the Inspirals' 'I Want You' video.

I thought the finished recording of 'Theme from Devil Hopping' was brilliant. Not the kind of thing any of our contemporaries were doing. For me, it was a great indicator of what our fifth album could sound like, and it got me excited at the thought of getting back into the studio to make our next album. The band felt invigorated again.

57/
No One Ever Said it Was Gonna Be Easy

In the mid-1990s Mute were quite fond of holding 'conference calls' to keep in touch with their bands. The internet was in its infancy and the easiest method for a group of people to chat remotely was still via the telephone. Mute would send us the details for the call and all five of us could 'dial in' from a landline at home or wherever we were based and discuss whatever band business needed to be agreed. The service was operated by British Telecom – although it sounds like prehistoric technology now, at the time it felt like something from the future. It reminded me of growing up in Oldham in the sixties, when we got our first phone, and you would often pick up the handset and hear your neighbours gossiping away on the communal 'party line'. The conference calls were a great way of discussing recording or rehearsal plans, artwork and video ideas, although they would often descend into chaos as we started winding each other up or taking the piss.

Daniel Miller, boss of Mute, would often join us. In my mind, he'd become something of a mentor and a father figure over the years. He started one call in early 1994, quite upbeat: 'Hi, guys! First of all, congratulations on getting *Top of the Pops* for "Saturn 5"!'

Us, in exaggerated-boredom voices: 'Thaaanks, Daaan!'

'Are you looking forward to it?'

Sarcastic mumbled replies from the band: 'Ooooh, yeah! Can't wait!'

We had planned to wear white turtleneck shirts for our forthcoming appearance on *Toppy*, as we had in the video for the single. The Mute team weren't enamoured by the idea. Dan, obviously having heard about our plans: 'What are you going to be wearing?'

Craig: 'We're gonna be stark bollock naked, Dan!'

Mass sniggers.

Dan, moving swiftly on: 'Let's discuss the next single, "Uniform". I want to add some more bits to it.'

Me: 'You're not gonna do rapping, are you, Dan?'

Dan: 'Drills and things, and samples like, *"Ah Yeaahhh!! DO NOT DETONATE! DO NOT DETONATE!!"*'

The conference calls could be quite surreal at times. Our moods could be anything from giddy and celebratory to quite serious if things weren't going to plan. Occasionally, during our conference calls with Dan, there'd be an anonymous, crackly and very camp, *'T.V.O.D.!'* from one of us, a reference to the pioneering single Dan recorded back in 1978 while still living at his mum's house. He released the single under the name 'The Normal'. It pretty much kickstarted Dan's career and, along with its B-side 'Warm Leatherette', which Grace Jones covered, was responsible for the birth of the mighty Mute Records. Daniel's contribution to the world of electronic music should never be underestimated.

'Leave him alone, lads! What do you want to put on it, Dan?' asked Tom.

A long pause . . . *'I plug the aerial into my skin . . .'* another snide young Daniel impression from one of us.

These more upbeat conference calls would usually be punctuated by all manner of burps, farts and animal impressions. It was the Inspirals at their mischievous, relentless peak. If only I'd realised when I bought the 'T.V.O.D.' single the week it came out in 1978, that the man behind it would one day change my life.

The excitement of doing *Toppy* hadn't faded for any of us over the four years since we first appeared on it: lots of jolly japes in the dressing rooms, hiding in the wardrobes as the 'runner' came to find us at call time was always a favourite and never stopped being funny. Our 'Saturn 5' performance looked great and went down a treat, not only with the audience in the studio, but the TV audience of millions at home. During the afternoon, we'd mentioned to the show's producer that we were considering releasing the Mark E Smith version of 'I Want You' as the next single. The producer got very animated: 'Yes! Do it! We'd love to get Mark on *Top of the Pops*!'

'D'ya think that's good idea?' I said, knowing that a day at *Top of the Pops* meant several hours of rehearsals, run-throughs, setting lights, planning camera angles, all activities carried out to a precise timetable and with military precision. Not the kind of work methodology that Mark was famous for. 'Do you really want us to bring him? Shouldn't we just do the album version?'

'Bring Mark! Bring him!! It'll be amazing TV!!!'

When I rang Mark to ask if he was up for doing *Top of the Pops* with us there was no hesitation at all: 'Sounds good, cock! I'm up for it. Shall I come down with you lot?'

We decided to go down to London the night before the filming and booked a hotel. We picked Mark up from his house in Prestwich in a minibus. He was already drunk, which wasn't a promising start. He climbed into the back with a carrier bag full of booze and cigarettes and drank and smoked from the moment we set off: the argumentative epitome of Mark E Smith at his very worst. At one point he started having a go at Craig, who was sat behind him in the van, drinking a can of beer, saying, 'Why are you pretending to drink beer, Craig?'

'What do you mean?' asked Craig.

'You're just pretending to drink beer,' sneered Mark. 'There's nothing in that can, it's an empty can.'

'It's full of beer, mate,' said Craig.

'Why are you pretending?' sneered Mark.

Craig had just had enough by this stage and emptied his can of beer over Mark's head in the van.

This seemed to calm Mark down for a few minutes. He reached into his carrier bag, pulled out another can of cheap lager, opened it and proceeded to neck it while staring out of the window and belching loudly. We hadn't even got to the M6 yet.

When we got to the hotel, Mark started to be really obnoxious to the girl on reception. It was nasty and vindictive; she burst into tears. It was at times like these that I found myself wondering what the fuck went on in this man's head.

The next day, within minutes of us setting up in the BBC studios, Mark was causing carnage. Upsetting the cameramen, who asked, 'Why is he standing in a different spot for every run-through?'

'Because he's Mark E Smith!'

'Why is he singing different words every time?'

'Because he's Mark E Smith!'

'Why is he messing with the guitar amplifier?'

'Because he's Mark E fuckin' Smith! That's what he does!'

Eventually, Nicki Kefalas, our TV plugger, came over and said a member of the show's production team needed a word. She led me and Graham through a fire escape into the alley behind the studio. The BBC person told us that the powers that be didn't want Mark on the show and suggested we send him home. We were told that the camera and lighting technicians couldn't handle his spontaneity and cantankerousness and had collectively decided they wouldn't work with him.

'Yeah, but that's what Mark does,' I explained. 'That's what makes him brilliant. That's why everyone loves him. That's why he's a legend!'

'Well, we don't want him on the show!'

'You begged us to bring him down last time we were here!' I explained we would only do the performance *with* Mark. 'If he goes home, we all go home.'

We got our way. The studio crew were told to persevere, be patient and get the best they could out of what was about to happen.

After another run-through, we retired to the BBC canteen where Mark set about abusing all kinds of celebrities and pop stars and causing a general atmosphere of discomfort and awkwardness. He had a real venomous go at Gillian Taylforth from *Eastenders*, for no apparent reason, then later had a go at Elvis Costello, who was also on the show that week. Morrissey was also filming for that *Top of the Pops*, but kept well away from us and Mark, probably for the best.

I was beginning to think that maybe we should have sent Mark home. Over the years, the programme changed formats regularly depending on the preferences of the producer in charge at the time. It was hardly ever broadcast live – maybe just the occasional Christmas special. It would be filmed on a Wednesday, to be transmitted on the Thursday evening. Sometimes, artists would have to mime everything, the music and the vocals; sometimes, depending on the producer, they could do the vocals live. On this occasion, Mark and Tom were to do live vocals over a pre-recorded instrumental backing track. I didn't have to do much except mime the keyboard-playing and pray that it would all go off without any major incident.

The time came and we headed out of the first-floor dressing room in the direction of the studio downstairs. Mark had just lit a cigarette. As we got halfway down the staircase, he stopped me, looked at me and said, 'Clint. Look at me. Are you OK?'

'Yeah, I'm fine, Mark. Why?'

I was wearing white jeans, grey suede ankle boots and a gorgeous denim shirt with a Harley-Davidson motorbike embroidered across the front. It was my favourite shirt at the time, and I'd been saving it for this occasion. As we stood face to face, the rest of the band watching on, Mark slapped me across the face, not particularly hard, but as if to wake me from a bad dream. Which wasn't the case at all. I was about to perform with my band, on *Top of the Pops*, with my all-time (still living) music hero as guest of honour. This was a good dream. In fact, it was all my dreams coming true at once.

I slapped him back. Across his face.

He leant forward and stubbed the end of his cigarette into the cylinder head of the Harley-Davidson on my chest, causing a small wisp of smoke to drift up onto my chin.

'You fuckin' dickhead!' I said, slapping him again.

The mutual slapping carried on for a few seconds longer until Craig said, 'C'mon, you fuckin' nobheads!'

Completely unfazed by this surreal moment, we made for the studio and pulled off one of our finest moments. Mark strutted around the stage, working around Tom's vocals just like on the record (but completely different at the same time). Mark had some lyrics written on a piece of paper in the pocket of his jacket. Throughout the performance, he kept pulling the sheet out and reading from it. The cameramen must have been fuming.

During the middle eight, there's a priceless Mark E Smith moment where he snarls a classic line straight into the camera to a television audience of roughly seven million people: 'You said you lost two stone in weight. So why are you so FAT?!!!'

Our appearance on *Top of the Pops* with Mark was a moment that went down in British pop-music history: the one and only appearance on *Top of the Pops* by one of the most influential British artists of all time. As the opening line of the song says so accurately: *'No one ever said it was gonna be easy!'*

58/
Sibling Rivalry

On 7 April 1994 we played at BBC Radio One's Sound City in Glasgow. It was an annual event where the Beeb would take over several venues in that year's chosen city for a week and showcase some of the best bands on the planet. We were booked to play at the Tramway, an old tram shed that had been converted into a live-music venue. Also on the bill that day were Oasis, Chumbawamba, Credit to the Nation, Baby Chaos and headliners The Boo Radleys.

Oasis were just a few days away from the UK release of their debut single 'Supersonic' and it was getting lots of airplay on the nation's radio stations. It was a great song that, apparently, Noel had knocked up in just one hour.

In the afternoon before the gig, we got to hang out with them backstage and have a nice catch-up. I'd not seen them for a few months but couldn't help but keep abreast of what was happening. They were getting loads of press and attention. They'd had an infamous trip to Amsterdam, where Liam and the rest of the band, apart from Noel, got into a fight with some football fans on the ferry and were arrested and put in cells on the boat. On arriving in Holland they were immediately deported. The music press had lapped it up.

By now they'd also recorded their debut album. Twice. Noel had got to know the Inspirals' front-of-house soundman Dave Batchelor while working with us and asked Dave to produce the album. Dave was a great soundman, a top bloke and lovely person to be around. As well as his live work, Dave had a history as a record producer, having worked, among others, with The Skids, Nazareth and The Sensational Alex Harvey Band. In the band's opinion, the first attempt at recording the Oasis album at Monnow Valley Studios in Wales, with Dave at the helm, failed to capture the energy of the band's live gigs, so they'd moved out and regrouped at Sawmills Studio in Cornwall.

For this session, they rerecorded all the tracks with a back-to-basics approach, recording it as live, with Noel's Inspiral crewmate Mark Coyle in charge. Mark was with them that day in Glasgow to do the front-of-house sound. It was great to see them both again.

'You lot are doin' all right, aren't you!' I said to Noel.

'All thanks to you lot, mate, innit!' he joked.

Then Liam came bounding over: 'How the fuck did you fuckers get fuckin' Mark E Smith on *Top of the* fuckin' *Pops*?!'

I told Liam the story of how me and Mark had ended up having a skirmish in the stairwell of the BBC studios, which Liam obviously loved – it was his type of story. The whole Oasis camp seemed happy and buzzing. They were the most talked-about new band in the UK, and it was obvious things were going to get even crazier for them. Jo Whiley from Radio One introduced their five-song set. I took up position next to Mark at the mixing desk as they kicked into the first song, 'Shakermaker'. 'Fuckin' 'ell, man! The volume!' I said to myself. Next up, 'Digsy's Dinner'. Even louder. 'Live Forever'. My head was throbbing now. Then 'Cigarettes and Alcohol'. The sheer volume was pummelling my entire frame. I'd seen Motörhead play at the Queens Hall in Leeds back in the early eighties, but this felt even louder than that. I leant over to Coyley and said, 'A bit loud innit, mate?!'

'Y'what?'

'I said, it's a bit fuckin' loud!'

'I can't hear you, Clint. It's just really fuckin' loud! Tell me in a minute.'

Over the years, Coyley has suffered worsening problems with his hearing. In helping one of the nation's most influential bands of all time shape their signature sound, and in helping create one of the most important albums of its age, Coyley sacrificed his hearing. Part of the appeal of early Oasis was just how loud and in-your-face they were. They couldn't help but cause a reaction. The debut album was also noticeably loud after Owen Morris mixed it. Jukeboxes were still a big thing in pubs then, and every time someone put an Oasis song on it sounded *huge*, much louder than the records on either side of it. Oasis finished their Glasgow set with the new single 'Supersonic' and set off into the night to carry on changing the world.

Later that evening, Noel and Liam went upstairs in the venue with music journalist John Harris to record an interview for the *NME*, an interview that became infamous and helped cement their reputation as sparring brothers in the music press and in the minds of many music fans. They'd never been at each other's throats when Noel worked for us and Liam would tag along. They'd slag each other off occasionally but always in a jokey way. Their mum Peggy said they always got on well as kids. But once they were in this insane pressure cooker of a band, the sibling rivalry came to the surface. Their recent escapades in Amsterdam were discussed. 'You're only gutted cos you were in bed, reading your books,' said Liam to Noel. Having written so many great songs in such a short time, Noel was getting annoyed that most of the band's press coverage seemed to revolve around their rock 'n' roll antics. John Harris suggested that the reason the music press were writing about Oasis was 70 per cent down to the music, 30 per cent because they seemed like a band who would always guarantee some rock 'n' roll stories of trouble and debauchery. Noel said he was only interested in the music, prompting Liam to tell Harris, 'He's teetotal! He's a fuckin' priest! He was born to be a priest!'

The interview was hilarious* and set the tone for much of the forthcoming press coverage and public perception of Noel and Liam. The music media couldn't get enough, and Noel and Liam gave them exactly what they wanted.

After that night in Glasgow, their trajectory went off the scale. Six months previously, they'd played the Duchess of York in Leeds, and nobody turned up. Not one person. But they still tore through their set to an empty room. Noel always said it's one of their greatest ever gigs, even though the only spectator was a bored barman, polishing glasses. A few days after the Tramway gig, they went back and played the Duchess of York again. This time it was absolutely rammed. Liam sarcastically introduced one song by saying, 'This one's for everyone who came last time we played here!' Most of the crowd cheered, as if they'd been there. 'You lying Yorkshire bastards,' said Noel.

---

* It was later released as a 7-inch single, 'Wibbling Rivalry', on Fierce Panda records, and made the charts.

Oasis were on the verge of something phenomenal, but nobody had the slightest inkling of just how mind-blowingly bonkers things were about to get. In hindsight, the scale of Noel and Liam's ambition in the interview they gave that night seems almost quaint. 'I like the way it's bubblin' up . . . it's remindin' me of the Roses all over again,' Liam said. 'I want to get 2,000 people in a nice fuckin' gaff who are there to see you.' Two thousand people? Within a year they'd be selling out arenas of 20,000. Within two years they would be playing Knebworth to 250,000.

59/ Pressing the Mute Button

That summer we played Glastonbury for the first time, and Oasis were also on the bill, making their debut at the festival. We played the *NME* stage, sandwiched between Pulp and Radiohead, and Oasis were below us on the bill, playing earlier in the afternoon. We didn't know it at the time, but it would be the last time the Inspirals and Oasis would appear on the same bill. Their debut album wasn't out yet and they weren't earning much money. Liam was just wearing a blue M&S woolly jumper that day, and on anyone else it would've looked like they'd borrowed it from their grandad, but Liam somehow carried it off. He always had this innate ability to make anything look cool, even when he couldn't afford smart clothes. In the backstage area, there were loads of bands and celebs milling about, but all eyes seemed to be on Liam. He was the up 'n' coming star, no question. As he walked through the backstage area in the afternoon, someone shouted, 'Where you going, Liam?' 'To the top, mate . . .' he replied, without even breaking his stride. Cool as . . .

The headliners that year were some of the old guard – The Levellers, Elvis Costello and Peter Gabriel – but those acts aside, it felt like 1994 was the year that Britpop arrived at Worthy Farm, with Oasis, Blur, Pulp and Radiohead all on the bill. For all those bands, it would be the start of a long relationship with the festival. It was interesting to see which bands ended up on the Britpop bandwagon. Bands like Suede and Elastica were coming through for the first time, but it was Blur's third crack at pop stardom. At first, in '90 and '91, they'd had a strong 'Madchester' vibe, Damon with his shaggy bowlhead and beads round his neck, then they'd had something of a mod phase, with the Doc Martens and drainpipe jeans. More recently, Damon had donned a Sergio Tacchini tracksuit top and the band shapeshifted again, becoming Britpop royalty in the process. Pulp had been around for years and spent most of the eighties as an overlooked bedroom indie band in Sheffield, before Jarvis moved to London.

As Oasis walked on stage, Liam had a can of Stella in one hand and a tambourine in the other, and taunted the crowd, 'Are you gonna wake up, then, yeah? For some real songs.' They were still figuring out their live dynamic as a band, and Noel didn't even have a mic for backing vocals, but, despite the early slot, they won over the crowd and rounded off with their swaggering cover of 'I Am the Walrus'. 'Nice one, see ya later,' said Liam, and sauntered off.

The Inspirals had hired a sleeper bus for Glastonbury so we could hang about on site and not have to trek back to some hotel miles away. Unfortunately for Oasis, they *were* booked into a hotel miles away, so after we played on Saturday night, Noel and Coyley came and hung out on the Inspirals' bus and started skinning up. It was the first time they'd been on our tour bus since we parted ways two years previously, and so much had changed in that time. I asked Noel how their set had gone.

'OK, mate. Crowd were hard work early on.'

'How was it for you, Mark?'

'Reeeally fuckin' loud, mate! Really loud!'

Our bands were now on different trajectories. Even though their star was in the ascendent, nobody would have predicted that the following year Oasis would be back at Glastonbury as headliners.

A few months after Glastonbury, in September 1994, we went into Britannia Row studios in Islington, north London, to record what should have been the Inspirals' fifth album. Britannia Row was an amazing studio that had been built by Pink Floyd in the seventies and was now owned by their drummer Nick Mason. We were in there for a couple of weeks, staying in accommodation just around the corner that was also owned by the studio. Joy Division had stayed there almost 15 years previously when they were recording their second and last album, *Closer*. The accommodation was basic, with four or five rooms; it felt more like a B&B than a hotel, but if it's good enough for Joy Division and Pink Floyd, it was good enough for the Inspiral Carpets. I was a massive Pink Floyd fan, and had only bought my first Farfisa because the bloke selling it had pointed out to me that Floyd had used it on all those early records. A decade later I was playing my Farfisa in the same studio where Floyd had recorded some of their records.

We were working with a producer called Ed Buller, who had done some great work with Suede. His dad was the famous composer John Buller, so he had a great music background. Ed was a brilliant producer, something of a genius in the studio. He could create these beautiful soundscapes from nothing just by manipulating the ambience of the room. He was great to work with, and I felt the demo tracks we were laying down were some of the most progressive music we'd ever produced.

It felt like the Inspirals were morphing into a slightly different entity. We felt like we were maturing and maybe reaching a different phase in our career. I sung lead vocals on a couple of tracks, Tom was playing guitar on others, Martyn was starting to play some synth lines and arpeggios. It was exciting, it felt like we were flexing our muscles and really changing into a different sort of musical unit. We all had stuff to get out of our creative systems and I think we all wanted to try something different – not just another pop album. Some of the songs were quite complete, with impressive, finished arrangements. We'd probably completed about 80 per cent of the album in around three weeks.

Our record deal with Mute had been for four albums, with an option for them to have the first claim on a fifth. That meant that if Mute decided they didn't want our fifth album, we'd be out of the contract and free to go elsewhere. Not that we'd really thought about that – after all, they were paying for this recording, so the fifth album would obviously be coming out on Mute. One afternoon, Daniel Miller came down to Britannia Row to have a listen to the recordings we'd done so far. We were between managers at the time, so it was just the band and Daniel there for the playback, and we were excited about what we had to play him. But not long after we started playing the recordings, I started to get an uneasy feeling. We were all watching him for his reaction, and the longer the listening session went on, we went from being confident he was going to love it, to getting the feeling that he wasn't really into it. As I sat there, watching Daniel out of the corner of my eye, I realised, 'Fuck! This is going to be a harder sell than I thought . . .' Daniel didn't give us an answer there and then; there was just a lot of pleasantries and words along the lines of, 'Great. I'll be in touch.' Not exactly the most reassuring of pleasantries.

Sure enough, within days, our worst fears were realised when we got a message from Daniel saying something along the lines of, 'I think what you're doing is great, you've still got a great future out there, but I don't think Mute is the label for you to go into your next stage with.' It was all very diplomatic, and Daniel had been kind enough not to tell us straight away at the studio, after we'd played him the songs, because that would have been a massive kick in the nads. Mute didn't officially drop us. Technically, they just didn't take up the option that they had. It was a gentle let-down. We tried to take it philosophically. The songs were going off in a slightly new direction, and maybe Daniel and Mute thought it would be a bit too much work for the label to make it all into a cohesive album and market it. They wouldn't be just selling a new Inspirals album, they would be selling a new artistic direction as well. If Daniel had heard more obvious singles, in the vein of 'Saturn 5' and 'I Want You', then maybe he would have taken up the option? It's also impossible to know what else was going on in Mute's world at that time. Einstürzende Neubauten were also going through a transition period, and Depeche frontman Dave Gahan was living out in LA with his ongoing struggles around mental health and drug abuse never far from the news. We'll probably never know what headaches the rest of the Mute roster might have been laying on Daniel's wobbly boardroom table. It could have been that the label didn't have the cashflow to support another album at the time. Or it might just have been that Daniel didn't like what he'd heard. Maybe the world had just moved on and our close connection with the whole Madchester scene had become something of a millstone around our necks. I've still got the tapes from those final sessions, and I still think there's some beautiful stuff in there. It's a real shame it never came out, but maybe it will one day.

The official line was that the record company had simply decided not to take up the option on the fifth album. But we knew the reality. No matter how you dress it up, Mute had just decided, after five years, that they didn't want the Inspiral Carpets any more. Somehow, unbelievably, even though it was hard to swallow, we had to recognise the stark truth. We'd been dropped.

60/
The Dream is Over

For a few weeks after Mute 'let us go' we stayed positive and convinced ourselves we'd be OK. We thought it would be only a matter of time before another label stepped in and offered us a deal. After all, only a few months earlier, we'd had a Top 10 album with *Devil Hopping*, two Top 20 singles with 'Saturn Five' and 'I Want You' and played a knockout set to a massive crowd at Glastonbury.

Over the following months, though, it started to feel like we were fighting for our lives. We were certainly fighting to save the band. We'd lost our record deal. Perhaps we'd also lost our direction. It didn't help that we were lacking a manager and were trying to manage ourselves. We felt a good manager would be the answer to our problems, particularly when it came to finding us a new record deal. We had meetings with a few potential managers, including Chris Morrison, who managed Blur, but, in the end, we agreed to be managed by Peter Felstead, and his company CEC Management. Peter also managed The Boo Radleys, which is how he came to our attention. Named after the character in *To Kill a Mockingbird*, the Boos were one of the UK's most loved 'new' British bands in the spring of '95, having scored a massive hit single with the exuberant 'Wake Up Boo!' and an accompanying number 1 album. We liked Peter and were chuffed that someone who knew the industry was happy to take a punt on us because, since our split with Mute, we'd began to sense that doors were starting to be closed in our faces. Early in our relationship with Peter, it came out in conversation one afternoon that, back in the day, he'd often appeared on *Top of the Pops* as a Womble, as he was friends with the songwriter Mike Batt, who wrote The Wombles' tunes. This made us like him even more, despite it not being the kind of backstory you'd find on the CVs of Brian Epstein, Malcolm McLaren or Simon Napier-Bell.

Peter was doing his best to find us a lifeline, but it felt as though the music industry in general wasn't interested in us any more. It also felt like it might have been more to do with the whole Madchester thing than our actual band. In the past year we'd had hit singles and been on *Top of the Pops* a couple of times, but in many people's eyes we were still linked to a Madchester scene that had happened four years earlier. Four years in pop years is a lifetime. Madchester had been usurped by grunge, which was now being usurped by Britpop. Instead of being allowed into the Britpop party, it felt like we were chained to a party that was long over. We were part of a scene that was now two scenes ago. It was as if the industry was thinking, 'It's 1995! Why would anybody want a bunch of lads from Manchester with shit haircuts and a fuckin' fairground organ any more?' Certain sections of the music press had turned on us and had taken to referring to us as 'the ugliest band in Britain', which was unnecessarily nasty, and far from true. I could think of at least three bands who were uglier than us! The 'ugliest band' comments quickly turned into 'where are they now?' comments once the news of Mute's decision started to filter through the industry.

The only money we had coming in was the occasional royalty cheque from the PRS and the PPL, which, by now, weren't substantial as we'd not been out gigging and weren't getting much radio support. We were in dispute with our accountants over a massive bill they'd just sent us. Our lawyer's fees were still huge even though we weren't earning the kind of sums we were three years earlier. Three of us had children. All of us had mortgages and bills to pay.

Peter, our new manager, was doing an admirable job of trying to save our sinking ship, and a couple of labels, Nude and Deceptive, did offer routes through which we could put some records out, but no one was offering the kind of financial stability we had enjoyed and come to depend on, courtesy of Mute since 1990.

We held a band meeting at Graham's house in Moston in the first week of April. We discussed, in detail, every aspect of our situation. We'd recorded some demos of new tunes in Suite 16 and we talked about releasing one of them, the prophetically titled 'Come Back Tomorrow' as a single to see if that would help us along. The bottom line, though, was that none of us could afford to carry on this fight for much longer without any steady income.

Even though the mood at the meeting was sombre and there was a definite sense of despondency, we stayed focused and methodical throughout it. No voices were raised, and there was still a genuine sense of unity between us. We talked about how we should probably wind the company down, even if we were to carry on with the band in some form or other. We talked about the pros and cons of splitting the band up and how to let our fans know if we decided to knock it on the head. As always, I was trying to be positive and encouraging: 'Lads, yesterday, when we were having that conference call with Peter Felstead, the sun came out and I thought to myself how symbolic it was and that everything will be all right!'

'Even if we do decide to carry on for a few months or a few years, there's too many loose ends,' Graham said. 'Everything's just hanging.'

Tom was very business-minded and always seemed at home getting involved with the company's administrative affairs. He'd brought along all the correspondence relating to the issue with our accountants. We'd managed to rack up a massive accountancy bill, which we were in the middle of contesting. We quite simply didn't have the kind of money they were demanding. Tom read every word of every page to us, as we grimaced in the realisation that we were probably fucked. It was the side of being in a household-name pop group that no fan would ever want to see. We were tangled up in the biggest bunch of loose ends and business bollocks we'd ever experienced. And with no wedge coming in.

It was a sad moment to experience. Only a year earlier, we were sharing a stage with Oasis at the Radio One gig in Glasgow, having just done *Top of the Pops* with Mark E Smith, and it felt like we were still at the top of our game. But that day in Graham's house, we all knew the band was in a dire position. To make things worse, that 'bunch of losers' my dad had shown me in the *Oldham Chron'* back in late 1989 were enjoying their sixth number 1 single with 'Back for Good'.

Graham and his wife, Karen, had a daughter, Yasmin, who'd just turned one. She kept us company through most of the meeting, which helped lighten the mood. Despite the gravity of the situation, we did have the occasional laugh. To his credit, Daniel Miller had kept in touch with us during the months after his decision to drop us. He genuinely wanted to see us get through this and was having regular phone calls with Peter to discuss our situation and explore options. On one of our trips to London around that time, we'd met up with Daniel for a catch up and a bite to eat. In a chat between Peter and Daniel a few days before our meeting at Graham's, Peter had asked Daniel how his meeting with us had gone. 'Well, they got a free meal out of it!' Daniel joked.

'Well, they bloody need it, Dan,' said Peter. 'Because there's not much of a band there at the moment.'

'Really? I didn't realise it was that bad.'

Daniel suggested Mute could put out a singles compilation album in the September of '95, but even though it was a nice gesture, we all knew that it wouldn't solve our financial problems. The fact was, we probably wouldn't be around to promote it.

The subject of going back to 'real jobs' cropped up. Graham mentioned how he'd consider getting some painting and decorating work if need be. He even said, 'Clint might end up playing keyboards for R.E.M.,' which totally flattered me but didn't fill me with any more confidence. The idea of approaching Tony Wilson to see if he'd consider putting something out on his new label, Factory Too was suggested.

'We could look at relaunching Cow Records and team up with a distribution company?' I suggested.

'The sheer amount of work that would involve would make it impractical,' said Tom.

He was right. We all knew that none of these options were going to pay for mortgages or nappies. Everything seemed to depend on a couple of meetings Peter was to have over the next two weeks.

'I think today, or this weekend, is too soon to make the decision on whether we should split the band or not,' I said. 'Let's give it two weeks.' We all agreed. Peter soldiered on for the fortnight, probably wishing he could go back to the good old days when life was so much more serene, underground, overground and wombling free. (For those wondering, he was Madame Cholet.)

A couple of weeks later we reconvened at Graham's house. There was nothing new to report: no good news, no new offers on the table. All we had was a bunch of demo tapes and a handful of university summer balls pencilled in the diary. As at the previous meeting, we spent some time discussing our plight before deciding this was it. Craig summed the mood up nicely in his own inimitable style: 'Let's just roll over and die!'

The Inspirals had been a dream come true in so many ways. I'd achieved more than I could ever have dreamt of, we'd toured the world, had hit records, headlined festivals and appeared on *Top of the Pops*, not once, not twice, but *seven* times. But now the dream was over. It was time to knock it on the head. We finished our brews, wished each other well, said our goodbyes and drove off in different directions. Back to the real world. Back to life, and back to reality.

LIFE IN TRANSITION

61/ Signing On

I felt a real sense of grief after we'd decided to split the Inspirals. What we'd achieved was incredible and there were times during the five-year period from 1989 to 1994 when I really thought it might last for ever. Our success had totally eclipsed that of scores of the bands we'd looked up to and were influenced by. Our music had touched people in all corners of the planet, and we'd got to travel the world at the same time. It had been all my dreams coming true.

But it had also been, over the full ten years of the journey, a trip of constant acceleration, which had left me tired and exhausted, almost shellshocked. I think all five of us were. So, although I was gutted that it was ending, there was also an element of relief, and I was excited about the idea that there was a new chapter starting and I could do some of the things that I'd not been able to do for the last ten years. There were conflicting waves of emotion. I was broke financially, but part of me started to feel exhilarated at the thought of a blank canvas where I could try my hand at absolutely anything without worrying about the constraints put on me by life in a successful pop group and all the commitments that go with it. For the best part of a decade I'd put every ounce of my time and energy into the band and I'd loved almost every minute. Yes, there were occasions when I would try to convince myself I didn't want this any more, but, usually, the little voice on my shoulder would step up with a firm, 'C'mon, Booney, you nob! This is what you've dreamt of all your life!' The voice was always right.

But that chapter of my life was over now, and a new one was starting. I didn't have a clue where I was going but I just got my head down and got busy. The most pressing matter was the fact that I was broke and had mouths to feed. Harley had just turned two and Max was only three months old.

The money had all gone but the bills were still there. The mortgage didn't seem too big when the Inspirals were at their peak, but when everything stopped, the realisation set in.

I knew that no matter what, I had to keep writing songs. It was the one thing I knew I could do well. I didn't have any fancy recording gear, just the old Tascam 234 Syncaset Portastudio that I'd had since 1983. I thought about getting back into DJing. My last DJ gigs had been at the Grey Horse in Oldham, where me and Chris Goodwin used to do our Back Trip Time Zones sets every Sunday night. But I'd hardly done any DJing since the band took off. Meg suggested I should try to get a residency at our local pub, the Slip Inn in Milnrow. She reckoned I could get £50 a night, which might help towards the bills. That's how bleak things had got, financially. I held off on the local pub idea as I thought it might look weird to the regular customers, most of whom were our neighbours and still thought I was loaded because of my 'success'. Instead, I started reaching out to other people who might be able to throw me a bone.

I thought about getting some TV work. I'd grown to feeling comfortable in front of the camera and wasn't as embarrassed about my speaking voice as I had been as a kid. I put together a VHS videotape showreel of my various TV appearances in an attempt to find some work as a presenter. I dug out some old interviews with the Inspirals – quirky bits to camera with Caroline Aherne, who was now becoming a household name as Mrs Merton – and some other bits of TV I'd done.

I even auditioned for a TV advert for one of the big sofa companies. The studio was in an annexe of Salford University. I had to strut around, excitedly exclaiming, 'These two sofas look exactly the same! But, they're not! One is half the price of the other!' You get the idea. Selling my soul to the devil for a few hundred quid. Thankfully, I didn't get that gig. I live in fear that one day the video of that audition will appear online and reduce the internet to fits of uncontrolled mirth. Fuck it, if it does pop up, that's me at a low point in my life where I was doing whatever to keep things going at home. Though it was soul destroying at the time, I'm not ashamed of exploring every avenue to feed my kids and keep a roof over our heads.

As the pile of unpaid bills got bigger and bigger, debt collectors started turning up at the house. At first, they caught me out, leading to awkward conversations on the doorstep where I'd promise them a quick repayment plan knowing full well there was no way in hell I could deliver what I was offering. We started to leave the black venetian blinds closed day and night. We didn't answer the door unless we knew someone was due to visit. Soon, there'd be bailiffs on the doorstep. We'd be on the living-room floor, hiding behind the couch until they left.

As I tried my hardest to keep some money coming in, Meg's parents, Doña and Dave, bailed us out by sending one of their credit cards over from Texas. It was a godsend. It helped with our groceries and nappies for baby Max, but the bigger picture was a scary one. I'd gone from being a high earner to being unemployed and broke. I still got recognised on my trips out of the house, by people wanting to chat, get my autograph, or ask me to draw the Inspirals cartoon cow on a cigarette packet. I was still a local celeb. But, financially, I was really struggling. I was on my arse.

Meg did her best to keep some money coming in, taking regular part-time work when the opportunity arose. On occasion, I'd find myself contemplating getting back into the furniture trade. I still had the skills to do it and could probably have made a decent income. The reality is, though, when you've supported Paul Simon in the River Plate Stadium and been photographed next to the Golden Gate Bridge for the front cover of the *NME*, it's hard to imagine ever putting a pair of overalls back on and firing up the welding set.

For the first time in my life, I turned to the state for help. Rochdale Jobcentre was a brutal place in 1995. Especially when the only entry on your CV for the last eight years was 'pop musician'. As part of the process for claiming Income Support, I had to register as being 'in search of and available for work'. I sat there with my poorly edited VHS showreel in hand while the condescending fucker on the other side of the desk smirked at the form I'd just filled out. I was genuinely eager to find work, ideally, in a field I was familiar with, but this bloke was treating me like an entitled prick, and deliberately talking way too loud so other people in the room could hear: 'Very nice, Mr Boon! *Top of the Pops* seven times! You must be very proud!!'

By the time I left the room, everyone behind me in the queue knew my backstory. I walked out of the jobcentre and crossed the road to where I was parked outside Rochdale Railway Station. I sat in my car, eyes watering, and stared into space. How the fuck did this happen? Exactly a year previously, I was at the top of my game, now I was at rock bottom.

Welcome back to the real world, Clinton David Boon, age 35. Brought down to earth with a bang. I was granted Income Support of £90 per week and another £90 towards the mortgage. I was also given free-milk tokens as we had two children under four years old. I counted my blessings that we lived in a country where social security was available. The whole experience was demoralising, but it was the lifeline me and the family needed. It would give me time to get back on my feet and, hopefully, re-establish my career. I still had to visit the jobcentre every week to sign on and explain my latest attempts at finding work. I'd still have to sit and listen to some unsympathetic bellend telling me I should stop dreaming and get back to the mills.

It was the most desperate personal thing I'd ever experienced and, all through it, the meteoric rise of Oasis continued. *Definitely Maybe* had become the fastest-selling debut of all time. They made worldwide headlines with their tours of Japan and America. They'd even released a brilliant 'Christmas' single, 'Whatever'. At the time the Inspirals split, Oasis had just scored their first number 1 single with 'Some Might Say'. They were on a fast track to becoming one of the most popular British bands of all time. Meanwhile, I was on a fast track to nowhere. I would be queuing at our local supermarket check-out in Milnrow with my milk tokens discreetly hidden in the palm of my hand so I could hand them over to the woman on the till when I was sure none of my neighbours were watching. All the while, Noel and Liam were laughing down at me from the news shelves. I was proper chuffed for them all but, at times, the irony crushed me. It felt like a cruel joke being played on me. Part of me wished some cheesy host from a TV prank show would just jump out from behind the vegetable rack and put me out of my misery with the words 'Clint Boon! You've been game for a laugh!'

The Stone Roses had spent ages making their second album, partly because of wrangles with their record company. They finally released the grandiosely titled *Second Coming* in December 1994, but all was not well in their camp either. Reni left the band in March 1995, reputedly after a fallout with Ian. They recruited a new drummer called Robbie Maddix, but the Roses were cemented in people's minds as the classic line-up of Ian, John, Mani and Reni, and as soon as one of those pieces was missing it didn't seem right. Bands are always about chemistry – after Reni left, things were never the same. The band were booked to headline Glastonbury in June, which some thought could have been an all-conquering triumphant return. Unfortunately, John Squire had got into mountain biking and injured himself crashing his bike in California, so they had to pull out of the festival. Pulp, who had just released their era-defining single, 'Common People', stepped in and smashed it.

Meanwhile, the *News of the World* somehow got hold of my home phone number and rang me up to see if I'd be up for telling my story. They wanted the story about the huge success our former roadie Noel was enjoying, now well on his way to making his first million, while me and the Inspirals appeared to have slid quietly off the edge of the world. I explained to the journalist on the phone that I wasn't interested. He offered me £500. I told him I still wasn't interested. He asked me why. I explained that, firstly, I didn't ever intend to make any money out of my relationship and friendship with Noel. Secondly, I didn't trust his publication and suspected that, if I agreed to accept the offer, I'd find myself being photographed with my bottom lip stuck out, standing outside the jobcentre, or my local rubbish dump, within a matter of hours. He doubled his offer to £1,000 on the spot. I refused again and hung up the phone. I knew full well that if I agreed to do the piece, they'd stitch me up. The journalist was relentless. He rang me at home every day, each time doubling the financial offer. When the offer got to £20,000, I told him to stick it and not contact me again.

It turns out I wasn't the only Mancunian ex-pop star having a rough time. I bumped into Mark Day from the Mondays one afternoon outside Dukes 92, a popular café-bar in Castlefield. Both our bands were over at this point.

'How are you gettin' on, Clint?' asked Mark.

'Strugglin', to be honest, brother. What about you?'

'Same here, mate. I'm on me fuckin' arse!'

I told him I was signing on and explained to him the extents I'd been going to in order to pay the bills, including trying to sell settees on a TV advert. He told me how he only had £1,500 in the bank and wasn't going to be able to pay his next mortgage payment.

'What're you going to do?' I asked him.

'I've started sellin' fuckin' cuddly toys out of my car boot, mate!'

'Cuddly toys?'

'Yep! And books for kids!'

'Are you doin' any music?' I asked him.

'AM I FUCK! I'm done with music, mate!'*

I had zero money in the bank and the debt was building. For me, it was a time of real awakening. It reminded me that this sort of constant, day-to-day stress and worrying about money was the norm for millions of people around the world – just not usually on upmarket newbuild streets like Lambourne Grove. I know now that being kicked back into reality in such a savage manner made me a stronger man. All my instincts told me that I needed to crack on with getting creative again. My dad helped me to build a cool recording studio in our attic to record my new songs. As well as the Tascam four-track recorder, I'd amassed other equipment over the years, including organs, synths, effects units and lots of rack-mounted 'outboard' gear. I cobbled up a practical and ergonomic setup where I could sit surrounded by my beloved machines and have access to almost every single control without leaving the comfort of my cheap Ikea office chair.

To keep the costs down, we decided not to install a separate staircase, and instead used a ladder to get in and out of the studio. The ladder was accessed by climbing into the airing cupboard on the landing of the house. The unusual method of entry added to the whole *The Lion, the Witch*

* Mark continued selling toys and books for the next 17 years, until he rejoined the Mondays in 2012.

and the Wardrobe magical vibe of a recording session at the Boon house. We widened the original loft hatch so I could get larger pieces of gear up into the attic. Dad fitted two Velux windows into the roof, so I had lots of daylight and fresh air when needed. He completely lined the room in woodgrain-effect hardboard from the local B&Q store. Dad and Mum paid for all the materials on the understanding that I'd pay them back when I got back on my feet. My latest studio was up and running and ready for action. I was in my own little Joe Meek heaven, right there in Milnrow, and open for business.

First, I started getting my new song ideas onto tape. It took me a while to realise there was a common thread running through my new tunes: 'You Can't Keep a Good Man Down', 'The Cool People Know Who the Cool People Are!', 'Climbing Back Inside the Dream'. Although I didn't realise it at the time, with 'Comet Theme Number One' – and its main chorus vocal, '*Even with the state of things I try, try, try!*' – I was writing songs about self-belief, hope, resilience and positivity.

The internet was still a relatively new thing to the man in the street. Technology was progressing incredibly fast, as it usually does. I decided to write a song that captured that moment in time when the world was waking up to this marvellous new thing called the 'World Wide Web'. The lyrics talked about how people were communicating with each other around the world using the internet and, in a lot of cases, the brand-new concept (which now seems prehistoric) of 'internet café bars'. At the time I wrote the song Manchester literally only had a handful of bars, which would function as cafés through the day then continue into the night with DJs and, in some instances, live music. I named three of them in the song – Atlas, Dry and Dukes of 92 – and also referenced my personal addiction to coffee, the fact that I would constantly have coffee with me, even when driving: '*It's taking me way high . . . when I ride on the highway*', the highway being the 'Information Super Highway'. I named the song 'White No Sugar' as a nod to my preferred way of taking my coffee. The song closes with a catchphrase coined by my good friend the legendary broadcaster Mark Radcliffe. We'd recently worked on a TV show together called *Mark Radcliffe's NWA* where the NWA stood for North West Arts. Mark was the host, and I was his 'house band', sitting constantly by his side through the show, at my organ waiting for my cue to play the odd jingle and the opening and closing theme tunes. He'd close each show by saying, 'So until next week, Mr Boon, Play that tune!!!' at which point I'd burst into action. I adapted the theme tune into another track called 'Push Me Back Down', which would go on to feature on my first 'solo' album.

Throughout that period, I wrote and recorded the foundations of what would later become the first album by The Clint Boon Experience! I took out a three-year loan of £1,500 to pay for a Fostex DMT-8VL digital multitrack recorder, which, at the time, was considered state-of-the-art technology for 'home studio' musicians like me. It meant my recordings would sound more professional and, hopefully, be of releasable quality further down the line. I was still using my old Atari ST computers, which were driving the original generation of the Cubase MIDI music-programming software – all very clunky, with stacks of floppy discs all over the desk. But I was loving it. Making music has been my happy place for most of my life.

I'd spend days on end up in the studio working on my latest masterpieces. Meg and the kids would spend a lot of time out in Texas with her parents, and I'd stay at home working on music, trying to get my career back on track. I'd be up there for hours, only stepping down the ladder for a coffee or the occasional bathroom break, not leaving the house unless I needed to get some food in. Occasionally, I'd catch my reflection and notice I'd grown a full beard, a look I've never been a fan of on such a gentle face as this. I'd regularly go to the John Milne pub in Milnrow for food, as it was cheap and convenient. The phrase 'Table for one, Mr Boon?' amused me at first, but after a short while started to haunt me.

All the while, the bills kept dropping onto my doormat, and still the bailiffs knocked on the door and pressed their faces up against the windows while I sat in silence in the kitchen or hid behind the couch if they happened to call when I was necking a kebab in the front room. They insisted on putting little notes through the door with things like 'MR BOON, YOU NEED TO CALL US IMMEDIATELY!' or 'WE KNOW YOU'RE HIDING BEHIND YOUR COUCH!!' written aggressively in serious capitals.

But I kept on writing songs – it was the only thing I knew. Shaun Ryder gave me some hope when I saw what he had just done: he'd made a huge comeback with his new band Black Grape and scored a number 1 album after being written off by everyone in the industry, and most of Manchester.

I had a friend called Karen Boardman, who I knew through the Manchester music scene, and she and her husband Gordon Biggins really helped me out when I was at my lowest – for which I will always be grateful. Gordon was head of A&R at EMI and was working with the Spice Girls. He gave me £2,000 to 'record some demos'. He knew my financial situation was desperate, that the money would be spent on debts and bills, and just said, 'Look, if you can send me a demo tape of something – anything – then at least I've got something to show for it, if anyone ever asks. But don't worry if you can't.' I think we both knew there was no chance of me signing to EMI as a solo act. They were too busy with huge acts like the Spice Girls to show any interest in an ex-Inspiral Carpet. But it was a magnificent gesture, which I've never forgotten. It felt like karma, in a way. We had given Noel £2,000 when we let him go, to help him on his way, and now £2,000 had found its way back to me when I needed it most.

62/
What's it All About?

In the summer of 1995, I got an answerphone message out of the blue one day, from Mark E Smith: ''Ello, Clint, it's Mark . . . listen, The Fall need a new keyboard player, so give us a call and we'll get you sorted out. All right, cock.'

I loved Mark E Smith and I loved The Fall, as I've already made clear. I'd loved them since I first saw them in 1978 at the Electric Circus, then got to know them a bit hanging around as a star-struck teenager. Mark was still my musical hero but, truth be told, I didn't want to join The Fall. Mark already had a long, chequered history of fall-outs with band members, which usually resulted in them leaving or being sacked. During live gigs he would antagonise them, messing with their amps and instruments during songs. He was always looking to get a rise. My personal experience of recording 'I Want You' with him at Parr Street, and all the promotion that went with it, including our *Top of the Pops* appearance together, had been stressful enough. There was no way I could handle that full time. I called Mark back. 'Mark, listen, I really appreciate the offer and everything,' I told him. 'I'm really flattered, but I'm too busy at the moment. I just haven't got the time. Cheers, though.'

That wasn't true, of course. I wasn't too busy. I was still on my arse. I could have really done with whatever income joining The Fall would have brought in, but I just couldn't do it. There's no way I could join that band. I loved The Fall too much to join The Fall. Plus, I had other things in mind.

Soon after, I got another call: 'Hi, Clint, my name's Sil Willcox and I manage The Stranglers.'

'Hi, Sil, what can I do for you, mate?'

'Well, the Stranglers are about to do a three-month tour of British Army bases around Europe . . . But Dave Greenfield is having some health issues and he's going to be out of action for a while.'

'Right . . .'

'He's suggested we get you in to cover for him until he's back on his feet. Whaddya reckon?'

I was speechless. After a few seconds, I told Sil I'd need to think about it. I knew right then that if I was to stand in for keyboardist Dave Greenfield, I'd need months to learn to emulate his style and play his parts – maybe a year. Though many people see the influence Dave's work has had on me, our playing styles couldn't be more different. Dave was a classically trained musician. I was just a punk with an organ. I called Sil back and explained that, even though this was one of the greatest offers I'd ever had, and that I was absolutely floored to be asked, my focus now was on getting my new songs out there, and that this wasn't the right time for me.

Even though I was on my arse, in the space of a few months I'd turned down £20,000 to talk to a tabloid about my former roadie, and the chance to play in two of my favourite bands of all time. Two of *the* bands that made me want to be in a band in the first place. I know now that these were the right decisions, but, looking back, I'm amazed at my presence of mind when I was in such a tight spot.

I got in touch with Oldham Council and presented them with a proposal to set up a free advice and support service on the music industry for the town's young unsigned bands and musicians. The council were up for the idea, and we secured some financial support from the European Social Fund. We decided to call the scheme 'Start '95'. I was going back to my roots, back to my mill days in a way. I organised some classes, seminars and sessions where unsigned artists could come along and listen to me and guest speakers like Janice Long, Mark Radcliffe and Terry Christian talking about our experiences in the business. We would offer advice and answer any questions. As far as I knew at the time, no other council in the country was providing a service like that.

We did one event at Werneth Park in Oldham, in the Grade II listed community centre that has its own music rooms. I invited Graham along as my main guest of the day and we talked to young musicians about life in the Inspirals, playing *Top of the Pops* and touring the world. We spent hours going through the ins and outs, the ups and downs of the music industry, and regaling them with tales of pop stardom. At the end of day, when we walked out to the car park to go home, neither of our cars would start because both our batteries were flat. We both had old 'classic' cars, which could be a bit unreliable – my 1971 VW Type 3 Fastback (BLG 724K), which I'd recently bought very cheap off a cousin, and Graham's 1960s Ford Anglia. We took it in turns pushing each other's cars, trying to bump-start them in front of some of the kids we'd just spent the day teaching how to be successful like us. Me and Graham saw the funny side, but I could see a couple of the kids watching us, thinking, 'Shit! Is this how it can all end?'

I was still on the lookout for unusual people to collaborate with on my new music. I put the word out through a few music-industry mates to watch out for anybody a bit out of the ordinary that I could work with. I wanted to make music that was quite different from what I'd done with the Inspirals. I was thinking of something a bit more abstract, a bit more cabaret, even.

I got a call from a friend of mine, Caroline Elleray of BMG Publishing. Caroline told me that her husband, a builder, had met a young lad from Fleetwood who was a budding opera singer. The lad had heard my name come up in conversation and sounded keen to be put in touch. Caroline sent me his number and I got on the phone to him. His name was Alf. He was only 23 and was still living with his mum and dad, the youngest of nine kids. He'd recently left his job paint-spraying cars for the TVR motor company in Blackpool, so he could go to college and study opera.

Me and Alf decided to get together and put some opera vocals on some of the new music I was working on. He came over to my house and we got to work in my attic studio. I was immediately blown away. His voice was incredible. I'd never stood next to someone who could sing like that. The combination of my psychedelic, retro, keyboard-led space pop and his perfect classical-opera vocal style was breathtaking. On the first session, I recorded several tracks of him singing along to my tunes. Some of his vocals, I chopped up and created samples to use in various songs. On other tracks, we'd duet, or he'd take on the lead vocal. To this day, I reckon my collaborations with him are some of the best work I've ever done.

Alf started coming to my house regularly. He didn't have a car, so he'd jump on the train to Rochdale, I'd pick him up in the VW and, when we'd finished recording, I'd drive him back home to Fleetwood. We'd often work with the roof windows wide open to allow the heat to escape. The house was in a tightly knit cul-de-sac surrounded by a couple of dozen other houses, so the whole neighbourhood could hear whatever I was working on. I'd be in the local supermarket the next day, and one of my neighbours would ask, 'Was that bongos I could hear last night, Clint?'

'Yeah, man!'

'Did you have a bloody opera singer up yer ladder yesterday, mate?'

'Oh yes!'

These were some of the first recordings of Alf's voice. I later released two albums that featured us working together.

One weekday afternoon at our house, in between recording, we were dancing around the living room to Elvis records. We were both really into Elvis. We were trying to breakdance, and I managed to break two ribs. Alf eventually got accepted into the Royal College of Music in London and I drove him down and helped him move into his flat. Alf did go on to become a huge superstar: Alfie Boe, an opera singer who is famous, even now, for loving to 'rock out'. After relocating to London, his bookings became more lucrative and higher profile. He went from singing at, among other things, private corporate events where rich women in expensive jewellery would swoon over him, to standing in at sound checks for The Three Tenors.

When I eventually got my new band The Clint Boon Experience! (aka the CBX!) together, I got in touch with Alf and asked if he'd like to do some gigs with us.

'I'd love to, mate! You know me, I've always wanted to be a rock star!'

I'd introduce him on stage part way through the gig. I christened him 'Opera Dude'. He wore full evening suit: white shirt, bow tie and big wraparound sunglasses. He'd do two or three songs with us then leave the stage. He totally brought the house down every single night. Even then it was obvious Alf would go on to bigger things. As he was catapulted towards worldwide success, we somehow lost touch, as you do. Occasionally, I'd chat to him on the phone or online for radio or podcast-based interviews. I never forgot about his infectious spirt and personality, though, and his huge talent, obviously. One of the many highlights of Alfie's career so far was when he sung on the roof of Buckingham Palace for the Queen's Diamond Jubilee in June 2012. I watched that performance and couldn't have been more chuffed for him – so proud of my old mate.

We've recently reconnected. In 2024 we met up for drinks in the Midland Hotel in Manchester. It was the first time we'd seen each other in 23 years, but it felt like only a couple of weeks had passed since our last gigs. The man hasn't changed one bit. He's still a diamond. As with Noel, Liam, Bonehead and Mani, it's such a beautiful thing to see these people remain true to their roots. Despite the wealth, the success, the fame – the big ups and massive downs – they are still decent human beings. Still men of the people.

Me and Alfie have also promised to make music together again.

63/ Changing Landscapes

The morning of Saturday 15 June, 1996, started like any other Manchester morning. It was a sunny day, in the middle of the Euro '96 football tournament, and England were due to play Scotland that afternoon at Wembley. There was a buzz around the England team that they might finally win something. I had a bit of running around to do that day, including nipping into Manchester city centre to pick up some free clothes from my mate Karl Campbell on Oldham Street. Karl had been our contact at Joe Blogg's back in the late eighties when he transformed us into a walking advertisement for the baggy generation's favourite clothing brand. On one of the Inspirals' early trips to Paris, we'd managed to abandon him at the hotel the morning after the gig when he overslept. He woke up to find his jeans were up on the roof and his passport was (inadvertently) back in Manchester with us.

I thought the Inspirals' re-release of 'Joe' was going to be featured on *The Chart Show* that day, so I set the video to record before I set off into the city. The first sign I noticed that something was wrong came as I was driving down Oldham Road and, as I got nearer to Manchester, there were more and more people walking or running away from the city centre. I couldn't work out what had happened. This sea of people escaping from something. Then I noticed the smoke. The IRA had detonated a bomb inside a truck on Corporation Street, between the Arndale and Marks & Spencer.

But that Saturday morning, not knowing the full extent of what had happened, I was just focused on getting my free gear. The whole city centre was cordoned off. Determined to get my swag, I dumped the car, sneaked past the police cordons and made my way to Karl's place on the corner of Oldham Street and Hilton Street. He was sat in the office, feet on the desk, smiling, having a brew. I got my gear and got out of town. Unbeknown to me, Shaun

Ryder was evading police cordons on the other side of town, also determined to get his gear, although a different type of gear to me. Me and Shaun were both on the blag at the same time. I was trying to get some free clobber; Shaun was trying to score some drugs.

By this time, Craig, the Inspirals' drummer, was a DJ at the Haçienda, at their indie night Stone Love. He was also in town that Saturday morning and ended up in Dry bar with Bobby Langley and Jon Drape from the Haç. There's a photograph of the three of them sat at the bar, in shock at what's just happened. When I got home, the videotape I'd put in to record *The Chart Show* had recorded the transmission of 'Joe', a new TV ad for the world's first ever in-car CD player, which featured our track 'I Want You', and a special lunchtime news broadcast about the events in Manchester. As I sat down and watched it, the enormity of what had happened began to sink in. We found out it was the biggest bomb the IRA had ever detonated on the British mainland, and the largest ever peacetime bomb in Britain. The IRA had given the police a warning, so they had been able to evacuate the immediate area. Miraculously, no one was killed, but hundreds were injured and no building within half a mile was unscathed.

People often say that the regeneration of Manchester started with the IRA bomb but, as this book has hopefully helped show, the city's rebirth was already well underway, culturally. The bomb did, however, give the city centre's bricks and mortar a chance to catch up.

The musical landscape of Manchester was changing too. The Mondays and the Inspirals had already split, and the Roses future was also now looking thorny. Reni had already left the year before, and then John Squire went in the spring of '96. After being forced to pull out of 1995's Glastonbury festival, the Roses had been booked to headline the 1996 Reading Festival on the Sunday evening, and I decided to go down to show some support. I drove down to Reading with Meg and the kids on the morning of the Roses gig. We were going to drive back home right after their set. Mani had put us on his guestlist. Even though John and Reni had left the band, there was still some of that magical vibe surrounding them, and there was a real sense of occasion when they arrived backstage in the afternoon. Mani, as always, was bouncing with enthusiasm, like a Manc Tigger. He came straight over to give me hugs when he saw me. Ian was dressed completely in purple and had the aura of a boxer who knew he was about to become the undisputed world champion. The atmosphere in the backstage VIP area was as celebratory as any I'd felt at previous Roses gigs. It felt like half of Manchester had come along as a show of support for the Roses.

Unfortunately, due to some technical issues to do with onstage monitoring, Ian's singing that night was way off key. From the very start of the set, it was an uncomfortable thing to be part of. People started leaving the site only three or four songs into the set, friends and supporters of the band included. The musicians among us knew exactly what the problem was. If you can't hear your voice coming back at you on stage, you've got no chance. You're dead in the water. It's something you'll only ever understand or experience when you're on stage singing in a large venue – and this was happening in front of 50,000 people. And the music press. The vultures had been circling since the release of the second album and the line-up changes. The Roses' Reading gig provided all the ammunition that their detractors needed. It was all over. Within weeks, they announced they were splitting up. Ian released a statement to the press, which read: 'Having spent the last ten years in the filthiest business in the universe, it's a pleasure to announce the end of The Stone Roses. May God bless all who gave us their love and supported us throughout this time. Special thanks to the people of Manchester who sent us on our way. Peace be upon you.'

Although the Roses weren't the band they once were after Reni and John had left, it was still a sad day. It also meant that the three leading lights of the Madchester scene – the Roses, the Mondays and the Inspirals – were no more. Having at one point reached such amazing heights, all three had seemingly flown too close to the sun – and had now come back down to Earth with a crash.

I spoke to Mani on the phone the day the news about the split broke. He was on his way to London: 'Clint, I've just got to sort some shit out with the lawyers, then I'm back up north and we'll get t'Mill back together! Pan pipes of the Andes!' It was a year since the Inspirals had split, so I was well up for it – it was exactly what I needed to hear.

However, on that visit to London, Mani bumped into Primal Scream frontman, Bobby Gillespie, who made him an offer he couldn't refuse. Within a week, Mani was announced as the Primals' new bass player. The next chapter in the career of Gary Mounfield had started, and it wasn't with t'Mill. I couldn't have been more pleased for my mate, though. Mani took the Scream to a new level. Bobby himself was very vocal about the new lease of life Mani's presence brought to the band. He'd gone from playing bass in one of the most important bands of all time to playing bass in another one of the most important bands of all time. T'Mill could wait.

64/
Boon Army

In early 1996 I was contacted by a guy called Pete Darnborough. He was based at Red Tape Studios in Sheffield and, on a trip to Manchester, a mutual friend had mentioned that I was making music again. Pete was an A&R scout, so he asked for my number. We chatted on the phone, and I sent him my new tunes. He liked what he heard, we got on, and he said he'd like to help me find a record deal. I drove over the Snake Pass to Sheffield one day because he had managed to secure me some free recording time in Red Tape Studios. It was a great opportunity to record some of my new music in a professional studio. During a break in the session, we went to the local pub, the Rutland Arms, behind Red Tape, where everybody working in the studios would go for a break or a celebration. As we approached the pub, we heard this massive explosion of laughter from inside, then the door flew open and a very pissed man with bleached hair stumbled out onto the street, like a scene from a cowboy film. After a few seconds, we realised it was Robbie Williams. It was in the period after he'd left Take That and just before his solo career took off. He spotted me and immediately shouted, 'Clint Boon, you legend!' and gave me a big hug before scurrying off down the street. It turned out he was working in Red Tape as well, with Eliot Kennedy, a Sheffield-based producer and songwriter who had worked with everyone from the Spice Girls to Celine Dion. Like myself, Robbie wasn't enjoying the best point of his career right then, and it was hard to imagine him ever regaining any of his previous success. My heart went out to him. Like many other characters in my journey, it's been a joy to witness the breathtaking success he went on to enjoy.

As with Pete Felstead and the Inspiral Carpets a few years earlier, Pete Darnborough did his best to help me find a record deal, but it still felt like it wasn't my time yet. I was writing what I thought were the best songs I'd ever written, but even though most industry people hearing them had only positive things to say, nobody seemed in a rush to offer me a deal. I was sending demo tapes off to everyone I knew. I sent one to Osman Eralp, a successful New York-based music executive, and someone we'd dealt with when we were signed to Mute. I'd always got on well with him. He'd grown up as part of the Atlantic Records family and, as a kid, had been present in the studio when the likes of the Rolling Stones and Aretha Franklin were recording. He was now head of A&R for A&M Records, so I sent him a demo thinking he might throw me a bone.

I got a reply within days along the lines of 'Clint, I hated the tape, much as I like and respect you! Best of luck . . .' – which took the wind out of my sails and just seemed to emphasise the reality of my situation.

After months of travelling to London for meetings, on a weekly basis, me and Pete realised we were pissing into the wind and agreed that, even though we'd become very close friends, our appeal as a music-industry double act was probably making the label executives think less about Elvis and Colonel Tom Parker and more about the Chuckle Brothers. We parted ways in a business sense, but our friendship continued.

Because I'd kept in touch with various people at Granada TV, I was getting regular requests to submit theme-tune ideas – some for the main terrestrial channel, some for their new digital channel, the more adult-focused 'Men and Motors'. Most of my tunes were being accepted and broadcast. It was bringing me some much-needed revenue. One afternoon in early '96, after dropping my latest batch of tapes off, I bumped into Caroline Aherne and her comedy-writing partner Craig Cash* in the bar at Granada, and we sat down for a drink. I first had the pleasure of getting to know Caroline back in the early nineties, when she was a fixture on the Manchester comedy scene. One of her first outings as 'Mrs Merton' was on a promo trip to Ireland with me, Graham and local musician turned TV presenter John Bramwell. Back then John fronted a band called the Ignition, who'd released a mind-bendingly

* They must have been working on *The Royle Family* at the time, which was first broadcast in 1998.

gorgeous single called 'Black and Blue' that was getting a lot of plays on Manchester's specialist music shows. We'd flown from Manchester Airport, spent a few hours filming around Dublin, then flown back to Manchester. Caroline had stayed in character for the entire day. It was lovely to see her again in the Granada bar, and she kindly asked me how the theme-tune writing was going. I told her it was going well, and I was enjoying doing something a bit different. She asked how many I'd written so far. I said, 'About 15 or 20, but I've written loads more . . . I've got theme tunes comin' out of my arse, Caroline!' Quick as anything, Caroline said, 'Well, to be honest, Clint, some of those theme tunes you've done *do* actually sound like they've come out of your arse!'

Thankfully, not everyone agreed with Caroline's judgement, as shortly after that, courtesy of another Caroline, I was offered a lifesaving solo publishing deal by BMG for my new music. Caroline Elleray had introduced me to her boss, Ian Ramage, who was a big fan of the Inspirals and loved the new music I was making. It wasn't a massive deal financially, but it would give me enough money to upgrade my home studio.

At this point, including outstanding tax, legal fees, bank overdrafts and other debts, I found myself owing around £50k. On top of that, I still had a large mortgage, was still in danger of going bankrupt and had fuck all in the bank. As a songwriter, you need to avoid bankruptcy at all costs. I mean, everyone wants to avoid bankruptcy, obviously, but it's even more important as a songwriter. If you're a songwriter and you go bankrupt you stand to lose all the publishing rights to your back catalogue as they are considered an asset, which means you're losing any future revenue from your songs. Through some delicate negotiation, I managed to avoid bankruptcy and, thanks to BMG advancing me £10,000, I did an Individual Voluntary Agreement (IVA), which meant I had to hand over £10,000 to my creditors, rather than the £50,000 in total that I owed. I arranged to pay monthly payments, which made things a lot easier, but, importantly, it meant I didn't need to go bankrupt and got to keep my songwriting copyrights and start again with a financial clean slate.

*

After I secured the BMG publishing deal, I set about putting a new band together. I had enough songs written, and I had a clear idea in my head about what the band would feel like. I wanted to make it more 'unbridled' than the Inspirals and toyed with the idea of going down more of a 'cabaret' route. It was time to find my new bandmates.

As part of the Start '95 scheme I'd created with Oldham Council, I had a regular unsigned-bands night at the Grey Horse, the same venue where me and Spud had run our Back Trip Time Zones club night a decade earlier. I was taking a back trip thru Clint Boon time zones already gone, to get to the Boon times ahead. Sometimes you've got to go backwards to go forwards. For my new unsigned-bands night, I painted a tin bucket gold, and local bands would drop their demo tapes in there. I called the event 'Get Yer Tapes Out!' I'd randomly pick a tape out, put it in the cassette player and me and whoever the guest was (I'd rope in old friends like Mani or Janice Long) would comment on it and offer advice. There was still a healthy local scene, including bands like The High Society and Mantraluna, and it was through this scene that I started to put together the band that became The Clint Boon Experience! – a fantastic line-up of exceptional musicians, including Richard 'Stubbsy' Stubbs on bass and backing vocals, his sister Kathryn (Sista-Stubbs) on trumpet, keyboards and backing vocals, Matt Hayden on guitar, and Tony Thompson on drums.

Stubbsy became my right-hand man throughout my CBX! years, and the rest of the CBX! tech crew consisted of a bunch of his mates: Danny Saville, Carl Chadwick and Steven 'Oakesy' Oakes. The whole team, except me, Tony and Matt, were still in their teens. Another brilliant local musician, Hollin Jones, guested on keyboards on a couple of recordings but never played live with us. Front-of-house sound and lights were sorted courtesy of Graham Smith from Sheffield and Tim 'Lampy' Harrison from Oldham respectively. Recording engineer Christophe Bride helped me to develop my home-studio recordings into full-blown 'radio-ready' tracks during several sessions at the Cutting Rooms recording studio in Crumpsall, Manchester. Here we added real drums and re-recorded some of my vocals. I made another close friend around this time when I met a chap called David 'Harry' Verth, who joined us as a roadie and occasional driver. 'H' was just four days older than me and we were like brothers. Like several other people in this story, he was taken from us way too soon.

At some point, I picked up a new manager called Spike, a portly chap from Liverpool with a big laugh and a big heart. One afternoon, on his first visit to my house in Milnrow, Spike asked where the bathroom was. I pointed it out to him and off he went. About a minute later, he popped his head around the living room door and, in his thick scouse accent said, 'Er, Clint. 'Ave ye got sumthin' I can read while I take a dump?'

Getting the new band together was an exciting time for me. After a few weeks of searching and getting people's recommendations, I had everyone in place. It was impossible to hold band rehearsals at home, so I was desperate to find a new base. I knew exactly what I needed. I needed another mill!

The band I assembled to finish the two albums I made and take the music out on the road were a bunch of good people and fantastic musicians. It's fair to say that, musically, their skills completely outshone mine.

The Clint Boon Experience! were one of the first bands to realise the importance of the internet and e-mail mailing lists. With the help of Oakesy, who was studying IT at university, we became one of the earliest bands to have an all-singing, all-dancing website, with such essential content as a fan-forum discussion page, a 'cut out and keep' Farfisa, and an interactive game where you could shoot the Spice Girls with tanks.

On one of our road trips with the CBX! Oakesy mentioned that while still at school he was made, very reluctantly, to play the tuba in the school orchestra. The next day, I acquired a tuba and, from then on, Oakesy would join us on stage to do a tuba solo during the song 'Me, I'm Just a Girl', while I'd pour a pint of lager into the tuba. I christened him 'Tuba Kid'. When Alf was no longer available to do the Opera Dude thing, I brought in another opera singer to do gigs with us, a soprano called Sara Cluderay. She became 'Opera Chick'.

It was quite a colourful stage show, to say the least. Our props included a life-size plywood cutout of me from an Inspirals' photoshoot, and the reindeer's head that had hung on my mum and dad's lounge wall when we lived over the shop, mounted on the front of my Farfisa. And lots of fairy lights. It was very much the 'cabaret' band I'd had in mind when I set about putting it all together. We had some amazing times and made memories that will stay with me for ever.

There's something quite unique about life in a band and everything that comes with it – creating the songs, making the records, touring, meeting the fans; it's all fabulous and it's everything I ever wanted – but the best bit, to me, is the camaraderie. You find your people and you set off on your trip together.

65/ Elbow Room

Alfie Boe wasn't the only incredible voice I had up the ladder in my attic. One day in 1997 I helped two fully grown blokes, one after the other, up into the airing cupboard then up the ladder into the studio. I followed them up and opened the windows in the roof to let the breeze in. This could be a hot one.

In the loft, I fired the equipment up and loaded up the backing track. The singer stepped up to the microphone and put on the headphones. I pressed the 'PLAY' and 'RECORD' buttons simultaneously.

He started to sing. *'I'll be the corpse in your bathtub . . .'*

'Bloody 'ell mate! That's a dodgy lyric!' I thought to myself. 'They'll struggle to get anywhere with lyrics like that!'

I'd been helping several local bands from Oldham, including Mantraluna, who were equal parts the Verve and mid-period Rolling Stones. I was producing quite a lot of recordings of them for no cost. I just believed they had the potential to be huge and wanted to help them on their way. Meg took on some of their management duties and was helping them get gigs around Manchester and beyond. One day I got a call from a lad called Phil Chadwick. He explained he'd first met me nearly ten years earlier when we mixed our debut album *Life* at Square One Studios in Bury. He'd been the tea boy there.

'Were we nice to you?' I asked.

'It was a bit weird at times. There always seemed to be at least one of you showing your arse or your balls,' he replied.

Being a tea boy back then didn't just mean brewing up for the visiting recording artists and producers. The job description also included such menial tasks as writing down all the settings on the mixing desk when the mix was finished, sticking a new VHS videotape into the video player in the lounge when the band couldn't be arsed to get up, going to the shop whenever the band got the munchies, and laughing at all the band's shit jokes. Phil told me he was now managing a band.

'What are they called?' I asked.

'Elbow.'

'That's a funny name! Are they any good?'

'Yeah, they're all right. They used to be called Soft. I was wondering if they could do any gigs, either with Mantraluna or The Clint Boon Experience!?'

Phil explained that the lads in the band had been playing together since 1990. Their 'fanbase' at the time I met Phil consisted mainly of family and friends.

I fell in love with Elbow's music from the moment I first heard it and told Phil I'd do my best to sort some supports slots. We started hanging out. We did a few gigs together and me and Phil became good friends.

As Elbow set about writing, rehearsing and gigging, Phil started to do the rounds of the record labels, mainly down in London, trying to find them a record deal. That's how it was back then. Every band's priority was to try to get a deal, get some money in the bank, and never have to do a proper job again.

Throughout the nineties, if a record company showed even the slightest bit of interest in your band, you could usually squeeze a wad of 'demo money' out of them. Anything between a few hundred quid and a few grand – usually with absolutely no obligation at all to sign a deal with the label that threw the money at you.

Phil came back home one night from London and said an A&R man at one of the labels he'd met with, Chrysalis Records, had slipped him a cheque for £750 for Elbow to record a couple of tracks. Chrysalis wanted to be the first major to hear this new Manchester band. The A&R man was leaving for an extended holiday the next day and would listen to the demos when he got back. I suggested to Phil that, rather than using the money for a couple of days in a local studio, we could record two or three songs on my recording setup. Then Elbow could use the £750 to buy the Portastudio they fancied to help with their writing and demoing. Hopefully, they'd also bag themselves a deal with Chrysalis in the process.

When I signed my publishing deal with BMG in 1996, I bought some new equipment for my studio. Some of the gear I bought was 'state of the art', especially the two Akai DR16s that sat at the heart of the setup: 16-track digital machines that gave people like me limitless scope to achieve all our multitrack dreams. Chaining two together in a small loft space at the top of a rickety ladder wasn't very common.

I'd recorded quite a lot of Clint Boon Experience! material at home and knew the quality was almost as good as some of the stuff the pro studios were putting out. Because my studio was too small to get a full drum kit in, we'd arranged to record Elbow's drums and bass at the Roadhouse in Manchester one afternoon. Most of the Elbow lads worked, or had worked, behind the bar at the Roadhouse, and the owner, Kate Mountain, had given them total access to use it for the recording session. We'd mic'd up the drums using the venue's microphones and recorded them and Pete's bass parts into one of my DR16s. When we'd finished recording the backing tracks we packed up and arranged to reconvene in Milnrow a few days later.

I'll never forget standing next to the young Guy Garvey in my little studio, while he belted out the two brand-new songs into the microphone. One was called 'Any Day Now', the other was called 'Newborn'.

We'd left the windows wide open, because the loft got really hot if you had more than two people up there. Imagine hearing the live sound of Guy Garvey singing the closing section of 'Newborn' emanating from underneath the roof of a small house in a little working-class town in the north of England.

We finished the recording, mixed the tracks to stereo, then Phil got busy circulating the demo.

Soon after, Elbow were offered a place on the bill at In The City, the legendary annual international music-industry convention that Anthony Wilson had set up with his partner, Yvette Livesey, in 1992. In The City was very much based in Manchester but, not long after Elbow's appearance, they were invited to play at a Best of In The City event in London. That night, an A&R person from Island Records was in the audience and signed them on the spot. The Chrysalis A&R chap must have been proper pissed off when he got back from his hols.

Partly by way of celebration, but also as a way of cracking on with creating their first album, Elbow decided to decamp to a quiet little village in France to get on with writing and demoing their debut album. Pete's parents had a villa down there. I hired a big black Mercedes Benz splitter bus (R884 RHL) from a company in Sheffield to drive the band and Phil out to France. The bus was gorgeous, inside and out – plush leather interior, blacked-out windows, a full electronic entertainment system – and a dream to drive.

The evening we set off for France started with a party at Bar Centro on Tib Street in Manchester for all the band's families, friends and people who had helped them along the way. At the end of the party, we all clambered into the splitter and headed off towards the M6. We made it to the end of Portland Street when someone in the back shouted, 'KFC's still open! Clint, pull over!'

We all jumped out and ordered our various fried chicken parts. As we sat eating, people who'd been at the Bar Centro send-off started to arrive at the KFC: a hungry flock of drunken disciples who were delighted to come across our unplanned late-night Manc supper. Before too long, we were enjoying our second party of the night. The cheering, the clapping and the roars of delight as we drove away from the KFC were louder and more hysterical than those on Tib Street an hour earlier.

I don't mind admitting that, as I'd stood there in my attic next to Guy on that day in 1997, the veins in his neck standing out as he belted out those amazing vocals, I didn't know where this would lead. I knew I loved the band. I knew they had a growing number of followers who loved the band, but I don't think any of us could have guessed what was coming next. As far as I knew, no one in the country was making this kind of music, and sometimes that makes something much harder to sell. There was no particular scene that this sound could be attached to. They had an almost progressive approach to their music, which bands hadn't done for years, maybe since Talk Talk back in the eighties, Pink Floyd and Genesis in the seventies – bands that weren't afraid of having huge swathes of silence around their lovingly crafted sounds and verse. Progressive music, quite simply, was not in demand in 1997; Britpop was still the most dominating force in the UK's music industry. What did happen, I believe, is that, over time, people's tastes changed. The music consumers of the UK started to want something more substantial. Maybe as a reaction against the sometimes shallow, laddish elements of the Britpop thing we'd been going through. Maybe people wanted something a bit more cerebral and challenging. Elsewhere, at the same time, Radiohead were doing a magnificent job of educating the masses on how a guitar band could evolve into a more abstract and cultured entity and still have hit singles.

Elbow recorded their debut album with producer Steve Osbourne but, before a single note of it was released, Island was taken over by Universal Records, who promptly dropped Elbow and a bunch of other Island artists. But within what seemed like a few days, Phil, the ultimate maverick, had set up another record deal, this time with the new V2 record label. And with a label that understood what this band were all about, Elbow found themselves perfectly poised to become that new band that everyone wanted but, as yet, no one knew they wanted. Eventually, they would record new versions of the two songs we'd demoed in Milnrow and release them first on their own Soft Records label, and then on Ugly Man Records, a small but much-loved Manchester-based record label owned by a chap called Guy Lovelady.

When Elbow's debut album *Asleep in the Back* was released in May 2001, the reception was incredible. It was nominated for a Brit Award and the Mercury Music Prize. They've gone on to become one of the most successful and enduring British bands of recent times, selling out arenas and headlining festivals. As people, they've never changed – they're still the same affectionate, cuddly, funny blokes from Bury. I used to greet them with big hugs and cat-like licks to their faces. Particularly Guy and Pete. I've stopped licking their faces in recent years. Partly because, they started getting a bit beardy and, at times, mainly after gigs, salty-tasting, but also, I think they found it all a bit weird. Oh, and there was the small matter of a worldwide pandemic. But Elbow: what a band. Long may they serenade us with majestic music.

I seem to have spent a big part of my life helping musicians get on the ladder to success. It's only in writing this that I've realised that, at times, an actual ladder was involved in my charitable efforts. Elbow went on to win the Mercury Music Prize in 2008, for their album *The Seldom Seen Kid*. Guy tells a great story about how he was brought down to Earth after partying in London following that awards ceremony. The next day, the band were all over the press. After Guy got off the train back in Manchester, he was crossing the road when a taxi driver beeped his horn and affectionately shouted, 'Elbow! Get a proper fucking job!'

Towards the winter of 1997 it felt like good things were starting to happen. I'd done the IVA thing, but money was still too tight to mention, and my bank manager was still being a pest. But I could see some glimmers of light breaking through. BMG were picking up the bill for the CBX!'s rehearsal room in the Orme Mill in Oldham, which was only 50 quid a week but helped things along. My old mate and legendary broadcaster Mike Sweeney got in touch and told me about a new TV show he was going to be hosting for Granada. It was a music-based quiz show with Mike as the quizmaster and Slade frontman Noddy Holder as one of the team captains. He asked if I'd like to be the other team captain. I jumped at the opportunity. The show was called *Elvis Has Just Left the Building*, and it got great reviews as well as bringing a bit more money into the Boon house. The theme-tune work was still coming in and Meg's parents were still helping us financially, but I'd stopped signing on by now as things were starting to pick up.

Then, one afternoon in October, another piece of good news came my way, when I got a call from Shed Seven drummer Alan Leach. The Sheds had supported the Inspirals on a run of shows in the spring of '94. We'd got on brilliantly and had some funny times together and made sure to keep in touch when the tour was finished. Over the next few years, the Boons, the Leaches and the Witters would be regularly jumping on the M62 to visit each other in Milnrow and York.

Alan asked if I'd like to make a guest appearance on the album they were recording down in London. They had a couple of tracks that they thought would sound great with my keys on. I genuinely think they knew I was struggling and needed a break, and I was over the moon to be asked. Partly because I loved the band, but partly because it was another sign that things were starting to pick up. I drove to Olympic Studios in Barnes, where Stephen Street was producing the album. I played keyboards on two tracks, 'She left Me on Friday' and 'Devil in Your Shoes', that both ended up on the Sheds' third album *Let it Ride*. 'She Left me on Friday' was released as a single on 2 March 1998 and entered the singles chart at number 11. Alan was back on the phone: 'Clint, fancy doing *Top of the Pops* with us?'

'Fuckin' too right I do, brother!'

66/
Sweet and Tender Hooligans

In the summer of 1998 I was approached to DJ at a cool new science-fiction-themed bar in Manchester called the Fab Café. It was a bizarre place, and although I didn't know it when I first walked in, past the full-size Dalek, it would play an important part in reigniting my DJ career over the next 20 years. It would also be the place in which a whole new chapter of my life was about to begin. When I first started DJing there, every Wednesday night, I think I got 30 quid a night and free beer, but, over time, as the night got more popular, they increased my fee until I was getting paid a sizeable chunk. It was another much-needed regular income stream for me.

At the time, the bar was home not only to a full-size Dalek and a giant Ice Warrior (the classic scaly *Dr Who* enemy), there were also display cabinets stacked full of all sorts of science-fiction and cult-television memorabilia. Fab was home to all sorts of misfits, nerds, punks and dropouts who couldn't get into (or didn't want to get into) the other bars in the city centre. It was Manchester's answer to the Cantina Bar in *Star Wars*, which might be why people like me always felt very much at home there. It became a tradition for many punters to give the Ice Warrior a punch in his ugly reptilian mush on the way out.

Fab Café was owned by a chap called Mike Royce, and twin brothers Steve and Paul Petricco, who had made a small fortune from their security and fire alarm business. That had been their day job, but they loved science fiction, and they loved celebrities, so decided to open the sci-fi-themed bar where, as well as guest DJs, they would also book evenings with people like Gerry Anderson, Warren Mitchell or Richard O'Brien. I was there for the Warren Mitchell night, and it was eye-opening, not what I expected at all. I only knew him as the actor who played Alf Garnett, the iconic but morally flawed fictional character on the famous TV comedy show *Till Death Us Do Part*. When he started talking, it became clear he'd had a fascinating life, coming from a Jewish family who had troubling stories about surviving the Holocaust. He had the whole place hanging on his every word. Another actor, David Soul, did an 'evening with' talk one night to another full house. He was still in Manchester the following night and popped back into Fab for a drink. Obviously, to anyone of my generation, it was a huge thing to meet one of *Starsky & Hutch*. I was DJing and he was sat at the bar, having a drink and enjoying the music, when this girl came up to talk to him and get his autograph. The girl's boyfriend, still sat at a table, got jealous, stood up, came over to the bar and started giving David Soul a load of earache. David tried to wave him away, but the lad kept getting in his face, so the actor just punched him once in the face and knocked him clean out, without even getting up off his stool. He then just turned back around, carried on drinking and listening to the music. I reached for my album of TV theme tunes and played the theme from *Starsky & Hutch*. When Richard O'Brien was booked to do a Q&A at the Fab, the Petricco twins weren't around to look after him through the day, so they asked me if I'd entertain him. I met up with him at the Fab and had a quick drink before heading out to show him Manchester. I spent the afternoon walking side by side and chatting with the guy that created *The Rocky Horror Show*.

Andy Rourke from The Smiths was another of the guest DJs at Fab, and we got on well and started hanging out together. I was getting offered more and more DJ work, and me and Andy started going out as a bit of a double act, DJing together in clubs all over the country, sharing our rock 'n' roll memories along the way. He was living in a first-floor flat in the middle of Chorlton-cum-Hardy at the time. His front-room window looked out over the traffic lights where Wilbraham Road crosses Barlow Moor Road. I'd recently bought a cool second-hand black Saab 9-3 (R663 VOK) for £4,500. I'd pick Andy up in it, and we'd head off on our travels. Andy loved David Bowie and we'd spend many of our journeys listening to Bowie's classic albums. On one occasion, I put a CD on in the car, and said, 'Here you go, Andy. I'll play you my favourite Smiths track.'

I put 'Half a Person' on.

'No way! That's my favourite Smiths track too!'

I also got to know Mike Joyce from The Smiths around this time, in bars and clubs or at the occasional music-industry event. He always had a big smile on his face and time for everybody. I went in the Night & Day Café on Oldham Street one evening and Mike and Bonehead were in a heap near the door completely battered. They were close back then and, like many of us, would often be out and about DJing together around the country and getting up to all sorts of mischief. 'Fucking hell!' I said. 'Look at the state of you two!'

Bonehead laughed, *'CLIIINT!! HOW ARE YA!!!'*

It's fair to say that Mike and Andy were two of the biggest Smiths fans in the world. Even years after the band split, and even through the legal disputes between the band members, they'd talk about those times with nothing but affection. They just never stopped loving their band. The three of us were chatting one day, a few years later, and Mike said, 'People who say, "Oooh! *Strangeways**, that's when it all started falling apart!" well, they don't know what they're on about. From the moment we met until the moment we split up, musically and friendship-wise it was an incredibly binding time. We'd be in the barn rehearsing, then we'd be in the studio, then we'd be out on tour, then we'd be on another plane. We were together constantly; it was an absolutely fantastic time. I've got nothing bitter to say about The Smiths.'

'Do you ever wake up in the mornin' and think, "Fuckin' 'ell, I'm a Smith!"?' I asked Mike.

'Absolutely!' Mike said. 'One of the great things for me was the unique view I had from the drum stool. I got to see this amazing band and the audience. One of the unusual things I noticed was that where, normally, the band's drummer would lock in with the bass player, I'd usually be watching Johnny and bouncing off him because, a lot of the time, the way Andy played was very much a melody on top of everything else that was going on.'

I once asked Andy and Mike what Sandie Shaw was like to work with when they recorded the alternative version of their 'Hand in Glove' single with her.

* *Strangeways, Here We Come,* was The Smiths' final studio album, released in September 1987.

'When we did *Top of the Pops,* she was dancing like a mum at a wedding. Rollin' about on the floor 'n' all that!' said Mike.

'She's a nutter!' said Andy.

Over the years, I got to know Johnny Marr too, and he's just the most generous bloke you could wish to meet. I met up with him one morning to get some stuff signed for a charity auction. I happened to mention that I was going to be spending a few hours that afternoon selling *The Big Issue* in Manchester city centre as part of an event to raise awareness of the homeless and their challenges. Later that day, Johnny came and found me outside Marks & Spencer's, bought a copy off me, and started helping me to sell them: 'Thought I'd come into town and support you!' Which just about sums up Johnny.

When I was working as a radio presenter for XFM Manchester, Mike Walsh, our head of music, asked if I'd like to interview Morrissey the night before his forthcoming headline slot at the V Festival in Staffordshire.

'Absolutely! I'd love to!' He was the only Smith I'd never met. (Apart from the time Graham tells me he stood with us watching James from the side of the stage at the Free Trade Hall in 1989.) My interview with Morrissey was set to take place at the Lowry Hotel in Manchester the night before his Saturday-night gig in Staffordshire. On the Friday afternoon, as I was getting ready to go and do the interview, we got a call saying there'd been a change of plan and Morrissey would now be doing all his interviews onsite at the festival on the Saturday afternoon. I explained to the XFM team that I couldn't do the Saturday as I had a big DJ gig down south that I needed to get to so instead, we arranged for our head of news, Sunta Templeton, to go along in my place.

Fast forward a couple of years: Morrissey announces another UK tour, which includes a Manchester date. 'Get Morrissey's people on the phone and tell them I want to interview him!' I told my producer, Kate Cocker. The reply from the Moz camp came quickly, explaining that Morrissey didn't want to speak to me because of the time I stood him up in Staffordshire. I wouldn't have had him down as one who bears a grudge. It's gruesome that someone so handsome should even care.

67/
Arthur Baker

In 1999 I took part in the *NME* 's Annual Pub Challenge. It was held at the Elbow Room in Islington, London. In attendance were a selection of the *NME* 's favourite bands, singers and general celebs, including myself, Bez, Manchester band Alfie and a few others. Alfie had a charming and very good-looking frontman in Lee Gorton and were signed to Badly Drawn Boy and Andy Votel's uber-cool Manchester label Twisted Nerve. Along with Elbow, I Am Kloot and Doves, Alfie were part of an exciting new wave of Manchester bands at the turn of the millennium.

NME get-togethers were usually just an excuse to get musicians like us drunk, record it all and, hopefully, sell a few extra copies on the strength of the controversial things we might say or do. On this occasion, for once, I kept things together and generally didn't make too much of a dick of myself. Which I was glad of, when I got to meet one of my all-time heroes that night, courtesy of Bez, who came over to me at one point and said, 'Clint, have you ever met Joe Strummer?'

'No, but I'd love to!'

'He's over here. C'mon, I'll introduce you.' Bez walked me to the other end of the room, and there was Joe Strummer. Bez introduced us, Joe shook my hand, looked me in the eyes and just said, 'Boon Army!' in his unmistakable rasp. We chatted for a few minutes, mainly about our kids. It was obvious he was a very devoted dad. I don't think we even touched on music.

I also got to meet another absolute legend that night, who became a close friend over the next couple of years. He was a co-owner of the Elbow Room. He came over and introduced himself, this huge American man with a long thick beard, big smile and the scruffiest pair of moon boots I've ever seen on a man. It looked like he'd just killed a wild animal, skinned it with his bare hands and teeth, and fashioned a pair of boots from the hide and sinews. 'Hey, Clint, I'm Arthur, Arthur Baker. Great to meet you, man. I fuckin' love your band!'

We sat and had drinks, in between me occasionally being dragged off for some more *NME* pub-game activities – darts, dominoes, pool, the usual kind of thing. Arthur asked if I'd be interested in working on some of the new music he was making. He was trying to break away from just being a world-famous electro and hip-hop producer and wanted to work on more 'indie'-type collaborations. Arthur Baker was a legend. He'd been present at the birth of hip-hop as we now know it. At the time, it wasn't even called hip-hop, it was just a bunch of kids in the Bronx with two turntables and a microphone. Arthur explained to me how, back in the late 1970s, he'd go to underground parties in the Bronx where kids would be making these incredible new sounds. 'There'd be all these amazing beats going on and some guy just talking into a microphone over the whole thing, man!'

He set up home in New York in 1981, moving everything he owned from his native Boston, where he'd become well known as a DJ and producer. Soon, he was totally immersed in New York's underground music community. Arthur is credited (along with his musical partner back then, Afrika Bambaataa) as making the first ever electro record, the seminal 'Planet Rock'. To this day, its seen as one of the most influential records of all time in the way it helped stylise and define what became electro, hip-hop and electronic dance music. Arthur also went on to work with the likes of Bob Dylan, Al Green and New Order. He was a bit of a mythical legend to us in Manchester, because we'd all heard the tales of New Order's trips to New York, and how Arthur taking them to clubs like Danceteria and the Fun House had inspired them to build the Haçienda. Arthur had played a part in kickstarting the whole cultural revolution of Manchester, even though he'd never been there at that point, because his then heavy cocaine habit meant he was scared of flying, so he rarely left America. Now, this New York legend was asking *me* if I'd like to collaborate with him!

'Er, hang on, mate, I'll just check my diary!' the little voice in my head joked. 'Of course I want to work with you, you massive legend. Despite your weird fuckin' yeti boots!'

Within a few days, I was loading my Vox Continental into my car ready for a trip down to London to work with Arthur. I arrived at his house in Camden, which was an unusual and very futuristic pad overlooking the Regent's Canal. I parked up in the underground car park and lugged my overnight bag and the Vox up to Arthur's place. He greeted me at his front door, standing tall in his trademark boots.

That night I recorded the organ and vocals for an instrumental tune Arthur had put together. He'd already produced a full backing track and it had the working title 'She Likes Noise'. Mani played bass on the track and Charlotte Hatherley from the band Ash had done some guitar. I'd written some lyrics that I felt worked, and we recorded a couple of vocal takes. The track was raucous and had a great energy. It was like nothing Arthur had put his name to before. I felt honoured to be part of the moment. Arthur was also working on another track, called 'Real Fuckin' Noise', which I put a Vox organ part on. Where 'She Likes Noise' was pure punk, 'Real Fuckin' Noise' had more of a big-beat vibe.

We started getting together on most of my London trips. We'd go out for food and drinks and, occasionally, to see bands playing. I'd stay at his place. He eventually gave me my own key so I could let myself in and out when he wasn't around. The house was one of a dozen or so laid out in a terrace fashion at the back of Camden Sainsbury's. From the canal, the homes looked like a line of robots, all gleaming steel, aluminium and smoked glass. The interior was bathed in daylight, with floor-to-ceiling windows and electronically controlled blinds that provided darkness or privacy when needed. Most of the place was open plan with a mezzanine level built directly above the kitchen, which is where Arthur had set up his studio. The legendary French-Swiss architect Le Corbusier once said, 'A house is a machine for living in.' That couldn't have been more appropriate for Arthur's pad. The home even came with its own instruction manual, a massive document to guide occupants through the technicalities of every aspect of life in the machine.

Sometimes when Arthur was away, I'd arrive to find a Post-it note on the fridge: 'Bro, help yourself to whatever's in here. Gone to Florida, might be back next week, AB.' When he was home, he'd be up at six or seven in the morning working in his studio on the mezzanine, knocking out his own brand of 'Really Fucking in Your Face Future Techno, MAN!!', or however he'd described it to me the night we'd met in the Elbow Rooms. Part of me felt privileged to be able to hear this true pioneer creating his art in real time, but part of me really wished he'd just fuck off back to bed so I could get a bit more sleep.

When he was working on a track, Arthur would enter a trance-like state, totally immersed in the rhythm, the bass, the sample, the ambience. There was no point shouting up to him, even in the brief moments of silence: 'Arthur! D'ya want a brew? . . . Arthur? . . . *Arthur!?*' The only way to get his attention would be to walk up there and tap him on the shoulder. More than any other individual I've ever met, Arthur was a music-making machine. There really didn't seem to be much space in his life for anything other than music. Apart from fine dining. He liked good-quality food and had recently launched his own soul-food restaurant called Harlem, which, unsurprisingly, also had its own DJ booth and dancefloor. I never went hungry when I hung out with Arthur.

As our lives changed direction, and my trips to London grew less frequent, I saw less and less of him. We've stayed in touch, and I hope we get to work together again. He's now a family man, living mainly out in Miami with his wife and daughter. The Yeti boots are long gone.

Arthur did a remix of my Clint Boon Experience! track 'Life in Transition'. The music is basically some of the stuff he was working on during all those mornings when I'd be lying in bed. He'd work his samplers, sequencers and drum machines until they were almost smoking. He sent me the backing track on a CDR through the post. I re-sung the lead vocal and asked Nicky Lockett (aka MC Tunes) to lay down some of his magical rap rhymes over it. Nicky stood there in my attic studio, wrote a stack of lyrics on the spot, and put it down in one take.

We laid down a second track of Nicky's vocal – a slightly lower tone to make it sound even more menacing. That version of 'Life in Transition' never got released, and I still consider it to be 'work in progress'. I planned on putting Alfie Boe's opera vocal (which featured on the original version) back in place but never got around to it. The remix, named 'Life in Transition: the Mission is On', will always take me back to those times. Me and Arthur Baker. A bloke I was incredibly honoured to meet, hang out and work with. An unlikely pairing if ever there was one. The king of New York electro and the organ player from Oldham.

68/ The Crash

M74 northbound, Scotland. Wednesday 28 April, 1999. I woke up feeling goosed as usual. 8.50am. Last night's CBX! gig in Derby was a stormer. Things were looking good, our luck seemed to be changing. I'd managed to offload a stack of debt I had through the IVA arrangement. Harley had just turned six and Max had just turned four. They were both blossoming and doing great at school. I heard Meg downstairs in the hallway getting them ready for school. I went down the stairs and helped the kids get their blazers and hats on. I kissed them both goodbye and told them I'd be back later that night as we'd be driving home after the Glasgow gig.

The tour bus was gorgeous: a Mercedes 'splitter', nine seats with a storage bay at the back for all the equipment. It was the same vehicle I'd hired to take Elbow to France a year earlier. In the lounge area were two TVs, a video player, a fridge, a PlayStation and a CD player. The paintwork was cool black, the engine was 2.8 litre, and it went like the proverbial shit off a shovel. I didn't mind driving the CBX! to and from gigs as I knew they were in safe hands. I didn't dick about, I stayed sober: no drugs and no speeding. Their lives were in my hands every time we set off for a gig. Spike had done some driving on this tour, including the Derby trip the day before, but he wasn't coming with us for the Scottish trip. I set off through the streets of Shaw to pick up Stubbsy and his sister Kathryn, then roadie Danny who lived around the corner, then on through Royton to pick up Tim 'Lampy' Harrison and roadie Karl Chadwick. The Manchester lads, drummer Tony and guitarist Matt, were the last ones on board, then off we went up the M6.

That night's gig was at King Tut's Wah Wah Hut in Glasgow, the seventh date on the tour. We were doing OK for time, slightly behind schedule, but everyone was upbeat because I'd told them all to expect a great reception:

'Glasgow never fails!' Danny was up front in the passenger seat, riding shotgun and enjoying the view. It was his twenty-first birthday. Behind us, some of the gang were watching *Lock, Stock and Two Smoking Barrels*, Karl was listening to Neil Young on his minidisc player, and Tim was slipping into a nice slumber.

Over the border, we stopped at Abington service station for a quick toilet break and to stock up on brews and snacks. I was feeling wide awake and unpressured. We phoned King Tut's to explain we were slightly behind schedule. 'Nah worry, man. Tek your time!'

Fifteen minutes later, at 4:35pm, we'd just passed junction 12 of the M74, a two-lane stretch of motorway. Ahead of us was hardly any traffic. We were in the outside lane passing a car on the inside lane, doing no more than 70mph. The weather was glorious, everything felt in order. On the other side of the barrier, the southbound carriageway was far busier, presumably with rush-hour traffic heading away from Glasgow.

Then there was an incongruous 'pop' from the back of the bus. I assumed it was someone popping a bag of crisps, or something. Or maybe another pile of videotapes falling on Kathryn's head. She'd not had much luck back there this week. But the bus started to sway, then swerve from side to side. I knew straight away it was a tyre problem: 'Fuck! We've got a puncture!'

I said it loud enough for Danny to hear but not those in the back. I thought I'd probably be able to control it. A second or so later, I realised we were out of control. Then a second loud bang, this time on the left side of the vehicle. Probably the passenger-side tyre exploding under the pressure. I shouted to everyone in the back to hold on tight. 'Hold on kids. I think we're goin' over!' I did my best to avoid going over the barrier into the traffic coming the other way. The rocking was intense, I knew we were going to crash but I carried on wrestling with the steering wheel, trying to steady the bus, but to no avail. We were still in the fast lane, with the busy southbound carriageway just a few feet away on the other side of a low steel barrier. I thought the longer I can hold it straight, the slower we'll be going if we roll over. I remember thinking, 'This isn't fair.' Not in a selfish way, but for all the others on board. It was obvious something grave was happening. I thought death had arrived. I tried one more time to steer the bus upright, but it just turned sharply to the left. I saw the road surface coming up towards my window. I saw Harley and Max in their school uniforms.

I waited for the first impact, convinced this was the end. In the moment, I accepted that was it. I didn't even contemplate the idea of there being any pain. I thought this would be quick death. As the driver's-side window shattered, the road surface coming at me, I let go of the steering wheel and wrapped my arms around my head. The first impact didn't kill me. We were still moving and still at some velocity. The noise of the bus screeching along the motorway on its side was sickening. The vehicle rolled completely over. Four tons of metal, music gear and people. I saw a flash of daylight and a lot of sparks. I felt intense heat on my right arm and waited for the next impact.

The second impact was even more violent than the first as the passenger side crashed down onto the road. Still rolling, we skidded down the hard shoulder backwards and hit the steep embankment rear end first, this third collision filling the cargo bay with clay, soil and foliage. The bus then flipped full length, nose over tail, and, with a fourth stomach-churning smash, came to rest. Silence. Then . . .

'Kathryn! *Where's Kathryn?!*'

The bus lay on its passenger side on the hard shoulder. I was suspended by my seatbelt, with Danny below me, his arm trapped between the edge of the door and the ground. I had wounds to my upper arm and scratches on my face but, apart from that, I was OK. Stubbsy desperately screaming his sister's name is a sound I'll never forget. I released my seatbelt, being careful not to land on Danny as I dropped. It was obvious he would be stuck in that position until the vehicle could be raised up somehow. He was in shock but kept saying, 'I'm OK! I'm OK!'

The diesel fuel was leaking, and the smell was growing more intense.

'Tony's gone too!' someone shouted.

I felt bad having to leave Danny in that situation but knew I had to get to Kathryn and Tony as quickly as possible. I kicked my way through what was left of the shattered windscreen and found Tony and Kathryn further down the hard shoulder behind where the bus had come to rest. They'd both been thrown from the vehicle during the crash. They were both alive but severely injured.

I heard Tony shouting, 'Clint, has my fuckin' eyeball gone?'

I played it down so as not to scare him too much, 'No mate, it's just your eyelid that's cut.'

Kathryn had a massive wound to her head, from her forehead, all the way around her scalp. I assumed she'd hit it against the sharp steel edge of the window frame as the glass and rubber trim came away. I decided to stay with her and asked a motorist who'd stopped at the scene to keep Tony talking. Kathryn's injury was too bad for me to leave her side. I was literally holding her head together. I'd never seen a wound this bad on a person. I wanted to keep it free of the dirt that was still hovering around us, and I didn't want the others to see how bad it was.

A number of motorists stopped to help. One of them produced a jack from his car and proceeded to release Danny. The emergency services were soon alerted.

Even though Tim hadn't been thrown from the vehicle, he'd been badly injured by the road surface as we skidded along the road. He'd lost a large part of his scalp and most of the skin on his back. As with Kathryn and Tony, he would be physically scarred for life because of his injuries. He sat on the embankment in shock, waiting for the paramedics while Karl and Matt looked after him.

Kathryn was complaining her back was in extreme pain. I couldn't stop thinking about her parents, Jeff and Jackie, and whether they'd ever forgive me for this. She stayed conscious throughout. I made her keep her eyes open and keep looking at me as we chatted. I knew help was on the way. I kept her talking. She was obviously in shock and in some distress, but still able to see the absurdity of the moment: 'Clint, is my trumpet bent?'

'No, but your head's a mess!'

I was still kneeling by her side, my white jeans covered in her blood. I reached underneath her with my left hand to clear the debris that was adding to her pain. I checked her mouth for any glass or dirt. I asked someone to get some water and a towel so that I could clean inside her mouth. She asked for a drink, but I persuaded her to hold off until the paramedics arrived.

When they did arrive, the paramedics saw Kathryn's state and immediately called for the air ambulance. I helped them get her onto a wooden stretcher then they put her into their ambulance to treat her until the helicopter arrived.

When the Strathclyde Police officers arrived, I was breathalysed. The result came back negative.

One of the officers then pointed out that the vehicles rear tyres hadn't actually punctured. They'd each lost their treads. Tyre failure. He explained it was something that had happened several times on this stretch of the motorway as the road surface changed from tarmac to a more unforgiving concrete type of compound, which can cause problems for warm tyres on long journeys.

The air ambulance arrived and landed near the wreckage. Kathryn was hastily taken away. As well as the massive head wound, she had a broken back. The rest of us were led to waiting ambulances and police cars and taken to Strathclyde Hospital in Motherwell.

It took a while for us all to recover from the accident, mentally as well as physically. Tony didn't lose his eye, but he lost his sense of smell as a result of his injuries. Kathryn would spend the next few weeks in hospital. Thankfully, after a long time, she made a good recovery. I can remember crying, with an overwhelming mixture of relief and happiness, two weeks after the crash, when I watched her take her first steps by her hospital bed.

LAST NIGHT, DJING SAVED MY LIFE

69/
'Bryan!'

After the motorway accident, it became increasingly difficult to keep the band going, even after we had mostly recovered from our physical injuries. There was, understandably, too much trauma when it came to travelling. Kathryn and Tim particularly struggled to even step onto a tour bus after the crash. We managed to limp along for a while, but not having a big budget to work with made things difficult.

The amount of DJ work I was getting also meant I was finding less time for the CBX! The income from the DJ work was helping me pay some of my debts off and pay the bills. The CBX! still wasn't making enough money to make things work. We were on a small independent record label called Artful Records. The label was owned by a charismatic chap called John Lennard, who was great to work with and loved our band but was limited in terms of the financial support he could give us. Though I was grateful for Artful's involvement, they could only fund a fraction of our activities: pressing the records, distributing and promoting them. The money I was giving the band members was barely enough to cover their expenses.

Despite all this, there was still the occasional ray of sunshine poking through the clouds. After playing a gig at the Monarch in London, we came offstage to find Mark E Smith waiting in the dressing room. He'd come to see us totally unannounced.

'Great gig that, Clint! Keep at it, cock!' he said.

I asked him if he fancied joining us for the encore.

'What song is it?'

I told him we ended every show with our cover of the Stooges 'I Wanna Be Your Dog'.

'Come on, then, what you waitin' for?' he laughed.

The following five minutes was one of the proudest moments of my life.

In the summer of '99 we supported the man who wrote 'The Summer of '69' in Hyde Park, London. Greater London Radio were giving the CBX! a lot of airplay (mainly 'White No Sugar', which was on 'heavy rotation') and we got the call to support Bryan Adams at a GLR gig in Hyde Park. I couldn't have been happier. The band was still suffering the after-effects of the motorway crash and needed something to lift us up. Plus, I was a fan of Bryan's, and I was looking forward to meeting him and thanking him for asking us to support him.

Our set in Hyde Park was well received, even though the crowd was mainly seated. The weather was great, and life couldn't have been better. After our set, I went off backstage hoping to meet Bryan, and maybe even Mel C (Sporty Spice), who he'd recently collaborated with on his hit single 'When You're Gone'. In the backstage paddock there was a small barrier separating Bryan's private area from the rest of us, which was not too unusual at an event like this – I mean, what world-famous rock star wants some nobhead from Oldham mithering him just before a massive gig? I'd been drinking all afternoon and was still going through the Red Stripes as I waited for the main man. Then, a limo pulled up, and I spotted Bryan step out and start strolling towards his dressing room. 'Bryan!' I yelled. 'Bryan! It's Clint . . . Clint Boon! . . . From The Clint Boon Experience!!'

He glanced over but kept walking.

'Bryan! . . . BRYAN! . . . 'BRYYYYAAAAAANEH!!!!' At which point, one of his security people came over and politely told me to fuck off.

In October 1999 we got invited onto Chris Evans' *TFI Friday* show, which, at the time, was one of the most watched TV programmes in the UK. 'White No Sugar' had been reissued and went into the Top 50. We pulled out all the stops for our *TFI* appearance, bringing all our stage props and hiring in a brass section. We even roped in our friend (and brilliant songwriter) Lee Griffiths to play acoustic guitar. We looked great and delivered a blazing, totally live performance. We ended the year with back-to-back tours supporting Travis and Echo and the Bunnymen.

I believe the two albums The Clint Boon Experience! made contain some of my best work as a writer and a performer. I was honoured to work with such amazing musicians who also happened to be wonderful people. In an ideal world, the CBX! would have landed a big record deal and, with it, enough financial support to take us on to the world stage.

Unfortunately for the band, that never happened. But life has a habit of giving you a break when you least expect it.

70/ Gone South

In 2001, it all went south for me. Bernard's Bar was one of the first gay bars in Manchester, having opened back in the 1970s. By the mid-1980s its name had changed to Stuffed Olives and earned the nickname Stuffed Bums (different times). It was mentioned by Morrissey in an interview in *Melody Maker*, when he said, 'The gay scene in Manchester was always atrocious. Do you remember Bernard's Bar? Now Stuffed Olives? If one wanted peace and to sit without being called a parade of names, then that was the only hope.' In 1987 Stuffed Olives became one of the first places in Manchester to play house music. Jon Dasilva had a house night there on Sundays, and the first ecstasy adopters like Shaun Ryder were regulars.

In the mid-1990s the bar was taken over by Paul Cons from the Haçienda, who changed the name of the venue to South (its address was 4a South King Street). One of the first club nights he launched took place on Fridays and was called the Rock 'n' Roll Bar, which is where Liam Gallagher first met Patsy Kensit. The resident DJ was Phil Beckett, but they also had guest DJs on. I'd been brought in to do a couple of slots, alongside regular guests like Jeff Hordley (who played Cain Dingle in *Emmerdale*) and Nev Cottee. Nev was in a band called Proud Mary, a band that Craig, the Inspirals' drummer, had also been in and who signed to Noel Gallagher's label Sour Mash. Craig also had some history with South nightclub, as he DJ'd there occasionally.

One day in May 2001 I got the answerphone message: 'Hi, it's Paul Cons from South. I'm looking for a new DJ for Saturday nights at South and wondered if you might be interested? Give me a call back when you can . . .'

I still didn't really have a steady income, so I was excited to get the call and phoned him straight back. We agreed I'd try a new Saturday-night residency, and would see how it went for a few weeks. The first night was amazing, a full house, with a queue down the street, and the punters loved it. I called the night 'Disco Rescue', and it quickly became established as one of the best club nights in Manchester. None of us had a clue, though, that it would last so long.

I always loved South as a club, from the first time I stepped into the place. It was a basement club, and the dancefloor took up pretty much the whole room. When you walked down the stairs and jumped off the bottom step, you were on the dancefloor and the music hit you. It was a magical place; all great clubs are in basements. South also felt like an island of cool in an otherwise mainstream part of the city, opposite a Pizza Express and just off King Street, a posh shopping street where you'd sometimes see the Beckhams with bags of expensive clobber. The atmosphere in South was like nowhere else. Wall-to-wall love. Simple as that. After my night was established, we'd bring in celebrity guest DJs now and again, including Andy Rourke, Tony Wilson, Tim Burgess, Shaun and John Peel. Peel was a real standout for me; getting to DJ with John Peel was bucket-list stuff. The doorway into the DJ booth was really low and with a rough brick lintel across the top, so you had to duck your head down to get in. Unfortunately, John smacked his head on his way in and cut it quite badly, just as he was about to start his set. He still went on, like a real trooper, and his first record was Sheena Easton's '9 to 5 (Morning Train)', which completely threw the crowd, who were expecting The Fall, or something. You could see all these bemused faces looking up at him, thinking 'What the fuck??' He wasn't being ironic either: he loved Sheena Easton. Sadly, John passed away not long after that, so it meant even more to me that I'd got the chance to DJ with the great man. Alan McGee was blown away by the night when he did a guest DJ slot, and went away almost evangelical about it, telling people, 'This is the best club in the fuckin' world!' He still talks about it to me now. Mani was always great as a guest DJ because he had no problem giving the crowd what they wanted, and would always play the classic Roses tracks, which the crowd obviously *loved*. I also booked Rick Witter from Shed Seven, who'd never really DJ'd before but got really into it. We became good mates and ended up DJing together all over the country.

The night quickly attracted a faithful bunch of regulars – 'the Boon Army' – many of who would come to South religiously for years. Because of the success of my South night, I started getting more DJ bookings around the country. On New Year's Eve 2001, I played for daft money, somewhere up north. The promoter who booked me had said on the phone, 'Play what you want, your usual set. No Showaddywaddy, though! Just make sure you do the bells at midnight. Pretty important, that. We must have the bells at midnight!'

'No probs, mate. I'll bring my *Chimes of Big Ben* sound-effects CD.'

'Seriously, we must have the bells. PLEASE don't forget.'

'Fuck's sake!' I thought. 'I do this for a livin'. I've been doing this DJ shit since 1975. Please don't tell me how to do my job.'

I turned up at the club on the night, and got my gear set up. The doors opened at ten, and people started piling in. It was a great atmosphere, and everyone set about getting battered. The promoter kept coming into the DJ booth to make sure everything was OK. He was really stressed out. He popped in around eleven o'clock with a couple of confetti cannons: 'Bells at midnight, Clint, yeah?'

'Mate, you don't need to mention the bells again. I've got my *Chimes of Big Ben* CD in my bag. It's always in there, you don't need to mention it again!'

I continued banging out the tunes. The crowd was getting more and more excited. At ten minutes to midnight the promoter appeared in the DJ booth again: 'Don't forget the bells!!'

'I'm on it, mate! Wind yer neck in! I know what I'm doin' here!'

I reached into my DJ bag to get the *Chimes of Big Ben* CD out. But there was no sign of it. What the fuck? I was sure it was there. The trouble was, it wasn't a CD I used every week. It dawned on me that I'd not actually used it or seen it for . . . well, exactly 12 months . . . almost to the minute. My arse went. Big time. I was getting a lot of money for this gig. The promoter was stood right behind me looking out at the punters with a big grin on his face, confetti cannon in his hand, mimicking ringing the bells like fuckin' Quasimodo: 'Five minutes, Clint! Five minutes! Bring it on!' he said to me, excitedly, bouncing like a child needing the toilet.

The flyer for the night actually said on it in big letters: 'Full New Year Big Ben Countdown!'

'Right,' I thought. 'I can either do an impression of a bell down the microphone, or think (pretty quickly) about whether there might be a record in my collection that's got a bell on it?' Then, in a moment of divine inspiration, a record came to mind: Daft Punk's recent second album had a bell chime at the start of the second track 'Aerodynamic'! I grabbed my 'DANCE' CD folder and desperately started wafting through it.

It was now two minutes to midnight. Waft. Waft. Waft. 'Why didn't I put all these in alphabetical order!' I thought. By now, my arse was puckering. I finally found the Daft Punk disc and slipped it into the CD player, trying not to look like I was stressing. I cue'd up the part of the disc with the bell on it. Got on the mic. Did the countdown: 'Ten, nine, eight . . . etc', shouted, 'Happy New Year!' and just started hitting 'play, pause, cue', 'play, pause, cue', for about a minute while the promoter fired his confetti cannons off left, right and centre. It worked. No one noticed. Next time you hear 'Aerodynamic' by Daft Punk, imagine me desperately digging through my DJ bag for that *Chimes of Big Ben* CD. The phrase 'prize bell' springs to mind.

I had no idea when I started DJing at South that it would last over 20 years. I spent every Saturday night in that DJ booth for well over two decades. It was my second home for a long time. It never became a chore, I loved every minute of it, playing my favourite records of all time to the most amazing bunch of party people in the greatest city in the world. I made many great friends in South over the years, staff and customers alike. I laughed, cried and danced with them and, on a couple of occasions, was carried out to my taxi by the bouncers after falling unconscious due to a heavy session. I hate to think how many cans of Red Stripe I drank in my years there. I still hold the South years very dear to my heart.

It was only after I'd been DJing there a few years that Paul Cons told me he'd left that original message on my answerphone by mistake. He'd meant to ring one of the club's other guest DJs and had dialled the wrong number from his phone book. But when I called him back, he thought, 'Clint might work, actually. What's the worst that can happen? I'll give him a chance . . .'

Getting the weekly residency at South was a big turning point for me. The regular income was a godsend, and the night soon started to gain a lot of attention, which started to bring more offers of work in. The downside, though, was that I got less time to visit Dallas. Meg and the kids were well and truly settled there. They'd been living with Meg's parents since early 2000, and Harley and Max had settled into a new school. We decided to carry on living apart and commuting whenever possible. It seemed like a good idea at the time but, ultimately, that decision would lead to the failure of our marriage and our eventual separation.

71/
Boon Aid

For a couple of years after the turn of the millennium, I had the pleasure of being booked for a monthly DJ residency at the legendary Razzmatazz club in Barcelona, a huge 5,000-capacity venue with various rooms playing different kinds of music. I'd fly out to Barcelona on Friday afternoon, check into my hotel and get my head down for a bit, then get up, have a quick shower and head off to the club. It was always a top gig. Good vibes. Good people. Good earner. The only downside to playing Razzmatazz every month was I always had to catch an 8am flight the next morning, as it was the *only* flight to Manchester each day. There were flights to other UK airports, but only one a day to Manchester.

On one occasion, my monthly trip to Barcelona coincided with the second anniversary of my weekly club night at South. I came up with the idea of doing a big 'Clint plays two gigs in two countries in one day!' concept to give my Manchester night a big push. The idea was I'd start DJing in Spain at 1am on Saturday morning and by 10pm the same night I'd be starting my set in Manchester. I even used the strap line 'Just like Phil Collins at Live Aid but without the Concorde!'

Things started fine. I got to my hotel in Barcelona, checked in, had a quick drink, got my head down, woke up, had a pint, then headed to the club and smashed it for a couple of hours on the decks. I got a great reaction from the punters, and loads of people wanted to hang out after my set, so I thought, 'OK, I'll hang out for a bit before I get off. Party a bit, but not too much because I've got to be up in three hours.'

Big mistake. One thing led to another. I got totally wasted in the club, vomited a lot and about 5am fell asleep under some seats in a room that was playing high-bpm hardcore techno. The room was completely black and had no lights on. Or maybe that was just me. I was so battered maybe my eyes had just packed in.

I had booked a taxi to pick me up from the hotel at 6.30am to get me to the airport for my 8am flight and a big day in Manchester. All the local press had run articles on my 'two gigs, two countries, one day, no Concorde!' story. I was still lying mashed and asleep under the seating in the club, thumb in mouth, when, just before 6am, some kind soul from the club woke me up, helped me to my feet and around the corner to the hotel. The promoter's mate carried my records, got me to my room, gave me my DJ cash in a big fat envelope, then got off. I shouldn't have even laid on the bed. I should have had a quick shower, put clean clothes on, got my taxi and gone straight to the airport. But I lay down, fell asleep, and missed both of the alarms I'd set on my Nokia 3210. I woke up, still fully dressed at 7.30am, and shit myself. I knew there was no way I'd catch the 8am plane now, but in a state of panic I grabbed my stuff and legged it down to reception, still wearing the same clothes that were filthy from sleeping on the floor of Razzmatazz: 'Taxi! Get me a taxi . . . soon as, man . . . need to get to Manchester . . . taxi now . . . taxi now, PLEASE . . . missed me fuckin' plane . . . why d'you not wake me up???'

Eventually, I got my message across, and I was soon in a taxi begging the driver to leg it as fast as he could so I could jump on the next plane headed for the UK. I'd never known a hangover this bad. On top of all this, I'd forgotten to charge my phone at the hotel, so was now stressing about that as well. My phone battery was only on 18 per cent.

Due to, let's say, 'anomalies' in my financial dealings, I didn't have a credit card at the time. I wasn't allowed one. But I figured when I got to the airport I'd go to the first airline desk that had a flight heading to England and buy a ticket with the big wad of cash I'd been given for DJing the night before. All I had to do was get a plane to anywhere on the British mainland, then get a train or a taxi to Manchester, for the Big Night. No problem. I knew that because I'd missed the flight due to my own fucking stupidity, I wouldn't get a refund. I got to the airport, ran into the departure hall, found the flight information board, and there was an EasyJet flight to Liverpool leaving in 55 minutes, but the display said it was 'BOARDING NOW'. The only other flight I could have got was flying to London that evening and I wouldn't have got to South in time. I had to get on that Liverpool flight. Whatever the cost.

Because the flight was already boarding, there was no queue at the check-in desk. I ran up, dropped my massive wheelie bag full of CDs and clothes on the conveyor belt, got the envelope out of my pocket, pulled out a big wad of £20 notes (I'd demanded Razzmatazz paid me in sterling because I'd been stung by shit exchange rates recently). I said to the check-in lady, 'I need to get to Liverpool, on that flight there . . . the one boarding now! I need to buy a ticket!'

She said, 'You need to go over there to the EasyJet ticket desk. But I honestly don't think you're going to make it.'

I ran over to the EasyJet ticket booth, wad of cash still in my hand: 'I need to get on that Liverpool flight, please. How much is it?'

'Sorry, sir, we don't take cash.'

'You what?'

'We don't take cash.'

'You don't take cash? What year is this? Have I gone forward in time to the year 3000, or summat?'

'We only take credit cards.'

'I've got a Solo card,' I said. 'Do you take them?'

'A Solo card,' she said, laughing. 'What's a Solo card?'

'They give 'em to people who can't get a credit card. I couldn't get a credit card.' I'd been turned down for a Switch card too.

A Solo card was a bit like a Fisher Price credit card. They were supposed to be for kids, to get them used to the idea of money. They weren't supposed to be used by ageing pop stars covered in sick, trying to book an emergency ticket to play their second gig of the day in another country.

Fuck. The plane was leaving in 38 minutes. I stood at the counter, scruffy as fuck, dirty hands, bedraggled, hair all over the place, thinking, 'Who do I know back home who's got a credit card, who can I call?'

First on my list was Matt Mellor, a good mate of mine who's wadded. But he didn't answer the phone. He NEVER answers his phone before 3pm. Next thought was to ring my mate Oakesy. He'd been helping me set this 'two gigs, two countries' gig up by designing the flyers. (They were based on the Live Aid logo, the guitar with its body as the shape of Africa with a guitar neck sticking out the top. Ours was the same, but with Spain instead of Africa. Yeah, I know, a bit insensitive now, looking back.) I thought Oakesy might be able to help me out, at least make some calls: 'Clint's stuck in Spain, we need to get him back!' That sort of thing.

Oakesy was working at Warburtons' bakery in Shaw at the time, so I knew he'd be up and about this early. I rang him and thankfully he answered.

'Oakesy, it's Clint. I'm in the shit, bro!'

'What's up?'

'I fuckin' fell asleep in t'club, didn't I.'

'Where are you now?'

'Still in fucking Barcelona, at the airport. Missed me plane!'

'What a nob! What you gonna do?'

'There's a flight leaving for Liverpool in 30 minutes. That's the only flight leaving Barcelona today that'll get me back in time for South tonight! D'ya know anyone who's got a credit card? They don't take cash and started laughing when I got my Solo card out.'

'Ha! You didn't get your fucking Solo card out, did you? They're for kids! I think my dad might have a credit card. Hang on . . .'

Oakesy's dad worked at Warburtons too. I heard Oakesy walking through the massive bakery, looking for his dad. 'Have you seen me dad? . . . Have you seen me dad? . . . Any of you seen me dad?' He sounded like a lost child. I was thinking, 'Fuck's sake! Just when I really need Oakesy's dad to be around, he's sneaked off for a shit, or summat.'

Eventually he found him.

'Have you got a credit card, Dad?'

'Yeah, course I've got a credit card. Why?'

'Clint's stuck in Spain. He needs to buy a ticket for a plane to Liverpool. He fell asleep in the club. He'll pay you back tonight!'

'What a nob! Here y'are.'

So Oakesy got the flight number off me and hung up so he could phone EasyJet and try to book me on the flight.

A few seconds later, I was back at the check-in desk, phone in hand, waiting for news, but down to 4 per cent on the battery. By now, the woman on the desk knew exactly what was going on. I'd filled her in, and she was with me on this. I'd told her all about 'two gigs, two countries, one day' and she really wanted me to make it home. She was feeling for me. I could see it in her eyes. Either that, or she wanted to get me out of the fucking way so she could finish her shift.

Twenty minutes to take off. I was shitting my keks. Phone went. It was Oakesy: 'Go! Go! Go! You're on . . .'

The check-in girl looked at her screen. Yep, thumbs-up. I grabbed my ticket and legged it like a proper desperate loser through the airport to gate 48: ''Scuse me, 'scuse me, let me past . . . can I just squeeze past, please . . . sorry, sorry.' I was proper stressed. Three women in EasyJet uniforms were waiting for me at the gate, looking totally bemused and proper vexed. They took my ticket, ripped a bit off and I ran through the door, down some stairs and out onto the runway where the plane was waiting for me. Engines going. Now ten minutes late because of some inconsiderate pisshead from Manchester. I thought, 'This is gonna go down great with a plane full of Scousers!' I could almost feel them all scowling at me through the windows as I climbed up the steps. A flight attendant shut the door the split second I walked over the threshold, just to prove a point. I knew they'd all been talking about me. I walked down the centre aisle, sweating my bollocks off, red as anything, nearly crying, partly through relief, partly through being distressed, looking for somewhere to sit. Someone started slow-clapping me, I'm thinking, 'Yeah, go on, fuck off!'

I spotted an empty seat next to a mum and a little girl. They looked Spanish. I sat down, next to the child. They were both staring at me, incredulous. I had white jeans on that were covered in nightclub slime from where I'd been crawling around on the floor in the techno room. I was wearing a black t-shirt with the words 'CHICK MAGNET' in big white letters across the chest, my hands were filthy, my hair was all stuck up, and I smelt like a swamp. On top of all that, I was burping a lot, and whenever I burped, it smelt like sick.

The little girl hastily switched places with her mum. I think she was a bit scared, and I didn't blame her. When the mother got settled in again,

I turned to her and started trying to explain to her that, 'despite how I look – and I know you never see dirty people on aeroplanes – I'm not going to be any trouble, I'm a reasonable chap and I've got kids of my own, but I fell asleep on the floor in a nightclub, and I've been a bit sick and. . . .' But the more I talked, the more weird it got, so eventually I just started intently studying the evacuation-procedure card and then pretended to go to sleep.

When we landed, I retrieved my bag from the luggage carousel and headed outside and walked past all the people waiting for their loved ones. All looking at this dirty bloke in sunglasses wearing a questionable t-shirt.

There, waiting on a grass verge outside Liverpool Airport, was my loyal partner in crime. Born on the same day as me but exactly 20 years later, Stephen Oakes. Oakesy in his little Fiat Punto with his big happy moon face. I thought, 'Clinterella . . . you *shall* go to the ball!' I was so happy I could've cried. I climbed in.

'Fuckin' 'ell, man, look at t'state of you!'

'I know, mate. Take me home, brother.'

72/ Pills 'n' Thrills with Dr Ryder

I got a call from Bez in 2001, asking if I could get Shaun Ryder some DJ work. Bez still called him 'X', a nickname that was a hangover from when they were young scallies selling a few drugs to get by, avoiding using their full names: 'Clint, X is on his arse and needs some wedge. Any chance you could help him out? Get him some work in the clubs?'

Shaun's profile at that time wasn't good. Neither was his health. He was still fighting addiction and, though making progress, was still showing the battle scars of years of serious drug abuse. He had also taken to wearing lots of fake tan to disguise his pale complexion and make himself look healthier than he was. He wasn't in a great place.

I'd always admired and looked up to Shaun so was obviously happy to help when I got the call from Bez. I was well established as a club DJ by that point, getting work all over the country and abroad, of course. I had a lot of contacts; my DJ work was bringing in some decent income at a time when I really needed it. The Clint Boon Experience! had ended and there was no sign of the Inspirals ever reforming. Along with the theme-tune work for Granada TV, I wasn't doing too bad, but Shaun was quite down on his luck. He was in a complicated legal battle with his ex-management team from his time with Black Grape. Every penny he was earning legitimately was being taken off him as part of the legal arrangement. It was a bizarre and heart-breaking position. I told Bez I'd be more than happy to help Shaun out: 'Yeah, man. Send me his number and I'll get on it.'

I got straight on the phone: 'Shaun, it's Clint!'

'Aw right, Clint! Cheers for ringin'.'

'How're you doin', brother?'

'Not bad, mate, not bad. Just need a bit of dosh!'

'Yeah, Bez told me. I'll try and get you some DJ gigs, no probs. What sort of stuff do you play?'

'I don't fuckin' know, mate! I've never been a disc jockey before!'

I started contacting all the agents, promoters and venue owners who'd been giving me work over the previous six years since the Inspirals had split. I explained Shaun's situation. He wasn't known as a DJ yet and didn't have a reputation as the most reliable of people, so there was a reluctance by some of those I spoke to at first.

'Look, I'll bring him along. I'll put the tunes on, and Shaun will shake hands, work the mic and generally be a man of the people!'

The bookings started coming in. At first, I'd be getting a grand for Shaun and £300 for me, plus accommodation. At the time, Shaun and Bez were next-door neighbours in a quaint and picturesque town called Hadfield, in Derbyshire. Just around the corner from Hadfield was Padfield, famous for being the village where the comedy-horror TV series *The League of Gentlemen* was filmed. Shaun, his then girlfriend Felicia and their little boy Joe lived in one little cottage, and in the cottage next door was Bez, his wife Debs, and their two lads. Shaun and Bez also shared a communal backyard. This bizarre neighbourly setting made for a far more surreal sitcom than anything in *The League of Gentlemen*, these two 24-hour party hellraisers living in pastoral, side-by-side cottages in the serene and melancholic countryside.

On gig days, I'd drive the Saab up to Shaun's house. Sometimes, he'd be home, sometimes he'd be in the local pub, a few doors down, enjoying a Guinness or two before the trip. One weekend, Shaun and I were booked to play in Brighton. Prior to the trip, I thought it'd be nice to get some new floormats in the car. The original ones were scruffy and threadbare, so I nipped up to Halfords and bought a set of plush floormats in sexy beige to match the interior of the car. 'Really expensive but worth every penny,' I thought. I put the mats in place, loaded the Shark up and headed off for Hadfield.

Shaun was sat in the pub, alone, nursing a Guinness. We walked round to his house, picked his bags up and set off. A few minutes into the trip he reached into his holdall on the back seat and pulled out a paper bag. He started fumbling around in the footwell next to his feet. I could see he was unscrewing the top off a bottle, which he then dropped.

'Oh fuck!! Sorry, Clint, I've fuckin' spilt it! Where's the fuckin' lid gone?!'

My new Halfords floormat was now decorated with a spectacular Pollock-style splash in bright orange.

'It's OK, Shaun. They're only cheap mats!'

He tried explaining to me what the medicine was, but I was too preoccupied to listen, already wondering if warm soapy water, baking soda, white vinegar or bleach would be the best option. Shaun's struggles with drugs over the years have been well documented, not least by the man himself. He'd recently conquered his heroin habit, and the spillage was his fluorescent opioid substitute. 'I reckon a bit of bleach will sort that, Booney!'

Cheers, brother.

I always enjoyed those road trips with Shaun. We'd listen to tunes and put the world and the music industry to rights. I'd pick him up, drive him to the town where we were playing, get him to his hotel room, wake him up for the gig, get him to the gig and play the tunes while he worked his magic. People were always delighted to see him in their local nightclub. They were overwhelmed that Shaun Ryder was in their quiet seaside town or forgotten working-class suburb. They weren't really interested in hearing him play records. They just wanted to meet him, shake his hand, have a photograph taken with him and share with him the stories of how he'd changed their lives. It was obvious the profound effect he'd had on his generation. I could relate to every single person in the room.

One night, we did a DJ gig in Newcastle. We checked into the hotel and, when the time came, headed off to the venue, which was just around the corner. Shaun was getting a bit more 'hands-on' with the actual DJing by now, but we were both still using my CD collection.

I did a short warm-up set while Shaun signed autographs and shook hands with his fans. When the time came, I got on the mic and introduced Shaun. The punters went wild. He had his first tune lined up and ready to go. I leant over to see what he'd chosen to start with. 'Wade in the Water' by Ramsey Lewis. 'Fuckin' 'ell! Bold move!' I thought to myself. Not the banging opener the crowd would be expecting but a nice groovy way to get things going. Shaun pressed play, the mellow northern-soul vibes kicked in and away he went, loving every moment. Next up, the Stones: 'Get Off of My Cloud'. Nice! Towards the end of the night, I took over the tunes again, playing a selection of Manc classics while Shaun regaled the crowd with his unique catalogue of lyrical catchphrases.

We got paid in cash most nights. When we did occasionally get paid by bank transfer, I'd have the money paid into my account then sort cash for Shaun. He once told me over a pint how he'd often hide the money in various cavities around his cottage: 'I used to be a burglar, so I know all the best places to hide the dosh! Trouble is, Booney, because of all the booze and drugs, I forget where I've hidden stuff!'

In early 2002 I'd met a woman called Charlie at the Fab Café. She'd been to the venue a few times with a friend of hers, Hannah, but apart from requesting the occasional tune, we'd not spoken much. One night, the three of us got chatting and I offered to drop them off on my way home. Charlie and I swapped numbers and stayed in touch. At first, it was just phone conversations, which then became longer and longer phone conversations, then we started meeting up. It soon became a full-on and very serious relationship.

Meg and the kids moved back to Manchester soon after, when she started a relationship with Scott, the brother of one of her close friends. I was overjoyed to have Harley and Max back in Manchester, and happy that Meg was able to settle down and build a new relationship. In Harley and Max, Meg and I created two of the most amazing human beings on the planet.

At the time, Charlie was studying nursing at Liverpool University. For the first few months of our relationship, I'd drive over to see her in a flat she had in the Kensington part of Liverpool. When she left uni, we moved into her mother's house in Middlewich. Around this time, Meg and I sold the house in Milnrow and were going through our divorce.

I sorted a booking for me and Shaun to DJ together at the Georgian Theatre in Stockton, and Charlie came with us. We picked Shaun up and set off up the M62. The gig was brilliant, Shaun played a blinder and got off to bed soon after our set. The next morning, we were in the hotel bar drinking Bloody Marys to try to cure our hangovers. Charlie was feeling particularly rough after a messy night. Doctor Ryder sprung into action. Shaun packed me off to the nearest pharmacist with a shopping list that included Nurofen, paracetamol, Rennies, and Lemsip extra strength. As I left the bar, he shouted, 'Clint. Get some Imodium too, cos she'll probably have the shits in a bit!' Then he leant over to Charlie and said, 'Make sure he gives you a good sorting out as well, cos I've always found that helps!'

I came back with a bag full of medicine and piled it all up on the table. Shaun started ripping boxes open and popping pills out of foil trays and announced loudly, 'Right. Whatever dosage it says on the packet, double it . . . if it says take one, take two. If it says take two, take four. If it says take two every four hours, take four every two hours. If it says don't take more than eight every twenty-four hours, ignore it. They only write that shit to cover their arses if you die!'

It was a little insight into the mind of one of the greatest British writers of our lifetime.

As for the floormats, I took Shaun's advice on that too and went for the bleach option. It completely fucked the mat up.

My manager at the time, Richard Jones, was based in Marple, just outside Stockport, and one day, knowing that I was house-hunting, he gave me a local newspaper with the 'property for sale' section at the back. We found a small semi-detached house for sale in Offerton in Stockport and decided to buy it. The first thing I did was get the attic converted into a studio. I brought in my old mate Lee Butterworth to do the conversion. Lee was one of Mani's best mates and had accompanied me, Mani and Spud on a lot of road trips to watch bands back in the eighties.

Me and Charlie would go on to have our first child, Oscar, in May of 2004. We married the year after at Manchester Town Hall. Peter Hook was my best man. I stood at the alter next to him as Charlie walked down the aisle to 'Everlasting Love' by the Love Affair. Then, another friend of mine, Mike Porter, played the classic sixties garage track 'Louie Louie' on his Farfisa Compact Duo as little Oscar walked down the aisle carrying our wedding rings on a cushion. Oscar's middle name is 'Louie Louie'. Mike was an Inspirals fan who used to write to me in the early 1990s. He lived in Newcastle. I'd always write back. It was quite normal back then to keep in touch with fans through letters or postcards – way before social media shoulder-charged its clingy way into our lives. Mike told me that he learnt to play keyboards by copying the parts I'd played on Inspirals records. When I'd started a weekly DJ residency in Newcastle in 1996, I got to know Mike and his mates. They had an amazing band called The Kustom Built. At that time, pre-internet, Newcastle-upon-Tyne was geographically just off the edge of the planet and down some steps. That's why the world never really got to hear about The Kustom Built. If they were based in London, or Manchester, they would have been huge. Seven years later, a band from Leicester with a similar sound, look and mindset, smashed into the country's mainstream music scene. They were called Kasabian.

Also during our wedding service, Mani did a reading of Candi Staton's 'You Got the Love' at the altar, and Rick Witter serenaded us all with a gorgeous rendition of one of our favourite songs, 'Chasing Rainbows', with Porter playing along on his keyboards. At the reception that evening, another hero of mine who I'd become mates with, Ian McNabb of The Icicle Works, performed an exquisite version of 'Love is a Wonderful Colour' for us. The following year, Hooky would become Oscar's godfather, or 'life roadie' as we prefer. At the time of writing, Oscar is Hooky's bass technician and roadie.

73/ Engie Benjy

Some of the pieces of music that had the most impact on me as a child, and have stayed with me through life, are the TV theme tunes of the 1960s. Those that the Barry Gray Orchestra recorded for Gerry Anderson's *Fireball XL5*, *Joe 90*, *Stingray* and *Supercar* are still some of my favourite tunes ever (even the song 'Aqua Marina' from *Stingray* deserves a mention). Probably because they conjure up memories and feelings of warmth, safety and innocence in terms of where in life we were when we first heard them: sat cross-legged in front of an electric fire in the living room of a corner shop in Oldham. Theme tunes for TV shows, films and stage shows are a massive part of popular culture and something I've always been fascinated by.

My relationship with Engie Benjy started back in 1997. One night when I was DJing in the Fab Café, a guy came over and introduced himself. His name was Chris Bowden, and he told me he worked at Cosgrove Hall Films, the Manchester-based animation company that had become a world-famous institution through its iconic stop-motion animation creations like *Danger Mouse*, *The BFG* and *Count Duckula*. They were based in the south Manchester suburb of Chorlton-cum-Hardy, which is where they got the name for the main character in *Chorlton and the Wheelies*. At various points in time, Stone Roses guitarist John Squire, New Order frontman Bernard Sumner and Alberto y Lost Trios Paranoias singer Jimmy Hibbert all worked in some capacity at Cosgrove Hall. Bernard even took on his short-lived stage surname 'Albrecht' from the manufacturer's name stamped in big letters on one of the stop-motion cameras in the studios.

Anyway, back in the Fab Café, Chris asked how I was getting on since the Inspirals had split. He knew that I was writing music for television and explained he was currently working on a pilot for a new kids' TV show called

Engie Benjy. He asked if I would like to come along to Cosgrove Hall and meet the show's creator and producer to talk about music.

'Count me in, mate!' I had time on my hands, and I had a nice home studio.

Engie Benjy was created by a woman called Bridget Appleby. I met up with her a few times to get my head around what Engie and his world were all about. 'So, he's got blue hair, and mends engines?' Engie was an 'engine doctor' in a surreal marzipan world where each of the characters had their own vehicle. Farmer Fred drove a tractor called Tractor; Astronaut Al piloted a rocket called Rocket; Dottie the bus driver had a double-decker bus called . . . you get the idea. Thinking back now, it all sounds a bit like a Happy Mondays song. Every episode of *Engie Benjy* revolved around the drama caused by certain vehicles breaking down or coming down with ailments like blue measles, then Engie's admirable efforts to make everything right again. As well as writing the theme music, I also auditioned to be the actual voice of Engie Benjy a few years later while the show was still being developed. Seemed like a good idea at the time. I thought the trial voice-over session went well and was so confident I went home with a VHS demo of the audition in my bag, and told Charlie, 'I nailed it. I reckon I'll deffo get the gig!'

But when we watched it back a couple of days later in the Cosgrove Hall studios it was all a bit weird. Engie sounded like some sort of deviant (with blue hair, and a set of spanners). I've still got the VHS tape of me as Engie Benjy. Hopefully, it'll never see the light of day. Along with that video of me auditioning for the DFS-couch TV advert.

The big scoop for Cosgrove Hall and ITV came when Ant & Dec agreed to provide the voices for the main characters. Engie (Dec) and his beloved dog Jollop (Ant) had found their perfect voices, although in Jollop's case, this was just an occasional growl, grunt or generic dog noise. Ant definitely got the easy gig. Comedian Les Dennis also came on board to provide the voice for Astronaut Al.

Although, on this occasion, my versatile voice-over skills weren't needed, the theme tune I wrote and sung was an instant hit with Cosgrove Hall, ITV and the nation's pre-school kids in general. The kids loved it because it was catchy as fuck, and parents loved it because it sounded like the Inspiral

Carpets. As with most of the music I've made since 1984, it featured my Farfisa quite prominently.

In the summer of 2003, I would start writing and recording the Engie Benjy album, a project that would take me 12 months to complete. I wrote songs for each of the characters, and their vehicles too. Fifteen songs in total. I seriously still see it as some of the best work I've ever created.

One of the *Engie Benjy* songs I wrote was for Trucker Troy and his truck. The song deals with all the great things about trucks. It's a very positive song, with a good strong message. Like most of the tracks on the *Engie Benjy* album, it didn't take me long to write and create. I burnt it onto a CD and took it down to Bridget at Cosgrove Hall to see what she thought. This was in the days before people like me could send music 'down the line'. No WeTransfer, SoundCloud or Dropbox knocking about back then! I sat down in Bridget's office, and she put the CD into the player.

'What's this one called, Clint?'

'It's called "Trucks Are Good".'

Song starts, quirky as anything. I was thinking, 'Another masterpiece here!', until I suddenly realised it sounded like I was singing, *'Drugs are good!'* Shit! That's not good! I was convinced Bridget was going to pick up on it, and was getting ready to apologise, but, instead, a big smile appeared across her face and she said, 'This is perfect, Clint. Once again, you've completely captured the spirit of Engie's world and its characters.'

'Well, thanks, Bridget. Glad you like it!'

The rest of the team at Cosgrove Hall loved 'Trucks Are Good' too and, for some strange reason, it became very popular at South nightclub, where I played it every week for the next few months.

The *Engie Benjy* series became a commercial success and was picked up by lots of other countries and territories – at one point, it was being broadcast in 66 different countries. Most of the international transmissions of the series were re-voiced by actors in the native language of the relevant territory. My vocal on the theme tune was also replaced in most non-English speaking countries. On one occasion, me and Charlie checked into a hotel in Barcelona. I was DJing that night. We put the TV on and there's *Engie Benjy* with some

Spanish bloke singing the Spanish version of the lyrics I'd written and sung back in Manchester. (If you're ever stuck for something to do and have 11 minutes to spare, go online and search 'Engie Benjy intro (multilanguage)' to hear my masterpiece sung in a dozen different languages, including Slovakian and Greek.) I still believe the *Engie Benjy* theme tune works best with the Oldham accent . . . although the German version is something to behold.

Engie Benjy turned out to be one of the last great stop-frame animation kids' TV series to be made in the UK. Soon afterwards, CGI took over as the new way of making this kind of television. Nothing would ever be the same again. Maybe the TV programmers and producers thought the kids wouldn't notice the shitness of this new format. Watching stop-frame classics like *Fireman Sam*, *Thomas the Tank Engine* and *Postman Pat* in their all-new, smooth, non-clunky slickness just didn't cut it in my world. These CGI reboots never sat well with me, and I could already imagine thousands of angry pre-schoolers, up and down the country, literally throwing their toys out of their prams in protest.

The *Engie* album never came out but 'Trucks Are Good' miraculously made it into the *Engie Benjy* stage show that toured the UK a couple of years later, playing to thousands of British toddlers and their families. It also made it onto a five-track CD that was on sale at the shows.

The *Engie Benjy* theme tune is probably the easiest song I've ever written. It's also, probably, the most lucrative piece of music I've made to date. Because the series was sold to so many countries worldwide, I would get paid every time an episode was broadcast. Which meant that, for several years, the royalties I got for a kids' theme tune were far bigger than my Inspirals royalties.

74/
I'm Crazy 'bout a Robot

After the success of the *Engie Benjy* TV series and the positive reaction to my theme tune, I was asked to submit ideas for another stop-frame animation series to be made by Cosgrove Hall. The new show was to be called *Little Robots*. When I found out Lego were behind the show, I thought, 'Kerching!!'

I drove to a Lego office in Slough to meet with the creators to go through the background of what these Little Robots were all about. Everything in their world was made up of bits and pieces of junk found in reclamation yards. If the message behind the *Engie Benjy* series was 'teamwork', the message behind *Little Robots* was simple too: 'recycling'.

The main character, Tiny, was a young robot. He was turquoise, with a pink aerial on top of his head and a pink button on his belly that opened the lid of his head to reveal the tools he used for fixing machines and robots. His responsibilities also included pulling the 'day–night lever' twice a day: 'morningtime' and 'nighttime'. Tiny lived on the 'Nut and Bolt Tree', right next to the 'day–night lever'. He was always very positive about things and constantly trying to help his friends to live in peace and harmony with each other. All of which I felt I could completely relate to.

I went away and wrote a theme tune based around the idea of Tiny having a bit of a crush on a lady robot. I don't know what I was thinking, but it made sense to me at the time. I think, to be honest, the success of *Engie Benjy* had gone to my head. I felt like the Hans Zimmer of children's TV, the Ennio Morricone of pre-school broadcasting. I was untouchable!

I recorded the track, burnt it to a CDR disc and, a few days later, headed south to play it to the people at Lego.

'This one's called "I'm Crazy 'bout a Robot" ' I explained to the assembled Lego executives.

As we sat and listened, it dawned on me that the song just sounded like Tiny wanted to shag a lady robot. *'I'm crazy 'bout a robot/She's got things other robots haven't got/And that's why I'm thinkin' 'bout her a lot/I'm just crazy 'bout a robot!'* followed by *'She wheels around/She wheels around/She makes my temperature go/up and then go down . . .'* It was much too raunchy for a pre-school audience. I'd given Tiny too strong a libido for a robot of his tender years. The idea of a Little Robot who wanted to get his leg over for the first time was far too much for children's television. I was shown to the car park quite swiftly and didn't get asked to do any more kids' TV theme tunes after that.

75/
24 Hour Party People

In 2001 I received a phone call from a casting director called Wendy Brazington who was working on a new film by Michael Winterbottom. The film was to be called *24 Hour Party People* and would be centred around the Manchester music scene, from the arrival of punk in 1976 and on through the rise and fall of Factory Records in the mid-1990s. It was to be based mainly around the stories of Joy Division, New Order, Happy Mondays, Factory Records and the Haçienda.

Wendy asked if I could spend a couple of hours with Michael so he could tap my brains for any memories and anecdotes I might have from that period. I happily obliged and met with him and Wendy at the Palace Hotel on Oxford Road the following week. We sat in the bar one afternoon and I talked at length about my journey through art college, seeing the Pistols on the Anarchy tour, having my life completely reshaped by punk, joining the Inspirals and on up to the present day. He wanted to know every detail. Wendy sat with us making notes on her laptop.

I went away not thinking too much of it, so I was pleasantly surprised to get a call from Wendy the next day, saying that Michael wanted to offer me a cameo role in the film. He wanted me to play a train conductor in a scene set in the 1970s where Tony Wilson takes a surreal train ride over the Pennines. We filmed the scenes one day in the summer of 2001 on a private train line in Bury, just outside Manchester, which had several vintage engines and carriages available and provided the perfect setting. I spent a couple of hours filming a short scene on the train with Steve Coogan, who was playing Tony.

I went to both the London and Manchester premières of the film in March 2002. When it was about to be released in Sweden, I was invited to attend a special press and media screening in Stockholm a few days before the official launch. I was also booked to DJ at a party immediately after the event. The screening was sponsored by Levi's, who had just launched a new range of jeans called 'Levi's Engineered Jeans'. These were a follow up to the ridiculous 'Levi's Twisted Jeans', which had been something of a hit with the younger generation but whose appeal was lost on the likes of me – it looked like whoever had sewn the denim panels together was on ketamine. The Engineered Jeans were a bit more conventional and quite smart-looking.

I was going to be the only member of the cast present at the event. I was told that the organisers were excited that I'd be there. They flew me and Charlie out to Stockholm and put us up in a top-notch hotel, all expenses paid, for a few days. We were treated like royalty.

In the afternoon, we visited the incredible Vasa Museum, which contains and tells the story of the world's only preserved 17th-century ship.

On the evening of the première, a limo picked us up from our hotel and drove us to a castle on a hill, which was home to a luxurious art-house cinema. We walked along the red carpet, me acting all full of myself, waving and shouting 'Boon Army!' while photographers snapped away. I felt like an indie Tom Cruise. After a couple of brief interviews, we were ushered to our seats, which were right in the middle of the audience. I was feeling a bit smug by now. I think it's right to say Charlie was fairly impressed too. People were pointing and nodding at us, smiling and all that. Then the film started. For the benefit of Swedish people who might be great at English but struggled to understand our Mancunian (or Oldham) accents, the Swedish version of *24 Hour Party People* had subtitles throughout.

My first appearance in the film comes at approximately 1 hour, 18 minutes and 42 seconds in, when the train sequence starts. Anthony Wilson/Steve Coogan climbs on board the train during a blizzard before Ernie, the train conductor/Clint Boon, shows him to a nice seat by a window. The best bit, though, comes later when Coogan (as Wilson) is doing a voice-over pointing out some of the cameo appearances by real-life celebs in the film: 'Here's the real Anthony Wilson, playing the part of a TV director . . . here's Mani of The Stone Roses playing a sound engineer . . . here's Mark E Smith of The Fall . . .' etc.

The Swedish subtitles scrolled away at the bottom of the screen: '*Det finns en hel del cameo-framträdanden i den här filmen, till exempel* . . . bla, bla, bla, Anthony Wilson; bla, bla, bla, Mani; bla, bla, Stone Roses . . .' Then the part of the film comes up were Coogan as Wilson says my name on screen. At the UK premières, I'd found it quite an emotional moment hearing Steve Coogan say the words 'And this chap here? Inspiral Carpets. What's his name? Clint Boon.'

So, I'm there, in a Swedish art-house cinema, excitedly waiting for the moment. Coogan says my name. But then I see, in slow motion, the subtitles pop-up. 'Here comes my name,' I'm thinking to myself.

'Bla, bla, bla . . . Clint Bone.'

I was *devastated*. Charlie says I literally sunk down in my chair. Not something that can be corrected, is it? Subtitles like that are burnt onto the image on the celluloid of the film. It's permanent. They're not going to go back and spend thousands of krona re-editing the film because I'm unhappy about a slight misspelling.

I pretended I hadn't noticed. The film ended. Everyone stood up and clapped. People were turning to me and clapping. Charlie pretended she wasn't with me and made a swift exit. It's funny to think that to the Swedish, I will be known for eternity as Clint Bone. The man who likes to dress up in funny uniforms for art-house films. Maybe that's an alternative career idea right there. I could get a new business card made:

Flexible and affordable actor, will consider anything.
Scandinavian art-house movies a speciality.
Contact Clint Bone, Manchester, England.

24 Hour Party People was a massive success. Although factually way off the mark here and there, it perfectly captured the utter madness of that period. One of the reviews said that Andy Serkis playing Martin Hannett was the actor's strangest role yet, and Tony Wilson pointed out that was really saying something, considering he was also playing Gollum in *The Lord of the Rings* trilogy. It's hard for me to be objective about a film that references the music movement I was part of, and a film that I had a small part in, but it's one of my favourite movies. I watched it recently and it's aged really well, arguably better than many of us musicians who featured in it!

76/
'Let's do it, boys!'

High Crompton sits on top of a big hill that separates the borough of Shaw and Crompton from the borough of Rochdale. Mum and Dad had moved to a modest bungalow on Cheviots Road, and the view from their kitchen window was like a picture postcard. It looked out over a typically green English valley: the village of Shaw snoozing down by the River Beal, the Pennines rising to the horizon on the other side. From that window you could the see the places where pretty much every important event in Mum and Dad's lives had taken place: the houses they were born in, the streets where they played as kids, the schools they attended, the mills they worked in and where they met, the places they went dancing, the churches they attended, and the graveyards where all their ancestors were laid to rest. In some ways, it felt like the most idyllic place for Marie and Cyril Boon to spend their final years together after 50 or more years of happy marriage.

Their house was always immaculately decorated. Dad was constantly working on making their perfect home: he'd done so at every address they'd had – Linney Lane, Higginshaw Lane, Polperro Close and Lambourne Grove – but Cheviots Road was a masterpiece. As the place was built on a steep slope, access from the street meant navigating a series of steps that a younger couple wouldn't have had an issue with. The back garden dropped steeply and unforgivingly in the direction of some properties further down the hill. As soon as they moved in, Dad got busy making the whole place more user friendly with some discreet but well-engineered concrete structures and a series of terraced paths and plant borders.

There was always an abundance of garden gnomes in Boon World because Dad had started making them as a hobby a few years earlier and couldn't seem to break the habit. The buggers were everywhere. One afternoon, a few dozen gnomes met a grizzly end when Dad found he didn't have enough rubble to use as a base for a concrete floor he was laying in the void under the garage. He converted the space into a workshop and, to this day, those unfortunate gnomes still lay entombed beneath 26 Cheviots Road, still smiling to themselves contentedly, fishing rods in hand.

Visiting Mum and Dad was always a pleasure but, when I started seeing Charlie, our visits became more frequent. We'd climb up the ladder into the loft where Dad had built a small art studio. He'd show us his latest work – a convincing Constable copy here, a snide Lowry there, and one of his finest pieces, a wooden model of the *Titanic* where, each week, a magazine would drop through his letterbox with lots of information about the doomed ship and a few bits of wood to glue into place. Cyril gave a good two years of his life to building his *Titanic*. The moment Dad proudly unveiled the finished model to me and Charlie, we both had a giggle. One of the brass letters from the nameplate at the bow of the ship had come unstuck leaving just the caption '*TIT NIC*'.

On a visit to Mum and Dad's in late 2002 Mum suggested we should show Charlie some of the Inspirals' old TV appearances on the video player. Our Booney, (Craig) and his partner, Julie, had come along to meet Charlie for the first time. Booney brought a dining chair into the lounge to make the most of the occasion, watching all these Inspirals vids that Mum had religiously recorded from 1990 to 1995 onto VHS tapes, which she'd then lovingly labelled and carefully stored away for a day like this.

I still had no desire to get the Inspirals back together, as I felt happier focusing on the new things in my life. I was enjoying composing music for TV, and presenting radio and TV shows. I was still making good money from my DJ work and getting more bookings than ever. Me and Charlie were spending endless, happy days cruising up and down the motorways of the nation on my DJing trips. We were having the time of our lives. Why would I want to change anything?

Richard, my manager, had recently been helping myself and the Inspirals tidy up some loose ends regarding our publishing deal, but there was absolutely no talk of a reunion. The Clint Boon Experience! had not long since ended, and I felt there was more chance of me revisiting that than getting back with the Inspirals.

That afternoon we watched some of our *Top of the Pops* performances, my appearance on *Star Test* from 1990, and a video from '93 where me and Tom were interviewed by Bonnie Burkert for one of the music TV channels (I was drunk, mumbling and half asleep). I'd seen all this footage many times over the years and, although I was always proud of what we'd achieved and was grateful that I'd been part of that monumental movement, it was always a bit like looking through old school photographs.

Mum put the last VHS tape in the machine: Inspiral Carpets on *The Word*, performing 'Saturn 5' in 1994. By the time of this TV appearance, my bowlhead was gone – I'd opted for a much more sensible and easy-maintenance hairstyle. The performance was recorded live at Teddington Studios in London for broadcast later. The vibe in the studio was electric. We were on a low stage, with the audience up close and dancing – going for it like it was 1968; a couple of professional dancers scattered around on podiums for added effect. Some psychedelic visuals were added later in post-production, courtesy of green-screen technology. We looked great, played great and the crowd loved us.

The presenter and co-creator of the show, Terry Christian, couldn't have been happier. His smile filled the room. He had tried so hard to get us on the show since its inception four years earlier. Terry believed in us since day one. We'd made a brief appearance in the first ever episode of *The Word* back in 1990 as part of their coverage of Manchester taking over LA, but we hadn't performed on that episode, just said a few words to camera about Manchester and its music. Then subsequently, for some reason, the show's producers and music programmers refused to give the Inspirals a slot.

Eventually, a combination of Terry's enthusiasm, and a stunning new single from us, made someone at Channel 4 give us the green light. That night, on *The Word*, we were the best band in the world. The way we sounded, the way we dressed, the way we moved, was equal parts mod, punk, pop and garage. It was all the ingredients of what became known as Britpop.

Mum slipped the VHS tape back in its sleeve and into the Granny Smith's apple box she stored her tape collection in. Me and Charlie said our goodbyes and headed off through the valley. As we drove along Oldham Road towards Heyside, past the spot where St Joseph's Primary School once stood, I said to Charlie, 'Watching that makes me want to do it again.'

'What do you mean? Do what again?'

'Seeing that clip of us on *The Word* makes me want to get the Inspirals back together.'

'Do it then!' she said, without any hesitation.

I phoned Richard the next day and told him how I felt. He sounded excited. He asked why I'd changed my mind.

'Blame my mum!' I laughed. 'And Charlie! . . . And Terry Christian!'

We decided we'd put the idea forward at the next meeting with the band.

Richard had a great knowledge of the music industry and a lot of experience. At various times in his career, he'd managed the Spice Girls and James among others. We agreed we should try to get the Inspirals around a table to discuss our publishing arrangements, our relationship with Mute and 'any other business'. We had a band meeting in Manchester a few weeks later and went through a couple of publishing-related and general housekeeping things before Richard casually addressed the elephant in the room: 'Once we've got a new publishing arrangement in place, what would any of you think about maybe doing some gigs?'

There was an air of surprise in the room.

I was the first to answer: 'I'm ready for it.' I even put my hand up as if to emphasise my eagerness and reinforce my message. The others followed in quick succession. It was obvious that our collective stars were perfectly aligned at that moment. I felt a rush, knowing how good this could be. There was obviously a chance that the public might not be arsed about us any more, or that our fanbase had completely moved on, but I didn't care.

We'd never officially announced our split back in May '95. We'd just drifted off into the background as Britpop started kicking the nation's back doors in. Our last gigs had been a short and underwhelming Mute package tour of Europe, with Moby and Miranda Sex Garden, followed by a surreal instrumental performance behind a contemporary dance troupe at the Royal Northern College of Music in Manchester. We didn't exactly go out with a bang. No manager, no record deal, no gigs, and with the music press asking, 'Where are they now!' before we'd even had time to pack our battered flight cases back into our respective garden sheds and garages. But none of that mattered now. It suddenly felt like we could be that brotherhood again. Day one of a new chapter. The Inspirals, with Richard now officially in the manager's seat, set about planning our return.

We decided to put a new single out. We opted for a song I'd given to the band just before we'd split in '95, a track called 'Come Back Tomorrow'. I'd written it with a northern-soul vibe. In my head, I wanted it to be like Edwyn Collins's 'A Girl Like You'. In reality, it turned out more like Elton John's 'Step into Christmas'. I'd subconsciously and unwittingly used a very similar top-line vocal melody to Elton's festive classic.

Filled with a fiery enthusiasm and overwhelming sense of excitement I set about rebuilding my live keyboard setup. I made space in the dining room and set up the Farfisa. I positioned the Ensoniq synth on top of the organ and, to the left, I started to rebuild my effects and amp rack. The recent arrival on the domestic market of the Iomega Zip drive meant that my Akai S3000 sampler could now be loaded in a matter of seconds from a single Zip cartridge as opposed to the previous method of having to upload data from six or seven floppy discs mid-set. I mounted the Tascam 234 four-track cassette machine into the rack and dug out all my old sound-effects tapes – the drunken homeless man singing his heart out on 'Memories of You', a tape of cows mooing and whale song I'd play in between numbers, and a boys' choir recorded at some abbey down south. I also dug out some weird clunky sounds from a Karlheinz Stockhausen album, and some clips of audio from porn films I'd copied at Square One Studios in 1989. I was in tech heaven. Charlie kept the coffee coming as I sat there through the first weeks of 2003, trying to remember the keyboard parts to songs I'd not played for eight years or more. Most of the parts came back quite quickly, with others I had to dig out old notebooks to be reminded of the chord progressions and lyrics. 'Joe', in particular, was a bastard to remember. Even though I'd written the words and music back in the mid-1980s, and we'd played the track at almost every show we'd done up until our split, I could not for the life of me figure out what I'd played on the bridges. I'd never learnt how to read or write music – when I composed a track, I'd just play by listening to what sounded right and remembering the shapes of the chords. It was only after I'd written a song that I'd work out what the chords were in order to show the rest of the band. I had no written notes for 'Joe', and trying to work out the bit immediately after the choruses was doing my head in. I asked Graham and Martyn, but they weren't sure what the notes or chords should be either. There was only one thing for it.

Phone Porter!

I got Mike Porter on the phone and told him the news: 'We're getting the band back together, Mike!' He sounded like he was about to cry. He'd always been one of our biggest fans. For the next two minutes I couldn't understand a word he said. Being a born and bred Geordie, he's hard to understand at the best of times, but when he'd just received the best news he'd ever heard in his life, forget it. He was overwhelmed with laughter and emotion. He was hysterical. I went on to explain my predicament regarding the bridges in 'Joe'. He totally cracked up. He couldn't believe that one of his favourite keyboard players of all time was asking him such a bizarre question: 'A cannae believe ye, Booney, y'absolute fuckin' lunatic!'

He fired up his keyboard right there, over the phone, and played me the part: 'Wayaye, man! Wi ye left hand it's the chords B, B minah, D 'n' A, 'n' wi ye right hand, it's a two-note riff, B, D, B, D . . . et-cet-era man!'

We rehearsed for the tour in a studio in Cheetham Hill, not far from Manchester city centre, which had once belonged to New Order. It was where they filmed the video for 'The Perfect Kiss'. The rehearsals went well. We sounded better than ever, energised by the time we'd spent away from the band.

A few weeks later, 27 March 2003, 8.57pm: I'm stood with Tom, Graham, Martyn and Craig immediately behind the stage at Sheffield Octagon. It's nine years since our last gig. The projection of the giant Inspirals cow logo flashes up on the backdrop. The audience start mooing. It's deafening. I'm tingling from the top of my head to the tip of my trainers. I can sense the celestial orb starting to spin slowly above us again: 'Let's do it, boys!'

77/
Jollop's Party People

Over the next couple of years, us Inspirals got our heads down and got busy reclaiming our rightful place as one of the best live bands to ever come from the northwest. In June 2006, 30 years after I'd joined the band, we played two sold-out nights at Oldham's Tokyo Project nightclub. We'd booked the Spacemen 3 to play the same venue back in 1987, when it was called the Hurricane Club. I think we paid them around £70 on the night and (obviously!) we were the support band.

The 2006 Oldham gigs were our way of saying thanks to our hometown and its people, an intimate affair in a venue where we had history, at a time when we could have filled any of the bigger venues down the road in Manchester. By now, 'Tokes' was owned by my old mate Aaron 'Matt' Mellor. Matt had really helped me out when I was struggling to find work after the Inspirals had split in '95. He helped me back into the world of DJing, booking me into the various venues he owned around the country. The Tokyo Project setup was so intimate that I had problems on one of the nights with some drunken nurses from a local hospital pulling the jack leads out of my keyboards throughout the gig. They thought it was piss funny. It was a pain in the arse for me, but a nice reminder of the grounded Oldham roots from which I'd grown.

My DJ trips with my mates around the UK and abroad continued through 2005 and into 2006. Mad times with Mani, Shaun, Bez, Andy Rourke, Rick Witter and Hooky, every outing bringing more memories for me to cherish forever. Our friendships continued to grow as our life journeys continued to run, seemingly, in parallel.

Following the success of the *Engie Benjy* TV series, ITV put together a touring stage show (called *Engie Benjy & Friends*), which turned out to be a major production that went around the UK, playing to thousands of children and their parents. The show featured all the characters from the television show, their vehicles and one new character called Learner Lucy, who was created to be the MC for the live performances. Lucy was the only character who wasn't in one of those massive suits that such productions usually feature. The stage show featured five or six of my *Engie Benjy* songs, which was nice, as I was basically getting paid loads of PRS royalties for songs I'd already written.

Charlie and I decided to go along with our baby, Oscar, to the *Engie Benjy* show at the Opera House in Manchester. I knew Shaun Ryder's little boy, Joe, was also a big *Engie Benjy* fan, so we thought it'd be nice to invite Shaun and his family along. Shaun also loved the *Engie* album I'd recorded, and we'd often listen to the tunes in the car when we were on the road on our DJ outings.

'Clint, put *Engie Benjy* on!'

I'd put the CD into the slot, hit play, and Shaun would sing along at the top of his voice, '*ENGIE BENJY, ENGINE MAN/ENGIE BENJY, JOLLOP AND DAN!!* . . . Clint! Put "DRUGS ARE GOOD!" on, mate!!' Shaun even suggested that we form an *Engie Benjy* band, so we could go out on the road and play a full set of the songs I'd written for the show: 'We'll get Mani on bass, Booney!'

It was midday when we arrived at the Opera House, and Shaun was already on the Guinness. He'd covered himself in nicotine patches because he knew there wouldn't be a smoking break during the show. It was the first time I'd been inside the Opera House for decades – a gorgeous building, in the classic theatre style, holding 1,900 people. It was where Mani had worked, 20 years earlier, as a lighting technician; it usually hosted more traditional musicals like Andrew Lloyd Webber's *The Phantom of the Opera*, so it felt slightly surreal that it would be reverberating to the music of Clinton David Boon's *Engie Benjy*! (A couple of years later, the Opera House would host Damon Albarn's Gorillaz with their *Demon Days* live show. But I got there first with *Engie Benjy*!) We had great seats, only four or five rows from the stage and right in the middle. They'd given us the full VIP treatment.

Me and Shaun had already drunk a couple of pints at this point, so my memory's a bit sketchy, but here goes. I seem to remember Lucy coming onstage before the rest of the cast. She stood waving enthusiastically at the crowd and opened with something along the lines of:

'Hello, boys and girls!'

Audience: *'Hello, Lucy!'*

'Are you all having a great time?'

'Yes, Lucy!'

She then asked the audience if they were good at keeping secrets.

'Yes, Lucy!'

You get the drift – this was proper pantomime stuff. Lucy went on to explain to the audience that today was a very special day because it was Jollop the Dog's birthday.

Hundreds of kids scream in unison: *'Ooooohh!!'*

'But when Jollop comes on stage in a minute,' Lucy continued, 'do you promise not to tell him we've organised a surprise party for him at the end of the show?'

'Yes, Lucy . . . we promise!'

'You see, children, Jollop thinks we've forgotten his birthday, so please don't tell him about the surprise party we've organised. Promise me?'

'We promise, Lucy!'

The intro to the *Engie Benjy* theme tune started to play out loud over the theatre's PA system, Engie came strutting out and the place went off. Hundreds of kids going wild. Then Dan the Van came out to massive applause, toddlers screaming and squealing with delight. Then, after a few minutes of ecstatic celebration, Lucy whispered down the mic:

'OK, boys and girls, it's time for Jollop to come onto the stage. Remember our secret. Don't mention his surprise birthday party, do you promise?'

The entire audience whisper back at Lucy, *'Yes Lucy, we promise!'*

Jollop entered, stage left, bouncing out to my song 'The Jollop Jump'. The crowd went wild again, kids completely losing it while waving those expensive flashing contraptions from the merchandise stall (ten quid a pop).

The intense level of drama and anticipation Lucy had created in the room was palpable.

The applause died down, Jollop standing centre stage, panting, tongue lolling out against his chin. Like dogs do.

At which point Shaun William Ryder shouted at the top of his voice, *'JOLLOP... IT'S YER PARTY!!!'*

The unified gasp of 1,900 incredulous parents and shocked kids that swept the auditorium was like nothing I'd ever heard before or since. Shaun Ryder, the Mancunian Phantom of the Opera House, leant over to me, chuckling: 'Fancy another drink, Booney?!'

Epilogue

The day after Mani's funeral, the *Manchester Evening News* changed its name to the *MANIchester Evening News*. What a tribute. The newspaper had been going over 150 years, since 1868, a decade before Manchester United was even founded, and it was the first time they'd ever changed the name of their paper to honour someone. They didn't do it when Tony Wilson, Matt Busby or George Best died, but they did it for my mate Mani. That would have made him laugh.

It made me think again how much Manchester has changed in my lifetime, and how much it has changed from an industrial city to a city of music and culture.

The arts organisation Factory International, named in tribute to Factory Records, produces the world-famous Manchester International Festival, and in 2023 opened a £185 million arts venue, Aviva Studios, on the site of the old Granada TV studios. Some of the original Granada buildings are still standing and have been incorporated into the new development. It stands on the exact spot where I made my TV debut with the Inspirals on *The Other Side of Midnight* in 1988, a bricks and mortar link from the old Manchester to the new Manchester. It's also the spot where Anthony H Wilson first met Alan Erasmus and started the conversations that would eventually lead to the birth of Factory Records, the Haçienda and all the beautiful chaos that came with it. Aviva Studios is the largest cultural project in Britain since the Tate Modern opened in 2000. Just this year, 2026, the Co-Op Live arena, the UK's biggest indoor live-music venue, hosted the Brit Awards in Manchester, the first time the national music showcase has been held outside London.

The skyline of the city is unrecognisable from the one I got to know as a young punk in the mid-1970s. Even by the time the Inspirals had an office there in the late 1980s, hardly anybody lived in the centre of Manchester. The entire population of the city centre was probably about 200 people, and most of them were musicians or artists, like Tony Wilson, Noel Gallagher and Mike Pickering, living in relatively cheap accommodation or housing-association flats. Today, there's around 100,000 people living in the city centre. There are huge glass skyscrapers of luxury apartments at the end of Deansgate, towering over the site of the little British Gas Board shed where Noel wrote songs like 'Live Forever'. The Haçienda was demolished long ago and replaced with yet more luxury apartments, marketed with the slogan, 'Now the party's over, you can come home!' Ancoats is unrecognisable from when we recorded our debut album there in 1989. Oldham Street was long ago rebranded as part of the 'Northern Quarter'. I've lost count of how many parts of Manchester have been rebranded as this 'quarter' or that 'quarter'. These days we've got the Civil Quarter, the Medieval Quarter, the Millennium Quarter, the Green Quarter, the University Quarter – as well as the Northern Quarter. I know I failed O-level maths, but I'm pretty sure you can only have four quarters!

Most of this redevelopment has been good progress, but there's a downside too. Many of the mills that were once homes to recording studios, rehearsal rooms and creative spaces with rent that any band could afford have been converted into expensive apartments way beyond the means of the same artists and creatives. Where there was once one original modern bar, Dry Bar, there's now hundreds. I always have a bit of a laugh to myself when I see yet another bar with the same slogan on the wall: 'Manchester, we do things differently here!' But I don't need to reiterate how much I love the place.

I love my life, and I've loved my life. I'm not a rich man, but I wouldn't trade what I've had. My journey has had its up and downs, but that's part of the fabric of life: what makes us human, and what make us feel alive. I'm lucky enough that the highs I've experienced have been incredible. I've achieved everything that wide-eyed kid who stood watching the Sex Pistols in 1976 could have wished for. And more. Way more. I've done all right, really.

From those early days in my first band t'Mill, the three of us went on to success in three different bands. I joined the Inspirals, Mani became the final piece in the Stone Roses jigsaw and went on to conquer the world, and Spud formed The High and scored a Top 10 album before going on to work with the likes of Electronic and Steve Diggle's Flag of Convenience.

I got to work with and befriend my musical hero, Mark E Smith, who passed away in 2016, having remained an uncompromising renegade to the end.

Rob Gretton died in 1999, aged only 46, and Tony Wilson died in 2007, aged only 57. The mark they made with Factory Records and the Haçienda, the legacy they left in music and in Manchester, is incredible. I was lucky enough to know them and witness that whole story.

New Order are still going strong, 50 years after they first formed as Warsaw, although Hooky left nearly 20 years ago. He now fronts the hugely successful Peter Hook & the Light and frequently tours the world, playing and celebrating the music of Joy Division and New Order.

The Inspirals are still at it, now managed by Alan McGee and with our original singer Ste Holt back on frontman duties after Tom and us went our separate ways in 2011. Ste's final gig before he left the band back in 1988 was to a small audience of around 40 people in a pub in London, but the first gig after he came back was to 8,000 people in Buenos Aires, Argentina.

We lost our drummer Craig, our little brother, in 2016, when he took his own life. We still believe his decades of suffering severe tinnitus might have contributed to his despair. We rallied round to help his family the best we could. It was crushing to see their pain. It floored us too. For a long time, we thought we'd never record or play live again. But, after six years, we picked ourselves up, brushed ourselves off and got on with it after we got an invitation to support the Happy Mondays on tour. A phenomenal Manchester-based drummer, Kev Clark, who'd been massively influenced by Craig, made our journey back onto the world stage much less difficult than it could have been.

As I'm writing this, the Mondays are about to go out on a thirty-fifth anniversary tour of *Pills, Thrills 'n' Bellyaches*. Shaun Ryder and Bez are now bona fide alternative national treasures, appearing regularly on reality TV shows. Bez won *Big Brother* and Shaun was the runner-up on *I'm a Celebrity Get Me Out of Here*, and they are regulars on *Celebrity Gogglebox*, watching TV shows while chuckling and gossiping away like Salford's answer to Waldorf and Statler. Shaun's brother, Paul, sadly passed away in 2022.

The Stone Roses reformed to huge acclaim in 2012 and reminded everyone why they were hailed as one of the greatest bands of all time. The seeds were sown when Mani was still playing with Primal Scream in 2011, and his dear mum, Anne, passed away. It was at her funeral that Ian Brown and John Squire started talking for the first time in years. Rumours started about a possible reunion after someone in the pub where the wake was held sent a photograph to one of the tabloids. People started messaging me on Twitter asking if I knew anything. I naively tweeted something along the lines of, 'It's true Ian and John met recently . . . it was at Mani's mum's funeral . . . they spent a couple of hours chatting . . . as a friend and a fan, I do hope it happens.' The press picked up on it, and the next day the headlines screamed, '*Clint Boon confirms Stone Roses reunion!*' I was gutted. They even put a picture of me next to it. Mani and Imelda were away on holiday, and I couldn't sleep for two nights until I got hold of them and explained how an innocent comment I'd made had been taken out of context. Mani and Imelda weren't bothered, they knew the score. The Roses would split again in 2016. 'Don't be sad it's over,' Ian Brown told the crowd at one of their final gigs, 'be happy it happened.'

Our cheeky scamp of a roadie, Noel, went on to have the fastest-selling debut album of all time, and his band became the biggest of their generation. As I was writing this book in the summer and autumn of 2025, the Oasis reunion was conquering the world. I could not be happier for them. Their songs are now the soundtrack to several generations, but I also think their appeal is about more than just Oasis: it's about the love and affection that people have for the 1990s. It was a much more optimistic time. Things feel a lot more fractured now, and people are desperate to feel that optimism again, even if it's just for one night. I feel hugely lucky to have been part of a scene that meant so much to so many people. The nineties are now as far away as the sixties were then but, in some ways, it all seems like yesterday.

My Farfisa organ featured on the final Oasis album *Dig Out Your Soul*. Noel got in touch to ask if he could borrow it for the recording, and I gladly obliged. He sent his roadie, Jason, to pick it up from my house in Stockport in his Range Rover, and he drove off to Abbey Road with it. He brought it back a few weeks later. I'd almost forgotten I'd lent it to Noel, until I got sent a copy of the first single from the album, 'The Shock of the Lightning', to play on my radio show on XFM. I could hear my Farfisa immediately, playing constantly through the track. Dirty, distorted, overdriven, beautiful – it was the same machine that Noel once spent his time setting up for our live shows, rehearsals and recording sessions. The same instrument I'd used to compose Inspirals standards like 'Saturn 5', 'This is How it Feels' and 'Joe'. The same instrument that Noel and Coyley had often used to smuggle drugs across borders around the world. Now there it was screaming out on the final Oasis album. The lyrics in the chorus to 'The Shock of the Lightning' talk about love being a time machine. There's something poetic about that.

It turns out the 1966 Farfisa Compact Duo I bought for a hundred quid back in 1983 is my time machine.

As I've got older, I've come to realise and understand certain things about life. You never know what fate has in store for you. After years of me saying, 'I don't need to, or want to, work with the Inspirals again!' I came around to realising, through stars aligning and my life's path changing direction, it was time to do it. Never say never. I've learnt you need to appreciate things you've created and not be afraid to celebrate them at every opportunity, whether it's a child, a song, or a band.

I'm deeply grateful for the hand I've been dealt in life and the people I've met along the way. Positivity, self-belief and passion are essential to artists like me. Even when times are shit. I have been, and still am, a lucky man. People and love are everything.

My life has changed beyond recognition over the last few decades. So has Manchester. I'm still DJing most weekends and loving it. If you told that 15-year-old who started on the record decks as the Royton Interchange Disco Roadshow in 1976 that he'd still be DJing 50 years later, I'd have thought you weren't right in the head.

I went on to enjoy a long and successful career as a radio presenter, talking to Manchester five and six days a week for over 20 years and meeting many of my idols along the way.

I feel incredibly blessed to have been born in the year I was born, to the two people I was born to, in a suburb of this city. Manchester is the greatest place in the world to me, and I'm glad to have not only played a little part in some of the city's halcyon days, but also to have helped make things a bit better for the next generation of people who may be born here or drawn here.

Speaking of the next generation, Charlie and I went on to raise three amazing sons, Oscar, Hector and Cassius. We also suffered the profound and devastating loss of our baby daughter, Luna Bliss, at just 34 days old in 2012. Meeting Charlie was a huge turning point in my life; we've loved and supported each other through some extremely dark moments and have always come out of the other side stronger and closer.

After Mani's funeral service at Manchester Cathedral, I talked with Liam Gallagher and Bobby Gillespie outside. It was good to see them, but we were all still in shock and just talking about how much we loved him and what a legend he was. Spending time with Spud on that day was particularly emotional. Some of the most powerful grief we've ever experienced. Mani's brother Greg had phoned me a few nights earlier and asked if I'd be one of Mani's pallbearers when he was brought out of the cathedral. I said I'd be honoured, and that it wouldn't be the first time I'd carried him out of some place or other. He called me the next day: 'Change of plan, Clint. I'd like you to carry him into the crematorium at Blackley Cemetery instead. Be there at 2pm.' So, after the service at the cathedral, I jumped into an Uber with my sons Oscar and Hector, not realising there were coaches laid on to take the congregation there. When we got near the cemetery, I was starving and realised it was only 1.20pm. I got the Uber to drop us outside a chippy in Blackley, which was only five minutes from the cemetery. I got my usual order – pudding, chips, peas and gravy, exactly as I would have ordered with Mani and Spud 40 years previously – my lads got their food, and we headed for the cemetery and found a bench in a quiet part of the grounds to sit and enjoy our chippy. I'd barely started on mine when I heard a big round of applause from the direction of the chapel. I checked the time and it was only 1.40pm, so I presumed it was the service before Mani's coming out, but I thought I'd better double check, so I dropped my chippy in a bin and legged it towards the crem.

'We'll catch you up in a minute, Dad,' shouted Oscar, polishing off his chips.

I passed two mods who'd been part of the cortège, stood next to a scooter. I said to them, 'Is that the service before Mani's coming out?' and they said, 'No, that's Mani goin' in!'

I legged it down to the chapel, but the hearse was already empty and the last of the congregation were walking in for the service. Mani had already gone in, and I'd missed him. Turns out, the start of the service was 1.30pm not 2pm and Greg had got mixed up. I slipped into the back of the chapel, still wiping gravy from my chin as the service started. I was gutted to have missed the chance to carry my old friend in, but I think Mani would have found it funny as fuck that, at the moment I was supposed to be putting him on my shoulder and carrying him on his way, I was sat necking pudding and chips behind some gravestones.

'Go on, Booney lad! You mad fucker!'

I'll miss you, brother. See you on the other side.

Pan Pipes of the Andes xxx

Text Credits

I'm in the Room

Lyrics are quoted from the song 'White Riot' by the Clash, written by Joe Strummer and Mick Jones (1977), © Universal Music Publishing Group.

The Groover

'You're wet'/'Yeah, but I'm getting drier' is taken from the film *Stardust* (1974) written by Ray Connolly, directed by Michael Apted, produced by David Puttnam and Sanford Lieberson and distributed by EMI Film Distributors Ltd and the song 'Wrote for Luck' by Happy Mondays/Shaun Ryder, Paul Ryder, Mark Day, Gary Whelan and Paul Davis (1988) © Universal Music Publishing Group.

Roses Start to Bloom

Lyrics from the Asia Fields song 'Miss Maxwell', written by Graham Maley (© Graham Maley), are quoted with permission.

'Clint, is this a fuckin' joke??'

Mike West's words are taken from 'Urbane Cowboys', by Mike West, *NME*, 25 June 1988.

The Baldricks

The quoted material from *i-D* magazine is taken from issue 57 ('The Surreal Issue'), published in April 1988 by Terry Jones.

Rave On

Lyrics are taken from 'She Bangs the Drums' by the Stone Roses, written by Ian Brown and John Squire (1989) © Silvertone Records.

The Boy from Burnage

Lyrics from the Inspiral Carpets song 'Whiskey', written by Inspiral Carpets (1990), © Mute Song Publishing, are quoted with permission.

On a Hillside, Desolate

The quoted material from Morrissey is taken from his *Autobiography* (Penguin Classics, 2013).

Sackville

Lyrics from the Inspiral Carpets song 'Joe', written by Inspiral Carpets (1989), © Mute Song Publishing, are quoted with permission.

Lyrics from the Inspiral Carpets song 'Sackville', written by Inspiral Carpets (1990), © Mute Song Publishing, are quoted with permission.

Halcyon Daze

John Squire's words are taken from 'NME's 100 Best Albums of All Time!', by combined *NME* writers, *NME*, 8 March 2003.

Ian Brown's words 'It takes time for people to fall in love with you . . . but it's inevitable' are taken from an interview with Ian Brown and John Squire of the Stone Roses that was broadcast on *Transmission* on Channel 4 on 25 July 1989. The interviewer was Rachel Davies.

Tony Wilson's comments about the city of Manchester are taken from 'The 10 best Mancunians – in pictures' by Luke Bainbridge, *Guardian*, 22 June 2013.

Danny Boyle's words come from the documentary film *The Class of '92* (2013), which was directed by Ben and Gabe Turner, produced by Leo Pearlman and F73 Productions and distributed by Universal Pictures.

Leo Stanley's words come from 'Madchester remembered: "There was amazing creative energy at the time"' by Luke Bainbridge, *Guardian*, 21 April 2012.

This is How it Feels

Lyrics from the Inspiral Carpets song 'This is How it Feels', written by Inspiral Carpets (1990), © Mute Song Publishing, are quoted with permission.

The 8:15 from Manchester

Lyrics from the Inspiral Carpets song 'Find Out Why', written by Inspiral Carpets (1989), © Mute Song Publishing, are quoted with permission.

Life's What You Make it

John Robb's comment is taken from a biog he wrote about the Inspiral Carpets ('John Robb biog') in October 2024.

'Clint, Shaun's got a knife!'

Martin Price and Danny Kelly's words are taken from *Manchester: The Sound of the North*, a TV special for the programme *Celebration* (1990), which was directed by Simon Massey and produced by Steven Lock for Granada Television.

'You'll get nowhere with a name like Oasis!'

Penny Anderson's words are taken from her article 'Oasis will go places', *Manchester Evening News*, 23 August 1991. Quoted with permission from Reach PLC Group.

I Want You

Lyrics from the Inspiral Carpets song 'I Want You' (featuring Mark E Smith), written by Inspiral Carpets (1994), © Mute Song Publishing, are quoted with permission.

Elbow Room

Lyrics from the Elbow song 'Newborn', written by Peter James Turner, Mark Potter, Guy Edward John Garvey, Craig Lee Potter and Richard Barry Jupp (2001), © Salvation Music Ltd, are quoted with permission. All rights administered by Warner Chappell Music Publishing Ltd.

Sweet and Tender Hooligans

The lyrics 'It's gruesome that someone so handsome should care' are taken from 'This Charming Man' by the Smiths, written by Morrissey and Johnny Marr (1984) © Morrissey/Marr Songs Ltd.

Gone South

Morrissey's words are quoted from his interview with Frank Owen, 'Home Thoughts from Abroad', *Melody Maker*, September 1988.

Love and Thanks . . .

To Jake Lingwood at Octopus Books for being, to date, the only human being capable of getting me to write a book. Others tried but failed. Thanks for teaching me all this new stuff, Jake.

To Leanne Bryan at Octopus for going through my final copy of the manuscript with the proverbial fine-tooth comb. Thanks for your patience, Leanne.

To Luke Bainbridge, for helping me get a 200,000-word book down to the 125,000 words that made the final edit.

To John Robb, not only for supporting the Inspirals from day one, but for your advice and guidance when I told you I was writing a book.

I'm also eternally grateful to all the other people in the team who helped me to make this book happen.

To my wife, Charlie, for your constant love and support, your unfaltering encouragement and your total understanding of how important writing this book was to me. Love you babe xxx

To my children, Harley Luv, Max Presley, Oscar Louie Louie, Hector Angel and Cassius Rudy. I've written some decent songs in my life, and made some great records, but the children I helped bring into this world are my greatest achievements. All my love to all of you, always.

To the absolute legend that is my mum, Marie Boon. You're a star on social media. You're a star in Aldi in Shaw. You're a star in real life. Mum, you're a woman of the people! Thousands of people love you, but none of 'em like I do.

To my brother and sister, Booney and Booney. We all did OK, didn't we?! I'm proud of you both and love you beyond words.

To my dad, Cyril, who passed away in 2011 but still talks to me through each minute of the day. Dad, you were God. I see your face in every mirror and I hear your voice in every word I speak.

To my mother-in-law, Jill, Grandad Malc and the rest of the Wilkinsons. Thanks for happily dropping everything whenever we've needed you.

To my second family, the Inspirals: Graham and Karen, Ste and Rachel, Martyn and Joanne, Kev, and our 2023–26 crew, Chris, Paul, Leigh, Snidge, Mia and Dave. Thanks also to other team members in recent years, Liam, Pete, Stocky and Rooky.

Extra special love to Rose Gill and her beautiful family. Rose, the Inspirals still feel Craig's presence whenever we're together and he still has us in stitches. Georgia, Orla and Levon, I hope this book helps in some small way to keep your dad's spirit alive and his star shining brightly.

To the people who have been there for the Boons at various times . . . Rob and Lucy Snowden (can you believe it, Robinson?! I wrote a book!), Iggy and Mel, Avril and Snidge, Dunc and April. Sarah Potts, Jo the Midwife and 'My Mark'.

To my 'lifelong' friends, Ken Berry, Dave Bradbury, Graham Maley and Karen Drinkwater. I hope you like the few memories that I chose to share here.

To the tutors at Rochdale College of Art from 1975–77, for seeing and nurturing my artistic qualities before I even did. Special mention to my fine-art tutor,

Keith Chadwick, who is undoubtedly one of the most influential people in my story. The way he recognized, appreciated and championed my extrovert tendencies made me change the way I thought about myself and my potential.

To my truly inspirational art-college friends, Cate Fashnact and Lesley Ann Albiston (Catty Da and Lesley Wesley), who I reconnected with after 50 years while writing this book. I honestly thought you'd both been taken off to another world by space-people.

To some others who helped me in ways I'll never forget: Aaron 'Matt' Mellor, Daniel Miller and his incredible Mute team from 1990–2026, Gordon Biggins and Karen Boardman, and Ian Ramage and Caroline Ellerey for giving me the BMG publishing deal when I was on my arse, drowning in debt and close to giving up.

To the Sheehan family: I'll never forget the important part you played in my life. Thank you.

Not mentioned in these chronicles but very important to my story are: Paul Fallon, for being a 'super roadie', a total grafter, and for helping me through many a difficult patch, often away from the music biz when times were tough. Bo Walsh, who drummed with the CBX! for a period in late '99, when 'Papa T' couldn't do it. Your drumming blew our minds, Bo. You're one of the greatest. I seriously think your big moment is still to come. Love you bro. John and Rosemary Barratt, I don't think you realise how much you inspire people like me. I'm proud to have you as mates.

To the broadcasters who not only supported me as a musician, but also inspired me in my years as a radio presenter: Pete Mitchell, Mike Sweeney, Phil Korbel, Tony the Greek, Terry Christian, Mark Radcliffe, Marc Riley, Andy and Liz Kershaw. To John Peel (and his beautiful wife, Sheila).

To Anthony H. Wilson.

There are scores of other people who helped me build a career in radio after the period covered in these pages. I'd like to mention you all by name, but that will be another book. You know who you are!

To my extended Manchester music family: musicians, industry folk and blaggers alike. I can't believe my luck in getting to share this amazing trip with you all!

To Hooky. Love you, mate.

Finally, thanks to anyone who ever supported or followed the Inspirals, the CBX!, my radio shows, or any of the other stuff I've had a go at over the years – thousands of people, most of whom I've never met and will probably never get to meet. You've given me and my family the wonderful life we have.

Lotsa love, Clint xxx

This monoray book was crafted and published by Jake Lingwood, Luke Bainbridge, Leanne Bryan, Ian Preece, Mel Four, Rachael Shone, Jack Smyth, Emily Campbell, Clare Sivell, Sarah Parry, Erin Brown and Karen Baker.

RAISING READERS
Books Build Bright Futures

Dear Reader,

We'd love your attention for one more page to tell you about the crisis in children's reading, and what we can all do.

Studies have shown that reading for fun is the single biggest predictor of a child's future life chances – more than family circumstance, parents' educational background or income. It improves academic results, mental health, wealth, communication skills, ambition and happiness.[1]

The number of children reading for fun is in rapid decline. Young people have a lot of competition for their time. In 2024, 1 in 10 children and young people in the UK aged 5 to 18 did not own a single book at home.[2]

Hachette works extensively with schools, libraries and literacy charities, but here are some ways we can all raise more readers:

- Reading to children for just 10 minutes a day makes a difference
- Don't give up if children aren't regular readers – there will be books for them!
- Visit bookshops and libraries to get recommendations
- Encourage them to listen to audiobooks
- Support school libraries
- Give books as gifts

There's a lot more information about how to encourage children to read on our website: www.RaisingReaders.co.uk

Thank you for reading.

hachette
LIVRE

---

[1] OECD. 2021. 21st-century readers: developing literacy skills in a digital world. Paris, France: OECD Publishing. https://www.oecd.org/en/publications/21st-century-readers_a83d84cb-en.html

[2] National Literacy Trust, Book Ownership in 2024, November 2024 https://nlt.cdn.ngo/media/documents/Book_ownership_in_2024